JEAN CROSS, currently at work
on several television scripts,
is a writer, artist, and photog-
rapher. Her articles and photo-
graphs have appeared nationally in
magazines and newspapers.

IN
GRANDMOTHER'S DAY

A LEGACY OF RECIPES, REMEDIES, & COUNTRY WISDOM FROM 100 YEARS AGO

JEAN CROSS

A SPECTRUM BOOK

PRENTICE-HALL, INC., Englewood Cliffs, New Jersey 07632

Library of Congress Cataloging in Publication Data
Main entry under title:

In grandmother's day.

  (A Spectrum Book)
  Includes index.
    1. Cookery. 2. Home economics, Rural. 3. Folk
medicine. I. Cross, Jean.
TX652I52   1980   640'.2   79-20325
ISBN 0-13-453704-1
ISBN 0-13-453696-7 pbk.

To Isabelle

friend and mentor,
whose golden advice, "Cool it, kid,"
puts me in print today

A SPECTRUM BOOK

10 9 8 7 6 5 4 3 2 1

Printed in the United States of America

Editorial/production supervision
by Norma Miller Karlin
Interior design by Michael Graves
Page layout by Dawn Stanley
Cover design by Michael Graves
Manufacturing buyer: Cathie Lenard

PRENTICE-HALL INTERNATIONAL, INC., *London*
PRENTICE-HALL OF AUSTRALIA PTY. LIMITED, *Sydney*
PRENTICE-HALL OF CANADA, LTD., *Toronto*
PRENTICE-HALL OF INDIA PRIVATE LIMITED, *New Delhi*
PRENTICE-HALL OF JAPAN, INC., *Tokyo*
PRENTICE-HALL OF SOUTHEAST ASIA PTE. LTD., *Singapore*
WHITEHALL BOOKS LIMITED, *Wellington, New Zealand*

CONTENTS

Part One
COOKERY RECEIPTS 3

* The easy recipes—usable today—are marked in the Cookery Section for the
fainthearted cook. The stouthearted connoisseur will likely try them all—with
Grandmother's blessing . . . and bicarb.

CONTENTS

Part Two
FOLK REMEDIES 205

Part Three
CARE OF THE HOUSE & FARM 279

Part Four
REMEDIES FOR FARM ANIMALS 327

Part Five
WEIGHTS & MEASURES 357

Liquid or wine measure—dry measure—avoirdupois weight—troy weight—
apothecaries' weight—cloth measure—miscellaneous table—long or linear measure—
surveyor's measure—square & cubic measure—circular measure. *How to Calculate:*
How to measure corn in the crib & grain in the bin—capacity of boxes—measuring
hay—how to find the weight of cattle—quantity of seed to sow per acre—harvest
wheat grain yields—how to measure capacity of tin vessels, round tanks, cones,
cylinders, & cisterns or wells. Sustaining power of ice—melting & boiling points of
various substances—Mother Shipton's prophecy.

Part Six
GLOSSARY 369

Part Seven
SOURCES OF SUPPLY 399

Sundries, tools, utensils, herbs, & chemicals—their availability & procurement.

PREFACE

One hundred years ago . . . men were men, held together with spit, glue, brine, and whisky, while women were made of even sterner stuff.

From the dusty recesses of Grandmother Artemisia's attic trunk spring sage receipts and time-honored homilies—to perk up the spirit, if not the stomach, and to bring full circle today's nostalgic reach for mellowed memories of simpler yesteryears.

These venerable and delicious receipts, having once been taken at full strength and faith in the Lord, are mostly untested by today's puny standards . . . but have withstood the test of time and tongue . . . and the sturdy generations who took them to their hearths, hearts, and innards.

Laugh if you will, but with a warm and kindly heart . . . remembering that your ways, too, may bring a smile to those to come . . . 100 years from now.

CREDITS

My eternal thanks goes to Lynne Lumsden, Shirley Covington, Jeannette Jacobs, Norma Karlin, and other kind souls at Prentice-Hall for doggedly hanging in there when Grandmother's prose gave them fits . . . and for miraculously turning her hodgepodge of recipes and nostrums into artful form.

My gratitude, also, goes to literary agent Richard Huttner, New York City, for his selfless assistance when the going got rough.

Bless, too, those good people who lent old drawings and lore to dress these pages of nostalgia. For their courtesies, credits must go to the Antique Guild of Los Angeles; Beefeater Gin®; Dover Publishing Company, New York City; Edwards Interiors, Costa Mesa, California; Forty Winks Sleep Products, Los Angeles; the Hurty-Peck Library of Beverage Literature, Irvine, California; *The Mother Earth News,* Hendersonville, N.C.; and lastly, to Marjorie Streeter, Reston, Virginia, for sharing her early *Enterprising Housekeeper* cookbook drawings.

Finally, for depicting Grandmother's day with such sensitivity, I am grateful to American artist Winslow Homer, that shining light from the nineteenth century's Golden Age of Illustrators, whose drawings herein first appeared in the following periodicals:

Every Saturday, Boston
    January 21, 1871   Deer-stalking in the Adirondacks in Winter,
                                     page 28

Harper's Bazaar
    August 28, 1875   The Family Record, page 204

Harper's Weekly
    June 11, 1870   The Dinner Horn, page 2
    August 22, 1874   Waiting for a Bite, page 18

INTRODUCTION

In copying these century-old receipts, I have been true, with purpose, to their arrangement, their spelling and punctuation, their wording and syntax, and to the general idiom of the day. This I have done in an effort to preserve the quaint charm of the originals.

Like receipts of farm women of her day, who had more chores than time, Grandmother's were the essence of brevity. Some were jotted down scantily, only to seed her memory, which would shame today's computers. Like those for butter and cheese, others were superfluous. No farm woman who knew one end of a cow from the other needed such reminders.

Grandmother cooked mostly from memory, relying on her experienced senses—not to mention honed intuition—to tell when things were "just right" in her mixing bowl and oven.

As for a thermometer, who needed it? An eye to the way waterdrops danced, sizzled, sputtered, and spatted on the stove—or a quick hand inside—told exactly how hot her oven was. Also, which kind of wood in the firebox gave the quickest oven, or which the slowest.

As for exact alphabetical order, forget it. If Grandmother could lay her finger instantly on any of the preserved foods "put by" in the cellar for the season, or if she could keep an eye on all the farm animals and family members—to say nothing of an ear to current countryside gossip and go-ings-on—who paid much mind to a receipt out of order?

A pragmatist at heart, Grandmother was split between puritanical mor-als and concern for her family's immediate earthly needs. She balanced both with inordinate skill.

Having attended to the spiritual salve for the familial soul, she would return from church of a Sunday morn, to stir the spirituous tonic for the familial stomach. Apron donned, she would trudge out back to the brew-house, to mix the mash for the still's next charge . . . trusting never to the whisky quacks and beer "doctors" of the day, who foisted on unsuspecting innards those "manufactured pot-house slops and washes."

And so, from an age of hand-me-downs, it is fitting and proper that Grandmother Artemisia's toothsome receipts, her rightful spirits and nos-trums be passed down to waiting generations—to spring full fresh again.

IN GRANDMOTHER'S DAY

Part One

COOKERY RECEIPTS

ALL ABOUT KITCHEN WORK

A lady who for the first time was compelled to do all of her own kitchen work says: "If every iron, pot, pan, kettle or any utensil used in the cooking of food, be washed as soon as emptied, and while still hot, half the labor will be saved." It is a simple habit to acquire, and the washing of pots and kettles by this means loses some of its distasteful aspects. No lady seriously objects to washing and wiping the crystal and silver, but to tackle the black, greasy, and formidable-looking ironware of the kitchen takes a good deal of sturdy brawn and muscle as well as common sense.

If the range be wiped carefully with brown paper, after cooking greasy food, it can be kept bright with little difficulty.

Stoves and ranges should be kept free from soot in all compartments. A clogged hot-air passage will prevent any oven from baking well.

When the draught is imperfect the defect frequently arises from the chimney being too low. To remedy the evil the chimney should be built up, or a chimneypot added.

It is an excellent plan for the mistress to acquaint herself with the practical workings of her range, unless her servants are exceptionally good, for many hindrances to well-cooked food arise from some misunderstanding of, or imperfection in, this article.

A clean, tidy kitchen can only be secured by having a place for everything and everything in its place, and by frequent scouring of the room and utensils.

A hand-towel and basin are needed in every kitchen for the use of the cook or house-worker.

Unless dish-towels are washed, scalded and thoroughly dried daily, they become musty and unfit for use, as also the dish-cloth.

Cinders make a hot fire—one particularly good for ironing days.

To scatter the Philadelphia brick over the scouring board on to the floor, to leave the soap in the bottom of the scrubbing pail, the Sappolio in the basin of water, and to spatter the black lead or stove polish on the floor are wasteful slatternly habits.

A clock in the kitchen is both useful and necessary.

How to tell oven temperature

If a hand be held without pain in a fired oven for 60 seconds, it be a slow *oven; if for 45 seconds, it be* moderate; *and if for only 20 seconds or so, it be* quick.

5

Chapter 1

To warm the cockles of the heart
BEVERAGES

ALE, SPICED

Is made hot, sweetened with sugar and spiced with grated nutmeg, and a hot toast is served in it. This is the wassail drink.

ALE TO MULL

Take a pint of good strong ale, and pour it into a saucepan with three cloves and a little nutmeg; sugar to taste. Set it over a fire, and when it boils take it off to cool. Beat up the yolks of four eggs exceedingly well, mix them first with a little cold ale, then add them to the warm ale, and pour it in and out of the pan several times. Set it over a slow fire, beat it a little, take it off again; do this three times until it is hot, then serve it with dry toast.

BEEF TEA

Cut a pound of fleshy beef in thin slices; simmer with one quart of water twenty minutes, after it has once boiled and been skimmed. Season if approved.

*ROSA'S BEEF TEA

To one pound of lean beef add one and one-half tumblers of cold water; cut the beef in small pieces, cover, and let it boil slowly for ten minutes, and add a little salt after it is boiled. Excellent.

*MRS. CRAVEN'S BEEF TEA

Cut lean, tender beef into small pieces, put them into a bottle, cork and set in a pot of cold water, then put on the stove and boil for one hour. Season to taste.

ANNIE'S BEEF TEA

When one pound of lean beef, free of fat, and separated from the bones, in a finely-chopped state in which it is used for mince-meat, or beef-sausages, is uniformly mixed

7

with its own weight of cold water, slowly heated till boiling, and the liquid, after boiling briskly for a minute or two, is strained through a towel from the coagulated albumen and the fibrine, now become hard and horny, we obtain an equal weight of the most aromatic soup, of such strength as cannot be obtained even by boiling for hours from a piece of flesh. When mixed with salt and other additions by which soup is usually seasoned, and tinged somewhat darker by means of roasted onions, or burnt bread, it forms the very best soup which can, in any way, be prepared from one pound of flesh.

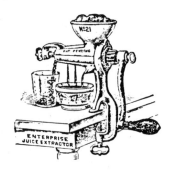

*BOSTON CREAM (a summer drink)
Make a syrup of four pounds of white sugar with four quarts of water; boil; when cold add four ounces of tartaric acid, and one and a half ounces of essence of lemon, and the whites of six eggs beaten to a stiff froth; bottle. Add a wine-glass of the cream to a tumbler of water, with sufficient carbonate of soda to make it effervesce.

*CHAMPAGNE CUP
One quart bottle of champagne, two bottles of soda-water, one liqueur-glass of brandy, two table-spoons of powdered sugar, a few thin strips of cucumber rind; make this just in time for use, and add a large piece of ice.

*CHOCOLATE
Scrape Cadbury's chocolate fine, mix with a little cold water and the yolks of eggs well beaten; add this to equal parts of milk and water, and boil well, being careful that it does not burn. Sweeten to taste, and serve hot.

*COFFEE
Is a tonic and stimulating beverage, of a wholesome nature. Use the best. For eight cups use nearly eight cups of water; put in coffee as much as you like, boil a minute and take off, and throw in a cup of cold water to throw the grounds to the bottom; in five minutes it will be very clear.

Or, beat one or two eggs which mix with ground coffee to form a ball; nearly fill the pot with cold water, simmer gently for half an hour, having introduced the ball; *do not boil,* or you will destroy the aroma.

*ICED COFFEE
The following is a delicious dish either for breakfast or dessert: Make a strong infusion of Mocha coffee; put it in a porcelain bowl, sugar it properly and add to it an equal portion of boiled milk, or one-third the quantity of rich

cream. Surround the bowl with crushed ice.

*LEMONADE

Take a quart of boiling water, and add to it five ounces of lump-sugar, the yellow rind of the lemon rubbed off with a bit of sugar, and the juice of three lemons. Stir altogether and let it stand till cool. Two ounces of cream of tarter may be used instead of the lemon, water being poured upon it.

*SUMMER DRINK

Boil together for five minutes two ounces of tartaric acid, two pounds white sugar, three lemons sliced, two quarts of water; when nearly cold add the whites of four eggs beaten to a froth, one tablespoonful of flour and half an ounce of wintergreen. Two tablespoonfuls in a glass of water make a pleasant drink; for those who like effervescence add as much soda as a ten-cent piece will hold, stirring briskly before drinking.

TEA

When the water in the teakettle begins to boil, have ready a tin tea-steeper; pour into the tea-steeper just a very little of the boiling water, and then put in tea, allowing one teaspoon of tea to each person. Pour over this boiling water until the steeper is a little more than half full; cover tightly and let it stand where it will keep hot, but not to boil. Let the tea infuse for ten or fifteen minutes, then pour into the tea-urn, adding more boiling water, in the proportion of one cup of water for every teaspoon of dry tea which has been infused. Have boiling water in a water-pot, and weaken each cup of tea as desired. Do not use water for tea that has been boiled long. Spring water is best for tea, and filtered water is next best.

*ICE TEA À LA RUSSE

To each glass of tea add the juice of half a lemon, fill up the glass with pounded ice, and sweeten.

*ALMA HASKIN'S HERB TEA

Take of any preferred herbs one half ounce; put to it one pint or one cupful of boiling fresh spring water, steep a little, then add clarified honey or brown sugar to sweeten as desirable.

Another Way—Take whatever herbs are desirous, put them in a saucepan and pour on them cold fresh water, place over a slow fire and heat to a boil; push aside to simmer for ten minutes. Most ladies prefer to take of herbs one teaspoonful in a teacupful of water, and find this to be very pleasant to the taste and more healthful than the imported teas.

Tea and Coffee are usually drank at 110 degrees.

9

Chapter 2

How to make soups & broths to stem the hunger

SOUPS

SOUP & SOUPS

It is not at all necessary to keep a special fire for five hours every day in order to have at dinner a first course of soup. Nor need a good, savory, nutritious soup for a family of five cost more than ten cents. There is no need hurling any remarks about "swillpails." Any housekeeper who knows anything about her kitchen and dining-room affairs, knows there are usually nice clean fragments of roasts and broils left over, and broth in which lamb, mutton, beef, and fowls have been boiled is in existence, and that twice a week or so there is a bowl of drippings from roasted meats. All these when simmered with rice, macaroni, or well-chosen vegetables, and judiciously seasoned, make good soups, and can be had without a special fire, and without sending to the butcher's for special meats. We name a few of the soups we make, and beg leave to add that they are pretty well received. We make them in small quantities, for nobody with three additional courses before him wants to eat a *quart* of soup, you know!

*1. One pint of good gravy, three cups of boiling water, a slice of turnip, and half an onion cut in small bits, two grated crackers. Simmer half an hour.

2. On ironing day, cut off the narrow ends from two or three sirloin steaks, chop them into morsels and put in a stewpan with a little salt, a tablespoonful of rice and a pint of cold water, and simmer

slowly for three hours. Then add water enough to make a quart of soup, a tablespoonful of tomato catsup, and a little browned flour mixed with the yolk of an egg.

*3. Pare and slice very thin four good sized potatoes, pour over them two cups of boiling water and simmer gently until the potatoes are dissolved. Add salt, a lump of nice butter, a pint of sweet milk with a dust of pepper. Let it boil up once, and serve. You wouldn't think it, but it is real good, and children cry for it.

4. One pint meat broth, one pint boiling water, slice in an onion, or a parsnip, or half a turnip—or all three if liked—boil until the vegetables are soft, add a little salt if needed, and a tablespoonful of Halford sauce.

5. Let green corn, in the time of green corn, be grated and to a pint of it put a pint of rich milk, a pint of water, a little butter, salt and pepper. Boil gently for fifteen or twenty minutes.

ARTICHOKE SOUP

Take Jerusalem artichokes according to the quantity of soup required to be made, cut them in slices, with a quarter of a pound of butter, two or three onions and turnips, sliced into a stewpan, and stew over a very slow fire till done enough, and thin it with good veal stock. Just before you serve, at the last boil, add a quarter of a pint of good cream. This is an excellent soup. Season to taste with a little salt and cayenne.

As it is necessary to vary soups, we shall give you a few to choose from according to season and taste. All brown soups must be clear and thin, with the exception of mock turtle, which must be thickened with flour first browned with butter in a stewpan. If the flour is added without previous browning, it preserves a raw taste that by no means improves the flavor.

*ASPARAGUS SOUP

Three or four pounds of veal cut fine, a little salt pork, two or three bunches of asparagus and three quarts of water. Boil one-half of the asparagus with the meat, leaving the rest in water until about twenty minutes before serving; then add the rest of the asparagus and boil just before serving; add one pint of milk; thicken with a little flour, and season. The soup should boil about three hours before adding the last half of the asparagus.

BEEF BROTH

Put two pounds of lean beef, one pound of scrag veal, one pound of scrag mutton, sweet herbs, and ten peppercorns, into a nice tin saucepan, with five quarts of water; simmer to three quarts, and clear from the fat when cold. Add onion, if approved.

Soup and broth made of different meats are more supporting, as well as better flavored.

To remove the fat, take it off, when cold, as clean as possible; and if there be still any remaining, lay a bit of clean blotting or cap paper on the broth when in the basin, and it will take up every particle.

*BEEF SOUP

Cut all the lean off the shank, and with a little beef suet in the bottom of the kettle, fry it to a nice brown; put in the bones and cover with water; cover the kettle closely, and let it cook slowly until the meat drops from the bones; strain through a colander and leave it in the dish during the night, which is the only way to get off all the fat. The day it is wanted for the table, fry as brown as possible a carrot, an onion, and a very small turnip sliced thin. Just before taking up, put in half a tablespoonful of sugar, a blade of mace, six cloves, a dozen kernels of allspice, a small tablespoonful of celery seed. With the

vegetables this must cook slowly in the soup about an hour; then strain again for the table. If you use vermicelli or pearl barley, soak in water first.

BROWN GRAVY SOUP

Shred a small plate of onions, put some drippings into a frying-pan and fry the onions till they are of a dark brown; then, having about three pounds of beef cut up in dice, without fat or bone, brown that in a frying-pan. Now get a saucepan to contain about a gallon, and put in the onions and meat, with a carrot and a turnip cut small, and a little celery, if you have it; if not, add two seeds of celery; put three quarts or three and one-half quarts of water to this, and stir all together with a little pepper and salt; simmer very slowly, and skim off what rises; in three or four hours the soup will be clear. When served, add a little vermicelli, which should have previously been boiled in water; the liquid should have been carefully poured off through a sieve. A large quantity may be made in the same proportions. Of course, the meat and onions must be stirred whilst frying, and constantly turned; they should be of a fine brown, not black, and celery-seed will give a flavor, it is so strong.

CARROT SOUP

Put some beef bones, with four quarts of the liquor in which a leg of mutton or beef has been boiled, two large onions, a turnip, pepper and salt into a sauce-pan, and stew for three hours. Have ready six large carrots, scraped and cut thin, strain the soup on them, and stew them till soft enough to pulp through a hair sieve or course cloth, then boil the pulp with the soup, which is to be as thick as pea-soup. Use two wooden spoons to rub the carrots through. Make the soup a day before it is to be used. Add cayenne. Pulp only the red part of the carrot, not the yellow.

*CLAM SOUP

Cut pork in small squares and fry light brown; add one large or two small onions cut very fine, and cook about ten minutes; add two quarts water and one quart raw potatoes, sliced; let it boil; then add one quart of clams. Mix one tablespoonful of flour with water, put it with one pint of milk, and pour into the soup, and let it boil about five minutes. Butter, pepper, salt. Worcestershire sauce to taste.

GAME SOUPS

Cut in pieces a partridge, pheasant, or rabbit; add slices of veal, ham, onions, carrots, &tc. Add a little water, heat a little over slow fire, as gravy is done; then add some good broth, boil the meat gently till it is done. Strain, and stew in the liquor what herbs you please.

Croutons
These are simply pieces of bread, fried brown and crisp, to be used in soups.

GAME SOUP

In the season for game, it is easy to have very good game soup at very little expense, and very nice. Take the meat from off the bone of any cold game left, pound it in a mortar and break up the bones, and pour on them a quart of any good broth, and boil for an hour and a half. Boil and mash six turnips, and mix with the pounded meat, and then pass them through a hair sieve; keep the soup-pot near the fire, but do not let it boil. When ready to dish the soup for the table, beat the yolks of five eggs very lightly, and mix with them half a pint of good cream. Set the soup on to boil, and, as it boils, stir in the beaten eggs and cream—but be careful that it does not boil after they are stirred in, as the eggs will curdle. Serve hot.

GRAND CONSOMMÉ SOUP

Put in a pot two knuckles of veal, a piece of leg of beef, a fowl, or an old cock, a rabbit, or two old partridges; add a ladleful of soup, and stir well; when it comes to a jelly, put in a sufficient quantity of stock, and see that it is clear, let it boil, skimming and refreshing it with water; season it as the above; you may add, if you like, a clove of garlic; let it then boil slowly or simmer four or five hours; put it through a towel, and use it for mixing in sauces or clear soups.

*JULIENNE SOUP

Put a piece of butter the size of an egg into a soup-kettle; stir until melted. Cut three young onions small, fry them a nice brown; add three quarts of good clear beef-stock, a little mace, pepper and salt, let it boil an hour; add three young carrots and three turnips cut small, a stalk of celery cut fine, a pint of French beans, a pint of green peas; let this boil two hours; if not a bright, clear color, add a spoonful of soy. This is a nice summer soup.

LAVENIA'S JULIENNE SOUP

Take some carrots and turnips, and turn them riband-like; a few heads of celery, some leaks and onions, and cut them in lozenges, boil them till they are cooked, then put them into clear gravy soup. Brown the thickening. N.B.: You may, in summer time, add green peas, asparagus tops, French beans, some lettuce or sorrel.

*LOBSTER SOUP

One large lobster, or two small ones; pick all the meat from the shell and chop fine; scald one quart of milk and one pint of water, then add the lobster, one pound of butter, a teaspoonful of flour, and salt and red pepper to taste. Boil ten minutes and serve hot.

*MOCK TURTLE SOUP

One soup-bone, one quart of turtle beans, one large spoonful of powdered cloves, salt and pepper. Soak the beans overnight, put them on with the soup-bone in nearly six quarts of water, and cook five or six hours. When half done, add the cloves, salt and pepper; when done, strain through a colander, pressing the pulp of the beans through to make the soup the desired thickness, and serve with a few slices of hard-boiled egg and lemon sliced very thin. The turtle beans are black and can be obtained from large grocers.

*OYSTER SOUP

Take one quart of water, one teacup of butter, one pint of milk, two teaspoons of salt, four crackers rolled fine, and one teaspoon of pepper; bring to a full boiling heat as soon possible, then add one quart of oysters; let the whole come to a boiling heat quickly, then remove from the fire.

*SARAH'S OYSTER SOUP

Pour one quart of boiling water into a skillet; then one quart of good, rich milk; stir in one teacup of rolled cracker crumbs; season with salt and pepper to taste. When all has come to boil, add one quart of fresh oysters; stir well, so as to keep from scorching; then add a piece of good sweet butter about the size of an egg; let it boil up once, then remove from the fire immediately; dish up and send to table.

*OX TAIL SOUP

Take two ox tails and two whole onions, two carrots, a small turnip, two tablespoonfuls of flour, and a little white pepper; add a gallon of water, let all boil for two hours; then take out the tails and cut the meat into small pieces, return the bones to the pot for a short time, boil for another hour, then strain the soup, and rinse two spoonfuls of arrowroot to add to it with the meat cut from the bones, and let all boil for a quarter of an hour.

ROYAL SOUP

Take a scrag or knuckle of veal, slices of undressed gammon of bacon, onions, mace, and a small quantity of water; simmer till very strong, and lower it with a good beef broth made the day before and stewed till the meat is done to rags. Add cream, vermicelli, almonds and a roll.

*SCOTCH BROTH

Take one-half teacup barley, four quarts cold water; bring this to the boil and skim; now put in a neck of mutton and boil again for half an hour, skim well the sides of the pot also; have ready two carrots, one large onion, a small head of cabbage, one bunch parsley, one sprig of celery top; chop all these fine, add your chopped vegetables,

pepper and salt to taste. This soup takes two hours to cook.

SOUP & BOUILLE

Stew a brisket of beef with some turnips, celery, leeks, and onions, all finely cut. Put the pieces of beef into the pot first, then the roots, and half a pint of beef gravy, with a few cloves. Simmer for an hour. Add more beef gravy, and boil gently for half an hour.

SPLIT PEA SOUP

Take beef bones or any cold meats, and two pounds of corned pork; pour on them a gallon of hot water, then let them simmer three hours, removing all the scum. Boil one quart of split peas two hours having been previously soaked, as they require much cooking; strain off the meat and mash the peas into the soup; season with black pepper, and let it simmer one hour; fry two or three slices of bread a nice brown, cut into slices and put into the bottom of the tureen, then on them pour the soup.

TOMATO SOUP

Boil chicken or beef four hours; then strain; add to the soup one jar of canned tomatoes and boil one hour. This will make four quarts of soup.

*TOMATO SOUP WITHOUT MEAT

Take one quart of tomatoes, one quart of water, one quart of milk. Butter, salt and pepper to taste. Cook the tomatoes thoroughly in the water, have the milk scalding (over the water to prevent scorching). When the tomatoes are done add a large spoonful of saleratus, which will cause violent effervescence. It is best to set the vessel in a pan before adding it to prevent waste. When the commotion has ceased, add the milk and seasoning. When it is possible, it is best to use more milk than water, and cream instead of butter. The soup is eaten with crackers and is by some preferred to oyster soup. This recipe is very valuable for those who keep abstinence days.

*TURKEY SOUP

Take the turkey bones and cook for one hour in water enough to cover them; then stir in a little dressing and a beaten egg. Take from the fire, and when the water has ceased boiling add a little butter with pepper and salt.

VARIOUS SOUPS

Good soups may be made from fried meats, where the fat and gravy are added to the boiled barley; and for that purpose, fat beef steaks, pork steaks, mutton chops, &tc. should be preferred, as containing more of the nutritious principle. When nearly done frying, add a little water, which will produce a gravy to be added to the barley broth; a little wheat flour should be dredged in also; a quantity of onion, cut small, should also be fried with the fat, which gives the soup a fine flavor, assisted, by seasoning, &tc.

Soups may be made from broiled meats. While the fat beef steak is doing before the fire, or the mutton chop, &tc., save the drippings on a dish, in which a little flour, oatmeal, with cut onions, &tc., are put.

VEAL SOUP

To a knuckle of veal of six pounds, put eight or nine quarts of water; boil down one half, skim it well. This is better to do the day before you prepare the soup for the table. Thicken by rubbing flour, butter and water together. Season with salt and mace. When done, add one pint new milk; let it just come to a boil; then pour into a soup dish, lined with macaroni well cooked.

*VEGETABLE SOUP

Pare and slice five or six cucumbers; and add to these as many Cos lettuces, a sprig or two of mint, two or three onions, some pepper and salt, a pint and a half of young peas and a little parsley. Put these with half a pound of fresh butter, into a saucepan, to stew in their own liquor, near a gentle fire, half an hour, then pour two quarts of boiling water to the vegetables and stew them for two hours; rub down a little flour into a teacupful of water, boil it with the rest twenty minutes and serve.

VERMICELLI SOUP

Boil tender one half pound of vermicelli in a quart of rich gravy; take half of it out, and add to it more gravy; boil till the vermicelli can be pulped through a hair sieve. To both put a pint of boiling cream, a little salt and a quarter pound Parmesan cheese. Serve with rasped bread. Add two or three eggs if you like.

BROWN VERMICELLI SOUP

Is made in the same manner, leaving out the eggs and cream, and adding one quart of strong beef gravy.

Worthwhile Hint
A handful of lettuce leaves, put to the boiling soup, will imbibe the grease and fat; then, when removed, will leave it clear and free.

Chapter 3

How to catch & cook fish of different kinds

FISH & SEA FOODS

Take the juice of smallage or lovage, and mix with any kind of bait. As long as there remains any kind of fish within yards of your hook, you will find yourself busy pulling them out.

HOW TO CHOOSE ANCHOVIES

They are preserved in barrels with bay salt; no other fish has the fine flavor of the anchovy. The best look red and mellow, and the bones moist and oily; the flesh should be high flavored, the liquor reddish, and have a fine smell.

BAKED BLACK BASS

Eight good-sized onions chopped fine; half that quantity of bread crumbs; butter size of hen's egg; plenty of pepper and salt; mix thoroughly with anchovy sauce until quite red. Stuff your fish with this compound and pour the rest over it, previously sprinkling it with a little red pepper. Shad, pickerel and trout are good the same way. Tomatoes can be used instead of anchovies, and are more economical. If using them, take pork in place of butter, and chop fine.

CHOWDER

Five pounds of codfish cut in squares; fry plenty of salt pork cut in thin slices; put a layer of pork in your kettle, then one of fish; one of potatoes in thick slices, and one of onions in slices; plenty of pepper and salt; repeat as long as your materials last, and finish with a layer of Boston crackers or crusts of bread. Water sufficient to cook with, or milk if you prefer. Cook one-half hour and turn over on your platter, disturbing as little as possible. Do clams and eels the same way.

*CLAM FRITTERS
Twelve clams chopped or not, one pint milk, three eggs, add liquor from the clams; salt and pepper, and flour enough for thin batter. Fry in hot lard.

*CLAM STEW
Lay the clams on a gridiron over hot coals, taking them out of the shell as soon as open, saving the juice; add a little hot water, pepper, a very little salt and butter rolled in flour sufficient for seasoning; cook for five minutes and pour over toast.

How to render boiled fish firm
Add a little saltpetre to the salt in the water in which the fish is to be boiled; a quarter of an ounce to one gallon.

TO BOIL CODFISH
If boiled fresh, it is watery; but it is excellent if salted, and hung for a day, to give it firmness. Wash and clean the fish well, and rub salt inside of it; tie it up, and put it on the fire in cold water; throw a handful of salt into the fish-kettle. Boil a small fish fifteen minutes; a large one thirty minutes. Serve it without the smallest speck or scum; drain. Garnish it with lemon, horseradish, the milt, roe, and liver. Oyster or shrimp sauce may be used.

EELS, TO STEW
Of this fish, that of the "silver" kind is preferable to its cogener, and, therefore, ought to be procured for all cuisine purposes. Take from three to four pounds of these eels, and let the same be thoroughly cleansed, inside and out, rescinding the heads and tails from the bodies. Cut them into pieces three inches in length each, and lay them down in a stew-pan, covering them with a sufficiency of sweet mutton gravy to keep them seething over a slow fire, when introduced into the pan, for twenty minutes. Add to the liquor, before you place your eels into it, a quarter of an ounce of whole black pepper, a quarter of an ounce of allspice, with one or two pieces of white ginger. Thicken with a light admixture of flour and butter, stirring it carefully round,

adding thereto, at the same time, one gill of good port wine, and half a gill of sweet ketchup. Lemon peel and salt may be added in accordance with your taste.

POTTED FISH

Take out the backbone of the fish; for one weighing two pounds take one tablespoonful of allspice and cloves mixed; these spices should be put into bags of not too thick muslin; put sufficient salt directly upon each fish; then roll in cloth, over which sprinkle a little cayenne pepper; put alternate layers of fish, spice and sago into an earthen jar; cover with the best cider vinegar; cover the jar closely with a plate and over this put a covering of dough rolled out to twice the thickness of pie crust. Make the edges of paste to adhere closely to the sides of the jar, so as to make it air-tight. Put the jar into a pot of cold water and let it boil from three to five hours, according to quantity. Ready when cold.

How to keep fish sound
To prevent meat, fish, &tc., going bad, put a few pieces of charcoal into the sauce-pan wherein the fish or flesh is to be boiled.

*FISH BALLS

Bone cooked fish, or salt fish, add double the quantity of mashed potatoes, one beaten egg, a little butter, pepper and salt to taste. Make into cakes or balls; dredge with flour and fry in hot lard.

FISH PIE

Pike, perch and carp may be made into very savory pies if cut into fillets, seasoned and baked in paste, with sauce made of veal broth, or cream put in before baking.

HOW TO BROIL OR ROAST FRESH HERRINGS

Scale, gut and wash; cut off the heads and steep them in salt and vinegar for ten minutes; dust them with flour and broil them over or before the fire, or in the oven. Serve with melted butter and parsley.

Herring is nice *jarred,* and done in the oven, with pepper, cloves, salt, a little vinegar, a few bay leaves, and a little butter.

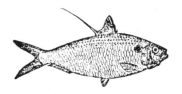

HOW TO FRY FRESH HERRINGS

Slice small onions, and lay in the pan with the herrings; add a little butter, and fry them. Perhaps it is better to fry the onions separately with a little parsley, and butter or drip.

HOW TO POT HERRINGS

Clean, cut off the heads, and lay them close in an earthen pot. Strew a little salt between every layer; put in cloves, mace, whole pepper, cayenne and nutmeg; fill up the jar with vinegar, water and a quarter of a pint of sherry, cover, tie down; bake in an oven, and when cold pot it for use. A few anchovies and bay leaves intermixed will improve the flavor much.

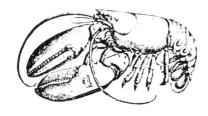

BUTTERED LOBSTER

Pick out the meat, cut it, and warm with a little brown gravy, nutmeg, salt, pepper and butter, with a little flour. If done white, use a little white gravy and cream.

CURRY OF LOBSTER

Take them from the shells, and lay into a pan, with a small piece of mace, three or four spoonfuls of veal gravy, and four of cream; rub smooth one or two teaspoonfuls of curry powder, a teaspoonful of flour, and an ounce of butter, simmer one hour; squeeze half a lemon in, and add salt.

LOBSTER CHOWDER

Four or five pounds of lobster, chopped fine; take the green part and add to it four pounded crackers; stir this into one quart of boiling milk; then add the lobster, a piece of butter one-half the size of a hen's egg, a little pepper and salt, and bring it to a boil.

*HOW TO BOIL MACKEREL

Rub them with vinegar; when the water boils, put them in with a little salt, and boil gently fifteen minutes. Serve with fennel and parsley chopped and boiled, and put into melted butter, and gooseberry sauce.

The secret art of catching fish
Put the oil of rhodium on the bait, when fishing with a hook, and you will always succeed.

SALT MACKEREL

Soak the fish for a few hours in lukewarm water, changing the water several times; then put into cold water loosely tied in cloths, and let the fish come to a boil, turning off the water once, and pouring over the fish hot water from the tea-kettle; let this come to a boil, then take them out and drain them, lay them on a platter, butter and pepper them, and place them for a few moments in the oven. Serve with sliced lemons, or with any fish sauce.

*HOW TO FRY OYSTERS

Use the largest and best oysters; lay them in rows upon a clean cloth and press another upon them, to absorb the moisture; have ready several beaten eggs; and in another dish some finely crushed crackers; in the frying pan heat enough butter to entirely cover the oysters; dip the oysters first into the eggs, then into the crackers, rolling them over, that they may become well encrusted; drop into the frying pan and fry quickly to a light brown. Serve dry and let the dish be warm. A chafing dish is best.

OYSTERS, SCALLOPED

Beard and trim the oysters, and strain the liquor. Melt in a stewpan, with a dredging of flour sufficient to dry it up, an ounce of butter, and two tablespoonfuls of white stock, and the same of cream; the strained liquor and pepper, and salt to taste. Put in the oysters and gradually heat them through, but be sure not to let them boil. Have your scallop-shells buttered, lay in the oysters, and as much liquid as they will hold; cover them well over with the bread crumbs, over which spread, or drop, some tiny bits of butter. Brown them in an oven, or before the fire, and serve them very hot.

OYSTERS, STEWED

In all cases, unless using shell oysters, wash and drain; mix half a cup of butter and a tablespoonful of corn starch; put with the oysters in a porcelain kettle; stir until they boil; add two cups of cream or milk; salt to taste; do not use the liquor of the oysters in either stewing or escaloping.

SUSIE'S OYSTERS, STEWED

Scald the oysters in their own liquor, then take them out, beard them, and strain the liquor carefully from the grit. Put into a stewpan an ounce of butter, with suffi-

cient flour dredged in to dry it up; add the oyster liquor, and a blade of pounded mace, a little cayenne, and a very little salt to taste, stir it well over a brisk fire with a wooden spoon, and when it comes to a boil, throw in your oysters, say a dozen and a half or a score, and a good tablespoonful of cream, or more, if you have it at hand. Shake the pan over the fire, and let it simmer for one or two minutes, but not any longer, and do not let it boil, or the fish will harden. Serve in a hot dish, garnished with sippets of toasted bread. Some persons think the flavor is improved by boiling a small piece of lemon peel with the oyster liquor, taking it out, however, before the cream is added.

SALMON, TO BOIL

Clean it carefully, boil it gently with salt and a little horse radish; take it out of the water as soon as done. Let the water be warm if the fish be split; if underdone it is very unwholesome. Serve with shrimp, lobster, or anchovy sauce, and fennel and butter.

SALMON, TO MARINATE

Cut the salmon in slices; take off the skin and take out the middle bone; cut each slice asunder; put into a saucepan and season with salt, pepper, six cloves, a sliced onion, some whole chives, a little sweet basil, parsley, and a bay leaf; then squeeze in the juice of three lemons or use vinegar. Let the salmon lie in the marinate for two hours; take it out; dry with a cloth; dredge with flour, and fry brown in clarified butter; then lay a clean napkin in a dish; lay the slices upon it; garnish with fried parsley.

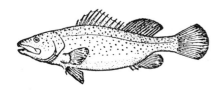

SALT COD, TO DRESS

Soak the cod all night in two parts of water, and one part of vinegar. Boil, and break into flakes on the dish; pour over it boiled parsnips, beaten in a mortar, and then boil up with cream, and a large piece of butter rolled in a bit of flour. It may be served with egg sauce instead of parsnip, or boiled and served without flaking with the usual sauce.

All *salt fish* may be done in a similar way. Pour egg sauce over it, or parsnips, boiled and beaten fine with butter and cream.

The value of cod
Of all fish, the cod lends itself most favorably to preservation, salting, curing, and drying.

HOW TO BOIL STURGEON

Take of water two quarts; vinegar, one pint; a stick of horse radish; a little lemon peel, salt, pepper, a bay leaf. In this boil the fish; when the fish is ready to leave the bones, take it up; melt one-half pound of butter; add an anchovy, some mace, a few shrimps, good mushroom ketchup, and lemon juice; when it boils, put in the dish; serve with the sauce; garnish with fried oysters, horseradish and lemon.

HOW TO DRESS FRESH STURGEON

Cut slices, rub egg over them, then sprinkle with crumbs of bread, parsley, pepper and salt; fold them in white paper, and carefully broil gently. Sauce: butter, anchovy and soy.

HOW TO BROIL STURGEON

After slicing fish, rub with a mixture of beaten egg and the juice of one-half lemon; dredge them in a powder of bread crumbs, herbs, parsley, salt and pepper. Wrap in paper and broil gently. Use for sauce Worcestershire, anchovy and butter.

HOW TO ROAST STURGEON

Put a piece of butter, rolled in flour, into a stewpan with four cloves, a bunch of sweet herbs, two onions, some pepper and salt, half a pint of water and a glass of vinegar. Set it over the fire till hot; then let it become lukewarm, and steep the fish in it an hour or two. Butter a paper well, tie it round, and roast it without letting the spit run through. Serve with sorrel and anchovy sauce.

TROUT, À LA GENEVOISE

Clean the fish well; put it into the stewpan, adding half champagne and half sherry wine. Season it with pepper, salt, an onion, a few cloves stuck in it, and a small bunch of parsley and thyme; put in it a crust of French bread; set it on a quick fire. When done, take out the bread, bruise it and thicken the sauce; add flour and a little butter, and boil it up. Lay the fish on the dish, and pour the sauce over it. Serve it with sliced lemon and fried bread.

HOW TO BROIL TROUT

Wash, dry, tie it, to cause it to keep its shape; melt butter, add salt, and cover the trout with it. Broil it gradually in a Dutch oven, or in a common oven. Cut an anchovy small, and chop some capers. Melt some butter with a little flour, pepper, salt, nutmeg, and half a spoonful of vinegar. Pour it over the trout and serve it hot.

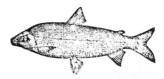

*BOILED WHITE FISH

Lay the fish open; put it in a dripping pan with the back down; nearly cover with water; to one fish put two tablespoonfuls salt, cover tightly and simmer (not boil) one-half hour; dress with gravy, butter, and pepper; garnish with sliced eggs.

For sauce, use a piece of butter the size of an egg, one tablespoonful of flour, one half pint of boiling water; boil a few minutes, and add three hard-boiled eggs, sliced.

*FRESH BROILED WHITE FISH

Wash and drain the fish; sprinkle with pepper and lay with the inside down upon the gridiron, and broil over bright coals. When a nice brown, turn for a moment on the other side, then take up and spread with butter. This is a very nice way of broiling all kinds of fish, fresh or salted. A little smoke under the fish adds to its flavor. This may be made by putting two or three cobs under the gridiron.

Fish ages
Carp live to be 70 to 150 years old; pike, 30 to 40 years; salmon, 16 years; codfish, 14 to 17 years; eel, 10 years.

Chapter 4

How to roast, broil or boil
POULTRY

HOW TO ROAST CHICKEN

Pluck carefully, draw and truss them, and put them to a good fire; singe, dust, and baste them with butter. Cover the breast with a sheet of buttered paper; remove it ten minutes before it is enough; that it may brown. A chicken will take fifteen to twenty minutes. Serve with butter and parsley.

When drawing a fowl, the prudent lady of the home will open its craw to search for possible gem stones scratched up and eaten by her farmyard poultry attracted to their brightness.

*HOW TO BOIL CHICKEN

Fasten the wings and legs to the body by threads tied round. Steep them in skim milk for two hours. Then put them in cold water, and boil over a slow fire. Skim clean. Serve with white sauce, or melted butter sauce, or parsley and butter. —Or melt one ounce of butter in a cupful of milk; add to it the yolk of an egg beat up with a little flour and cream; heat over the first, stirring well.

CHICKEN PIE

Cut the chicken in pieces, and boil nearly tender. Make a rich crust with an egg or two to make it light and puffy. Season the chicken and slices of ham with pepper, salt, mace, nutmeg, and cayenne. Put them in layers—first the ham, chicken, force-meat balls, and hard eggs in layers. Make a gravy of knuckle of veal, mutton bones, seasoned with herbs, onions, pepper, &tc. Pour it over the contents of the pie, and cover with paste, bake an hour.

SCALLOPED COLD CHICKENS

Mince the meat very small, and set it over the fire, with a scrape of nutmeg, a little pepper and salt, and a little cream, for a few minutes. Put it into the scallop shells, and fill them with crumbs of bread over which put some bits of butter, and brown them before a fire. Veal and ham eat well done the same way, and lightly covered with crumbs of bread, or they may be put on in little heaps.

*ROAST CHICKEN, HERBED

Crush with a small garlic clove a half teaspoonful of peppercorns; rub in a lump of butter the size of a hen's egg; add a little salt, pepper, about a half teaspoonful each of ginger, cinnamon, powdered cumin, and sweet herbs as favored to taste. Pluck, draw, and singe over an open fire a large roasting bird; then pierce it sharply where its flesh is the thickest. Rub thoroughly over the body and inside cavity the butter and herb admixture. Then set aside a while that the seasoning may infuse. Add a few bay leaves to the bird when put in a dripping pan and roast in a medium oven an hour or so; turning it over once when half done, and basting with butter drippings. Roast till skin is crisp and savory brown. Serve with lemon slices and sauce of drippings.

GOOSE À LA MODE

Skin and bone the goose; boil and peel a dried tongue, also a fowl; season with pepper, salt and mace, and then roll it round the tongue, season the goose the same way, and lay the fowl and tongue on the goose, with slices of ham between them. Beef marrow, rolled between the fowl and the goose, will greatly enrichen it. Put it all together in a pan, with two quarts of beef gravy, the bones of the goose and fowl, sweet herbs and onions; cover close, and stew an hour slowly; take up the goose, skim off the fat, strain, and put in a glassful of good port wine, two tablespoonfuls of ketchup, a veal sweetbread cut small, some mushrooms, a piece of butter rolled in flour, pepper and salt; stew the goose half an hour longer; take up and pour the ragout over it. Garnish with lemon.

HOW TO ROAST PIGEONS
Take a little pepper and salt, a piece of butter, and parsley cut small; mix and put the mixture into the bellies of the pigeons, tying the necks tight; take another string; fasten one end of it to their legs and rumps, and the other to a hanging spit, basting them with butter; when done, lay them in a dish and they will swim with gravy.

HOW TO BOIL PIGEONS
Wash clean; chop some parsley small; mix it with crumbs of bread, pepper, salt, and a bit of butter; stuff the pigeons, and boil fifteen minutes in some mutton broth or gravy. Boil some rice soft in milk; when it begins to thicken, beat the yolks of two or three eggs, with two or three spoonfuls of cream, and a little nutmeg; mix well with a bit of butter rolled in flour.

HOW TO BROIL PIGEONS
After cleaning, split the backs, salt and pepper them, and broil them very nicely; pour over them either stewed or pickled mushrooms, in melted butter, and serve as hot as possible.

HOW TO ROAST TURKEY
The sinews of the legs should be drawn whichever way it is dressed. The head should be twisted under the wing; and in drawing it, take care not to tear the liver, nor let the gall touch it.

Put a stuffing of sausage meat; or, if sausages are to be served in a dish, a bread stuffing. As this makes a large addition to the size of the bird, observe that the heat of the fire is constantly to that part; for the breast is often not done enough. A little strip of paper should be put on the bone to hinder it from scorching while the other parts roast. Baste well and froth it up. Serve with gravy in the dish, and plenty of bread sauce in a sauce tureen. Add a few crumbs, and a beaten egg to the stuffing of the sausage meat.

Chapter 5

How to choose & cook
GAME

How to choose ducks
A young duck should have supple feet, breast and belly hard and thick. A tame duck has dusky yellow feet. They should be picked dry, and ducklings scalded.

HOW TO ROAST DUCK
Carefully pick, and clean the inside. Boil two or three onions in two waters; chop them very small. Mix the onions with about half the quantity of sage leaves, bread crumbs finely powdered, a spoonful of salt, and a little cayenne pepper; beat up the yolk of an egg and rub the stuffing well together. With a brisk fire roast about 35 minutes. Serve with gravy sauce.

HOW TO STEW DUCKS
Lard two young ducks down each side the breast; dust with flour; brown before the fire; put into a stewpan with a quart of water, a pint of port wine, a spoonful of walnut ketchup, the same of browning, one anchovy, a clove of garlic, sweet herbs and cayenne pepper. Stew till they are tender, about half an hour; skim and strain, and pour over the duck.

GAME PIE
Divide the birds, if large, into pieces or joints. They may be pheasants, partridges, &tc. Add a

little bacon or ham. Season well. Cover with puff paste, and bake carefully. Pour into a pie half a glass of melted butter, the juice of a lemon, and a glass of sherry, when rather more than half baked.

HOW TO HASH PARTRIDGE

Cut up the partridges as for eating; slice an onion into rings; roll a little butter in flour; put them into the tossing pan, and shake it over the fire till it boils; put in the partridge with a little port wine and vinegar; and when it is thoroughly hot, lay it on the dish with sippets around it; strain the sauce over the partridge, and lay on the onion in rings.

HOW TO POT PARTRIDGE

Clean them nicely; and season with mace, allspice, white pepper and salt, in a fine powder. Rub every part well; then lay the breast downward in a pan, and pack the birds as closely as you possibly can. Put a good deal of butter on them, then cover the pan with a coarse flour paste and a paper over, tie it close, and bake. When cold, put the birds into pots, and cover with butter.

HOW TO ROAST PARTRIDGE

Roast them like a turkey, and when a little under roasted, dredge them with flour and baste them with butter; let them go to the table with a fine froth; put gravy sauce in the dish, and bread sauce on the table.

HOW TO STEW PARTRIDGE

Truss as for roasting; stuff the craws, and lard them down each side of the breast; roll a lump of butter in pepper, salt and beaten mace, then put them inside; sew up the vents; dredge them well and fry a light brown; put them into a stewpan with a quart of good gravy, a spoonful of sherry wine, the same of mushroom ketchup, a teaspoonful of lemon pickle, and a little mushroom powder, one anchovy, half a lemon, a sprig of sweet marjoram; cover the pan close, and stew half an hour; take out, and thicken the gravy; boil a little, and pour it over the partridge, and lay round them artichoke buttons, boiled, and cut in quarters, and the yolks of four hard eggs, if agreeable.

HOW TO ROAST PHEASANT

Roast them as turkey; and serve with a fine gravy (into which put a very small bit of garlic) and bread sauce. When cold, they may be made into excellent patties, but their flavor should not be overpowered by lemon.

HOW TO ROAST PLOVERS

Roast the *green* ones in the same way as woodcocks, and quails, without drawing, and serve on toast. *Gray* plovers may be either roasted or stewed with gravy, herbs and spice.

HOW TO FRICASSEE QUAILS

Having tossed them up into a sauce-pan with a little melted butter and mushrooms, put in a slice of ham, well beaten, with salt, pepper, cloves and savory herbs; add good gravy, and a glass of sherry; simmer over a slow fire; when almost done, thicken the ragout with a good cullis (i.e. a good broth, strained, gelatined, &tc.) or with two or three eggs, well beaten up in a little gravy.

HOW TO ROAST QUAILS

Roast them without drawing and serve on toast. Butter only should be eaten with them, as gravy takes off the fine flavor. The thigh and the back are the most esteemed.

HOW TO ROAST RABBITS

Baste them with butter, and dredge them with flour; half an hour will do them at a brisk fire, and if small, twenty minutes. Take the livers, with a bunch of parsley, boil them, and chop them very fine together; melt some butter, and put half the liver and parsley into the butter; pour it into the dish, and garnish the dish with the other half; roast them to a fine brown.

HOW TO MAKE RABBIT TASTE LIKE HARE

Choose one that is young, but full grown; hang it in the skin three or four days; then skin it, and lay it, without washing, in a seasoning of black pepper and allspice in a very fine powder, a glass of port wine, and the same quantity of vinegar. Baste it occasionally for forty hours, then stuff it and roast it as a hare, and with the same sauce. Do not wash off the liquor that it was soaked in.

ROMAN PUDDING

Oil a plain tin mold, sprinkle it with vermicelli, line it with a thin paste; have some boiled macaroni ready cut into pieces an inch long; weigh it, and take the same weight of Parmesan cheese, grated; boil a rabbit, cut off all the white meat in slices, as thin as paper; season with pepper, salt, and shalot; add cream sufficient to moisten the whole; put it into the mold, and cover it with paste; bake in a moderate oven for an hour, turn the pudding out of the mold, and serve it with a rich brown gravy.

HOW TO ROAST SNIPES

Do not draw them. Split them; flour them; and baste with butter. Toast a slice of brown bread; place it in the dish under the birds for the trail to drop on. When they are done enough, take up, and lay them on the toast; put good gravy in the dish. Serve with butter, and garnish with orange or lemon.

SNIPE PIE

Bone four snipes, and truss them. Put in their insides finely chopped bacon, or other forcemeats; put them in a dish with the breasts downward, and put forcemeat balls around them. Add gravy made of butter, and chopped veal and ham, parsley, pepper, and shalots. Cover with nice puff paste; close it well to keep in the gravy. When nearly done, pour in more gravy, and a little sherry wine. Bake two or three hours.

HOW TO FRY VENISON

Cut the meat into slices and make a gravy of the bones; fry it of a light brown, and keep it hot before the fire; put butter rolled in flour into the pan, and stir it till thick and brown; add one-half pound of loaf sugar powdered, with the gravy made from the bones, and some port wine. Let it be as thick as cream; squeeze in a lemon; warm the venison in it; put it in a dish, and pour the sauce over it.

Chapter 6

How to select & cook
MEATS

HOW TO DISTINGUISH GOOD MEAT FROM BAD

1. It is neither of a pale pink nor of a deep purple tint, for the former is a sign of disease, and the latter indicates the animal has not been slaughtered, but has died with the blood in it, or has suffered from acute fever.

2. It has a marked appearance from the ramifications of little veins of fat among the muscles.

3. It should be firm and elastic to the touch and should scarcely moisten the fingers—bad meat being wet and sodden and flabby with the fat looking like jelly or wet parchment.

4. It should have little or no odor, and the odor should not be disagreeable, for diseased meat has a sickly cadaverous smell, and sometimes a smell of physic. This is very discoverable when the meat is chopped up and drenched with warm water.

5. It should not shrink or waste much in cooking.

6. It should not run to water or become very wet on standing a day or two, but should, on the contrary, dry upon the surface.

7. When dried at a temperature of 212°, or thereabouts, it should not lose more than 70 to 74 per cent of its weight, whereas bad meat will often lose as much as 80 per cent.

OBSERVATIONS ON MEAT

In all kind of provisions, the best of the kind goes the farthest; it cuts out with more advantage, and affords more nourishment. Round of beef, fillet of veal, and leg of mutton are joints of higher price; but as they have more solid meat they deserve the preference. But those joints which are inferior may be dressed as palatably.

1. In loins of meat, the long pipe that runs by the bone should be taken out, as it is apt to taint; as also the kernels of beef. Do not purchase joints bruised by the blows of drovers.

2. Save shank bones of mutton to enrich gravies and soups.

3. When sirloin of beef, or loins of mutton or veal, come in, part of the suet may be cut off for puddings, or to clarify.

4. Drippings will baste anything as well as butter; except fowls and game; and for kitchen pies, nothing else should be used.

5. The fat of the neck or loin of mutton makes a far lighter pudding than suet.

6. Frosted meats and vegetables should be soaked in *cold water* two or three hours before using.

7. If the weather permits, meat eats much better for hanging two or three days before it is salted.

8. Roast beef bones, or shank bones of ham, make fine pea soup; and should be boiled with the peas the day before eaten, that the fat may be taken off.

*Batter to be used for all sorts of roasting meat

Melt good butter; put to it three eggs, with the whites well beaten up, and warm them together, stirring them continually. With this you can baste any roasting meat, and then sprinkle bread crumbs thereon; and so continue to make a crust as thick as you please.

CALF'S LIVER & BACON

Cut the liver into slices, and fry it first, then the bacon; lay the liver in the dish, and the bacon upon it; serve it up with gravy, made in the pan with boiling water, thickened with flour and butter, and lemon juice; and, if agreeable, a little parsley and onion may be chopped into it, or a little boiled parsley strewed over the liver. Garnish with slices of lemon.

NICE FORM OF COLD MEATS

Remains of boiled ham, mutton, roast beef, &tc., are good chopped fine with hard boiled eggs, two heads of lettuce, a bit of onion, and seasoned with mustard, oil, vinegar, and, if needed, more salt. Fix it smoothly in a salad dish, and adorn the edges with sprigs of parsley or leaves of curled lettuce. Keep by the ice or in a cool place until wanted.

FRICASSEE OF COLD ROAST BEEF

Cut the beef into very thin slices; shred a handful of parsley very small, cut an onion into quarters, and put all together in a stewpan, with a piece of butter, and some strong broth; season with salt and pepper, and simmer very gently a quarter of an hour; then mix into it the yolks of two eggs, a glass of port wine, and a spoonful of vinegar; stir it quickly, rub the dish with shalot, and turn the fricassee into it.

ROLLED BEEF

Hang three ribs three or four days; take out the bones from the whole length, sprinkle it with salt, roll the meat tight and roast it. Nothing can look nicer. The above done with spices, &tc., and baked as hunters' beef, is excellent.

BEEF, ROLLED TO EQUAL HARE

Take the inside of a large sirloin, soak it in a glass of port wine and a glass of vinegar mixed, for 48 hours; have ready a large fine stuffing, and bind it up tight. Roast it on a hanging spit, and baste it with a glass of port wine, the same quantity of vinegar, and a teaspoonful of pounded allspice. Larding it improves the look and flavor; serve with a rich gravy in the dish; also with currant jelly and melted butter in tureens.

Aberdeen-Angus cattle run to fatter beef than Jerseys.

ROUND OF BEEF

Should be carefully salted and wet with the pickle for eight or ten days. The bone should be cut out first, and the beef skewered and tied up to make it quite round. It may be stuffed with parsley, if approved, in which case the holes to admit the parsley must be made with a sharp pointed knife, and parsley coarsely cut and stuffed in tight. As soon as it boils, it should be skimmed, and afterwards kept boiling very gently.

*ROAST BEEF SHOULDER

Take a good-sized joint of beef—shoulder has the strongest flavor most desirable of all beef cuts. Rub over meat with a mix of one half teaspoonful flour and the same of salt. A few holes to admit small pieces of shalots must be made in the meat with a sharp pointed knife (a boning knife will do nicely). Poke in the shalots, then close over with small plugs of salt pork. Put it in a deep iron pot or Dutch oven; brown all over quick in hot fat. Put to it two teacupfuls tomato juice seasoned with pepper and salt and a sprig of thyme or dill weed chopped fine. Let it just boil, cover close,

and simmer gently about two hours over a slow fire. Meat should be tender but not dry. Lay it on a hot dish and keep warm; skim fat from drippings; thicken with a little flour; pour sauce over roast. Boiled celery, strained through a hair sieve, goes nicely with it.

*ROAST SIRLOIN OF BEEF

Of a two to five pound beef sirloin gash the top thin layer of fat; rub it well with pepper and salt. Roast in a medium oven about one or one and a half hours. Serve on a hot dish with a gravy of its own drippings, made of one cupful brown gravy sauce with a glass of good port wine; put together in a saucepan and boiled down to half its quantity. In a skillet brown two or three shalots chopped fine, in two tablespoonfuls butter till soft; add several mushrooms chopped fine,

and cook tender. Mix into wine sauce, season with pepper and salt as desired. Serve in a sauce dish sprinkled with minced parsley.

SPICED BEEF

Take a round of an ox; or young heifer, from twenty to forty pounds. Cut it neatly, so that the thin flank end can wrap nearly round. Take from two to four ounces of salt-petre, and one ounce of coarse sugar, and two handfuls of common salt. Mix them well together and rub it all over. The next day salt it well as for boiling. Let it lie from two to three weeks, turning it every two or three days. Take out of the pickle, and wipe dry. Then take cloves, mace, well powdered, a spoonful of gravy, and rub it well into the beef. Roll it up as tightly as possible; skewer it, and tie it up tight. Pour in the liquor till the meat is quite saturated, in which state it must be kept.

STEWED BEEF

Take five pounds of buttock, place it in a deep dish; half a pint of white wine vinegar, three bay leaves, two or three cloves, salt and pepper; turn it over twice the first day, and every morning after for a week or ten days. Boil half a pound or a quarter of a pound of butter, and throw in two onions, chopped very small, four cloves, and some peppercorns; stew five hours till tender and a nice light brown.

BEEF STEAK, STEWED

Peel and chop two Spanish onions, cut into small parts four pickled walnuts, and put them at the bottom of a stewpan; add a teacupful of mushroom ketchup, two teaspoonfuls of walnut ketchup, one of shalots, one of Chile vinegar, and a lump of butter. Let the rump steak be cut about three-quarters of an inch thick, and beat it flat with a rolling-pin, place the meat on top of the onions, &tc., let it stew for one hour and a half, turning it every twenty minutes. Ten minutes before serving up, throw in a dozen oysters with the liquor strained.

BEEF STEAK & OYSTER SAUCE

Select a good, tender rump steak, about an inch thick, and broil it carefully. Nothing but experience and attention will serve in broiling a steak; one thing, however, is always to be remembered, never salt or season broiled meat until cooked. Have the gridiron clean and hot, grease it with either good butter or lard, before laying on the meat, to prevent its sticking or marking the meat; have clear, bright coals, and turn it frequently. When cooked, cover tightly, and have ready nice stewed oysters; then lay the steak in a hot dish and pour over some of the oysters. Serve the rest in a tureen. Twenty-five oysters will make a nice sauce for a steak.

AMY KISSWETTER'S IRISH STEW

Take a loin of mutton, cut it into chops, season it with very little pepper and salt, put it into a saucepan, cover it with water, and let it cook half an hour. Boil two dozen potatoes, peel and mash them, and stir in a cup of cream while they are hot; then line a deep dish with the potatoes, and lay in the cooked mutton chops; cover them over with the rest of the potatoes; then set in the oven to bake. Make some gravy of the broth in which the chops cooked. This is a very nice dish.

IRISH STEW

Cut off the fat of part of a loin of mutton, and cut it into chops. Pare, wash, and slice very thin some potatoes, two onions, and two small carrots; season with salt and pepper. Cover with water in a stewpan, and stew gently till the meat is tender, and the potatoes are dissolved in the gravy. It may be made of beef steaks, or mutton and beef mixed.

LEG OF LAMB

Should be boiled in a cloth to look as white as possible. The loin fried in steaks and served round, garnished with dried or fried parsley;

spinach to eat with it; or dressed separately or roasted.

LAMB PASTY

Bone the lamb, cut it into square pieces, season with salt and pepper, cloves, mace, nutmeg, and minced thyme; lay in some beef suet, and the lamb upon it, making a high border about it; then turn over the paste close, and bake it. When it is enough, put in some claret, sugar, vinegar, and the yolk of eggs, beaten together. To have the sauce only savory, and not sweet, let it be gravy alone, or the baking of bones in claret.

HOW TO HASH MUTTON

Cut thin slices of dressed mutton, fat and lean; flour them; have ready a little onion boiled in two or three spoonfuls of water; add to it a little gravy and the meat seasoned; and make it hot, but not to boil. Serve in a covered dish. Instead of onions, a clove, a spoonful of currant jelly, and half a glass of port wine will give an agreeable flavor of venison, if the meat be fine.

Serve with pickled cucumber, or walnut cut small, warm in it for change.

Hash smoothly plastered down will sour more readily than if left in broken masses in the chopping bowl, each mass being well exposed to the air.

BOILED LEG OF MUTTON

Soak well for an hour or two in salt and water; do not use much salt. Wipe well and boil in a floured cloth. Boil from two hours to two and a half. Serve with caper sauce, potatoes, mashed turnips, greens, oyster sauce.

To preserve the gravy in the leg, do not put it in the water till it boils; for the sudden contact with water causes a slight film over the surface, which prevents the escape of the gravy, which is abundant when carved.

LOIN OF MUTTON

Take off the skin, separate the joints with the chopper; if a large size, cut the chine-bone with a saw, so as to allow it to be carved into smaller pieces; run a small spit from one extremity to the other, and affix it to a larger spit, and roast it like the haunch. A loin weighing six pounds will take one hour to roast.

How to keep meat sound
To prevent meat going bad, put a few pieces of charcoal into the saucepan wherein the meat is to be boiled.

HOW TO DRESS BACON & BEANS

When you dress beans and bacon, boil the bacon by itself, and the beans by themselves, for the bacon will spoil the color of the beans. Always throw some salt into the water and some parsley nicely picked. When the beans are done, throw them into a colander to drain. Take up the bacon and skin it; throw some raspings of the bread over the top, and if you have a salamander, make it red hot, and hold it over it to brown the top of the bacon; if you do not have one, set it before the fire to brown. Lay the beans in the dish, and the bacon in the middle on the top, and send them to the table, with butter in a tureen.

BRAWN
Clean a pig's head, and rub it over with a little salt and saltpetre, and let it lie two or three days; then boil it until the bones will leave the meat; season it with salt and pepper, and lay the meat hot in a mold, and press and weight it down for a few hours. Boil another hour, covering. Be sure to cut the tongue, and lay the slices in the middle, as it much improves the flavor.

HAM & CHICKEN, IN JELLY
This is a nice dish for supper or dinner. Make with a small knuckle of veal some good white stock. When cold, skim and strain it. Melt it, and put a quart of it into a saucepan with the well-beaten whites of three eggs; a dessertspoonful of chili powder, or a tablespoonful of tarragon vinegar, and a little salt. Beat the mixture well with a fork till it boils; let it simmer till it is reduced to a little more than a pint; strain it; put half of it into a mold; let it nearly set. Cut the meat of a roast chicken into small thin pieces; arrange it in the jelly with some neat little slices of cold boiled ham, and sprinkle chopped parsley between the slices. When it has got quite cold, pour in the remainder of the jelly, and stand the mold in cold water, or in a cool place, so that it sets speedily. Dip the mold in boiling water to turn it out. Do not let it remain in the water more than a minute, or it will spoil the appearance of the dish. Garnish with a wreath of parsley.

*FRIED HAM & EGGS
Cut thin slices, place in the pan, and fry carefully. Do not burn. When done break the eggs into the fat; pepper slightly; keep them whole; do not turn them.

Ham rasher may be served with spinach and poached eggs.

*TO COOK HAM
Scrape it clean. Do not put in cold nor boiling water. Let the water become warm; then put in the ham. Simmer or boil lightly for five or six hours; take out, and shave off the rind. Rub granulated sugar into the whole surface of the ham, so long as it can be made to receive it.

Place the ham in a baking dish with a bottle of champagne or prime cider. Baste occasionally with the juice, and let it bake an hour in a gentle heat.

A slice from a nicely cured ham thus cooked is enough to animate the ribs of death.

Or, having taken off the rind, strew bread crumbs or raspings over it, so as to cover it; set it before the fire, or in the oven till the bread is crisp and brown. Garnish with carrots, parsley, &tc. The water should simmer all the time, and never boil fast.

HOW TO PREPARE PIG'S CHEEK FOR BOILING

Cut off the snout, and clean the head; divide it and take out the eyes and brains; sprinkle the head with salt, and let it drain 24 hours. Salt it with common salt and saltpetre; let it lie nine days if to be dressed without stewing with peas, but less if to be dressed with peas, and it must be washed first, and then simmer till all be tender.

CHINE OF PORK

Salt three days before cooking. Wash it well; score the skin, and roast with sage or onions finely shred. Serve with apple sauce. The chine is often sent to the table boiled.

HOW TO COLLAR PORK

Bone a breast or spring of pork; season it with plenty of thyme, parsley and sage; roll it hard; put in a cloth, tie both ends, and boil it; then press it; when cold, take it out of the cloth, and keep it in its own liquor.

PIG'S FEET & EARS

Clean carefully, and soak some hours, and boil them tender; then take them out; boil some vinegar and a little salt with some of the water, and when cold put it over them. When they are to be dressed, dry them, cut the feet in two, and slice the ears; fry and serve with butter, mustard and vinegar. They may be done either in batter, or only floured.

PORK, LOIN OF

Score it, and joint it, that the chops may be separated easily; then roast it as a loin of mutton. Or, put it into sufficient water to cover it; simmer till almost enough; then peel off the skin, and coat it with yolk of egg and bread crumbs, and roast for fifteen or twenty minutes, till it is done enough.

HOW TO ROAST A LEG OF PORK

Choose a small leg of fine young pork; cut a slice in the knuckle with a sharp knife; and fill the space with sage and onion chopped, and a little pepper and salt. When half done, score the skin in slices, but don't cut deeper than the outer rind. Apple sauce and potatoes should be served to eat with it.

PORK, ROLLED NECK OF

Bone it; put a forcemeat of chopped sage, a very few bread crumbs, salt, pepper and two or three berries of allspice over the inside; then roll the meat as tight as you can, and roast it slowly, and at a good distance from the fire at first.

PORK AS LAMB

Kill a young pig of four or five months; cut up the forequarter for roasting as you do lamb, and truss the shank close. The other parts will make delicate pickled pork; or steaks, pies, &tc.

*SPIT ROASTED PORK LOIN

Mix one half cupful soy with same amount of tomato juice; a quarter cupful clear honey, a clove of garlic chopped, a tablespoonful of ginger finely chopped. Pour over pork and let set in a warm place two or three hours. Roast it slowly on a hanging spit till done. Baste often with the drippings and saved marinate.

A Chinese sauce can be made by putting a tablespoonful of dry mustard to enough sherry wine to make a paste; mix in one quarter cupful each of tomato sauce and toasted sesame seeds, browned with shaking in a heavy skillet over a brisk fire. This roast and sauce are nice with rice and mustard greens cut small before boiling.

PORK SAUSAGES

Take six pounds of young pork, free from gristle or fat; cut small, and beat fine in a mortar. Chop six pounds of beef suet very fine; pick off the leaves of a handful of sage and shred it fine; spread the meat on a clean dresser, and shake the sage over the meat; shred the rind of a lemon very fine, and throw it, with sweet herbs, on the meat; grate two nutmegs, to which put a spoonful of pepper, and a large spoonful of salt; throw the suet over, and mix all well together. Put it down close in the pot; and when you use it, roll it up with as much egg as will make it roll smooth.

*SAUSAGE ROLLS

One pound of flour, half a pound of the best lard, quarter of a pound of butter, and the yolk of three eggs well beaten. Put the flour into a dish, make a hole in the middle of it, and rub in about one ounce of the lard, then the yolks of the eggs, and enough water to mix the whole into a smooth paste. Roll it out about an inch thick; flour your paste and board. Put the butter and lard in a lump into the paste, sprinkle it with flour, and turn the paste over it; beat it with a rolling-pin until you have got it flat enough to roll; roll it lightly until very thin; then divide your meat and put it into two layers of paste, and pinch the ends. Sausage rolls are now usually made small. Two pounds of sausage meat will be required for this amount of paste, and it will make about two and a half dozen rolls. White of the eggs should be beaten a little, and brushed over the rolls to glaze them. They will require from twenty minutes to half hour to bake; and should be served on a dish covered with a neatly-folded napkin.

HOW TO MAKE MEAT PIES & PUDDINGS OF VARIOUS KINDS

BEEF STEAK PIE

Prepare the steak, as stated under *Beefsteaks,* and when seasoned and rolled with fat in each, put them in a dish with puff paste around the edges; put a little water in the dish and cover it with a good crust.

BEEF STEAK PUDDING

Take some fine rump steaks; roll them with fat between; and, if you approve, a little shred onion. Lay a paste of suet in a basin, and put in the chopped steaks; cover the basin with a suet paste, and pinch the edges to keep the gravy in. Cover with a cloth, tie close, let the pudding boil slowly for two hours.

*BAKED BEEFSTEAK PUDDING

Make a batter of milk, two eggs and flour, or, which is better, potatoes boiled and mashed through a colander; lay a little of it at the bottom of the dish; then put in the steaks very well seasoned; pour the remainder of the batter over them, and bake it.

LENA'S BEEF STEAK PUDDING

Prepare a good suet crust, and line a cake-tin with it; put in layers of steak with onions, tomatoes, and mushrooms, chopped fine, a seasoning of pepper, salt and cayenne, and half a cup of water before you close it. Bake from an hour and a half to two hours, according to the size of the pudding and serve very hot.

GIBLET PIE

Clean the giblets well; stew with a little water, onion, pepper, salt, sweet herbs, till nearly done. Cool, and add beef, veal or mutton steaks. Put the liquor of the stew to the giblets. Cover with paste, and when the pie is baked, pour into it a large teacupful of cream.

KIDNEY PIE

If kidney, split and soak it, and season that or the meat used. Make a paste of suet, flour, and milk; roll it, and line a basin with some; put the kidney or steak in, cover with paste, and pinch round the edge.

Cover with a cloth and boil a considerable time.

MEAT & POTATO PUDDING

Boil some mealy potatoes till ready to crumble to pieces; drain; mash them very smooth. Make them into a thickish batter with an egg or two, and milk, placing a layer of steaks or chops well-seasoned with salt and pepper at the bottom of the baking dish; cover with a layer of batter, and so alternately, till the dish is full, ending with batter at the top. Butter the dish to prevent sticking or burning. Bake to a fine brown color.

PORK PIE, TO EAT COLD

Raise a common boiled crust into either a round or oval form, which you choose, have ready the trimmings and small bits of pork cut off the sweet bone when the hog is killed, beat it with a rolling pin, season it with salt and pepper, and keep the fat and lean separate; put it in layers close to the top, lay on the lid, cut the edge smooth, round, and pinch it; bake in a slow-soaking oven, as the meat is very solid. Observe, put no bone or water in the pork pie; the outside pieces will be hard if they are not cut small and pressed close.

*VEAL & HAM PIE

Cut about two pounds of veal into thin slices; as also a quarter of a pound of cooked ham; season the veal rather lightly with white pepper and salt, with which cover the bottom of the dish; then lay over a few slices of ham, then the remainder of the veal, finishing with the remainder of the ham; add a wine-glassful of water, and cover with a good paste, and bake; a bay leaf will be an improvement.

VEAL PIE

Take some of the middle, or scrag, of a small neck; season it, and either put to it, or not, a few slices of lean bacon or ham. If it is wanted of a high relish, add mace, cayenne, and nutmeg, to the salt and pepper; and also forcemeat and eggs; and if you choose, add truffles, morels, mushrooms, sweetbread, cut into small bits, and cocks'-combs blanced, if liked. Have a rich gravy ready, to pour in after baking. (It will be very good without any of the latter additions.)

COMMON VEAL PIE

Cut a breast of veal into pieces; season with pepper and salt, and lay them in the dish. Boil hard six or eight yolks of eggs, and put them into different places in the pie, pour in as much water as will nearly fill the dish; put on the lid, and bake. *Lamb Pie* may be done this way.

HOW TO BOIL TONGUE

If the tongue be a dry one, steep in water all night. Boil it three hours. If you prefer it hot, stick it with cloves. Clear off the scum, and add savory herbs when it has boiled two hours; but this is optional. Rub it over with the yolk of an egg; strew over it bread crumbs; baste it with butter; set it before the fire till it is of a light brown. When you dish it up, pour a little brown gravy or port wine sauce mixed the same way as for venison. Lay slices of currant jelly around it.

*HOW TO FRICASSEE TRIPE
Cut into small square pieces. Put them into the stewpan with as much sherry as will cover them, with pepper, ginger, a blade of mace, sweet herbs and an onion. Stew fifteen minutes. Take out the herbs and onion, and put in a little shred of parsley, the juice of a small lemon, half an anchovy cut small, a gill of cream and a little butter, or yolk of an egg. Garnish with lemon.

*HOW TO FRY TRIPE
Cut the tripe into small square pieces; dip them in yolks of eggs, and fry them in good dripping, till nicely brown; take out and drain, and serve with plain melted butter.

BREAST OF VEAL, STUFFED
Cut off the gristle of a breast of veal, and raise the meat off the bones, then lay a good forcemeat, made of pounded veal, some sausage meat, parsley, and a few shalots chopped very fine, and well seasoned with pepper, salt, and nutmeg; then roll the veal tightly and sew it with a fine twine to keep it in shape, and prevent the forcemeat escaping; lay some slices of fat bacon in a stewpan, and put the veal roll on it; add some stock, pepper, salt, and a bunch of sweet herbs; let it stew three hours, then cut carefully out the twine, strain the sauce after skimming it well, thicken it with brown flour; let it boil up once, and pour it over the veal, garnish with slices of lemon,

each cut in four. A fillet of veal first stuffed with forcemeat can be dressed in the same manner, but it must first be roasted, so as to brown it a good color; and forcemeat balls, highly seasoned, should be served around the veal.

VEAL CUTLETS, MAINTENON
Cut slices about three quarters of an inch thick; beat them with a rolling pin, and wet them on both sides with egg; dip them into a seasoning of bread crumbs, parsley, thyme, knotted marjoram, pepper, salt and a little nutmeg grated; then put them in papers folded over, and broil them; and serve with a boat of melted butter, with a little mushroom ketchup.
Another Way—Prepare as above, and fry them; lay into a dish, and keep them hot; dredge a little flour, and put a bit of butter into the pan; brown it, then pour some boiling water into it and boil quickly; season with pepper, salt, and ketchup and pour over them.
Another Way—Prepare as before, and dress the cutlets in a Dutch oven; pour over them melted butter and mushrooms.

FILLET OF VEAL
Veal requires a good, bright fire for roasting. Before cooking, stuff with a forcemeat, composed of two ounces of finely powdered bread crumbs, half a lemon peel chopped fine, half a teaspoonful of salt, and the same quantity of mixed mace and cayenne pepper, powdered pars-

ley, and some sweet herbs; break an egg, and mix all well together. Baste your joint with fresh butter, and send it to table well browned. A nice bit of bacon should be served with the fillet of veal, unless ham is provided.

VEAL PATTIES

Mince some veal that is not quite done with a little parsley, lemon peel, a scrape of nutmeg, and a bit of salt; add a little cream and gravy just to moisten the meat; and add a little ham. Do not warm this sauce till the patties are baked.

STEWED VEAL

Cut the veal as for small cutlets; put into the bottom of a pie dish a layer of the veal, and sprinkle it with some finely-rubbed sweet basil and chopped parsley, the grated rind of one lemon with the juice, half a nutmeg, grated, a little salt and pepper, and cut into very small pieces a large spoonful of butter; then another layer of slices of veal,

with exactly the same seasoning as before; and over this pour one pint of Lisbon wine and half a pint of cold water; then cover it over very thickly with grated stale bread; put this in the oven and bake slowly for three quarters of an hour, and brown it. Serve it in a pie dish hot.

Chapter 7

For meats, fish, game, &tc.

SAUCES

*ANCHOVY SAUCE

Chop one or two anchovies, without washing, put to them some flour and butter, and a little water; stir it over the fire till it boils, once or twice. If the anchovies are good, they will dissolve.

*ESSENCE OF ANCHOVIES

Take two dozen of anchovies, chop them, and without the bone, but with some of their liquor strained, add to them sixteen large spoonfuls of water; boil gently till dissolved, which will be in a few minutes. When cold, strain and bottle it.

*APPLE SAUCE

Pare, core, and quarter half a dozen good sized apples, and throw them into cold water to preserve their whiteness. Boil them in a saucepan till they are soft enough to mash—it is impossible to specify any particular time, as some apples cook much more speedily than others. When done, bruise them to a pulp, put in a piece of butter as large as a nutmeg, and sweeten them to taste. Put into saucepan only sufficient water to prevent them from burning. Some persons put the apples in a stone jar placed in boiling water; there is no danger of their catching.

APPLE SAUCE FOR GOOSE OR ROAST PORK

Pare, core, and slice some apples, and put them in a strong jar, into a pan of water. When sufficiently boiled, bruise to a pulp, adding a little butter, and a little brown sugar.

BECHAMEL SAUCE

Put a few slices of ham into a stew-pan, a few mushrooms, two or three shalots, two cloves, also a bay leaf and a bit of butter. Let them stand a few hours. Add a little water, flour and milk or cream; simmer forty minutes. Scalded parsley, very fine, may be added.

SAUCE FOR HOT OR COLD ROAST BEEF

Grate, or scrape very fine, some horseradish, a little made mustard, some pounded white sugar and four large spoonfuls of vinegar. Serve in a saucer.

*ELSIE JACK'S BREAD SAUCE

Break three quarters of a pound of stale bread into small pieces, carefully excluding any crusty and outer bits, having previously simmered till quite tender, an onion, well peeled and quartered in a pint of milk. Put the crumbs into a very clean saucepan, and, if you like the flavor, a small teaspoonful of sliced onions, chopped, or rather minced, as finely as possible. Pour over the milk, taking away the onions simmered in it, cover it up, and let it stand for an hour to soak. Then, with a fork, beat it quite smooth, and season with a very little powdered mace, cayenne and salt to taste, adding one ounce of butter; give the whole a boil, stirring all the time, and it is ready to serve. A small quantity of cream added at the last moment makes the sauce richer and smoother. Common white pepper may take the place of cayenne; or a few peppercorns may be simmered in the milk, but they

should be extracted before sending to table.

*BREAD SAUCE

Grate some old bread into a basin; pour boiling new milk over it; add an onion with five cloves stuck in it, with pepper and salt to taste. Cover it, and simmer it in a slow oven. When enough, take out the onions and cloves; beat it well, and add a little melted butter. The addition of cream very much improves the sauce.

CAPER SAUCE

Melt some butter, chop the capers fine, boil them with the butter. An ounce of capers will be sufficient for a moderate size sauce-boat. Add, if you like, a little chopped parsley, and a little vinegar. More vinegar, a little cayenne, and essence of anchovy, make it suitable for fish.

As a substitute for capers, some use chopped pickled gherkins.

*ESSENCE OF CELERY

Soak the seeds in spirits of wine or brandy; or infuse the root in the same for 24 hours, then take out, squeezing out all the liquor, and infuse more root in the same liquor to make it stronger. A few drops will flavor broth, soup, &tc.

*CELERY SAUCE

Wash well the inside leaves of three heads of celery; cut them into slices a quarter inch thick; boil for six minutes, and drain; take a tablespoonful of flour, two ounces of butter, and a teacupful of cream; beat well, and when warm, put in the celery and stir well over the fire about twelve minutes. The sauce is very good for boiled fowl, &tc.

COCOA SAUCE

Scrape a portion of the kernel of a cocoa nut, adding the juice of three lemons, a teaspoonful of the tincture of cayenne pepper, a teaspoonful of shalot vinegar, and half a cupful of water. Gently simmer for a few hours.

SAUCE FOR DUCKS

Serve a rich gravy in the dish; cut the breast into slices, but don't take them off; cut a lemon, and put pepper and salt on it, then squeeze it on the breast, and pour a spoonful of gravy over before you serve.

Sauce, plain, and for immediate use, should not be put into a jar and covered when warm, else it will change and ferment very quickly. It will keep some days with care in the putting up. Let it stand until perfectly cold, then put into a stone jar.

*EGG SAUCE

Boil two eggs hard, half chop the whites, put in the yolks, chop them together, but not very fine, put them with one quarter pound good melted butter.

*COUSIN AVIS' EGG SAUCE

Four eggs boiled twelve minutes, then lay them in fresh water, cold, put off the shells, chop whites and yolks separately, mix them lightly in a half-pint melted butter, made in proportions of quarter pound of butter to a large tablespoonful of flour, with four of milk and hot water; add powdered mace or nutmeg; to be eaten with pork, boiled, or poultry; or can use chicken gravy or the water the chicken was boiled in.

QUIN'S FISH SAUCE

Half a pint of mushroom pickle, the same of walnut, six long anchovies pounded, six cloves of garlic, three of them pounded; half a spoonful of cayenne pepper; put them into a bottle, and shake well before using. It is also good with beefsteaks.

SAUCE FOR FOWL OF ANY SORT

Boil some veal gravy, pepper, salt, and the juice of a Seville orange and a lemon, and a quarter as much of port wine as of gravy; pour it into the dish or a boat.

MINT SAUCE

Pick, wash, mash and chop fine green spearmint; to two tablespoonfuls of the minced leaves, put eight of vinegar, adding a little sugar. Serve cold.

*AUNT MYRTLE'S MINT SAUCE

Wash fresh gathered mint; pick the leaves from the stalks; mince them very fine, and put them into a sauceboat with a teaspoonful of sugar, and four tablespoonfuls of vinegar. It may also be made with dried mint or mint vinegar.

ONION SAUCE

Peel the onions, and boil them tender; squeeze the water from them, then chop them, and add to them butter that has been melted, rich and smooth, but with a little good milk instead of water; boil it up once, and serve it for boiled rabbits, partridge, scrag, or knuckle of veal, or roast mutton. A turnip boiled with the onions makes them milder.

SAUCE FOR COLD PARTRIDGE, MOOR-GAME, &TC.

Pound four anchovies and two cloves of garlic in a mortar; add oil and vinegar to taste. Mince the meat, and put the sauce to it as wanted.

SAUCE FOR SALMON

Boil a bunch of fennel and parsley, chop them small, and put into it some good melted butter. Gravy sauce should be served with it; put a little brown gravy into a saucepan, with one anchovy, a teaspoonful of lemon pickle, a tablespoonful of walnut pickle, two spoonfuls of water in which the fish was boiled, a stick of horseradish, a little browning, and salt; boil them four minutes; thicken with flour and a good lump of butter, and strain through a hair sieve.

SAUCE FOR SAVOURY PIES

Take some gravy, one anchovy, a sprig of sweet herbs, an onion, and a little mushroom liquor; boil it a little, and thicken it with burnt butter, or a bit of butter rolled in flour; add a little port wine, and open the pie, and put it in. It will serve for lamb, mutton, veal or beef pies.

FRENCH TOMATO SAUCE

Cut ten or a dozen tomatoes into quarters, and put them into a saucepan, with four onions, sliced, a little parsley, thyme, a clove and a quarter pound of butter; then set the saucepan on the fire, stirring occasionally for three quarters of an hour; strain the sauce through a horse-hair sieve, and serve with the directed articles.

ETHEL SMYTHE'S TOMATO SAUCE

Take twelve tomatoes, very red and ripe; take off the stalks, take out the seeds, and press out the water. Put the expressed tomatoes into a stewpan, with one and one half ounces of butter, a bay leaf, and a little thyme; put it upon a moderate fire, stir it into a pulp; put into it a good cullis, or the top of broth, which will be better. Rub it through a searcher, and put it into a stewpan with two spoonfuls of cullis; put in a little salt and cayenne.

Another Way—Proceed as above with the seeds and water. Put them into a stewpan, with salt and cayenne, and three tablespoonfuls of beef gravy. Set them on a slow stove for an hour, or till properly melted. Strain, and add a little good stock; and simmer a few minutes.

SAUCE FOR A TURKEY

Open some oysters into a basin, and wash them in their own liquor, and as soon as settled pour into a saucepan; add a little white gravy, a teaspoonful of lemon pickle; thicken with flour and butter; boil it three or four minutes; add a spoonful of thick cream, and then the oysters; shake then over the fire till they are hot, but do not let them boil.

VEAL GRAVY

Put into the stewpan bits of lard, then a few thin slices of ham, a few bits of butter, then slices of fillet of veal, sliced onions, carrots, parsnips, celery, a few cloves upon the meat, and two spoonfuls of broth; set it on the fire till the veal throws out its juices; then put it on a stronger fire till the meat catches to the bottom of the pan, and is brought to the proper color; then add a sufficient quantity of light broth, and simmer it upon a slow fire till the meat is well done. A little thyme and mushroom may be added. Skim and sift it clear for use.

WHITE SAUCE

One pound of knuckle of veal, or any veal trimmings, or cold white meat, from which all brown skin has been removed; if meat has been cooked, more will be required. It is best to have a little butcher's meat fresh, even if you have plenty of cold meat in the larder; any chicken bones greatly improve the stock. This should simmer for five hours, together with a little salt, a dozen white peppercorns, one or two small onions stuck with cloves, according to taste, a slice or two of lean ham, and a little shred of celery and a carrot (if in season) in a quart of water. Strain it, and skim off all the fat; then mix one dessertspoonful of flour in a half pint of cream; or, for economy's sake, half milk and half cream, or even all good new milk; add this to the stock, and if not salty enough, cautiously add more seasoning. Boil all together very gently for ten minutes, stirring all the time, as the sauce easily burns and very quickly spoils. This stock, made in large quantities, makes white soup; for this an old fowl, stewed down, is excellent, and the liquor in which a young turkey has been boiled is as good a foundation as can be desired.

*ECONOMICAL WHITE SAUCE

Cut up fine one carrot, two small onions, and put them into a stewpan with two ounces of butter, and simmer till the butter is nearly absorbed. Then mix a small teacupful of flour in a pint of new milk, boil the whole quietly till it thickens, strain it, season with salt and white pepper, or cayenne, and it is ready to serve. Or mix well two ounces of flour with one ounce of butter;

49

with a little nutmeg, pepper and salt; add a pint of milk, and throw in a strip of lemon peel; stir well over the fire till quite thick, and strain.

*WINE SAUCE

One and one half cupfuls sugar, three quarters cupful of good port wine, a large spoonful flour, and a large piece of butter. Mix together and simmer slowly over a slow fire, after carefully rubbing in the flour.

SAUCE FOR WILD FOWL

Simmer a teacupful of port wine, the same quantity of good meat gravy, a little shalot, a little pepper, salt, a grate of nutmeg and a bit of mace for ten minutes; put in a bit of butter and flour, give it all one boil, and pour it through the birds. In general, they are not stuffed as tame, but it may be done so if liked.

HOW TO MANUFACTURE WORCESTERSHIRE SAUCE

Mix together one and one half gallons white wine vinegar, one gallon walnut ketchup, one gallon mushroom ketchup, one half gallon Madeira wine, one half gallon Canton soy, two and one half pounds moist sugar, nineteen ounces salt, three ounces powdered capsicum, one and one half ounces each of pimento, coriander, and chutney, three quarters ounce each of cloves, mace, and cinnamon, and six and one half drachms assafoetida dissolved in a pint of brandy 20 above proof. Boil two pounds hog's liver for twelve hours in one gallon of water, adding water as required to keep up the quantity, then mix the boiled liver thoroughly with the water, strain it through a horse hair sieve, coarse. Add this to the sauce.

Chapter 8

How to prepare & serve

COOKED VEGETABLES

*HOW TO BOIL ARTICHOKES

If the artichokes are very young, about an inch of the stalk can be left; but should they be full grown, the stalk must be cut quite close. Wash them well and put them into strong salt water to soak for a couple of hours. Pull away a few of the lower leaves, and snip off the points of all. Fill a saucepan with water, throw some salt into it, let it boil up, and then remove the scum from the top; put the artichokes in with the stalks upward, and let them boil until the leaves can be loosened easily; this will take from thirty to forty minutes, according to the age of the artichokes. The saucepan should not be covered during the time they are boiling.

Rich melted butter is always sent to the table with them.

*NEW MODE TO DRESS ASPARAGUS

Scrape the grass, tie it up in bundles, then cut the ends off an even length. Have ready a saucepan, with boiling water, and salt in proportion of a heaped saltspoonful to a quart of water. Put in the grass, standing it on the bottom with the green heads out of the water, so that they are not liable to be boiled off. If the water boils too fast, dash in a little cold water. When the grass has boiled a quarter of an hour it will be sufficiently done; remove it from the saucepan, cut off the ends down to the edible part, arrange it on a dish in a round pyramid with the heads toward the middle of the dish, and boil some eggs hard; cut them in two, and place them around the dish quite hot. Serve melted butter in a sauce tureen; and those who like it rub the yolk of a hard egg into the butter, which makes a delicious sauce to the asparagus.

*HOW TO BOIL ASPARAGUS

Scrape the asparagus spears; tie them in small bunches; boil them in a large pan of water with salt in it; before you dish them up, toast some slices of bread, and then dip them into the boiling water; lay the asparagus on the toasts; pour on them rich melted butter and serve hot.

RAGOUT OF ASPARAGUS

Cut small asparagus spears like green peas, the best method is to break them off first; then tie them into small bunches to cut, boil them till half done; then drain them and finish with butter, a little broth, herbs, two cloves, and a sprig of savory. When done, take out the cloves, herbs, &tc., mix two yolks of eggs, with a little flour, and broth, to garnish a first course dish. But if you intend to serve it in a second course mix cream, a little salt, and sugar.

Batter for frying vegetables
Cut four ounces of fresh butter into small pieces, pour on it half a pint of barley water, and when dissolved, add a pint of cold water; mix by degrees with a pound of fine dry flour, and a small pinch of salt. Just before it is used, stir into it the whites of two eggs beaten to a solid froth; use quickly, that the batter may be light.

*FRENCH BEANS, À LA CREME

Slice the beans, and boil them in water with salt. When soft, drain. Put into a stewpan two ounces of fresh butter, the yolks of three eggs, beaten into a gill of cream, and set over a slow fire. When hot, add a spoonful of vinegar; simmer five minutes.

STEWED BEANS

Boil them in water in which a lump of butter has been placed; preserve them as white as you can; chop a few sweet herbs with some parsley very fine; then stew them in a pint of the water in which the leaves have been boiled, and to which a quarter of a pint of cream has been added; stew until quite tender, then add the beans, and stew five minutes, thickening with butter and flour.

*HOW TO BOIL BROCCOLI

Peel the thick skin of the stalks, and boil for nearly a quarter of an hour, with a little bit of soda, then put in salt, and boil five minutes more. Broccoli and savoys taste better when a little bacon is boiled with them.

*HOW TO BOIL CABBAGE

Cut off the outside leaves, and cut it in quarters; pick it well, and wash it clean; boil it in a large quantity of water, with plenty of salt in it; when it is tender and a fine light green, lay it on a sieve to drain, but do not squeeze it—it will take off the flavor; have ready some very rich melted butter, or chop it with cold butter. Greens must be boiled the same way. Strong vegetables like turnips and cabbage, &tc., require much water.

*CABBAGE SALAD

Three well beaten eggs, one cupful of vinegar, two tablespoonfuls of mustard, salt and pepper, one tablespoonful of butter; let this mixture come to a boil, when cool add seven tablespoonfuls of cream, and half a head of cabbage shaved fine.

*HOW TO BOIL CAULIFLOWERS

Strip off the leaves which you do not intend to use, and save same for the hogs; put the other cauliflowers into salt and water some time to force out snails, worms, &tc. Boil them twelve minutes on a drainer in plenty of water, then add salt, and boil five or six minutes longer. Skim well while boiling. Take out and drain. Serve with melted butter, or a sauce made of butter, cream, pepper and salt.

HOW TO FRY CAULIFLOWERS

Wash as before. Boil twenty or thirty minutes; cut it into small portions, and cool. Dip the portions twice into a batter made of flour, milk and egg, and fry them in butter. Serve with gravy.

*CORN-OYSTERS

Take a half dozen ears of sweet corn (those which are not too old); with a sharp knife split each row of the corn in the center of the kernel lengthwise; scrape out all the pulp; add one egg, well beaten, a little salt, one tablespoonful of sweet milk; flour enough to make a pretty stiff batter. Drop in hot lard, and fry a delicate brown. If the corn is quite young, omit the milk, using as little flour as possible.

*CUCUMBERS FOR IMMEDIATE USE

Slice, sprinkle with salt; let them stand several hours, drain, and then put to them sliced onions, vinegar to cover them, and salt, pepper, &tc. Cayenne pepper and ground mustard render them wholesome.

*STEWED CELERY

Wash and clean six or eight heads of celery, let them be about three inches long; boil tender and pour off all the water; beat the yolks of four eggs, and mix with half a pint of cream, mace and salt; set it over the fire with the celery, and keep shaking until it thickens, then serve hot.

*COLD SLAW

Take half a head of cabbage chopped fine, a stalk of celery chopped very fine—or a teaspoonful of celery seed, or a tablespoonful of celery essence—four hard boiled eggs, whites chopped very fine, a teaspoonful of mustard, a tablespoonful of butter, the yolks of the boiled eggs, salt and pepper, mix well; take an egg well beaten and stir in a cup of boiling vinegar, pour over and cover for a few minutes.

*EGG PLANT

Slice the egg plant an eighth of an inch in thickness, sprinkle a thin layer of salt between the slices, and lay them one over the other; and let them stand an hour. This draws out the bitter principal from the egg plant, and also a part of the water. Then lay each slice in flour, put in hot fat and fry it brown on both sides. Or boil the egg plant till tender, remove the skin, mash fine, mix with an equal quantity of bread or cracker crumbs, and salt, pepper and bake half an hour. This makes a delightful dish, and a very digestible one, as it has so little oily matter in it.

HOW TO BROIL MUSHROOMS

Pare some large, open mushrooms, leaving the stalks on, paring them to a point; wash them well, and turn them onto the back of a drying sieve to drain. Put into a stewpan two ounces of butter, some chopped parsley, and shalots, then fry them for a minute on the fire; when melted, place your mushroom stalks upward on a saucepan, then pour the butter and parsley over the mushrooms; pepper and salt them well with black pepper, put them in the oven to broil; when done, put a little good stock to them, give them a boil and dish them, pour the liquor over them, adding more gravy, but let it be put in hot.

HOW TO FRICASSEE PARSNIPS

Boil in milk till they are soft, then cut them lengthwise in bits two or three inches long, and simmer in a white sauce, made of two spoonfuls of broth, and a bit of mace, half a cupful of cream, a bit of butter, and some flour, pepper and salt.

*HOW TO MASH PARSNIPS

Boil them tender, scrape, then mash them in a stewpan with a little cream, a good piece of butter, and pepper and salt.

HOW TO STEW PARSNIPS

Boil them tender; scrape and cut into slices; put them into a saucepan with cream enough; for sauce, a piece of butter rolled in flour, and a little salt; shake the saucepan often, when the cream boils, pour them into a dish.

*PARSNIPS PATTIES

Boil young ones till tender, scrape, then pulp fine through a sieve; put to them two eggs well beaten, salt and pepper to season; then form into little patties, roll in fine flour seasoned, and fry in good butter to a nice brown. Place on a dish and garnish well.

*HOW TO BOIL PEAS

Peas should not be shelled long before they are wanted, nor boiled in much water; when the water boils, put them in with a little salt (some add loaf sugar, but if they are sweet themselves, it is superfluous) ; when the peas begin to dent in the middle they are boiled enough. Strain, and put in a piece of butter, then stir, before turning out into the dish. A little mint should be boiled with the peas.

*HOW TO BOIL POTATOES

Boil in a saucepan without lid, with only sufficient water to cover them; more would spoil them, as the potatoes contain much water, and it requires to be expelled. When the water nearly boils, pour it off, and add cold water, with a good portion of salt. The cold water sends the heat from the surface to the center of the potato, and makes it mealy. Boiling with a lid on often produces cracking.

*SAVORY POTATO CAKES

Take one quarter of a pound of grated ham, one pound of mashed potatoes, and a little suet; mixed with the yolks of two eggs, pepper, salt and nutmeg. Roll it into little balls, or cakes, and fry it of a light brown. Sweet herbs may be used in place of ham. Plain potato cakes are made of potatoes and eggs only.

*NEW POTATOES

Have them fresh dug as may be convenient; the longer they have been out of the ground the less well-flavored they are. Wash them well, rub off the skins with a coarse cloth or brush, and put them into boiling water, to which has been added salt, at the rate of one heaped teaspoonful to two quarts. Let them boil till tender—try them with a fork; they will take from ten or fifteen minutes to half an hour, according to size. When done, pour away the water, and set by the side of the fire, with the lid aslant. When they are quite dry, have ready a hot vegetable dish, and in the middle of it put a piece of butter the size of a walnut—some people like more;

heap the potatoes around it and over it, and serve immediately. You can do very young potatoes, no larger than marbles, parboiled, then fried in cream, with pepper, salt, a very little nutmeg, and a flavoring of lemon juice. Both make a very pretty little supper dish.

New potatoes
Should be cooked soon after having been dug; wash well, and boil.

The Irish, who boil potatoes to perfection, say they should always be boiled with their *jackets* on; as peeling them for boiling is only offering a premium for water to run through the potato, and rendering it sad and unpalatable; they should be well washed and put into cold water.

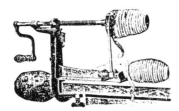

POTATO PASTY
Boil, and peel, and mash potatoes as fine as possible; mix them with salt, pepper and a good bit of butter. Make a paste; roll it out thin like a large puff, and put in the potato; fold over one half, pinching the edges. Bake in a moderate oven.

POTATO PIE
Skin some potatoes, and cut them in slices; season them; and also slice some mutton, beef, pork or veal, and a lump of butter. Put layers of them and of the meat. A few eggs boiled and chopped fine improves it.

PUREE OF POTATOES
This differs from mashed only in the employment of more milk and butter, and in the whole being carefully reduced to a perfectly smooth, thick, cream-like mixture. Where economy is a great object, and where rich dishes are not desired, the following is an admirable mode of mashing potatoes: Boil them till thoroughly done, having added a handful of salt to the water, then dry them well, and with two forks placed back to back beat the whole up until no lumps are left. If done rapidly, potatoes thus cooked are extremely light and digestible.

*POTATO RIBBONS
Cut the potatoes into slices, rather more than half an inch thick, and then pare round and round in very long ribbons. Place them in a pan of cold water, and a short time before wanted, drain them from the water. Fry them in hot lard, or good dripping, until crisp and browned; dry them on a soft cloth, pile them on a hot dish, and season with salt and cayenne.

*POTATOES ROASTED UNDER THE MEAT

These are very good. They should be nicely browned. Half boil large, mealy potatoes; put into baking dish, under the meat roasting; ladle the gravy upon them occasionally. They are best done in an oven.

POTATO ROLLS

Boil three pounds of potatoes; crush and work them with two ounces of butter and as much milk as will cause them to pass through a colander; take half a pint of yeast and half a pint of warm water; mix with the potatoes; pour the whole upon five pounds of flour; add salt, knead it well; if too thick, put to it a little more milk and warm water; stand before the fire for an hour to rise; work it well and make it into rolls. Bake it half an hour.

POTATO RISSOLES

Boil the potatoes floury; mash them, seasoning them with salt and a litle cayenne; mince parsley very fine, and work up with the potatoes, adding eschalot, also chopped small. Bind with yolk of egg, roll into balls, and fry with fresh butter over a clear fire. Meat shred finely, bacon or ham may be added.

POTATOES, SAUTÉED

These are even more agreeable with meat than fried potatoes. Cold boiled potatoes are sliced up, and tossed up in a saucepan with butter, mixed with a little chopped parsley, till they are lightly browned. Pure goose or other dripping is by many cooks preferred to butter for this purpose.

*POTATO SOUFFLES

The delicious blistered potatoes are prepared as follows: The potatoes, if small, are simply cut in halves; if large, cut in three or more slices; these are fried in the usual way, but are taken out before they are quite done, and set aside to get cold; when wanted, they are fried a second time, but only till they are of a light golden color, not brown.

*RICE FRITTERS

One pint of cooked rice, half cupful of sweet milk, two eggs, a tablespoonful of flour, and a little salt. Have the lard hot in the skillet, allow a tablespoonful to each fritter, fry brown on each side, then turn same as griddle cakes. If you find the rice spatters in the fat, add a very litle more flour. You can judge after frying one.

*RICE CROQUETTES

Make little balls or oblong rolls of cooked rice; season with salt, and pepper if you like; dip in egg; fry in hot lard.

*TOMATOES

Cut ripe tomatoes in slices, put them in a buttered dish with some bread crumbs, butter, pepper and salt, and bake till slightly brown on top.

FORCED TOMATOES

Prepare the following forcemeat: Two ounces of mushroom, minced small, a couple of shalots, likewise minced, a small quantity of parsley, a slice of lean ham, chopped fine, a few savory herbs, and a little cayenne and salt. Put all these ingredients into a saucepan with a lump of butter, and stew all together until quite tender, taking care that they do not burn. Put it by to cool, and then mix with them some bread crumbs and the well beaten yolks of two eggs. Choose large tomatoes, as nearly of the same size as possible, cut a slice from the stalk end of each, and take out carefully the seeds and juice; fill them with the mixture which has already been prepared, strew them over with bread and some melted butter, and bake them in a quick oven until they assume a rich color. They are a good accompaniment to veal or calf's head.

TOMATO TOAST

Remove the stems and all the seeds from the tomatoes; they must be ripe, mind, not *over ripe;* stew them to a pulp, season with butter, pepper and salt; toast some bread (not new bread), butter it, and then spread the tomato on each side, and send it up to the supper or dinner table, two slices on each dish, the slices cut in two; and the person who helps it must serve with two half-slices; do not attempt to lift the top slice, otherwise, the appearance of the under slice will be destroyed.

*TO MASH TURNIPS

Boil them very tender. Strain till no water is left. Place in a saucepan over a gentle fire, and stir well a few minutes. Do not let them burn. Add a little cream, or milk, or both, salt, butter and pepper. Add a tablespoonful of fine sugar. Stir and simmer five minutes longer.

*TO BOIL OR STEW VEGETABLE MARROW

This excellent vegetable may be boiled as asparagus. When boiled, divide it lengthways into two, and

serve it upon a toast accompanied by melted butter; or when nearly boiled, divide it as above, and stew gently in gravy like cucumbers. Care should be taken to choose young ones not exceeding six inches in length.

BOILED PASTES

*LEMON DUMPLINGS

Two tablespoonsfuls flour; one half pound of bread crumbs; six ounces beef suet; the grated rind of a large lemon; four ounces sugar, pounded; four eggs well beaten and strained, and the juice of three lemons, strained. Make into dumplings, and boil in a cloth for one hour.

*SUET DUMPLINGS

Shred one pound of suet; mix with one and one quarter pounds of flour; two eggs beaten separately, a little salt, and as little milk as will make it. Make it into two small balls. Boil twenty minutes. The fat of loins or necks of mutton finely shred makes a more delicate dumpling than suet.

MACARONI, AS USUALLY SERVED

Boil it in milk, or a weak veal broth flavored with salt. When tender, put it into a dish without the liquor, with bits of butter and grated cheese, and over the top grate more, and put a little more butter. Put the dish into a Dutch oven a quarter of an hour, and do not let the top become hard.

*MACARONI, DRESSED SWEET

Boil two ounces in a pint of milk, with a bit of lemon peel, and a good bit of cinnamon, till the pipes are swelled to their utmost size without breaking. Lay them on a custard dish, and pour a custard over them hot. Serve cold.

MACARONI PUDDING

Take an equal quantity of ham and chicken, mince fine, half the quantity of macaroni which must be boiled tender in broth, two eggs beaten, one ounce of butter, cayenne pepper and salt to taste; all these ingredients must be mixed thoroughly together; put in molds and boil two hours.

*VERMICELLI PUDDING

Boil four ounces of vermicelli in a pint of new milk till soft, with a stick or two of cinnamon; then put in half a pint of thick cream, a quarter pound of butter, the same of sugar, and the yolks of four eggs. Bake without paste in an earthen dish.

Another Way—Simmer two ounces of vermicelli in a cupful of milk till tender; flavor it with a stick or two of cinnamon or other spice. Beat up three eggs, one ounce of sugar, half a pint of milk, and a glass of wine. Add to the vermicelli. Bake in a slow oven.

Chapter 9

How to prepare & serve
COOKED FRUITS

To skin apples
By pouring scalding water on apples, the skins may be easily slipped off, and much labor saved.

*APPLE FANCY
Pare and core apples, stew with sugar and lemon peels, beat four eggs to a froth, add a cupful of grated bread crumbs, a little sugar, and nutmeg, lay the apples in the bottom of a dish and cover with the bread crumbs, laying a few pieces of butter over the top, bake in a quick oven, when done turn out upside down on a flat dish, scatter fine sugar over the top of apples. A good companion dish can be made of boiled potatoes, beat fine with cream, large pieces of butter and salt, dropped on tin, made smooth on top, and scored with knife. Lay a thin slice of butter on top, then put in oven till brown.

*BAKED APPLES
Take a dozen tart apples, pare and core them, place sugar and small lump of butter in centre of each, put them in a pan with half pint of

water, bake till tender, basting occasionally with syrup while baking, when done, serve with cream.

*APPLE FRITTERS

One pint of milk, three eggs, add salt to taste, as much flour as will make a batter, beat yolks and whites of eggs separately, add yolks to milk, stir in the whites when mixing the batter; have tender apples, pare, core, and cut in large thin slices; around the apple, to be fried in hot lard, ladle batter into spider; lay slice of apple in centre of each quantity of batter; fry to a light brown.

*STEWED FIGS

Take four ounces of fine sugar, the thin rind of a large lemon, and a pint of cold water, when the sugar is dissolved add one pound of turkey figs, and place the stewpan over a moderate fire where they may heat and swell slowly, and stew gently for two hours, when they are quite tender, add the juice of one lemon, arrange them in a glass dish and serve cold.

*BOILED PEARS

Boil pears in water till soft, then add one pound of sugar to three pounds of fruit.

*STEWED PEARS

Pare and halve or quarter a dozen pears, according to their size; carefully remove the cores, but leave the sloths on. Place them in a clean baking jar with a closely fitting lid; add to them the rind of one lemon, cut in strips, and the juice of half a lemon, six cloves, and whole all-spice, according to discretion. Put in just enough water to cover the whole, and allow half a pound of loaf sugar to every pint. Cover down close, and bake in a very cool oven for five hours, or stew them very gently in a lined saucepan from three to four hours. When done, lift them out on a glass dish without breaking them; boil up the syrup quickly for two or three minutes; let it cool a little, and pour it over the pears. A little cochineal greatly enhances the appearance of the fruit; you may add a few drops of prepared cochineal; and a little port wine is often used, and much improves the flavor.

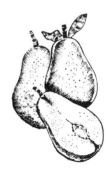

*QUINCES FOR THE TEA TABLE

Bake ripe quinces thoroughly; when cold, strip off the skins, place them in a glass dish, sprinkle with white sugar, and serve them with cream. They make a fine-looking dish for the tea table, and a more luscious and inexpensive one than the same fruit made into sweetmeats. Those who once taste the fruit thus prepared, will probably desire to store away a few bushels in the fall to use in the above manner.

STRAWBERRY & APPLE SOUFFLE

Stew the apples with a little lemon peel; sweeten them, then lay them pretty high round the inside of a dish. Make a custard of the yolks of two eggs, a little cinnamon, sugar and milk. Let it thicken over a slow fire, but not boil; when ready, pour it into the inside of the apple. Beat the whites of the eggs to a strong froth, and cover the whole. Throw over it a good deal of pounded sugar, and brown it to a fine brown. Any fruit made of the proper consistence does for the walls—strawberries, when ripe, are delicious.

*BRANDIED MELONS

Bring from the garden several nice melons, ice cream melons do particularly well; cut a well deep into the heart meat, leaving a small cave therein; fill with good apricot brandy, or any fruit liqueurs you have in the pantry; then replace the rind plug and set aside in a cold place, preferably in the ice chest if there is room. After a couple of hours, open up and pour in more liqueur, doing the same for the next day or so. Before serving, slice up on a chilled platter. Your dinner guests will never forget such excellent cuisine.

Batter for frying fruits
Cut four ounces of fresh butter into small pieces, pour on it half a pint of barley water, and when dissolved, add a pint of cold water; mix by degrees with a pound of fine dry flour, and a small pinch of salt. Just before it is used, stir into it the whites of two eggs beaten to a solid froth; use quickly, that the batter may be light.

Chapter 10

DAIRY PRODUCTS

How to make, keep, & cook

HOW TO KEEP MILK

Milk may be preserved in stout, well-corked and wired bottles by heating them to the boiling point in a water bath; by which the small quantity of enclosed air becomes decomposed. Milk, or green goose-

berries, or peas, thus treated, will keep for two years. Some persons add a few grains of calcined magnesia to each bottle of milk before corking it.

Milk keeps from souring longer in a shallow pan than in a milk pitcher. Deep pans make an equal amount of cream.

*A SUBSTITUTE FOR CREAM

Beat up the whole of a fresh egg in a basin, and then pour boiling tea over it gradually to prevent its curdling; it is difficult from the taste, to distinguish it from rich cream.

HOW TO MAKE BUTTER & BUTTERMILK

Rest thick new cream, fresh from the separator, covered in a warm place eighteen to twenty-four hours till congealed. Then fill a clean churn less than half full with the

cooled cream (or, if desired, use two parts whole milk and one part cream). Cover churn and work the paddle briskly, one-half to an hour—longer in inclement weather —keeping the mixture cool, till the butter flecks are the size of peas. Pour off the buttermilk, and wash the butter particles once or twice with a like quantity of cool spring water, working it well in with the paddle till the butter be clean. Turn out in a large wooden butter bowl and, if desired salted, cut in with the ladle one ounce of table salt to a pound.

The butter will keep excellently as mentioned aforehand; but the buttermilk must be used immediately while fresh and flavorful. When mixed with gruel or swill, it makes the hogs' meat more tender and savory.

The best churn made today comes from England. It is an iron-hooped white oak barrel, with thick staves sadiron waxed inside, having a firm clamped end-opening head, which hangs in a cradle and tumbles end for end when turned by a crank handle on one side and a pivot axel on the opposite. These churns are said to make better butter quicker with less cream, and to last a lifetime.

Cows fed long hay give richer milk.

HOW TO PRESERVE BUTTER

1. The best method to preserve butter from the air is to fill the pot to within an inch of the top, and to lay on it common coarse-grained salt, to a depth of one-half an inch or three-quarters of an inch, then to cover the pot up with any flat article that may be convenient. The salt by long keeping will run to brine, and form a layer on the top of the butter, which will effectually keep out the air, and may at any time be easily removed by turning the pot on one side.

2. Fresh butter, sixteen pounds; salt, one pound.

3. Fresh butter, eighteen pounds; salt, one pound; saltpetre one and one-fourth ounces; honey or fine brown sugar 2 ounces.

Butter as medicine
Like some other foods, butter
was originally used not as a food
but as a medicine. Although the
early Greeks and Romans did
not eat butter, they utilized it as
a remedy for skin injuries, as we
still use it for burns.

HOW TO PACK & PRESERVE BUTTER

Packing up butter gathered from an abundant churn is a nice operation, and needs to be carefully performed. As it is of all shades of color, from white to pale yellow generally, depending upon the kind of milk cow from whence it came, a coloring may be prepared by melting some of the butter and dissolving in it a prepared annatto, which may be procured at any drug store. This should be kept for use as it is wanted. To use it, take a quantity of the butter to be colored in the mixing-bowl, cut it into gashes with the butter ladle (don't touch it with the hands), place a small portion of the coloring preparation in each of these gashes, and mix until the color is evenly spread and no streaks are to be seen. Then gash it once more with the ladle, sprinkle one ounce of salt to the pound of butter, and leave it twenty-four hours. Then pour off any water collected on it, and pack it in a new oak tub that has been soaked with brine for a day and night. Water should never be used for working butter at any time.

*HOW TO MAKE SCHMIERKAESE CHEESE

Let skimmed milk fresh from the cream separator set still a day or so in a warm place by the fire till clabbered; slightly warm the mixture, stirring a little, for one-half to an hour till the curds are quite firm and whey rises to the top. Strain the mixture through a fine hair sieve; hang in a clean muslin bag to drain overnight. When the curds are very dry, whip to crumbles and the cheese is ready to eat.

*HOW TO MAKE CLABBERED CHEESE

Put to fresh made Schmierkaese enough thick sweet cream to make it the consistence of tapioca pudding.

How to tell the age of eggs

We recommend the following process (which has been known for some time, but has been forgotten) for finding out the age of eggs, and distinguishing those that are fresh from those that are not. This method is based upon the decrease in the density of eggs as they grow old.

Dissolve two ounces of common kitchen salt in a pint of water. When a fresh-laid egg is placed in this solution it will descend to the bottom of the vessel, while the one that has been laid on the day previous will not quite reach the bottom. If the egg be three days old it will swim in the liquid, and if it is more than three days old it will float on the surface, and project above the latter more and more in proportion as it is older.

*HOW TO PRESERVE EGGS

Pour one quart of waterglass dissolved in two and a half gallons of boiling water into a large earthen keg and set aside. When cooled sufficiently, throw in several dozen fresh laid eggs, taking care the liquid covers them thoroughly. Cover the crock with a head and store in a cool part of the cellar till needed.

Hens stand to lay their eggs, cocks fly to fertilize them.

VALUE OF EGGS FOR FOOD & OTHER PURPOSES

Every element that is necessary to the support of man is contained within the limits of an egg shell, in the best proportions, and in the most palatable form. Plain boiled, they are wholesome. It is easy to dress them in more than 500 different ways, each method not only economical, but salutary in the highest degree. No honest appetite ever yet rejected an egg in some guise. It is nutriment in the most portable form, and in the most concentrated shape. Whole nations of mankind rarely touch any other animal food. Kings eat them plain as readily as do the humble tradesmen. After the victory of Muhldorf, when the Kaiser Ludwig sat at a meal with his *burggrafs* and great captains, he determined on a piece of luxury —"one egg to every man and two to the excellently valiant Schwepperman." Far more than fish—for it is watery diet—eggs are the scholar's fare. They contain phosphorus, which is brain food, and sulphur, which performs a variety of functions in the economy. And they are the best of nutriment for children, for, in a compact form, they contain everything that is necessary for the growth of a youthful frame. A raw egg in shell, stood on end, will support a weight of thirty-two pounds.

Eggs are, however, not only food —they are medicines also. The white is the most efficacious of remedies for burns, and the oil extractable from the yolk is regarded by the Russians as an almost miraculous salve for cuts, bruises, and scratches. A raw egg, if swallowed in time, will effectually detach a fish bone fastened in the throat, and the white of two eggs will render the deadly corrosive sublimate as harmless as a dose of calomel. They strengthen the consumptive, invigorate the feeble, and render the most susceptible all but proof against jaundice in its more malignant phase. They also can be drunk in the shape of that "egg flip" which sustains the oratorical efforts of modern statesmen.

The merits of eggs do not even end here. In France alone the wine clarifiers use more than 80,000,000 a year, and the Alsatians consume fully 38,000,000 in calico printing and for dressing the leather used in making the finest of French kid gloves.

Finally, not to mention various other employments for eggs in the arts, they may, of course, almost without trouble on the farmer's part, be converted into fowls, which, in any shape, are profitable to the seller and welcome to the buyer. Even egg shells are valuable, for allopath and homeopath alike agree in regarding them as the purest of carbonate of lime.

ASPARAGUS OMELET
Boil a dozen of the largest and finest asparagus heads you can pick; cut off all the green portions, and chop it in thin slices; season with a small teaspoonful of salt, and about one-fourth of that quantity of soluble cayenne. Then beat up six eggs in a sufficient quantity of new milk to make a stiffish batter. Melt in the frying pan a quarter of a pound of fresh sweet butter (or good clean dripping), and just before you pour on the batter place a small piece of butter in the center of the pan. When the dripping is quite hot, pour on half your batter, and as it begins to set, place on it the asparagus tops, and cover over

with the remainder. This omelet is generally served on a round of buttered toast, with the crusts removed. The batter is richer if made with cream.

*BUTTERED EGGS

Beat four or five eggs, yolks and whites together, put a quarter of a pound of butter in a basin, and then put that in boiling water, stir it till melted, then pour the butter and the eggs into a saucepan; keep a basin in your hand, just hold the saucepan in the other over a slow part of the fire, shaking it one way, as it begins to warm; pour it into a basin, and back, then hold it again over the fire, stirring it constantly in the saucepan, and pouring it into the basin, more perfectly to mix the egg and butter until they shall be hot without boiling. Serve on toasted bread, or in a basin, to eat with salt fish, or red herring.

*CHEESE OMELET

Mix to a smooth batter three tablespoonfuls of fine flour, with half a pint of new milk. Beat up well the yolks and whites of four eggs, a little salt, and a quarter of a pound of grated old English cheese. Add these to the flour and milk, and whisk all the ingredients together for half an hour. Put three ounces of butter into a frying pan, and when it is boiling pour in the above mixture, fry it for a few minutes, and then turn it carefully; when it is sufficiently cooked on the other side, turn it onto a hot dish and serve.

*OMELET

Six eggs beaten separately, beaten hard; two teaspoonfuls of corn starch, two tablespoonfuls of milk; whites of eggs, put in slow at last. Fry in butter.

*POACHED EGGS

Break an egg into a cup, and put it gently into boiling water; and when the white looks quite set, which will be in about three or four minutes, take it up with an egg slice, and lay it on toast and butter, or spinach. Serve them hot; if fresh laid, they will poach well, without breaking.

How to distinguish raw eggs from cooked ones

The housewife can easily distinguish between her raw eggs and those which are cooked. She should lay her egg on a table, then give it a vigorous twirl; the cooked egg spins rapidly several *times, while the raw egg wallows shortly to a stop.*

*RUMBLED EGGS

This is very convenient for invalids, or a light dish for supper. Beat up three eggs with two ounces of fresh butter, or well-washed salt butter; add a teaspoonful of cream or new milk. Put all in a saucepan and keep stirring it over the fire for nearly five minutes, until it rises up like a soufflé, when it should be immediately dished on buttered toast.

*EGGS WITH CROUTONS

Melt fresh sweet butter in an iron skillet; add small pieces of bread and fry of a golden brown; mix in three eggs, broken but not beaten, with a gill of sweet milk, cayenne and a little salt, parsley chopped fine, and a few scrapes of nutmeg. Cover close, and simmer over a slow fire till just set. Serve on a warm dish with a sprinkle of turmeric powdered.

*HOW TO DRY EGGS

The eggs are beaten to uniform consistency, and spread out in thin cakes on batter plates. This dries them in a paste, which is to be packed in close cans and sealed. When required for use, the paste can be dissolved in water and beaten to a foam like fresh eggs. It is said that eggs can be preserved for years in this way and retain their flavor.

HOW TO STORE EGGS

Wright's *Illustrated Book of Poultry* says that a systematic trial for two seasons has shown that, for purposes of long keeping for eating or breeding, eggs should be packed with the large end downward, instead of being placed on the small end, as is commonly done. The longer the eggs are kept the greater difference will be found in the results of the two methods. Experiment has proved that eggs placed as recommended may be set and successfully hatched, with remarkable uniformity, at ages which with the usual method of storing would render success almost hopeless. The practical philosophy of the case is alleged to consist in delaying the spread of the air bubble and its detachment from the membraneous lining of the egg, thus retarding alterations destructive to its vitality.

TEN WAYS TO KEEP EGGS

1. Parties in the egg business in a large way build brick vats made water-tight, in which is lime water, made by putting lime in water, and when it is slacked and settled to the bottom, drawing off the liquor. Into this liquor the eggs are placed and kept beneath the surface. They are kept as cool as possible. These are the limed eggs with which the market is supplied during the winter.

2. Another mode of keeping eggs, tested by the Agriculture Department, is as follows: Rub the eggs with flaxseed (linseed) oil, and place them, large end down, in sand. Eggs so prepared were found at the end of six months to have the same taste and smell of perfectly fresh eggs, and to have lost in weight only three percent. Greasing eggs with lard or tallow has not been successful in preserving them, except for short periods.

3. Take a thin board of any convenient length and width and pierce it full of holes (each one and a half inches in diameter) as you can. (A board two feet and six inches in length and one foot wide, has five dozen holes in it—say, twelve rows of five each.) Then take four strips two inches broad and nail them together edgewise into a rectangular frame of the same size as your other board. Nail this board upon a frame and the work is done unless you choose to nail a heading around the top. Put your eggs in this board as they come from the hen house, the large end down, and they will keep good for six months, if you take the following precautions: Take care that the eggs do not get wet, either in the nest or afterwards. Keep them in a cool room in summer, and out of reach of frost in winter. If two boards be kept, one can be filling while the other is emptying.

4. Eggs can easily be kept from October to March in the following manner: A piece of lime, as large as a quart dipper, is put into five gallons of water, and salt added until an egg will float. This is strained and put into a clean keg, into which a loose head is made to fit easily; a knob fitted to the head for a handle. The eggs are put, as they are gathered, into the liquid, and the loose head placed on them to keep them below the surface. The keg should be kept in a cool place in the cellar. The liquor will not freeze except at a lower temperature than freezing point. Eggs thus preserved will sell readily as limed eggs until fresh eggs come, and are almost as good as fresh ones.

5. Take one quart of unslacked lime, pour to it water enough to make it the consistency of white-

wash, add one teaspoonful of cream of tartar; let this be in a wooden or stone vessel, and put the eggs into it.

6. Hang them by hooks in strong cabbage nets, and every day hook them on a fresh mesh, so as thereby to turn the eggs.

7. Apply with a brush a solution of gum arabic to the shells, or immerse the eggs therein, let them dry, and afterwards pack them in dry charcoal dust. This prevents their being affected by alterations of temperature.

8. Mix together in a tub, or vessel, one bushel Winchester measure of quick lime, 32 ounces of salt, eight ounces of cream of tartar, with as much water as will reduce the composition to a sufficient consistence to float an egg. Then put and keep the eggs therein, which will preserve them perfectly sound for two years at least.

9. Eggs can be preserved by keeping them at a temperature of 40° or less in an icebox. Eggs have been tested when kept in this manner for two years and found to be perfectly good.

10. Dissolve three or four ounces of beeswax in seven ounces of warm olive oil; put in this the tip of your finger and anoint the egg all over. Keep the eggs in a cool place and they will keep fresh for five years.

How to keep pans from darkening

When boiling eggs in aluminum kettles, add a little vinegar to the water; this will keep the vessel from darkening and yolk from oozing out should an egg crack during heating.

Chapter II

How to can, cure, pickle, store, & dry

PRESERVING FOODS

MEATS, FOWLS, & SEA FOOD

In this section, methods of food conservation are listed in rank of importance to Grandmother Artemisia, unblessed with the refrigeration, quick freeze, and vacuum flash-dry processing available to today's provenders.

In those times, she gave prime attention to beef preservation, since large, long-lasting quantities of meat dressed from butchery required long-time keeping.

Like cattle, hogs put not only meat on Grandmother's table but money in her family pocket as well. Unlike cows, pigs required little room to raise or to market, either on the hoof or as hams and bacon . . . whereas she valued sheep and goats more for their wool and milk than as handy meat sources.

She found that poultry, fish, and seafood called for little conservation and storage, since they were always on hand fresh in quantities needed.

As for fruits, Grandmother Artemisia knew bumper crops exacted harvest in season and not at will; so they demanded much thought to their over-winter protection and preservation.

On the whole, vegetables kept well in the ground where grown, and she could pull or dig them as wanted. Over hard winters, her convenient—though not infallible—root cellar enhanced their storage prospects.

Vinegar from the apple orchard, salt, sugar, and Grandmother's seasoned, country savvy combined to give her the clout needed to mediate the extremes in her otherwise feast-or-famine environment.

HOW TO PRESERVE MEAT IN CANS

There is a new method of preserving meat in cans which is favorably accepted by many. In this process the meat is first packed in its raw state into tins of any desired size. The lids are then soldered down, the top of each lid having a small tin tube inserted into it, which communicates with the interior of the tin. These tubes are next inserted into the exhauster, which is a receptacle connected with a machine designated a "Torricellian vacuum," an apparatus in which the air is exhausted by the action of water. The tins are then placed in the cooking bath, and at the proper juncture the vacuum is created and the meat most thoroughly cooked, at a temperature varying from 180° to 228°. At this stage, another feature of the invention comes into play. The vacuum

having been created, a supply of gravy is turned on from the receptacle, and the tins filled with nutritious fluid. The feed pipes of the tins are then nipped and the cases hermetically sealed. By thus filling the tins with the gravy, the difficulty of collapse, which has always hitherto prevented large tins from being used, is obviated, while the whole space of the can is utilized. Testimonials from ship captains, and others who have used it, are furnished by the inventor, certifying as to the excellent quality of the meat. By this improved process, overcooking the meat is prevented, and as now prepared it would seem to merit general approbation.

HOW TO KEEP MEAT FRESH IN WINTER

In Minnesota, where winter thaws are not much to be feared, it is quite common to hang up a porker or a leg of venison or beef, and cut from it as it hangs, week after week. But it seems that meat so kept must greatly deteriorate in flavor. It is best to cut the beef or venison into good pieces for cooking in various ways, and pack them down in snow. Of course they freeze, but thawing a piece brought in to cook is a simple thing. Put frozen poultry or meat in cold water, and all the frost will shortly leave it. A coating of ice will be found on the outside, which will easily cleave off.

HOW TO PROTECT MEAT FROM FLY

An effectual way of excluding the fly is by using a wire meat-safe, or by covering the joints with a long loose gauze, or some thin cloth, and hanging them from the ceiling of a dry room. Pepper and ginger should be sprinkled on the parts likely to be blown by the fly, but should be washed off before the joint is put to the fire.

HOW TO CURE MEAT

To one gallon of water add one and a half pounds of salt, half a pound of sugar, half an ounce of saltpetre, half an ounce of potash, in this ratio, the pickle to be increased to any quantity desired. Let these be boiled together until all the dirt from the sugar rises to the top and is skimmed off. Then throw it into a tub to cool, and when cold pour it over your beef or pork, to remain the usual time, say four or five weeks. The meat must be well covered with pickle, and should not be put down for at least two days after killing, during which time it should be slightly sprinkled with powdered saltpetre, which removes all the surface blood, &tc., leaving the meat fresh and clean. Some omit boiling the pickle, and find it to answer well, though the operation of boiling purifies the pickle by throwing off the dirt always to be found in salt and sugar. If this receipt is properly tried, it will never be abandoned. There is none that surpasses it, it is so good.

HOW TO PICKLE BEEF

Rub each piece of beef very lightly with salt; let them lie singly on a tray or board for 24 hours, then wipe them very dry. Pack them closely in a tub, taking care that it is perfectly sweet and clean. Have the pickle ready, made thus: Boil four gallons of soft water with ten pounds of coarse salt, four ounces of saltpetre, and two pounds of coarse brown sugar; let it boil fifteen minutes, then skim it while boiling very clean. When perfectly cold, pour it on the beef, laying a weight on the top to keep the meat under the pickle; this quantity is sufficient for 100 pounds of beef if closely packed.

A GOOD BEEF PICKLE

Take of moist sugar, two pounds; bay or common salt, four pounds; saltpetre, one-half pound; fresh ground allspice, two ounces; water, six to eight quarts. Dissolve. Used to pickle meat, particularly beef to which it imparts a fine red color and a superior flavor.

CORNED BEEF

Make the following pickle: Water, two gallons; salt, two and a half pounds; molasses, a quarter pound; sugar, one pound; saltpetre, one and a quarter ounces; pearlash, one quarter ounce. Boil all together; skim, and pour the pickle on about 25 pounds of beef. Let it stay in four weeks. Boil in plenty of water when cooked to remove the salt, and eat with it plenty of vegetables. It is nice to eat cold, and makes excellent sandwiches.

*MINCE MEAT

There are various opinions as to the results of adding meat to the sweet ingredients used in making this favorite dish. Many housewives

think it an improvement, and use either the under-cut of a well-roasted surloin of beef or a boiled fresh ox tongue for the purpose. Either of these meats may be chosen with advantage, and one pound, after it has been cooked, will be found sufficient; this should be freed from fat, and well minced. In making mince meat, each ingredient should be minced separately and finely before it is added to the others.

For a moderate quantity, take two pounds of raisins (stoned), the same quantity of currants, well washed and dried, ditto of beef suet, chopped fine; one pound of American apples, pared and cored, two pounds of moist sugar, half a pound of candied orange peel, and a quarter pound of citron, the grated rinds of three lemons, one grated nutmeg, a little mace, half an ounce of salt, and one teaspoonful of ginger. After having minced the fruit separately, mix all well together by hand; then add half a pint of French brandy and the same of good sherry. Mix well with a spoon, press it down in jars, and cover with a bladder.

*BETSY HOBBS' MINCE MEAT

Take three pounds of stoned raisins; three of currants; three pounds of beef suet, chopped fine; one pound of bread crumbs; three quarters of a pound of mixed candied peel; one and a half pounds of fillet of beef, previously cooked; salt, sugar, spices and ginger to taste. Each ingredient must be chopped up separately and very fine. Mix all well together, and take especial care that the beef is well mixed with the other ingredients. Moisten with a large bottle of brandy and stir occasionally.

*HELEN WILLIAMS' MINCE MEAT

Take half a pound of candied peel, cut in delicate slices, then chopped; add two wineglassfuls of brandy. Mix well together with a wooden spoon, and put the mince meat, well pressed down, into a covered jar, tied over very well. The mince meat should be made some days before it is wanted, and when about to be used a little more brandy should be stirred into it.

*MAVIS MAAS' MINCE MEAT

One quarter of an ounce of fine salt; half an ounce of mixed spice; three pounds of moist sugar, three pounds of well cleaned currants; two pounds of stoned raisins, chopped; two and a half pounds of beef suet, finely chopped; the thinnest peel of two lemons and their juice; two pounds of apples, baked to a pulp, and weighed when cold.

HOW TO CUT UP & CURE PORK

Always kill your hog in the morning, and let it remain from twenty-four to thirty-six hours before cutting it up. Have the hog laid on his back on a stout, clean bench; cut off the head close to the base. If the hog is large, there will come off a considerable collar, between head and shoulders, which, pickled or dried, is useful for cooking with vegetables. Separate the jowl from the face at the natural point; open the skull lengthwise and take out the brains, esteemed a luxury. Then with a sharp knife remove the back-bone the whole length, then the long strip of fat underlying it, leaving about one inch of fat covering the spinal column.

The leaf lard, if not before taken out for the housewife's convenience, is removed, as is also the tenderloin—a fish-shaped piece of flesh —often used for sausage, but which makes delicious steaks. The middling, or sides, are now cut out, leaving the shoulders square-shaped and the hams pointed, or they may be rounded to your taste. The spareribs are usually wholly removed from the sides, with but

little meat adhering. It is the sides of small, young hogs cured as hams that bear the name of breakfast bacon. The sausage meat comes chiefly in strips from the backbone, part of which may also be used as steaks. The lean trimmings from about the joints are used for sausage, the fat scraps rendered up with the backbone lard.

The thick part of the backbone that lies between the shoulders, called the griskin or chine, is separated from the tapering, bony part, called backbone by way of distinction, and used as flesh. The chines are smoked with jowls, and used in late winter or spring.

When the meat is to be pickled it should be dusted lightly with salt-petre sprinkled with salt, and allowed to drain 24 hours; then plunge it into pickle, and keep under with a weight. It is good policy to pickle a portion of the sides. They, after soaking, are sweeter to cook with vegetables, and the grease fried from them is much more useful than that of smoked meat.

If the meat is to be dry salted, allow one teaspoonful of pulverized

saltpetre to one gallon of salt, and keep the mixture warm beside you. Put on a hog's ear as a mitten, and rub each piece of meat thoroughly. Then pack skin side down, ham upon ham, side upon side, strewing on salt abundantly. It is best to put large and small pieces in different boxes for the convenience in getting at them to hang up at the different times they will come into readiness. The weather has so much to do with the time that meat requires to take salt, that no particular time can be specified for leaving it in.

The best test is to try a medium-sized ham; if salt enough, all similar and smaller pieces are surely ready, and it is well to remember that the saltness increases in drying.

Ribs and steaks should be kept in a cold, dark place, without salting, until ready for use. If you have many, or the weather is warm, they keep better in pickle than dry salt. Many persons turn and rub their meat frequently. Others who never practiced this, claim to have never lost any.

When the meat is ready for smoking, dip the hocks of the joints in ground black pepper and dust the raw surface thickly with it. Sacks, after this treatment, may be used for double security, and the bacon, hung high and dry, is sweeter than packed in any substance. For sugar-cured hams, the following receipt is the best ever used, though troublesome.

ENGLISH RECEIPT FOR SUGAR-CURED HAMS

As soon as the meat comes from the butcher's hand, rub it thoroughly with salt. Repeat this four

days, keeping the meat where it can drain. The fourth day rub it with saltpetre and a handful of common salt, allowing one pound of saltpetre to seventy pounds of meat. Now mix one pound of brown sugar and one of molasses, rub over the hams every day for a fortnight, and then smoke with hickory chips or cobs. Hams should be hung highest in the meat-house, because there they are less liable to attacks of insects, for insects do not so much infest high places—unlike human pests.

Pickle—Make eight gallons of brine strong enough to float an egg; add two pounds of brown sugar, and a quart of molasses, and four ounces of saltpetre; boil and skim clean, and pour cold onto the meat. Meat intended for smoking should remain in pickle about four weeks. This pickle can be boiled over, and with a fresh cupful of sugar and salt used all summer. Some persons use as much soda as saltpetre. It will correct acidity, but some think it impairs the meat. Some persons use a little sal prunella and a little vinegar.

Portly Berkshires dress out more lard and bacon. Lean razorbacks give better hams and chops.

HOW TO CURE HAMS

Hams cured by the following methods have been judged remarkable for their excellent flavor, while at the same time were juicy and tender.

MRS. GEORGE POTTS' HAMS

To each green ham of eighteen pounds, one dessertspoonful of saltpetre, one fourth pound of brown sugar, applied to the fleshy side of the ham and about the hock; cover the fleshy side with fine salt half an inch thick, and pack away in tubs; to remain from three to six weeks, according to size. Before smoking, rub off any salt that may remain on the ham, and cover well with ground pepper, particularly about the bone and hock. Hang up and drain for two days; smoke with green wood for eight weeks, or until the rind assumes a light chestnut color. The pepper is an effectual preventive of the fly.

ALVA HOLLOPETER'S HAMS

When the hams are cool, salt them down in a tight cask, putting a bushel of salt, well mixed with six ounces of saltpetre, to about one thousand pounds of pork; after it has been salted down four or five days, make a brine strong enough to float an egg, and cure the meat with it, then let it remain five weeks longer; then hang it up, dusting the fresh sides with black pepper; then smoke with green wood.

W. H. LEASE'S HAMS

After cutting out the pork, rub the skin-side with about half a teaspoonful of saltpetre, well rubbed in. Rub the pieces all over with salt, leaving them well covered on the fleshy side. Then lay the hams in large, tight troughs, skin-side down. Continue this process until it is all salted down. Let them remain in the troughs without touching or troubling them for four or five weeks, according to the size of the hog, no matter how warm or changeable the weather is. Then take them out of the trough, and string them on white oak spits; wash all the salt off with the brine, if sufficient; if not, with water; then rub them well and thoroughly with wood ashes. Let them hang up and remain 24 hours or two or three days before making the smoke under them, which must be made of green chips, and not chunks. Make the smoke under them every day, and smoke them five or six weeks. After the smoking stops, let the hams remain hanging all the time. Shoulders cure in the same manner.

HOW TO KEEP SMOKED HAMS

Make sacks of coarse cotton cloth, large enough to hold one ham, and fill it with chopped hay all around about two inches thick. The hay prevents the grease from coming in contact with the cloth, and keeps all insects from the meat. Hang in the smokehouse, or other dry, cool place, and they will keep a long time.

HOW TO MAKE & KEEP SAUSAGE

To make family sausage, the trimmings and other lean and fat portions of pork are used, taking care that there is about twice as much lean as fat; some consider it an improvement to add about one-sixth of the weight of lean beef. As to seasoning, that is a matter of taste. Most people use salt, pepper, and sage only, some use only salt and pepper, while others, in addition to the above, put in thyme, mace, cloves, and other spices. There is something repulsive about the intestines, or "skins," used for stuffing sausage, and the majority preserve the meat in bulk. In cold weather it will keep for a long time, but if it is desired to preserve it beyond cold weather it needs some care. It has been found that muslin bags,

made of a size to hold a roll two and a half to three inches in diameter, keep the meat very satisfactorily. These bags, when filled with sausage meat, are dipped into melted lard, and hung up in a dry, cool place. For seasoning, use to one hundred pounds of meat forty ounces salt, and from eight to ten ounces pepper.

HOW TO MAKE LARD

Cut the fat up into pieces about two inches square; fill a vessel holding about three gallons with the pieces; put in a pint of boiled lye made from oak and hickory ashes, and strained before using; boil gently over a slow fire, until the cracklings have turned brown; strain and set aside to cool. By this process you will get more lard, a better article, and whiter than by any other process.

HOW TO TRY OUT LARD

This should be done in the open air. Set a large kettle over the fire, in some sheltered place, on a still day. It will cook much quicker in large quantities. Put into the kettle, while the lard is cold, a little saleratus, say one tablespoonful to every twenty pounds of lard; stir almost constantly when nearly done, till the scraps are brown and crisp, or until the steam ceases to rise—then there is no danger of its molding; strain out into pans, and the first will be ready to empty into crocks when the last is strained.

HOW TO KEEP LARD FROM MOULDING

It is not likely to melt if properly tried and kept in a cool, dry place. Earthen crocks or pans well tinned are good to put lard in for keeping. Lard made from intestinal fat will not keep so long as leaf fat. It should be soaked two or three days in salted water, changed each day.

HOW TO KEEP LARD SWEET

Even during the warmest weather lard can be kept sweet by the following plan: When rendering (melting) it, throw into each kettle a handful of fresh slippery elm bark. No salt must be added to it at any time. The jars in which the lard is to be kept must be thoroughly cleansed.

HOW TO BLEACH LARD
Lard may be bleached by applying a mixture of bichromate of potassa and muriatic acid, in minute proportions, to the fat.

HOW TO KEEP SUET
Suet may be kept a year, thus: Take the firmest and most free from skin or veins, remove all traces of these, put the suet in the saucepan at some distance from the fire, and let it melt gradually; when melted, pour into a pan of cold spring water; when hard, wipe it dry, fold it in white paper, put it in a linen bag, and keep it in a cool, dry place; when used, it must be scraped, and it will make an excellent crust with or without butter.

*HOW TO PRESERVE BIRDS
Birds may be preserved in a fresh state for some time by removing the intestines, wiping out the inside quite dry with a towel, and then flouring them. A piece of blotting paper, on which one or two drops of creosote have been placed, is now to be put inside them, and a similarly prepared paper tied around them. They should then be hung up in a cool, dry place, and will be found to keep much longer than without undergoing this process.

*OYSTERS, TO PICKLE
Take 200 of the plumpest, nicest oysters to be had, open them, saving the liquor, remove the beards, put them, with the liquor, into a stewpan, and let them simmer for twenty minutes over a very gentle fire, taking care to skim them well. Take the stewpan off the fire, take out the oysters, and strain the liquor through a fine cloth, returning the oysters to the stewpan. Add to a pint of the hot liquor half an ounce of mace, and half an ounce of cloves; give it a boil, and put it in with the oysters, stirring the spices well in amongst them. Then put in about a spoonful of salt, three quarters of a pint of white wine vinegar, and one ounce of whole pepper, and let the oysters stand until they are quite cold. They will be ready for use in about twelve to twenty-four hours; if to be kept longer, they should be put in wide-mouth bottles, or stone jars, and well drawn down with bladder. It is important that they should be quite cold before they are put into the bottles, or jars.

FRUITS

HINTS ON PRESERVING

A very common discovery made by those who preserve fruits, &tc., is, that the preserves either ferment, grow moldy, or become candied.

These three effects arise from three separate causes. The first, from insufficient boiling; the second, from being kept in a damp place, assisted in some degree by the first cause; and the third, from being too quick and too long in boiling.

Preserves of all kinds should be kept entirely secluded from the air, and in a dry place. In arranging them on the shelves of a storage closet, they should not be suffered to come in contact with the walls. Moisture in winter and spring exudes from some of the driest walls, and preserves invariably imbibe it, both in dampness and taste. It is necessary occasionally to look at them, and if they have been attacked by mold boil them up gently again. To prevent all risks, it is always as well to lay a brandy paper over the fruit before tying down. This may be renewed in the spring.

Fruit jellies are made in the ratio of a quart of fruit to two pounds of sugar. They must not be boiled quick, nor very long. Practice, and a general discretion, will be found the best guide to regulate the exact time, which must be necessarily affected, more or less, by local causes.

HOW TO PRESERVE SMALL FRUITS WITHOUT COOKING

Strawberries, raspberries, blackberries, cherries, and peaches can be preserved in this manner: Lay the ripe fruit in broad dishes, and sprinkle over it the same quantity of sugar used in cooking it. Set it in the sun, or a moderately heated oven, until the juice forms a thick syrup with the sugar. Pack the fruit in tumblers, and pour the syrup over it. Paste writing paper over the glasses, and set them in a cool dry place. Peaches must be pared and split, and cherries stoned. Preserved in this manner, the fruit retains much more of its natural flavor and healthfulness than when cooked.

HOW TO PRESERVE FRUITS WITHOUT SUGAR OR VINEGAR

Pick the fruits from the stalks; put them into bottles. Put one drachm of alum into four gallons of boiling water; let it stand till it is cold; then fill the bottles with this liquor, bung them tight, and put them into a copper of cold water, and heat to 176°; and then tie them over with a bladder and seal them.

HOW TO PRESERVE FRUITS BY SYRUP WITHOUT HEAT

Many fruits when preserved by boiling lose much of their peculiar and delicate flavor, as for instance pineapples; and this inconvenience may, in some instances, be remedied by preserving them without heat. Cut the fruit in slices, about one-fifth of an inch thick; strew powdered loaf sugar an eighth of an inch thick in the bottom of the jar, and put the slices on it. Put more sugar on this, and then another layer of slices, and so on, till the jar is full. Place the jar with the fruit up to the neck in boiling water, and keep it there until the sugar is completely dissolved, which may take half an hour, removing the scum as it rises. Lastly, tie a wet bladder over the mouth of the jar, or cork and wax it.

FRUIT IN BRANDY

Gather your fruit before it is quite ripe; prick them with a pin on each side and put them into a stewpan of fresh spring water, and stew them gently until you can pass a pin with facility to the stone of the fruit, when you take them from the pan and put them to drain on a sieve. Whilst draining, prepare a syrup, which, when the fruit is nicely arranged in a tureen, should be thrown on it boiling hot, and so left for 24 hours, when the fruit is again put to drain, and the syrup boiled for one hour, and poured boiling hot all over the fruit once more. On the third day arrange the fruit in the preserving pots, and boil the syrup to a proper consistency; when cool mix with brandy, in the proportion of two-thirds syrup to one-third brandy, and pour it over the fruit.

HOW TO BOTTLE FRUIT

Cherries, strawberries, sliced pineapples, plums, apricots, gooseberries, &tc., may be preserved in the following manner, to be used as fresh fruit. Gather the fruit before it is very ripe; put it in wide-mouthed bottles made for the purpose; fill them as full as they will hold, and cork them tight; seal the corks; put some hay in a large saucepan; set in the bottles with hay between them to prevent their touching; then fill the saucepan with water to the necks of the bottles, and set it on the fire until the water is nearly boiling, then take it off; let it stand until the bottles are

83

cold; then keep them in a cool place until wanted, when the fruit will be found equal to fresh.

HOW TO KEEP FRUIT FRESH IN JARS

Self-sealing jars should be used. Put the fruit in a porcelain-lined preserving kettle, sufficient to fill four quart jars; sprinkle on sugar, one half pound, place over a slow fire and heat through, not boiled.

While fruit is being heated, keep the jars filled with moderately hot water. As soon as the fruit is ready, empty the water from the jars, fill to the brim with fruit, and seal immediately. As it cools a vacuum is formed, which prevents bursting. In this way every kind of fruit will retain its flavor. Sometimes a thick, leathery mold will form on the top —if so, all the better. The plan of keeping the jars full of hot water is merely to prevent the danger of cracking when the hot fruit is inserted. Some prefer to set the bottles full of cool water in a boiler of water, and heating all together gradually; but the other way is much simpler and equally effective.

HOW TO PRESERVE FRUITS WITHOUT SELF-SEALING CANS

Prepare a cement of one ounce resin, one ounce gum shellac, and a cubic inch of beeswax; put them in a tin cup and melt slowly; too high or too quick heat may cause it to scorch.

Place the jars where they will become warm while the fruit is cooking. If they are gradually heated there is no danger of breaking.

As soon as the fruit is thoroughly heated, and while boiling hot, fill the jars full, letting the juice cover the fruit entirely. Have ready some circular pieces of stout, thick cotton or linen cloth, and spread over with cement a piece sufficient to cover the mouth and rim of the jar. Wipe the rim perfectly dry, and apply the cloth while warm, putting the cement side down, bring the cover over the rim, and secure it firmly with a string; then spread a coating of cement over the upper surface. As the contents of the jar cool, the pressure of the air will depress the cover, and give positive proof that all is safe.

HOW TO CAN FRUITS

The principle should be understood, in order to work intelligently. The fruit is preserved by placing it in a vessel from which the external air is entirely excluded. This is effected by surrounding the fruit by liquid, and by the use of heat to rarefy and expel the air that may be entangled in the fruit or lodged in its pores. The preservation does not depend upon sugar, though enough of this is used in the liquid which covers the fruit to make it palatable. The heat answers another purpose; it destroys the ferment which fruits naturally contain, and as long as they are kept from contact with the external air they do not decompose.

The vessels in which fruits are preserved are tin, glass, and earthenware. Tin is used at the factories where large quantities are put up for commerce, but is seldom used in families, as more skill in soldering is required than most people possess. Besides, the tins are not generally safe to use more than once. Glass is the preferable material, as it is readily cleaned and allows the interior to be frequently inspected. Any kind of bottle or jar that has a mouth wide enough to admit the fruit and that can be securely stopped, positively air-tight—which is much closer than water-tight—will answer. Jars of various patterns and patents are made for the purpose, and are sold at the crockery and grocery stores. These have wide mouths and a glass or metallic cap which is made to fit very tightly by an India-rubber ring between the metal and the glass. The devices for these caps are numerous, and much ingenuity is displayed in inventing them. We have used several patterns without much difference

in success, but have found there was some difference in the facility with which the jars could be opened and closed. The best are those in which atmospheric pressure helps the sealing, and where the sole dependence is not upon screws or clamps. To test a jar, light a slip of paper and hold it within it. The heat of the flame will expand the air and drive out a portion of it. Now put on the cap; when the jar becomes cool the air within will contract, and the pressure of the external air should hold the cover on so firmly that it cannot be pulled off without first letting in the air by pressing aside the rubber or by such other means as is provided in the construction of the jar. When regular fruit jars are not used, good corks and cement must be provided.

Cement is made by melting one and a quarter ounces of tallow with one pound of rosin. The stiffness of the cement may be governed by the use of more or less tallow. After the jar is corked, tie a piece of stout drilling over the mouth. Dip the cloth on the mouth of the jar into the melted cement, rub the cement on the cloth with a stick to break up the bubbles, and leave a close covering.

The Process—Everything should be in readiness, the jars clean, the covers well fitted, the fruit picked over or otherwise prepared, and the cement and corks, if these are used, at hand. The bottles or jars are to receive a very hot liquid, and they must be gradually warmed beforehand, by placing warm water in them, to which boiling water is gradually added. Commence by making a syrup in the proportion of a pound of white sugar to a pint of water, using less sugar if this quantity will make the fruit too sweet. When the syrup boils, add as much fruit as it will cover, let the fruit heat in the syrup gradually, and when it comes to a boil, ladle it into the jars or bottles which have been warmed as above directed. Put in as much fruit as possible, and then add the syrup to fill up the interstices among the fruit; then put on the cover or insert the stopper as soon as possible.

Have a cloth at hand dampened in hot water to wipe the necks of the jars. When one lot has been bottled, proceed with more, adding more sugar and water if more syrup is required. Juicy fruits will diminish the syrup much less than others. When the bottles are cold, put them away in a cool, dry and dark place. Do not tamper with the covers in any way. The bottles should be inspected every day for a week or so, in order to discover if any are imperfect. If fermentation has commenced, bubbles will be seen in the syrup, and the covers will be loosened. If taken at once, the contents may be saved by thorough reheating.

Another Way—Prepare a syrup and allow it to cool. Place the fruit in the bottles, cover with the syrup and then set the bottles nearly up to their rims in a boiler of cold water. Some wooden slats should be placed at the bottom of the boiler to keep the bottles from contact with it. The water in the boiler is then heated and kept boiling until the fruit in the bottles is thoroughly heated through, when the covers are put on, and the bottles allowed to cool. It is claimed that the flavor of the fruit is better preserved in this way than by any other.

WHAT WILL PRESERVE

All the fruits that are used in their fresh state or for pies, &tc., and rhubarb, or pie-plant, and tomatoes. Green peas, and corn, cannot be readily preserved in families as they require special apparatus. Strawberries—hard-fleshed sour varieties, such as the Wilson, are better than the more delicate kinds.

Currants need more sugar than the foregoing. Blackberries and huckleberries are both very satisfactorily preserved, and make capital pies. Cherries and plums need only picking over. Peaches need peeling and quartering. The skins may be removed from ripe peaches by scalding them in water or weak lye for a few seconds, and then transferring them to cold water.

Some obtain a strong peach flavor by boiling a few peach meats in the syrup. We have had peaches keep three years, and were better then than those sold at the stores. Pears are pared and halved, or quartered, and the core removed. The best high-flavored and melting varieties only should be used. Coarse baking pears are unsatisfactory. Apples—very few put up these. Try some high-flavored ones, and you will be pleased with them. Quinces—there is a great contrast between quinces preserved in this way and those done up in the old way of pound for pound. They do not become hard, and they remain of a fine light color. Tomatoes require cooking longer than the fruits proper. Any intelligent person, who understands the principle upon which fruit is preserved in this way, will soon find the mechanical part easy of execution and the results satisfactory.

HOW TO KEEP CANNED FRUITS

The preservation of canned fruits depends very much on the place where they are stored. If put in the cellar, unless it is exceptionally dry, they will gather mould and lose all the fine, fresh flavor it is so desirable to retain. If kept in too warm a spot, they will ferment and burst the cans, and in that case, even if the fruit has not been spilled over the shelves, it will have been made so sour that no re-scalding, &tc., can make it good. Severe

cold does not injure it unless the weather is below zero.

One stinging cold morning, we entered our milk room to find long rows of grenadiers in red coats, standing triumphantly amid the fragments of numerous defeated bottles.

The tomatoes, being preserved entirely without sugar or spice, were frozen to a solid red ice, but the fruits put up with a small quantity of sugar were only slightly frozen, and as we immediately immersed the jars in cold water until the frost was extracted, they did not burst. The tomatoes were saved by an immediate re-bottling.

A double-walled closet in a fireless room on the second floor is one of the best places for storing canned fruits in the winter; and in summer, a cool milk room will be found safe.

*HOW TO PROTECT DRIED FRUIT FROM WORMS

It is said that dried fruit, put away with a little bark of sassafras—say, a large handful to a bushel—will save for years, unmolested by those troublesome little insects which so often destroy hundreds of bushels in a single season. The remedy is cheap and simple, but we venture to say a good one.

HOW TO DRY APPLES

The most general method adopted in drying apples is, after they are pared, to cut them in slices, and spread them on cloths, tables, or boards, and then dry them outdoors. In clear and dry weather, this is perhaps the most expeditious and best way; but in cloudy and stormy weather this way is attended with much inconvenience, and sometimes, loss, in consequence of the apples rotting before they dry. To some extent, they may be dried in this way in the house, though this is attended with much inconvenience. The best method that we have ever used to dry apples is to use frames. These combine the most advantages with the least inconvenience of any way, and can be used with equal advantage either in drying in the house or out in the sun. In pleasant weather the frames can be set outdoors against the side of the building, or any other support, and at night, or in cloudy and stormy weather, they can be brought into the house, and set against the side of the room near the stove or fireplace. Frames are made in the following manner: Two strips of board, 7 feet long, 2 to 2½ inches wide—two strips 3 feet long, 1½ inches wide, the whole ¾ inch thick—nail the short strips across the ends of the long ones, and it makes a frame 3 by 7 feet, which is a convenient size for all purposes. On one of the long strips nails are driven three inches apart, extending from the top to the bottom. After the apples are pared, they are quartered and

cored, and with a needle and twine, or stout thread, strung into lengths long enough to reach twice across the frame; the ends of the twine are then tied together, and the strings hung on the nails across the frames. The apples will soon dry so that the strings can be doubled on the nails, and fresh ones put on or the whole of them removed, and others put in their place. As fast as the apples become sufficiently dry, they can be taken from the strings, and the same strings used to dry more on. If large apples are used to dry, they can be cut into smaller pieces. Pears and quinces, and other fruits that can be strung, may be dried this way.

HOW TO KEEP APPLES

The following is a good plan: The apples should be placed in glazed earthenware vessels, each containing about a gallon, and surrounding the fruit with paper. The vessels being perfect cylinders, about a foot each in height, stand very conveniently upon each other, and thus present the means of preserving a large quantity of fruit in a very small room. If the space between the top of one vessel and the base of another be filled with cement, composed of two parts of the curd of skimmed milk and one of lime, by which the air will be excluded, the winter kind of apples will preserve with little change in their appearance from October to March. A dry and cold place in which there is little change of temperature is the best.

HOW TO PACK APPLES IN A BARREL

When the farmers find out that the manner of packing apples in barrels greatly influences the price of the same, they will take more care than they usually do. A neatly packed barrel will bring from one to two dollars more than one in which the apples are thrown in without any effort to make a good show. When you begin to pack the barrel, turn it upside down, the head resting on the ground or floor; then take the bottom out, leaving the head in. Then choose about a peck of your prettiest and finest apples; wipe them clean, being certain that there are no spots on them, or in any other manner disfigured; then place them in the barrel with their stems down, first placing them

around the rim of the barrel, entirely round the same, after which make another ring, until the whole is covered. Then throw in your apples, and when your barrel is full, press them down and put in the bottom, after which turn them head upwards. When the barrel is opened from the top, your apples will be found in good condition, even, and nicely packed.

*HOW TO PRESERVE APPLES

Pare and core and cut them in halves or quarters; take as many pounds of the best brown sugar; put a teacupful of water to each pound. When it is dissolved set it over the fire; and when boiling hot put in the fruit and let it boil gently until it is clear and the syrup thick; take the fruit with a skimmer on to flat dishes; spread it to cool; then put it in pots or jars and pour the jelly over. Lemons boiled tender in water and sliced thin may be boiled with the apples.

APPLE BUTTER

Select two bushels of sour apples, and peel, core, and quarter them. Take a barrel of good, sweet apple cider, and boil it in a copper kettle until all the impurities have arisen

89

to the surface. After this is done, and the impurities skimmed off, take out two-thirds of the cider. Then put in the apples, and as the quantity boils down put in the rest of the cider. After putting in the apples, the butter must be stirred without interruption until it is taken off. It will take about five hours' boiling after the apples are put into the cider. It should be boiled until the whole mass becomes smooth and of the same consistency, and of a dark brown color. Spice with ground cloves and cinnamon to taste. The butter can then be taken off and put into vessels for use. Earthen crocks are best for this purpose. Tie the vessels over with heavy paper and set them away in a dry place. The butter will keep a year if wanted.

HOW TO MAKE PENNSYLVANIA APPLE BUTTER

Let three bushels of fair sweet apples be pared, quartered, and the cores removed. Meanwhile, let two barrels of new cider be boiled down to one-half. When this is done, commit the prepared apples to the cider, and let the boiling go on briskly and systematically, stirring the contents without cessation, that they do not become attached to the side of the kettle and be burned. Let the stirring go on till the amalgamated cider and apples become as thick as hasty-pudding; then throw in pulverized allspice, when it may be considered as finished,

and committed to pots for future use.

*HOW TO PRESERVE CRAB APPLES

Take off the stems and core them with a sharp knife without cutting them open; weigh a pound of white sugar for each pound of apples; put a teacupful of water to each pound of sugar, and then put it over a slow fire. When the sugar is dissolved and hot put the apples in; let them boil gently until they are clear, then skim them, cut and spread them on flat dishes. Boil the syrup until it is thick; put the fruit in whatever they are to be kept, and when the syrup is cold and settled, pour carefully over the fruit. Slices of lemon boiled with the fruit is to some an improvement; one lemon is sufficient for several pounds of fruit. Crab apples may be preserved whole with three-quarters of an inch of stem on, three-quarters of a pound of sugar for each pound of fruit.

HOW TO PRESERVE WHOLE APRICOTS

Take the largest and cleanest apricots to be got; pick out the stones with a silver skewer, or slit them down the sides with a silver knife; take nearly their weight in good lump sugar; dip each lump in water and put over the fire; let it just boil; skim and put by till cold; then pour it over the fruit in the preserving can, warm very gently and only allow them to simmer; then put them by till the next day, and warm them again, continuing this till they look clear; then take the fruit from the syrup; the latter must now be well boiled and skimmed, and when cold poured over the fruit.

HOW TO DRY CHERRIES

Take the stems and stones from ripe cherries; spread them on flat dishes, and dry them in the sun or warm oven; pour whatever juice may have run from them, a little at a time, over them, stir them about that they may dry evenly. When they are perfectly dry, line boxes or jars with white paper, and pack them close in layers; strew a little brown sugar, and fold the paper over, and keep them in a dry place; or put them in muslin bags, and hang them in an airy place.

*HOW TO PRESERVE CHERRIES

Take fine large cherries, not very ripe; take off the stems and take out the stones; save whatever juice runs from them; take an equal weight of white sugar; make the syrup of a teacupful of water for each pound; set it over the fire until it is dissolved and boiling hot; then put in the juice and cherries, boil them gentle until clear throughout; take them from the syrup with a skimmer and spread them on flat dishes to cool; let the syrup boil until it is rich and quite thick; set it to cool and settle; take the fruit into jars or pots and pour the syrup carefully over; let them remain open until the next day;

then cover as directed. Sweet cherries are improved by the addition of a pint of red currant juice and half pound of sugar to it for four or five pounds of cherries.

HOW TO KEEP SWEET CIDER

Use only sound apples. Make the cider when the weather is almost cold enough to freeze the apples. Expose the cider during weather, and stir it till the whole of it is reduced as near the freezing point as possible without freezing. Then barrel it, bung up tight, and place in a cellar kept nearly down to the freezing point. As long as you can keep it cold enough it will not ferment, and as long as it does not ferment it will remain sweet.

*HOW TO PRESERVE CITRON MELON

Pare, core, and cut into slices some fine citron melons. Weigh them. To each six pounds of melons allow six pounds of refined sugar, the juice and grated rind of four large lemons, and a quarter pound of root ginger. Boil the slices of melon half an hour or more, till they look quite clear and are so tender that a broom straw will pierce them.

Then drain them, lay them in a pan of cold water, cover them, and let them stand all night. In the morning tie the root ginger in a thin muslin cloth, and boil it in three pints of clear water till the water is highly flavored; take out the bag of ginger and pour the water over the pieces of sugar, which is previously broken and put in a preserving kettle. When the sugar is melted, set it over the fire, put in the grated peel of the lemons and boil and skim it till no more scum rises. Then put in the sliced citrons and the juice of the lemons; boil them in the syrup till all the slices are quite transparent, and so soft that a straw will go through them, but do not break them. When done put the slices, still warm, into jars, and gently pour over the syrup. This will be found delicious.

HOW TO PRESERVE CUCUMBERS TO IMITATE GINGER

Take small cucumbers, with flowers and stalks on them, and some large ones gathered dry; put them in a stone jar with salt and water enough to cover them; then put cabbage leaves on the top to cover them close, and set them in the chimney corner for a fortnight, until they are turned yellow; then drain the water away and throw away the cabbage leaves, which will smell very strong, almost to putrefaction; split the large ones, take out the seed, put them in an earthen pipkin over the fire with weak salt and water; cover them close, and let them simmer gently for ten hours, when they will look a little green, and are very clean; take them off the fire and drain them, and put them into cold water, shifting them twice a day for two days; then drain them and dry them in a fine cloth. Have ready a thin syrup with a good deal of whole ginger boiled in it, and some lemon peel; when it is cold, put it on the cucumbers. Boil up the syrup every day for a fortnight, and when it is cold, pour it on as before. Tie them down with a bladder, and a leather, and a paper under it, and keep them in a cool, dry place. A pint of water to a pound of sugar is a good proportion for the syrup.

*HOW TO PRESERVE CURRANTS

Take ripe currants, free from stems; weigh them, and take the same weight of sugar; put a teacupful of water to each pound of it; boil the syrup until it is hot and clear; then turn it over the fruit; let it remain one night; then set it over the fire and boil gently, until they are cooked and clear; take them into the jars or pots with a skimmer; boil the syrup until rich and thick; then pour it over the fruit. Currants may be preserved with ten pounds of fruit to seven of sugar. Take the stems from seven pounds of the currants, and crush and press the juice from the remaining three pounds; put them into the hot syrup and boil until thick and rich; put it in pots or jars, and the next day secure as directed.

*HOW TO PRESERVE BLACK CURRANTS

Let the currants be ripe, dry and well picked; to every pound and a quarter of currants put a pound of sugar into a preserving pan, with as much juice of currants as will dissolve it; when it boils, skim it, and put in the currants, and boil them till they are clear; put them into a jar, lay brandy paper over them, tie them down, and keep in a dry place. A little raspberry juice is an improvement.

*HOW TO PRESERVE DAMSONS

Put a quart of damsons into a jar with a pound of sugar strewed between them; set the jar in a warm oven, or put it into a kettle of cold water and set it over the fire for an hour, then take it out, set to become cold, drain the juice off, boil it until it is thick, then pour it over the plums; when cold, cover as directed for preserves.

HOW TO PRESERVE DEWBERRIES

Pick your berries very early in the morning, weigh them, then spread them on dishes; sprinkle them with sugar in the due proportion as-

signed them (pound for pound). When the juice settles from them in the dishes, pour it off, and with it moisten the remainder of the sugar; simmer this over a slow fire, and, while simmering, drop in a portion of the berries; let them become clear, and return them to the dishes to cool, while the remainder take their place in the kettle. When all are clear, and the syrup boiled down to a rich consistency, pour it over them, and when cool enough, transfer them to glass jars.

*HOW TO PRESERVE GREEN GINGER

Scrape and clean your green ginger well; to each pound of green ginger put a pint and a half of water; boil it down one-third; skim carefully while boiling, then strain off the liquid; and add a pound of sugar-candy, and boil the ginger in it until quite tender.

*HOW TO PRESERVE IMITATION OF GINGER

Boil, as if for the table, small, tender, white carrots; scrape them until free of all spots, and take out the hearts. Steep them in spring water, changing it every day, until all vegetable flavor has left them. To every pound of carrots so prepared add one quart of water, two pounds of loaf sugar, two ounces of whole ginger, and a rind of lemon shred fine. Boil for a quarter of an hour every day, until the carrots clear, and when nearly done, add red pepper to taste. This will be found a good imitation of West Indian preserved ginger.

HOW TO PRESERVE MOCK GINGER

Cut off the stocks of lettuce just going to seed, and peel off the strings, cut them in pieces two or three inches long, and throw them into water; after washing them, put them into sugar and water, mixed in the proportion of one pound of sugar to five pints of water, add to this quantity two large tablespoonfuls of pounded ginger. Boil the whole together for twenty minutes, and set it by for two days. Then boil it again for half an hour, and renew this five or six times in the same syrup. Then drain the stalks upon a sieve, and wipe them dry; have ready a thick syrup boiled, and make strong with whole ginger. Pour it upon the stalks boiling hot, boil them in it once or twice, or until they look clear, and taste like the West India ginger.

*HOW TO DRY GOOSEBERRIES

To seven pounds of red gooseberries add a pound and a half of powdered sugar, which must be strewed over them in the preserving pan; let them remain at a good heat over a low fire till they begin to break; then remove them. Repeat this process for two or three days; then take the gooseberries from the syrup and spread them out on sieves near the fire to dry. This syrup may be used for other preserves. When the gooseberries are quite dry, store them in tin boxes on layers of paper.

HOW TO PRESERVE GOOSEBERRIES

Take full-grown gooseberries before they are ripe, pick them and put them in wide-mouthed bottles; cork them gently with new, soft corks, and put them in an oven from which the bread has been drawn; let them stand till they have shrunk nearly a quarter, then take them out and beat the corks in tight; cut them off level with the bottles and resin them down close. Keep in a dry place.

*HOW TO KEEP RED GOOSEBERRIES

Pick gooseberries when fully ripe, and for each quart take a quarter of a pound of sugar and a gill of water; boil together until quite a syrup; then put in the fruit, and continue to boil gently for fifteen minutes; then put them into small stone jars; when cold cover them close; keep them for making tarts or pies.

WAYS TO KEEP GRAPES

1. They must not be too ripe. Take off any imperfect grapes from the bunches. On the bottom of a keg put a layer of bran that has been dried in the oven, or in the sun. On the bran, put a layer of grapes, with bran between the bunches so that

94

they may not be in contact. Proceed in the same way with alternate layers of grapes and bran, till the keg is full; then close the keg so that no air can enter; they will keep nine or ten months. To restore them to their original freshness, cut the end off each bunch stalk, and put into wine, like flowers.

2. Or, bunches of grapes may be preserved through winter by inserting the end of the stem into a potato. The bunches should be laid on dry straw, and turned occasionally.

3. In a box first lay a paper, then a layer of grapes, selecting the best bunches and removing all imperfect grapes, then another paper, then more grapes, and so on until the box is full; then cover all with several folds of paper or cloth. Nail on the lid, and set in a cool room where it will not freeze. It is best to use small boxes, so as not to disturb more than you want to use in a week or so. Give each bunch plenty of room so they will not crowd, and do not use newspapers. Some seal the stems with sealing wax and wrap each bunch by itself, but you can get along without that trouble. The grapes should be looked to several times during the winter. Should any mould or decay, they should be removed and the good ones again repacked. By this means, you can have, with your pitcher of cider and basket of apples, your plate of grapes daily, besides distributing some among your

friends and the sick of the neighborhood.

4. (Chinese Method) It consists of cutting a circular piece out of a ripe pumpkin or gourd, making an aperture large enough to admit the hand. The interior is then completely cleaned out, the ripe grapes are placed inside, and the cover replaced and pressed in firmly. The pumpkins are then kept in a cool place—the grapes will be found to retain their freshness for a very long time. However, a very careful selection of the pumpkin must be made, the common field pumpkin, though, being well adapted for the purpose in question.

HOW TO PRESERVE GRAPES IN BUNCHES

Take out the stones from the grapes with a pin, breaking them as little as possible; boil some clarified sugar nearly to candy height; then put in sufficient grapes to cover the bottom of the preserving pan, without laying them on each other, and boil for five minutes, merely to extract all the juice; lay them in an earthen pan, and pour the syrup over them; cover with paper, and the next day boil the syrup, skimming it well for five minutes; put in the grapes, let them boil a minute or two; put them in pots, and pour the syrup over them after which tie down.

*HOW TO PRESERVE GRAPES IN VINEGAR

Grapes are preserved in vinegar by the Persians after the following fashion: The grapes are gathered when half ripe, and put into bottles half filled with vinegar, which so macerates them that they lose their hardness, and yet do not become too soft. The grapes have a sweet acid taste, which is not unpalatable, and is especially refreshing during the great heats.

HOW TO PRESERVE GREENGAGES

Select well-grown greengages, but not the least ripe; prick them with a fork to the stone, and as soon as pricked, put them in water in a preserving pan. When they are all done, put them over a slow fire to simmer very gently, so as to make them tender without breaking; try them with a fork, and when tender to the stone, put them in cold water, and as some will get soft before others, they must be watched carefully; let them lie in water a day and a night; strain them, and when well drained, put them in an earthen pan, and pour over them some boiling hot clarified sugar sufficient to cover them; put a paper over them; the next day pour off the syrup and boil it; if three quarts or thereabouts, boil for ten minutes, then pour it over the fruit, and again lay the paper over them. Boil the syrup every other day in the same manner until it is about the consistence of cream (in five or six boilings). If the syrup shrinks, so as not to keep the fruit well covered, add a fresh supply. While boiling the syrup the third time, put the greengages in, and let them simmer gently for a short time, which will bring them green; and the last time of boiling the syrup, let them simmer a little in it.

HOW HARRIET PRESERVES GREENGAGES

Choose the largest when they begin to soften; split them without paring; strew upon them part of the sugar. Blanch the kernels with a sharp knife. Next day pour the syrup from the fruit, and boil it with the other sugar six or eight minutes gently; skim and add the plums and kernels. Simmer till clear, taking off the scum; put the fruit singly into small pots, and pour the syrup and kernels to it. To candy it, do not add the syrup, but observe the directions given for candying fruits; some may be done each way.

*HOW TO PRESERVE HUCKLEBERRIES

The huckleberries may be easily kept for winter use by putting them in bottles or cans, without adding anything to them, and without cooking. The mouths of the cans should be tightly closed, and the cans should be buried mouth downward, in a box of sand. When taken out of the sand for use in the winter, the color of the berries is slightly changed, but the shape and flavor is preserved in perfection. They make excellent pies.

HOW TO PRESERVE MELON LIKE GINGER

When the melon is nearly ripe, pare it thin, and cut it into pieces about the size of ginger; cover it with salt water, changing every day for three days; then put in clear spring water, changing it twice a day for three days. Then make a thin syrup, and boil it together with the melons once a day for three

days; next make a thick syrup, adding the rind of one or more lemons, according to the quantity of melons, cut into narrow strips, and the juice squeezed in; then add some best white ginger, with the outside cut off, so as to make the syrup strong of the ginger. This should be boiled, and when cold put to the melons.

HOW TO PRESERVE MUSHROOMS

The small open mushrooms suit best. Trim and rub them clean, and put into a stewpan a quart of the mushrooms, three ounces of butter, two teaspoonfuls of salt, and half a teaspoonful of cayenne pepper and mace mixed; stew until the mushrooms are tender; take them carefully out, and drain them on a sloping dish. When cold, press into small pots, and pour clarified butter over them. Put writing paper over the butter, and on that pour melted suet, which will exclude the air, and preserve them for many weeks, if kept in a dry, cool place.

HOW TO PRESERVE WHOLE SEVILLE ORANGES

Cut a hole at the stem end of the oranges the size of a half dime, take out all the pulp, put the oranges into cold water for two days, changing it twice a day; boil them rather more than an hour, but do not cover them, as it will spoil the color; have ready a good syrup, into which put the oranges, and boil them till they look clear; then take out the seeds, skins, &tc., from the pulp first taken out of the oranges, and add to it one of the whole oranges previously boiled, with an equal weight of sugar to it and the pulp; boil this together till it looks clear over a slow fire, and when cold, fill the oranges with this marmalade, and put on the tops, cover them with syrup, and put brandy paper on the top of the jar. It is better to take out the inside at first, to preserve the fine flavor of the juice and pulp, which would be injured by boiling in the water.

*HOW TO PRESERVE ORANGE PEEL

Clean carefully; cut into thin strips; stew in water until the bitterness is extracted; drain off the water and stew again for half an hour in a syrup of sugar and water, allowing a half pint of water and a pound of sugar to each pound of peel. Put it aside in jars, and keep in a cool place. If desired, a little cinnamon and ginger may be stewed with the peel, but it is more delicately cooked simply with sugar. Lemon peel may be prepared in the same manner, either alone or mixed with orange peel. These form pleasant "relishes" eaten with cake or break, or if chopped finely when prepared, they form excellent flavoring for puddings and pies.

*HOW TO DRY PEACHES

Never pare peaches to dry. Let them get mellow enough to be in good eating condition, put them in boiling water for a moment or two, and the skins will come off like a charm. Let them be in the water long enough, but no longer. The gain is at least sixfold—saving of time in removing the skin, great saving of the peach, the part of the peach saved is the best part, less time to stone the peaches, less time to dry them, and better when dried. A whole bushel can be done in a boiler at once, and the water turned off.

HOW TO CAN PEACHES BY THE COLD PROCESS

Pare and halve your peaches. Pack them as closely as possible in the can without any sugar. When the can is full, pour in sufficient pure cold water to fill all the interstices between the peaches, and reach the brim of the can. Let them stand long enough for the water to soak into the crevices—say six hours—then pour in water to replace what has sunk away. Seal up the can, and all is done. Canned in this way, peaches retain all their freshness and flavor.

There will not be enough water in them to render them insipid. If preferred, a cold syrup could be used instead of pure water, but the peaches taste more natural without any sweet.

HOW TO PRESERVE PEACHES

Take the peaches when ripe, pare them, and if you desire to preserve them whole, throw them into cold water as you pare them, so as to prevent them losing color. When you have everything ready, place the peaches in a can, adding as much sugar to each layer as will make them palatable. Then set the can in a vessel containing hot water, and allow it to remain in boiling water until the fruit becomes heated through. This will require, if a quart can be used, from twenty to thirty minutes. When heated sufficiently, seal at once by heating the cover and pressing it at once firmly into place, and allowing a weight sufficient to keep down the cover to remain upon it until the cement hardens. The proper temperature of the lid is easily and conveniently ascertained by putting a piece of resin, about the size of a small pea, on the cover when it is put on the stove; as soon as the resin melts, the cover is ready to put in place. This precaution is necessary, as the solder with which the parts of the lid are joined easily melts. It is not absolutely necessary to use sugar in this process, but as it asssists in the preservation of the fruit, they can be sealed at a lower temperature than if not used. As sugar is used to render the fruits palatable, there can be no objection to using it when preparing the fruit for family use, as it will, in any case, be necessary, and there is no reason why the sugar should not be used before the can is sealed.

If soft peaches are preferred, they should be cut up as if intended to be eaten with cream, and must not be placed in water. When ready, they should be put in cans and heated as described above. It is not necessary to heat them in the can, but a larger quantity may be more conveniently heated together and put into the cans or jars while hot and sealed. A flat stewpan, lined with porcelain, will be found well adapted to this purpose. It must not, of course, be placed directly over the fire, but in a vessel of water which is set directly over the fire. By this means soft peaches may readily and certainly be preserved for winter use in such condition as scarcely to differ at all from the fresh peach. A most delicious dessert may thus be secured much more readily and at less expense, and much more palatable than the ordinary preserve. This method of preserving fresh peaches has been fully tested and may be relied upon.

HOW TO PRESERVE PEARS

Take six pounds of pears to four pounds of sugar, boil the parings in as much water as will cover them, strain it through the colander, lay some pears in the bottom of your kettle, put in some sugar, and so on, alternately, then pour the liquor off the pear-skins over them, boil them until they begin to look transparent, then take them out, let the juice cool, and clarify it; put the pears in again, and add some ginger, prepared as for preserving orange peel; boil till done; let the liquor boil after taking them out, until it is reduced to a syrup.

*HOW TO PRESERVE PINE-APPLE

Choose ripe but sound ones, and cut them in slices about an inch in thickness, and cut off the rind. Weigh the slices, and to every two pounds of fruit put one pound and three quarters of sifted white sugar. Boil them together in a preserving pan for thirty minutes, and if the slices are tender, take them out carefully with a wooden spoon, and place them on a wooden dish; boil the syrup for a short time longer, and then pour it over the slices of pine-apple. This process must be repeated for three successive days, after which the preserves may be put into jars and covered.

HOW TO PRESERVE PURPLE PLUMS

Make a syrup of clean brown sugar; clarify it of all impurities; when perfectly clear and boiling hot, pour it over the plums, having picked out all unsound ones and stems; let them remain in the syrup two days, then drain it off; make it boiling hot, skim it, and pour it over again; let them remain another day or two, then put them in a preserving kettle over the fire, and simmer gently until the syrup is reduced, and thick or rich. One pound of sugar for each pound of plums. Small damsons are very fine, preserved as cherries or any other ripe fruit; clarify the syrup; and when boiling hot put in the plums; let them boil very gently until they are cooked, and the syrup rich. Put them in pots or jars; the next day secure as directed.

QUINCES, PRESERVED, WHOLE OR HALF

Into two quarts of boiling water, put a quantity of the fairest golden pippins, in slices not very thin, and not pared, but wiped clean. Boil them very quickly, close covered, till the water becomes a thick jelly; then scald the quinces. To every pint of pippin jelly, put one pound of the finest sugar; boil it and skim it clear. Put those quinces that are to be done whole into the syrup at once, and let it boil very fast; and those that are to be in halves by themselves; skim it, and when the fruit is clear, put some of the syrup into a glass to try whether it jellies, before taking it off the fire. The quantity [weight] of quinces is to be equal to one pound of sugar and one pound of jelly, already boiled with the sugar.

*HOW TO PRESERVE RASPBERRIES

Take raspberries that are not too ripe, and put them to their weight in sugar, with a little water. Boil softly, and do not break them; when they are clear, take them up, and boil the syrup till it be thick enough; then put them in again, and when they are cold, put them in glasses or jars.

RASPBERRIES, PRESERVED

These may be preserved wet, bottled, or made jam or marmalade of, the same as strawberries. Raspberries are very good dried in the sun or in a warm oven. They are delicious stewed for table or tarts.

*RHUBARB, PRESERVED

Cut without peeling or splitting, six pounds of ordinary-sized rhubarb, into pieces about an inch long; put it in with the rind of a lemon, into the stewpan, in which must be about a tablespoonful of water to keep it from burning; let it boil till tender, then, with a strainer, take out the fruit, and add to the juice five pounds of sugar;

boil this forty minutes, then again put in the fruit and boil ten minutes. This is a delicious preserve.

STRAWBERRIES, PRESERVED

Use ripe strawberries, but not soft. Make a syrup of one pound of sugar to a pound of berries. Sugar should be double-refined (though refined sugar will answer), as it makes the preserves have a more brilliant color than simply refined sugar. To each pound of sugar take a teacupful of water; set it over a gentle fire and stir it until totally dissolved. When boiling hot put in the fruit, having picked off every hull and imperfect berry; then boil very gently in a covered kettle, until by cutting one open, you find it cooked through; that will be known by it having the same color throughout. Take them from the syrup with a skimmer, and spread them on flat dishes, and let them remain till cold, boil the syrup until quite thick; then let it cool and settle; put the fruit into jars or pots, and strain or pour the syrup carefully over, leaving the sediment which will be at the bottom of the pitcher. The next day cover with several papers wet with sugar boiled to candy; set them in a cool airy place. Strawberries keep perfectly well made with seven pounds of sugar to ten of fruit. They should be done as directed above, and the syrup cooked quite thick. A pint of red currant juice and a pound of sugar for it to three pounds of strawberries make the syrup very beautiful.

HOW TO PRESERVE WHOLE STRAWBERRIES

Take equal weights of the fruit and refined sugar, lay the former in a large dish, and sprinkle half the sugar in fine powder over, give a gentle shake to the dish that the sugar may touch the whole of the fruit; next day make a thin syrup with the remainder of the sugar, and instead of water allow one pint of red currant juice to every pound of strawberries; in this simmer them until sufficiently jellied. Choose the largest scarlets, or others when not dead ripe.

*HOW TO PRESERVE STRAWBERRIES IN WINE

Put a quantity of the finest large strawberries into a gooseberry-bottle, and strew in three large spoonfuls of fine sugar; fill up with Madeira wine or fine sherry.

PRESERVED TOMATOES

Add one pound of sugar to one pound of ripe tomatoes boiled down; flavor with lemon.

WALNUTS, PRESERVED

Pierce your nuts several times with a fork, and boil them in water until they begin to be tender; take them out of the water, and when cold make a hole through every one with a pretty large bodkin, and introduce a piece of candied lemon or citron. Make a syrup of brown sugar and a little water (the sugar to the weight of your nuts), and boil your nuts well until the sugar has penetrated to the center; then put them into preserving pots, filling them with a thick syrup, and tie them up like jellies.

VEGETABLES & HERBS

HOW TO KEEP VEGETABLES

Sink a barrel two-thirds of its depth into the ground (a box or cask will

answer a better purpose); heap the earth around the part projecting out of the ground, with a slope on all sides; place the vegetables that you desire to keep in the vessel; cover the top with a water-tight cover; and when winter sets in, throw an armful of straw, hay, or something of that sort, on the bar-

rel. If the bottom is out of the cask or barrel, it will be better. Cabbages, celery, and other vegetables, will keep in this way as fresh as when taken from the ground. The celery should stand nearly perpendicular, celery and earth alternating. Freedom from frost, ease of access, and especially freshness, and freedom from rot, are the advantages.

HOW TO KEEP FRENCH BEANS FRESH FOR WINTER

Procure a wide-mouthed stone jar or a little wooden keg; throw onto the bottom a layer three inches deep of young, freshly-pulled French beans; and over them put a layer of salt, fill up the vessel in this manner with alternating layers of beans and salt to a height you think proper. The beans need not all be put in at the same time, but they are better if the salt be put on while they are quite fresh. Lay over them a plate, or cover of wood that will go into the keg, and put a heavy stone on it. A pickle will rise from the beans and salt. They will keep good all through the winter. When ready to use them, steep for some hours in fresh cold water. If they are too salted, the soaking and boiling will not be sufficient to make them pleasant to the taste.

*HOW TO DRY STRING BEANS

Dried string beans are very excellent in winter. Cut the beans up in the usual length, dry them on handles, and put them in a bag. In winter, soak them, then cook them in the usual way.

HOW TO KEEP CABBAGE

Gather them before the severe fall frosts. Let the coarse outside leaves remain on them. Fix a strong string around each stalk, and suspend the cabbages from the timbers of the ceiling, heads downward. The cellar should be cool and dry. This will preserve them with a certainty. *Another Way*—Cut the cabbage from the stump, pack close in a cask, taking care to fill up all the vacancies with dry chaff, or bran, and keep in a dry cellar.

HOW TO KEEP CAULIFLOWER

They can be kept in a cellar by covering the roots and stalks with earth, till February. Or they may be placed in a trench in the garden, roots down, and covered with earth, up close to the heads, and then covered with hay or straw, four or five inches thick, placing just enough soil on the straw to keep it in its position. This method does well in the latitudes of New York; but in colder climates, a thicker covering would be required.

HOW TO KEEP CELERY

This may be kept in good condition through the winter in a cool, dry cellar, by setting it in earth.

When a small quantity only is wanted, take a box and stand the celery up in it, placing a little earth about the roots. The farmers who raise quantities of it often keep it in their old hot-beds; standing it up, and protecting it from frost. There is no vegetable more relished than this, and every person who has a garden should raise enough for his own use, if no more.

*HOW TO DRY HERBS

They should be gathered in a dry season, cleansed from discolored and rotten leaves, screened from earth and dust, placed on handles covered with blotting paper, and exposed to the sun or the heat of a stove, in a dry, airy place. The quicker they are dried the better, as they have less time to ferment or grow moldy; hence they should be spred thin and frequently turned. When dried, they should be shaken into a large meshed sieve to rid them of the eggs of any insects. Aromatic herbs ought to be dried quickly with a moderate heat, that their odor may not be lost. Cruciferous plants should not be dried, as in that case they lose much of their anti-scorbutic qualities. Some persons have proposed to dry herbs in a water bath, but this occasions them, as it were, to be half boiled in their own water.

*HOW TO DRY SAGE

After sage is harvested in a dry season, it should be thoroughly cleansed from insects, rotted leaves and discolored ones; then tied by the stems in small bunches and hung, tops down, from the rafters of a warm, dry room or shed, with space between to allow a sufficient circulation of air between them. The room should be kept from 75° to 90° for the first 24 hours or so; and the cuttings should be turned daily to dispell rotting or brittling of the leaves or flowers.

HOW TO KEEP ONIONS

Gather in the fall, and remove the tops; then spread upon the barn floor or in any open shed, and allow them to remain there until thoroughly dry. Put into barrels, or small bins or boxes and place in a cool place, and at the approach of cold weather cover with straw or chaff, if there is danger of very severe freezing. Onions are often injured in winter by keeping them in too warm a place. They will seldom be injured by frost if kept in the dark, and in tight barrels or boxes, where not subjected to frequent changes of temperature. It is the alternate freezing and thawing that destroys them, and if placed in a position where they will remain frozen all winter, and then thawed out slowly and in a dark place, no considerable injury would result from this apparently harsh treatment. Onions should always be stored in the coolest part of the cellar, or put in chaff or set in the barn or some out-house.

HOW TO KEEP PARSNIPS

The almost universal practice among farmers is to allow their parsnips to remain in the ground through winter, just where they were grown. It is believed the quality of this root is improved by being frozen, or at least kept cool, but it is not necessary to leave them in the open garden during winter, where, if the ground remains frozen, they cannot be got at until it thaws in spring, and then used in a very few weeks or not at all. If the roots are dug up late in the fall, leaving all the tops on, then carefully heeled in thickly together in rows, after which cover with a little coarse litter, they can be reached whenever wanted during winter.

HOW TO DRY GREEN PEAS

When full grown, but not old, pick and shell the peas. Lay them on dishes or tins in a cool oven, or before a bright fire; do not heap the peas on the dishes, but merely cover them with peas. Stir them frequently, and let them dry very gradually. When hard, let them cool, then pack them in stone jars, cover close, then keep them in a very dry place. When required for use, soak them for some hours in cold water till they look plump and nice before boiling; they are excellent for soup.

HOW TO PRESERVE GREEN PEAS FOR WINTER USE

Carefully shell the peas; then place them in canisters, not too large ones; put in a small piece of alum, about the size of a horse-bean, to a pint of peas. When the canisters are full of peas, fill up the interstices with water, and solder on the lids perfectly air-tight, and boil the canisters for about twenty minutes; then remove them to a cool place, and by the time of January they will be found but little inferior to fresh, new-gathered peas. Bottling is not so good; at least, it has not been found so; for the air gets in, the liquid turns sour, and the peas acquire a bad taste.

HOW TO PRESERVE GREEN PEAS

Shell, and put them in a kettle of warm water when it boils; give them two or three warms only, and pour them into a colander. Drain, and turn them out on a cloth, and then on another to dry perfectly. When dry, bottle them in wide-mouthed bottles; leaving only room to pour clarified mutton suet upon them an inch thick, and for the cork. Rosin it down; and keep in the cellar, or in the earth, as directed for gooseberries. When they are to be used, boil them until tender, with a bit of butter, a spoonful of sugar, and a bit of mint.

HOW TO STORE POTATOES

Potatoes should not be exposed to the sun and light any more than is necessary to dry them after digging from the hill. Every ten minutes of such exposure, especially in the sun, injures their edible qualities. The flesh is thus rendered soft, yellowish or greenish, and injures the flavor. Dig them when dry, and put them in a dark cellar immediately; and they will keep there till wanted for use, and there would not be so much fault found about bad quality. This is also a hint to those grocers and market-men who keep their potatoes in barrels in the sun —that is, if they wish to furnish their customers with a good article.

*HOW TO KEEP POTATOES FROM SPROUTING

To keep potatoes intended for use at the table from sprouting until new potatoes grow, take boiling water, pour into a tub, turn in as many potatoes as the water will cover; then pour off all the water; handle the potatoes carefully, laying up in a dry place on boards, only one layer deep; and see if you do not have good potatoes the year around, without hard strings, and watery ends caused by growing.

HOW TO KEEP SWEET POTATOES IN BULK

A sweet potato grower in Southern Illinois states that sweet potatoes will keep in bulk. He has kept seven hundred bushels in one pile. The potatoes should be dug before the vines are injured by frost, sunned until dry, and then placed in a cellar on a clay floor, putting fine hay or flax straw between the potatoes and the wall, and covering with the same material. The deeper and larger the pile, the better. The hay or straw should be covered with clay, a thickness of one or two inches being sufficient for the climate of that region. At the top should be left one or more air-holes, according to the size of the pile, for escape of steam. In damp, warm weather open a window or door in the daytime.

HOW TO KEEP SWEET POTATOES

Sweet potatoes can be kept by placing them in bulk in a bin or box (the more the better) without drying, and maintaining for them a uniform temperature of 45° to 50°. Putting something between, among, or around them may serve to keep them at the proper temperature, but it is of no value whatsoever aside from this; and if it should retain dampness, it will be a positive injury. After the sweat takes place, say in three to four weeks, scatter over them a light covering of dry loam or sand. In this way it is easier to keep sweet potatoes for table use or for seed, as well as "the inferior and less nourishing Irish potato."

Another Way—Pack sweet potatoes in barrels, and pour in kiln-dried

sand until the intervals are full; or in boxes of uniform size, piled up on the side of the room where the temperature never falls to the freezing point, which is a condition of first importance. This wall of boxes may be papered over, and left undisturbed until spring, when the potatoes will command the highest prices.

*HOW TO DRY PUMPKINS

Take the ripe pumpkins, pare, and cut into small pieces, stew soft, mash and strain through a colander, as if for making pies. Spread this pulp on plates in layers not quite an inch thick; dry it down in a stove oven, kept at so low a temperature as not to scorch it. In about a day it will become dry and crisp. The sheets thus made can be stowed away in a dry place, and they are always ready for use in pies or sauce. Soak the pieces over night in a little milk; and they will return to nice pulp, as delicious as the fresh pumpkin. The quick drying after cooking prevents any portion from slightly souring, as is always the case when the uncooked pieces are dried; the flavor is much better preserved, and the after-cooking is saved.

HOW TO CAN TOMATOES

The most thorough and reliable mode of canning tomatoes is as follows: They are just sufficiently steamed, not cooked, to scald or loosen the skin, and are then poured upon the table and the skin removed, care being taken to preserve the tomato in as solid a state as possible. After being peeled, they are placed in large pans, with false bottoms perforated with holes, so as to strain off the liquid that emanates from them. From these pans they are carefully placed by hand into the cans, which are filled as solidly as possible—in other words, all are put in that the cans will hold. They are then put through the usual process, and then hermetically sealed. The cans, when opened for use, present the tomatoes not only like the natural vegetable in taste and color, but also in appearance; and moreover, when thus sealed, they are warranted to keep in any climate, and when opened will taste as natural as when just picked from the vine.

How tomatoes became vegetables

In 1893, the United States Supreme Court declared that the tomato is a vegetable, not a fruit.

*TOMATOES PRESERVED

Scald them, take off the skins. Weigh the tomatoes, which must be full grown and ripe. Allow to every two pounds of the best, two pounds of brown sugar, a large spoonful of ground ginger, and the juice and rind of one large lemon. Mix the tomatoes and sugar and white of one egg together, and put in a porcelain kettle. Boil slowly till the scum ceases to appear; then add gradually the juice and grated rind of the lemons, and boil slowly for an hour or more. The tomatoes must all have burst by this time. When done, take them off, and when cool put them in jars.

Chapter 12

How to make various kinds

JAMS, JELLIES, & PRESERVES,

Chemists say that it takes more than twice as much sugar to sweeten preserves, sauces, &tc., if put in when they begin to cook as it does to sweeten after the fruit is cooked.

HOW TO PUT JAM UP WHILE HOT

It is said that ordinary jam—fruit and sugar which have been boiled together some time—keeps better if the pots into which it is poured are tied up while hot. If the paper can act as a strainer, in the same way as cotton wool, it must be as people suppose. If one pot of jam be allowed to cool before it is tied down, little germs will fall upon it from the air, and they will retain their vitality, because they fall upon a cooled substance; they will be shut in by the paper and will soon fall to work decomposing the fruit. If another pot, perfectly similar, be filled with a boiling hot mixture, and immediately covered over—though, of course, some of the outside air must be shut in—the germs which are floating in it will be scalded, and in all probability destroyed so that no decomposition can take place.

APPLE JAM

Fill a wide jar nearly half full of water; cut the apples unpeeled into quarters, take out the core, then fill the jar with the apples; tie a paper over it and put it into a slow oven. When quite soft and cool pulp them through a sieve. To each pound of pulp put three quarters of a pound of crushed sugar, and boil it gently until it will jelly. Put it into large tart dishes or jars. It will keep for five or more years in a cool, dry place. If, for present use, or a month hence, half a pound of sugar is enough.

BARBERRY JAM

The barberries for this preserve should be quite ripe, though they should not be allowed to hang until they begin to decay. Strip them from the stalks; throw aside such as are spotted, and for one pound of fruit allow eighteen ounces of well-refined sugar; boil this, with about a pint of water to every four pounds, until it becomes white, and falls in thick masses from the spoon; then throw in the fruit, and keep it stirred over a brisk fire for six minutes only; take off the scum, and pour it into jars or glasses.

Another Way—Sugar, four and a half pounds; water, a pint and a quarter; boil to candy height; barberries, four pounds; six minutes.

*CHERRY JAM

Pick and stone four pounds of May-duke cherries; press them through a sieve; then boil together half a pint of red currants or raspberry juice, and three-quarters of a pound of white sugar; put the cherries into them while boiling; add one pound of fine white sugar. Boil quickly 35 minutes; jar and cover well.

FRUIT JAM

Let the jam be drawn on a dry day; wipe the fruit clean but do not wash it; peel off the skin and coarse fibres, and slice the fruit thin. To each pound thus prepared allow a pound of fine sugar in fine powder; put the fruit in a pan, and strew a quarter of the sugar amongst it and over it; let it stand until the sugar is dissolved, when boil it slowly to a smooth pulp; take it from the fire, and stir in the remainder of the sugar by degrees; when it is dissolved, boil the preserves quickly until it becomes very thick, and leaves the bottom of the pan visible when stirred. The time required for preparing this preserve will depend on the kind of fruit used, and the time of year it is made. It will vary from an hour to two hours and a quarter. The juice should be slowly drawn from it first.

GREENGAGE JAM

Peel and take out the stones. To one pound of pulp put three-quarters of a pound of loaf sugar; boil half an hour; add lemon juice.

RASPBERRY JAM

One pound of sugar to four pounds fruit, with a few currants.

To color jelly red

Boil fifteen grains of cochineal in the finest powder, with a drachm and a half of cream of tartar, in half a pint of water, very slowly half an hour. Add, in boiling, a bit of alum the size of a pea.

*APPLE JELLY

Cut off all spots and decayed places on the apples; quarter them, but do not pare or core them; put in the peel of as many lemons as you like, about two to six or eight dozen apples; fill the preserving pan, and cover the fruit with spring water; boil them till they are in pulp, then pour them into a jelly bag; let them strain all night, do not squeeze them. To every pint of juice put one pound of white sugar; put in the juice of the lemons you had before pared, but strain it through muslin. You may also put in about a teaspoonful of essence of lemon; let it boil for at least twenty minutes—it will look redder than at first—skim it well at the time. Put it either in shapes or pots, and cover it the next day. It ought to be quite stiff and very clear.

*APPLE JELLY, PIPPINS

Prepare twenty of the fairest golden; boil them in a pint and a half of water from the spring till quite tender; then strain the liquor through a colander; to every pint put a pound of fine sugar; add cinnamon, grated orange or lemon; then boil fifteen minutes hard to a jelly.

Another Way—Prepare apples as before, by boiling and straining; have ready half an ounce of isinglass boiled in half a pint of water to a jelly; put this to the apple-water and apple, as strained through a course sieve; add sugar, a little lemon juice and a peel; boil all together, and put into a dish. Take out the peel.

ARROW-ROOT JELLY

To a dessert-spoonful of the arrow-root, add as much cold water as will make it into a paste, then pour on half a pint of boiling water, stir briskly and boil it a few minutes, when it will become a clear smooth jelly; a little sugar and sherry wine may be added for debilitated adults; but for infants, a drop or two of essence of caraway seeds or cinnamon is preferable, wine, being very liable to become acid in the stomachs of infants, and to disorder the bowels. Fresh milk, either alone or diluted with water, may be substituted for the water.

CALF'S FOOT LEMON JELLY

Boil four quarts of water with three calf's feet, or two cow's heels, till half wasted; take the jelly from the fat and sediment, mix with it the juice of a Seville orange and twelve lemons, the peels of three ditto [lemons], the whites and shells of twelve eggs, sugar to taste, a pint of raisin wine, one ounce of coriander seeds, one quarter ounce of allspice, a bit of cinnamon, and six cloves, all bruised, after having mixed them cold. The jelly should boil fifteen minutes without stirring; then clear it through a flannel bag.

CHERRY JELLY
Take cherries, five pounds; stone them; red currants, two pounds; strain them, that the liquor may be clear; add two pounds of sifted loaf sugar, and two ounces of isinglass.

CURRANT JELLY, RED OR BLACK
Strip the fruit, and in a stone jar stew them in a saucepan of water or directly over the fire; strain off the liquor, and to every pint weigh one pound of loaf sugar; put the latter in large lumps into it, in a stone or China vessel, till nearly dissolved; then put it into a preserving pan; simmer and skim. When it will jelly on a plate, put it in small jars or glasses.

HOW TO MAKE JELLY WITH FRUIT IN
Put in a basin a half pint of calf's foot jelly, and when it has become stiff, lay in a bunch of grapes, with the stalks upwards, or fruit of any kind; over this put a few vine leaves, and fill up the bowl with warm jelly; let it stand till next day, and then set the bowl in water up to the brim for a moment; then turn out carefully. It is an elegant looking dish.

*HOW TO MAKE JELLY WITH GELATINE
Take two ounces and three-quarters of gelatine, dissolved in about a quart of water, four lemons, one pound of loaf sugar, nearly half a bottle of raisin wine, or a little brandy, and less of the wine; a little white of egg is necessary to clear it, as the egg takes from the stiffness of the jelly. Boil together, strain through a jelly-bag, and put into a mold.

JENNY'S GELATINE JELLY
To make a quart, soak one ounce of gelatine in a pint of cold water for twenty minutes, then add the same quantity of boiling water, stir

until dissolved; add the juice and peel of two lemons, with enough sugar to sweeten; have ready, well beaten, the white and shell of one egg; stir these briskly into the jelly, then boil for two minutes without stirring it; remove it from the fire and allow it to stand twenty minutes; then strain through a coarse flannel bag; this jelly may be flavored or colored according to taste.

GREEN GOOSEBERRY JELLY

Place the berries in hot water on a slow fire until they rise to the surface; take off; cool with a little water, add also a little vinegar and salt to green them. In two hours drain, and put them in cold water a minute; drain, and mix with an equal weight of sugar; boil slowly for twenty minutes; sieve, and put into glasses.

ICELAND MOSS JELLY

Take of moss, one-half to one ounce; water, one quart; simmer down to one-half pint. Add fine sugar and a little lemon juice. It may be improved with one-quarter ounce of isinglass. The moss should first be steeped in cold water an hour or two.

HOW TO MAKE ISINGLASS JELLY

Take two ounces of isinglass to a quart of water; boil till it is dissolved; strain it into a basin upon a slice of lemon peel pared very thin, six cloves and three or four lumps of sugar; let this stand by the fire for an hour; take out the

lemon and cloves, and then add four tablespoonfuls of brandy.

Another way—Boil one ounce of isinglass in a quart of water, with one quarter ounce of Jamaica peppercorns or cloves, and a crust of bread, till reduced to a pint. Add sugar. It keeps well, and may be taken in wine and water, milk, tea, soup, &tc.

*LEMON JELLY

Take one and a half packages of gelatine, one pint of cold water, soak two hours, then add two teacupfuls sugar, one pint of boiling water; stir all together, add the juice of two lemons or one wineglassful of wine, strain through a cloth, and put in a shape.

ORANGE JELLY

It may be made the same as lemon jelly, which see. Or grate the rind of two Seville and of two China oranges, and two lemons; squeeze the juice of three of each, and strain, and add to the juice a quarter of a pound of lump sugar, a

quarter of a pint of water, and boil till it almost candies. Have ready a quart of isinglass jelly made with two ounces; put to it the syrup, boil it once up; strain off the jelly, and let it stand to settle as above, before it is put into the mold.

How to preserve jelly from mold
Cover the surface one quarter of an inch deep with fine pulverized loaf sugar. When thus protected, the jellies will keep for years in good condition, and free from moldiness.

*QUINCE JELLY

Cut in pieces a sufficient quantity of quinces; draw off the juice by boiling them in water, in which they ought only to swim, no more. When fully done drain, and have ready clarified sugar, of which put one spoonful to two of the juice; bring the sugar to the *soufflé;* add the juice, and finish. When it drops in a sheet from the skimmer it is enough; take it off, and pot it.

*JELLY OF SIBERIAN CRABS

Take off the stalks, weigh and wash the crabs. To each one and a half pounds, add one pint of water. Boil them gently until broken, but do not allow them to fall to a pulp. Pour the whole through a jelly bag, and when the juice is quite transparent weigh it; put it into a clean preserving pan, boil it quickly for ten minutes, then add ten ounces of fine sugar to each pound of juice; boil it from twelve to fifteen minutes, skim it very clean, and pour into molds.

Another Way—Mash the crabapples, take off stems and heads, put in a pot, cover with spring water, let them boil to a pulp, then turn them into a flannel bag, and leave all night to strain, then add one pound of sugar to a pint of juice, boil ten to fifteen minutes, skim and put in jelly glasses.

Another Way—Fill a large flannel bag with crabs. Put the bag in a preserving pan of spring water, and boil for about seven hours; then take out the bag, and fill it so that all the syrup and the water that remains in the pan can run through; and to each pint of syrup add one pound of loaf sugar, and boil for about an hour, and it will be clear, bright red jelly.

*MARMALADE OF APPLES

Scald apples till they will pulp from the core; take an equal weight of sugar in large lumps, just dip them in water, and boil it till it can be well skimmed, and is a thick syrup; put to it the pulp, and simmer it on a quick fire for a quarter of an hour. Grate a little lemon peel before boiled, but if too much it will be bitter.

*CHERRY MARMALADE

Take some very ripe cherries; cut off the stalks and take out the stones; crush them and boil them well; put them into a hand sieve, and force them through with a spatula, till the whole is pressed through and nothing remains but the skins; put it again upon the fire to dry; when reduced to half, weigh it, and add an equal weight of sugar; boil again; and when it threads between the fingers, it is finished.

*FRUIT MARMALADE

Pare and cut up the fruit into small pieces, and to a pound of fruit add a pound of sugar; when the sugar is dissolved, set it over the fire, and let it boil till it is a smooth paste. Stir it all the time it is boiling. If you wish a flavor, add any essence you desire. Put it in the jars while warm, and paste them over the next day.

TRANSPARENTLY BEAUTIFUL ORANGE MARMALADE

Take three pounds of bitter oranges; pare them as you would potatoes; cut the skin into fine shreds, and put them into a muslin bag; quarter all the oranges; press out the juice. Boil the pulp and shreds in three quarts of water two and a half hours, down to three pints; strain through a horsehair sieve. Then put six pounds of sugar to the liquid, the juice and shreds, the outside of two lemons grated, and the insides squeezed in; add three cents worth of isinglass. Simmer altogether slowly for fifteen to twenty minutes.

*SUNSHINE STRAWBERRY PRESERVES

Pick enough near-ripe berries, when stemmed and culled of unfit fruit and hulls, to allow three pounds of ready fruit. Boil over a slow fire in a preserving kettle two and one-third pounds white sugar to a clear syrup, with as little water as needed. Throw in the berries and let come only to a boil. Pour onto low pans, set outside on a table to thicken in the sun. If the weather be hot, three or four days will do, but leave the trays out, bringing in nightly, till sufficiently thickened. It is best to cover the pans tightly with thin cloths or screens to prevent insects and vermin from infesting the preserves. Small berries are best for they candy through more quickly. A bit of currant juice instead of water gives the syrup a beautiful color. Take in, take up in glasses or jars, cover close, tie down.

*TOMATO MARMALADE

Take ripe tomatoes in the height of the season; weigh them and to every pound of tomatoes add one pound of sugar. Put the tomatoes into a large pan or small tub, and scald them with boiling water, so as to make the skin peel off easily. When you have entirely removed the skin, put the tomatoes (without any water) into a preserving kettle, wash them, and add the sugar, with one ounce of powdered ginger to every three pounds of fruit, and the juice of two lemons, the grated rind of three always to every three pounds of fruit. Stir up the whole together, and set it over a moderate fire. Boil it gently for two or three hours; till the whole becomes a thick, smooth mass, skimming it well, and stirring it to the bottom after every skimming. When done, put it warm into jars, and cover tightly. This will be found a very fine sweetmeat.

How to keep preserves
Apply the white of an egg, with a brush, to a single thickness of white tissue paper, with which cover the jars, lapping over an inch or two. It will require no tying, as it will become, when dry, inconceivably tight and strong, and impervious to the air.

*CHOCOLATE CARAMEL

One pint of milk, half a pound of butter, half a pound of Cadbury's chocolate, three pounds of sugar, two spoonfuls of vanilla. Boil slowly until brittle.

A RECEIPT FOR MARSHMALLOWS, AS MADE BY CONFECTIONERS

Dissolve one half pound of gum arabic in one pint of water, strain, and add one half pound of fine sugar, and place over the fire, stirring constantly until the syrup is dissolved, and all of the consistency of honey. Add gradually the whites of four eggs well beaten. Stir the mixture until it becomes somewhat thin and does not adhere to the finger. Flavor to taste, and pour into a tin slightly dusted with powdered starch, and when cool divide into small squares.

*BLACKBERRY & OTHER FRUIT SYRUP

To one pint of blackberry or other fruit juice put one pound of white sugar, one half ounce of powdered cinnamon, one fourth ounce mace, and two teaspoonfuls cloves; boil all together for a quarter of an hour, then strain the syrup, and add to each pint a glass of French brandy.

Honey will not freeze
Persons who are engaged in the baking industry and also those in the tobacco business use it because it absorbs and retains moisture.

HOW TO KEEP HONEY

After the honey is passed from the comb, strain it through a sieve, so as to get out all the wax; gently boil it, and skim off the whitish foam which rises to the surface, and then the honey will become perfectly clear. The vessel for boiling should be earthen, brass, or tin. The honey should be put in jars, when cool, and tightly covered.

TO KEEP HONEY IN THE COMB

Select combs free of pollen, pack them edgewise in jars or cans, and pour in a sufficient quantity of the boiled and strained honey (as above) to cover the combs. The jars or cans should be tightly tied over with thick cloth or leather. These processes have been in use some twenty years with unvarying success.

Chemical composition of honey
It is principally of saccharin matter and water, about as follows: Levulose 33½ to 40 percent; dextrose 31¾ to 39 percent; water 20 to 30 percent, besides ash and other minor constituents.

*HOW TO MAKE ARTIFICIAL HONEY

To ten pounds of good brown sugar, add four pounds of spring water; gradually bring it to a boil, skimming it well. When it has become cool, add two pounds of bees' honey and eight drops of peppermint.

A better article can be made with white sugar instead of common, with one pound less of water and one pound more of honey.

Another Way—To twenty pounds of coffee sugar add six pounds of water, four ounces cream of tartar, four tablespoonfuls of strong vinegar, the white of two eggs, well beaten, and one pound of bees' honey, Lubin's extract of honeysuckle, twenty drops. Place the sugar and water in a kettle, and put it over a fire; when lukewarm add the cream of tartar, stirring it at the time; then add the egg, and when the sugar is melted, put in the honey and stir it well until it comes to a boil; then take it off, let it stand five minutes, then strain, adding the extract. Let it stand overnight, and it is ready for use.

Ages of bees
Queen bees live four years,
Drones four months, and
Working Bees six months

Chapter 13

How to make & put up PICKLES, KETCHUPS, & VINEGARS

HOW TO PRESERVE PICKLES

The strongest vinegar must be used for pickling; it must not be boiled, or the strength of the vinegar and spices will be evaporated. If parboiled in brine, the pickles will be ready in much less time than when done in the usual manner of soaking them in cold water for six or eight days. When taken out of the hot brine, let them get cold and quite dry before you put them into the pickle.

To assist the preservation of pickles, a portion of salt is added, and for the same purpose, and to give flavor, long pepper, black pepper, allspice, ginger, cloves, mace, eschalots, mustard, horse radish and capsicum.

The following is the best method of preparing pickle, as cheap as any, and requires less care than any other way: Bruise in a mortar four ounces of the above spices, put them into a stone jar with a quart of the strongest vinegar, stop the jar closely with a bung, cover that with a bladder soaked with pickle, set it on a trivet by the side of the fire for three days, well shaking it up at least three times in the day; the pickle should be at least three inches above the pickles. The jar being well closed, and the infusion being made with mild heat, there is no loss by evaporation.

To enable the articles pickled more easily and speedily to imbibe the flavor of the pickle they are immersed in, previous to pouring it on them, run a larding-pin through them several places.

Pickles should be kept in a dry place in unglazed earthenware or glass jars, which are preferable, as you can, without opening them, observe whether they want filling up; they must be carefully stopped with well-fitted bungs, and tied over closely as possible with a bladder wetted with the pickle; and if it be preserved a long time after that is dry, it must be dipped in bottle cement.

Jars should not be more than three parts filled with the articles pickled, which should be covered with the pickle at least two inches above their surface; the liquor wastes, and all of the articles pickled that are not covered are soon spoiled.

When they have been done about a week, open the jars and fill them up with pickle.

Tie a wooden spoon, full of holes, round each jar, to take them out with.

If you wish to have gherkins, &tc., very green, this may be easily accomplished by keeping them in vinegar, sufficiently hot till they become so.

If you wish cauliflowers, onions, &tc., to be white, use distilled vinegar for them.

To entirely prevent the mischief arising from the action of the acid upon metallic utensils usually employed to prepare pickles, the whole of the process is directed to be performed in unglazed stone jars.

WALNUT LIQUOR
To walnut liquor may be added a few anchovies and eschalots; let it stand till it is quite clear, and bottle it; thus you may furnish the table with an excellent savory-keeping sauce for hashes, made dishes, fish, &tc., at very small cost.

*HOW TO PICKLE BEETS
Boil your beets till tender, but not quite soft. To four large beets, boil three eggs hard and remove the shells; when the beets are done, take off the skin by laying them for a few minutes in cold water, and then stripping it off; slice them a quarter of an inch thick, put the eggs at the bottom, and then put in the beets with a litle salt. Pour on cold vinegar enough to cover them. The eggs imbibe the color of the beets and look beautiful on the table.

CABBAGE, PICKLED
Choose a fine, close cabbage for the purpose of pickling, cut it as thin

as possible, and throw some salt upon it. Let it remain for three days, when it will have turned a rich purple; drain from it the salt, and put it into a pan with some strong vinegar, a few blades of mace, and some white peppercorns. Give it a scald, and when cold, put it into the jars, and tie it up.

HOW TO PICKLE RED CABBAGE

Slice it into a colandar, and sprinkle each layer with salt; let it drain two days, then put into a jar, with boiling vinegar enough to cover it, and put in a few slices of beet-root. Observe to choose the purple red-cabbage. Those who like the flavor of spice will boil some peppercorns, mustard seed, and other spice, *whole,* with the vinegar. Cauliflower in branches, and thrown in after being salted, will color a beautiful red.

Another Way—Choose a sound large cabbage; shred it finely, and sprinkle it with salt, and let it stand in a dish for a day and night. Then boil vinegar (from a pint) with ginger, cloves, and cayenne pepper. Put the cabbage into jars, and pour the liquor upon it when cold.

CAULIFLOWER & BROCCOLI

These should be sliced and salted for two or three days, then drained, and spread upon a dry cloth before the fire for 24 hours; then put into the jar and covered with spiced vinegar. Some say that if vegetables are put into cold salt and water (a quarter of a pound of salt to a quart of water), and gradually heated to boiling, it answers the same purpose as letting them lie some days in salt.

*CHERRIES PICKLED

Take the largest and ripest red cherries, remove the stems, have ready a large glass jar, fill it two-thirds full with cherries, and fill up to the top with the best vinegar; keep it well covered, and no boiling or spice is necessary, as the cherry flavor will be retained, and the cherries will not shrivel.

CHOPPED PICKLES

What is called chopped pickle goes also under the name of chow-chow, picklette, higdum, &tc. It is liked by most persons, is readily made, and admits of the use of a number of articles. There is no particular rule for making it, and the bases may be of whatever pickle-making material is most abundant. One of the best receipts is made as follows: Green tomatoes furnish the largest share, then there are nearly ripe cucumbers with the seeds removed, cabbage, onion, and green peppers. These are chopped in a chopping machine, and mixed, sprinkled freely with salt, and allowed to stand until the next day. The abundant juice is then thoroughly drained off, and enough spiced vinegar is prepared to cover the material. No rule can be given for the spice, which may be according to taste. Whole pepper, cloves, mustard seed, broken cinnamon, or whatever spice is fancied, may be boiled in the vinegar. It is excellent with the addition of sugar. Some mix up mustard and add to the pickle when cold, and others boil vinegar with one ounce of mixed pepper, half an ounce of ginger, and some salt, and pour it cold over the beet-root and onions.

CHOW-CHOW

Take two quarts of small white onions, two quarts of gherkins, two quarts of string beans, two small cauliflowers, half a dozen ripe, red peppers, one half pound mustard seed, one half pound whole pepper, one pound ground mustard, and, as there is nothing so adulterated as ground mustard, it's better to get it at the druggist's; twenty to thirty bay leaves (not bog leaves, as some one of the ladies facetiously remarked), and two quarts of good cider, or wine vinegar. Peel the onions, halve the cucumbers, string the beans, and cut in pieces the cauliflower. Put all in a wooden tray, and sprinkle well with salt. In the morning wash and drain thoroughly, and put all into the cold vinegar, except the red peppers. Let boil twenty minutes slowly, frequently turning over. Have wax melted in a deepish dish, and, as you fill and cork, dip into the wax. The peppers you can put in to show to the best advantage. If you have more than six jars full, it's good to put the rest in a jar and eat from it for every dinner. Some add a little turmeric for the yellow color.

*PICKLED CITRON

One quart vinegar, two pounds sugar, cloves and cinnamon each one tablespoonful, boil the citron tender in water, take them out and drain, then put them in the syrup and cook until done.

HOW TO COLOR PICKLES GREEN

A beautiful green coloring, entirely destitute of any poisonous qualities, may be made by dissolving five grains of saffron in one fourth ounce distilled water; and in another vessel dissolving four grains of indigo carmine in one-half ounce distilled water. After shaking each up thoroughly they are allowed to stand for 24 hours, and on being mixed together at the expiration of that time, a fine green solution is obtained, capable of coloring five pounds of sugar.

CORN, GREEN, PICKLING

When the corn is a little past the tenderest, roasting-ear stage, pull it, take off one thickness of the husk, tie the rest of the husk down at the silk end loosely, place the ears in a clean cask compactly together, and put on a brine to cover them of about two-thirds strength of meat pickle. When ready to use in winter, soak in cold water over night, and if this does not appear sufficient, change the water and freshen still more. Corn, prepared in this way, is excellent, very much resembling fresh corn from the stalk.

*CRAB-APPLES, SWEET, PICKLED
Boil the fruit in clear water until it becomes a little soft; then drain them on a large dish; then to every pound of fruit add one of sugar, and boil hard until they are preserved.

To make the pickles, take one-half syrup and one-half vinegar; fill the jar with the preserves, and pour on the syrup and vinegar; add spices to suit the taste.

CUCUMBERS, PICKLED
Make a brine by putting one pint of rock salt into a pail of boiling water, and pour it over the cucumbers; cover tight to keep in the steam, and let them remain all night and part of a day; make a second brine as above, and let them remain in it the same length of time, then scald and skim the brine, as it will answer for the third time, and let them remain in it as above; then rinse and wipe them dry, and add boiling hot vinegar; throw in a lump of alum as large as an oil-nut to every pail of pickles, and you will have a fine, hard, green pickle; add spices if you like, and keep the pickles under the vinegar. A brick on the top of the cover, which keeps the pickles under, has a tendency to collect the scum to itself, which may arise.

*SPICED CURRANTS
Six pounds of currants, four pounds of sugar, two tablespoonfuls of cloves, and two of cinnamon, and one pint of vinegar; boil two hours until quite thick.

GHERKINS, PICKLED
Steep them in a strong brine for a week, then pour it off, heat it to a boiling point, and again pour it on the gherkins; in 24 hours drain the fruit on a sieve, put it into wide-mouthed bottles or jars, fill them up with strong pickling vinegar, boiling hot, bung down immediately, and tie over with a bladder. When cold, dip the corks into melted bottle wax. Spice is usually added to the bottles, or else steeped in the vinegar.

In a similar way are pickled: onions, mushrooms, cucumbers, walnuts, samphires, green gooseberries, cauliflowers, melons, barberries, codlins, red cabbage (without salt and with cold vinegar), beet-roots (without salt), garlic, peas, peaches, lemons, tomatoes, beans, radish pods, &tc; observing that the softer and more delicate articles do not require so long soaking in brine as the harder and coarser kinds, and may be often advantageously pickled by simply pouring very strong pickling vinegar over them, without applying heat.

*GREEN GINGER, PICKLED

Clean and slice the ginger; sprinkle with salt; let it remain a few hours; then put it into a jar or bottle, and pour boiling vinegar over it; cork it up when cool.

PICKLED EGGS

At the season of the year when eggs are plentiful, boil some four or six dozen in a capacious saucepan, until they become quite hard. Then, after carefully removing the shells, lay them in large-mouthed jars, and pour over them scalding vinegar, well seasoned with whole pepper, allspice, a few races of ginger, and a few cloves of garlic. When cold, bung down closely, and in a month they are fit for use. Where eggs are plentiful the above pickle is by no means expensive, and is a relishing accompaniment to cold meat.

*HOW TO PICKLE EGGS

The jar is to be of moderate size: a wide-mouthed earthen jar, sufficient to hold one dozen eggs; let the latter be boiled, quite hard, when fully done, place the same, after taking them up, into a pan of cold water. Remove the shells from them and deposit them carefully in the jar. Have on the fire a quart or more of good white vinegar, into which put one ounce of raw ginger, two or three blades of sweet mace, one ounce of allspice, half an ounce of whole black pepper and salt, half an ounce of mustard seed, with four cloves of garlic. When it has simmered down, take it up and pour the contents into the jar, taking care to observe that the eggs are wholly covered. When quite cold, stopper it down for use. It will be ready after a month. When cut into quarters, they serve as a garnish, and afford a nice relish to cold meat of any kind.

INDIAN PICKLE

One gallon of the best vinegar, quarter of a pound of bruised ginger, quarter of a pound of shalots, quarter of a pound of flour of mustard, quarter of a pound of salt, two ounces of mustard seed, two ounces of turmeric, one ounce of black pepper, ground fine, one ounce of cayenne. Mix all together and put in cauliflower sprigs, radish pods, French beans, white cabbage, cucumber, onions, or any other vegetable; stir it well two or three days after any fresh vegetable is added, and wipe the vegetable with a dry cloth. The vinegar should not be boiled.

LEMON-LIMES, PICKLED

They should be small, and with thin rinds. Rub them with pieces of flannel, then slit them half down in four quarters, but not through to the pulp; fill the slits with salt, hard pressed in; set them upright in a pan for four or five days until the salt melts, turn them three times a day in their own liquor until tender; make a sufficient quantity of pickle to cover them, of vinegar, the brine of the lemons, pepper and ginger; boil and skim it, and when cold put it to the lemons with two ounces of mustard seed and two cloves of garlic to every six lemons. In boiling the brine, care should be taken to use a well-tinned copper saucepan only, otherwise it will be discolored.

HOW TO PICKLE MUSHROOMS

To preserve the flavor, buttons must be rubbed with a bit of flannel and salt; and from the larger take out the *red* inside, for when they are black they will not do, being too old. Throw a little salt over, and put them into a stewpan with some mace and pepper; as the liquor comes out, shake them well, and keep them over a gentle fire till all of it be dried into them again; then put as much vinegar into the pan as will cover them, give it one warm, and turn all into a glass or stone jar. They will keep two years, and are delicious.

*OLIVES, GARLICKED

Choose only the finest, largest ones free from bruises or blemishes when taken from their brine. Drain them and put them into a stone

crock or earthen jar. Fill the jar to cover the tops of the olives with olive oil, having added a clove or two of garlic, lightly bruised; let stand in a cold place for three days. Again drain off the oil, and save it for other uses. Serve drained olives in a dish sprinkled over with minced parsley. The saved oil may be used again, after throwing out the garlic, for cooking other things wherein a garlic flavoring is desirous.

*HOW TO PICKLE ONIONS

Scald one gallon of small onions in salt water of the strength to bear an egg. Only just let them boil; strain them off, and peel them after they are scalded, place them in a jar, and cover them with the best cold vinegar. The next day pour the vinegar off, add two ounces of bruised ginger, one ounce of white pepper, two ounces of flour of mustard seed, half an ounce of chillies; boil them twenty minutes, turn all together, boiling hot, to the onions; let them remain ten days, turn the vinegar out again, boil as before, turn them hot on the onions again. They will be ready for use as soon as quite cold.

*HOW TO MAKE PEACH PICKLES

Take any quantity of fine peaches just before they are ripe, stick into each five or six cloves; make a syrup of three pints of vinegar to three pounds of peaches; add cinnamon if you like. Bring the syrup to a boil, and pour hot over them; repeat the process for three days, or until they are shrunk on the pit. After the last scald, they should be well covered and put away in a very cool cellar until cold weather sets in. They will be ready for use, however, in a few days after they are pickled.

*PICKLED PEARS

Take three pounds of sugar to a pint of vinegar, spices in a bag and boil; then cook the pears in the vinegar till done through.

HOW TO PICKLE PEPPERS

Soak fresh, hard peppers in salt and water for nine days, in a warm place; changing the brine every day; then put them in cold vinegar. If the pickles are not required very hot, take out the seeds from the greater portion of the peppers.

PICCALILLI, INDIAN METHOD

This consists of all kinds of pickles mixed, and put into one large jar —sliced cucumbers, button onions, cauliflowers, broken in pieces. Salt them; or put them in a large hair sieve in the sun to dry for three days, then scald them in vinegar a few minutes, when cold put them together. Cut a large white cabbage in quarters, with the outside leaves taken off and cut fine, salt it and put in the sun to dry three or four days, then scald it in vinegar, the same as cauliflower; carrots, three parts, boiled in vinegar and a little bay salt. French beans, radish pods, and nasturtiums, all go through the same process as capsicums, &tc. To one gallon of vinegar put four ounces of ginger bruised, two ounces of whole white pepper, two ounces of allspice, one-half ounce of chillies bruised, four ounces of turmeric, one pound of the best mustard, one half pound of shallots, one ounce of garlic, and one-half pound of bay salt. The vinegar, spices, and other ingredients, except the mustard, must boil half an hour; then strain it into a pan; put the mustard into a large basin with a little vinegar; mix it quite fine and free from lumps, then add more. When well mixed, put it into the vinegar just strained off, and when quite cold put the pickles into a large pan, and the liquor over them; stir them repeatedly, so as to mix them all. Finally, put them into a jar, and tie them over first with a bladder, and afterwards with leather. The capsicums want no preparation.

*MIXED PICCALILLI, PICKLED

To each gallon of strong vinegar put four ounces of curry powder, four ounces of good flower mustard, three ounces of bruised ginger, two ounces of turmeric, eight ounces of skinned shallots, and two ounces of garlic (the last two slightly baked in a Dutch oven), one quarter pound of salt and two drachms of cayenne pepper. Digest these near the fire, as directed above for spiced vinegar [LEMON-LIMES, PICKLED]. Put into a jar, gherkins, sliced cucumbers, sliced onions, button onions, cauliflower, celery, broccoli, French beans, nasturtiums, capsicums, large cucumbers, and small lemons. All, except the capsicums, to be parboiled in salt water, drained, and dried on a cloth before the fire. Pour on them the above pickle.

MIXED PICKLES

One large white cabbage, beans, green tomatoes, gherkins and green pepper (the veins to be cut out), without regard to quantity; chop them up finely, and place in sepa-

rate vessels; salt them, and let them stand 24 hours; squeeze them through a sieve; mix all together, and flavor with mustard-seed spice, cloves, black pepper and horse radish; pour on scalding vinegar; cut up two large onions and throw in, and let them stand 24 hours; then pour off the vinegar and fill up with cold.

*HOW TO PICKLE SWEET PLUMS

Take seven pounds of fruit, put them in a jar with three and one-half pounds of sugar, one quart best vinegar, two ounces stick cinnamon, two ounces cloves; the whole boiled together and thrown over the fruit three days.

HOW TO PICKLE ROOTS

Roots, such as carrots, salsify, and beet-root, may be pickled by being sliced, or cut into small pieces; and slightly boiled in vinegar without destroying their crispness, and adding the common spices; with beet-root, put button onions, or cut some Spanish onions in slices, lay them alternately in a jar; boil one quarter ounce of turmeric in the vinegar to give it a uniform yellow color. It is a pickle that can be made according to fancy rather than accepted rule. In winter, cabbage, celery and onions, treated in the same way make a very fine pickle. As with other pickles, the vinegar should be poured off and boiled, at intervals of a few days, two or three times before it is put away for the winter.

ELSIE CHENOWITH'S PICKLED BEET ROOTS

Beet roots are a very pretty garnish for made dishes, and are thus pickled. Boil the roots till they are tender, then take off the skins, cut them in slices, gimp them in the shape of wheels, or what form you please and put them in a jar. Take as much vinegar as you think will cover them, and boil it with a little mace, a race of ginger sliced, and a few slices of horse radish. Pour it hot upon your roots and tie them down tight.

*BEET ROOT, PICKLED

Simmer the roots till three parts done (from one and a half to two and a half hours) ; then take them out, peel and cut them in thin slices. Put them into a jar, and pour on sufficient cold spiced vinegar to cover them.

PICKLE SAUCE

Slice green tomatoes, onions, cabbage, cucumbers, and green peppers. Let all stand covered with salt over night. Wash, drain and chop fine. Be careful to keep as dry as possible. To two quarts of the hash, add four tablespoonfuls of American mustard seed and two of English; two tablespoonfuls ground allspice, one of ground cloves, two teaspoonfuls of ground black pepper, one teaspoonful of celery seed. Cover with sharp vinegar, and boil slowly an hour. Put away in stone jar, and eat when wanted.

*HOW TO MAKE SWEET PICKLES

For pickling all kinds of fruit to keep good the year around, the following rule is safe: To three pounds of sugar add one pint of good vinegar, spices to your taste; boil it together, then let it cool; fill the jars with clean and sound fruit, such as peaches, pears, plums, cherries, and grapes (each kind in a separate jar) ; then, when the vinegar is cool, put it on the fruit; let it stand all night, then turn off the liquor, and boil it down a little; then let it cool, and pour it in the jars; cover them nicely, and put them in a cool place. If, in time you discover a white scum on the top, skim it off, turn off the vinegar, add a little sugar, and boil it; when cool, pour it on the fruit again, and you will have a delightful pickle.

For peach mangoes, these are excellent. Take sound, ripe, free-stone peaches; wipe off the fur; split them open; take out the pits; have ready some fine chopped tomatoes, cabbage, horse radish, and mustard seed; fill the vacancy in the peaches; then place them together, and tie them with a string; fill your jars with prepared vinegar.

HOW TO PICKLE TOMATOES

Always use those which are thoroughly ripe. The small, round ones are decidedly the best. Do not prick them, as most recipe books direct. Let them lie in strong brine three or four days, then put them down in layers in your jars, mixing with them small onions and pieces of horse radish; then pour on the vinegar (cold), which should be first spiced as for peppers; let there be a spice bag to throw into every pot. Cover them carefully, and set them by in a cellar for a full month before using.

HOW TO PICKLE GREEN TOMATOES

To one peck of tomatoes add a handful of salt, and enough water to cover them. Let them remain in this 24 hours. Put them in a kettle (porcelain-lined is the best), fill up with vinegar, and set upon the stove until the vinegar begins to boil, then set away to cool. When cool, set the kettle again upon the stove, and bring it to the boiling point. Then skim the tomatoes, and put them into a jar; fill up with some new, cold vinegar, and

flavor with mustard seed, allspice, cloves, &tc.

The same vinegar first used will do to scald more tomatoes in.

*SPICED TOMATOES

Eight pounds of tomatoes, four pounds of sugar, one quart vinegar, one tablespoonful each of cloves, cinnamon and allspice, make a syrup of the sugar and vinegar. Tie the spice in a bag and put in syrup, take the skins off the tomatoes, and put them in the syrup; when scalded through skim them out and cook away one-half, leave the spices in, then put in your tomatoes again and boil until the syrup is thick.

TOMATO LILLY

Prepare one peck of green tomatoes by slicing and laying them in a jar over night, with a little salt, then chop them and cook in water until you think them sufficiently tender, then take them up in a colander and drain nicely; then take two large cabbages, chop and cook same as tomatoes, then chop six green peppers and add one quart vinegar, put all in kettle together and boil a short time; add fresh vinegar and spice with one ounce each cinnamon and cloves, one pound sugar and half pint molasses. Onions can be used instead of cabbage if preferred.

*HOW TO PICKLE WALNUTS

When a pin will go through them, as they hang on the trees in their outer green husks, put into a brine of salt and water boiled, and strong enough to bear an egg, being quite cold first. Let them soak six days; then change the brine, let them stand six more; then drain, and pour over them in a jar a pickle of the best vinegar, with plenty of pepper, pimento, ginger, mace, cloves, mustard seed, and horse radish; all boiled together, but cold. To every hundred of walnuts put six spoonfuls of mustard seed, and two or three heads of garlic or shalot, but the latter is least strong. In this way they will be good for several years, if closely covered. They will not be fit to eat under six months. This pickle makes good ketchup.

A GOOD KETCHUP

Boil one bushel of tomatoes until soft enough to rub through a hair sieve. Then add to the liquid a half gallon of vinegar, one and a half pints of salt, two ounces of cloves, one quarter pound allspice, three ounces good cayenne pepper, five heads of garlic, skinned and separated, one pound of sugar. Boil slowly until reduced to one-half. It takes about one day. Set away for a week, boil over once, and, if too thick, thin with vinegar; bottle and seal as for chow-chow.

HOW TO KEEP KETCHUP TWENTY YEARS

Take one gallon of strong, stale beer, one pound of anchovies, washed from the pickle; one pound of shalots, one-half ounce each of mace and cloves; one-quarter ounce of whole pepper, one-half ounce of ginger, two quarts of large mushroom flaps, rubbed to pieces; cover all close, and simmer till it is half wasted, strain, cool, then bottle. A spoonful of this ketchup is sufficient for a pint of melted butter.

*A GOOD GOOSEBERRY KETCHUP

To ten pounds of finest sugar dissolved in two quarts of boiling apple cider vinegar, add ten quarts of the finest, unblemished gooseberries, not too ripe, and one ounce each of powdered allspice, cinnamon, cloves and pepper mixed; cook over moderate fire till thick. When they are sufficiently cooled to handle, rub through a hair sieve; bottle, close down for later use.

MUSHROOM KETCHUP

Sprinkle mushroom flaps, gathered in September, with common salt, stir them occasionally for two or three days; then lightly squeeze out the juice, and add to each gallon bruised cloves and mustard seed, of each, half an ounce; bruised allspice, black pepper, and ginger, of each, one ounce; gently heat to the boiling point in a covered vessel, macerate for fourteen days, and strain; should it exhibit any indication of change in a few weeks, bring it again to the boiling point, with a little more spice.

OYSTER KETCHUP

Beard the oysters; boil them up in their liquor; strain and pound them in a mortar; boil the beards in spring water, and strain it to the first oyster liquor; boil the pounded oysters in the mixed liquors, with beaten mace and pepper. Some add a very little mushroom ketchup, vinegar, or lemon juice; but the less the natural flavor is overpowered the better; only spice is necessary for its preservation. This oyster ketchup will keep perfectly good longer than oysters are ever out of season.

*TOMATO KETCHUP

Put them over the fire, crushing each one as you drop it into the pot; let them boil five minutes; take them off, strain through a colander, and then through a hair sieve, get them over the fire again as soon as possible, and boil down two-thirds; when boiled down add to every gallon of this liquid one ounce of cayenne pepper, one ounce of black pepper, one pint of vinegar, four ounces each of cinnamon and mace, two spoonfuls of salt.

*HOW TO MAKE TOMATO CATSUP

Take of perfectly ripe tomatoes a half bushel; wash them clean and break to pieces; then put over the fire and let them come to a boil, and remove from the fire; when they are sufficiently cool to allow your hands in them, rub through a wire sieve; and to what goes through, add salt two teacupfuls; allspice and cloves, ground, of each, one teacupful; best of vinegar, one quart. Put on to the fire again and cook one hour, stirring

with great care to avoid burning. Bottle and seal for use. If too thick when used, put in a little vinegar. If they were very juicy, they may need boiling over an hour.

VERY FINE WALNUT KETCHUP

Boil a gallon of the expressed juice from green tender walnuts, and skim it well; then put in two pounds of anchovies, bones and liquor, two pounds of shalots, one ounce each of cloves, mace, pepper, and one clove of garlic. Let all simmer till the shalots sink; then put the liquor into a pan till cold; bottle and divide the spice to each. Cork closely, and tie a bladder over. It will keep twenty years, but is not good the first. Be very careful to express the juice at home; for it is rarely unadulterated, if bought.

*HOW TO KEEP HORSE RADISH

Grate a sufficient quantity during the season, while it is green, put it in bottles; fill up with strong vinegar, cork them tight, and set them in a good place.

HOW TO MAKE SAUERKRAUT

In the first place, let your "stand," holding from half a barrel to a bar-

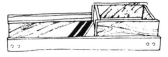

rel, be thoroughly scalded out; the cutter, the tub, and the stamper also well scalded. Take off all the outer leaves of the cabbages to slop the hogs, halve them, remove the heart, and proceed with the cutting. Lay some clean leaves at the bottom of the stand, sprinkle with a handful of salt, fill in half a bushel of cut cabbage, stamp gently until the juice just makes its appearance, then add another handful of salt, and so on until the stand is full. Cover over with cabbage leaves, place on top a clean board fitting the space pretty well, and on top of that a stone weighing twelve or fifteen pounds. Stand away in a cool place, and when hard freezing comes on, remove to the cellar. It will be ready for use in from four to six weeks. The cabbage should be cut tolerably coarse. The Savoy variety makes the best article, but it is only half as productive as the Drumhead and Flat Dutch.

WAYS TO MAKE CIDER VINEGAR

1. The most profitable return from such apples as are made into cider is the further transformation of the juice into vinegar. To do this, the barrels should be com-

pletely filled, so that all impurities that "working"—fermenting— throws off will be ejected through the bung-hole. This process should be completed before the barrel is put in the cellar, and when this is done, the purified juice should be drawn out of the original cask and put into others where there is a small amount of old vinegar, which will amazingly hasten the desired result. If no vinegar can be obtained to "start" the cider, it must remain in a dry cellar six months, and perhaps a year (the longer the better), before it will be fit for the table.

2. Save all your apple parings and slice in with them all waste apples and other fruits; keep them in a cool place till you get a pailful, then turn a large plate over them, on which a light weight should be placed, and pour on boiling water till it comes to the top. After they have stood two or three days pour off the liquid, which will be as good cider as much that is offered for sale; strain and pour it into a cask or some other convenient vessel (anything that can be closely covered will do), and drop in a piece of "mother," or vinegar plant, you procure from someone who has good vinegar. If set in a warm place, the vinegar will be fit for use in three or four weeks, when it can be drawn off for use, and the cask filled with cider made from time to time by this process. The parings should be pressed compactly into a tub or pail, and only water enough poured over to come to their surface, otherwise the cider would be so weak as to require the addition of molasses. By having two casks, one to contain the vinegar already made, and the other to fill into from time to time, one never need be without good vinegar. The rinsings of preserve kettles, sweetmeat jars, and from honey, also stale beer and old cider, should all be saved

for the vinegar cask; only caution should be used that there be sufficient sweetness, or body, to what-

ever is poured in, or the vinegar may die from lack of strength.

3. A barrel or cask of new sweet cider, buried so as to be well covered with fresh earth, will turn to sharp, clear, delicious vinegar in three or four weeks, as good as ever sought affinity with cabbage, pickles, or table sauce, and better than is possible to make by any other process.

*RASPBERRY VINEGAR
Fill a jar with red raspberries picked from their stalks. Pour in as much vinegar as it will hold. Let it stand ten days, then strain it through a hair sieve. Don't press the berries, just let the juice run through. To every pint add one pound of loaf sugar. Boil it like other syrup; skim, and bottle when cold.

Chapter 14

Yeast, quick, baked, steamed, & griddled

BREADS

GENERAL DIRECTIONS FOR MAKING BREAD

In the composition of good bread, there are three important requisites: Good flour, good yeast (and here let us recommend Gillett's Magic Yeast Cakes. They keep good for one year in any climate, and once used you will not do without them. All grocers keep them), and strength to knead it well. Flour should be white and dry, crumbling easily again after it is pressed in the hand.

A very good method of ascertaining the quality of yeast will be to add a little flour to a very small quantity, setting it in a warm place. If in the course of ten or fifteen minutes it raises, it will do to use.

When you make bread, first set the sponge with warm milk or water, keeping it in a warm place until quite light. Then mold this sponge, by adding flour, into one large loaf, kneading it well. Set this to rise again, and then when sufficiently light, mold it into smaller

loaves; let it rise again, then bake. Care should be taken not to get the dough too stiff with flour; it should be as soft as it can be to knead well. To make bread or biscuits a nice color, wet the dough over top with water just before put-

ting it into the oven. Flóur should always be sifted.

*BEULAH'S BROWN BREAD

For those who can eat cornmeal: Two cupfuls Indian meal to one cup flour; one-half teacupful syrup, two and a half cupfuls of milk; one teaspoonful salt; three teaspoonfuls of Gillett's baking powder. Steam an hour and a half. To be eaten hot. It goes very nicely with a corn-beef dinner.

BROWN BREAD

Stir together wheat meal and cold water (nothing else, not even salt) to the consistency of a thick batter. Bake in small circular pans, from three to three and a half inches in diameter, (ordinary tin patty-pans do very well) in a quick, hot oven.

It is quite essential that it be baked in this size cake, as it is upon this that the raising depends. In this article, there are none of the injurious qualities of either fermented or superfine flour bread; and it is so palpably wholesome food, that it appeals at once to the common sense of all who are interested in the subject.

*EASY BROWN BREAD

Take part of the sponge that has been prepared for your white bread, warm water can be added; mix it with graham flour (not too stiff).

*BOSTON BROWN BREAD

One and a half cupfuls of graham flour, two cupfuls of corn meal, a half cupful of molasses, one pint of sweet milk, and one-half tea-spoonful of soda; steam three hours.

Bread is steam-cooked by placing the sponge in a tin which when sealed is stood in a covered pot of boiling water. Or the sponge can be put into a cloth bag and hung above boiling water in a covered pot. The steam or cook time will vary with the bulk of the sponge. A good cook will know when it be done.

*DORIS MILLER'S BOSTON BROWN BREAD

To make one loaf: Rye meal unsifted, half a pint; Indian meal sifted, one pint; sour milk, one pint; molasses, half a gill. Add a teaspoonful of salt, one teaspoonful of soda, dissolved in a little hot water; stir well, put in a greased pan, let it rise one hour; then steam four hours.

*CORN BREAD

One-half pint of buttermilk (fresh churned), one-half pint of sweet milk; sweeten the sour milk with a half teaspoonful of soda; beat two eggs, whites and yolks together;

pour the milk into the eggs, then thicken with about nine tablespoonfuls of sifted corn meal. Put the pan on the stove with a piece of lard the size of an egg; when melted, pour it in the batter; this lard, by stirring it, will grease the pan to bake in; add a teaspoonful of salt.

*CHEESE CORN BREAD

Cut from tender, freshly picked ears of sweet corn the kernels from three ears; then with a good rasping knife, scrape the cobs dry of all milk; mix with it in a large vessel one cupful of Indian corn meal; then add one and a half teaspoonfuls of salt and one tablespoonful of Gillett's baking powder. Throw into the mix one cupful of well-soured cream; melt a large lump of fresh sweet butter the size of two eggs or better, and pour into two large eggs well beaten. Add the latter to the corn mixture; then to this very thin batter add one quarter pound cottage cheese, very dry and crumbly. Pour into a baking pan and put in a moderate oven for about an hour or so.

*EXCELLENT BREAD

Four potatoes mashed fine, four teaspoonfuls of salt, two quarts of lukewarm sweet milk, one-half cake of Gillett's Magic yeast dissolved in one-half cupful of warm water, flour enough to make a pliable sponge; mold with hand well greased with lard; place in pans, and when sufficiently light, it is ready for baking.

FRENCH BREAD

With a quarter of a peck of fine flour mix the yolks of three and the whites of two eggs, beaten and strained, a little salt, half a pint of good yeast that is not bitter, and as much milk, made a little warm, as will work into a thin light dough. Stir it about, but don't knead it. Have ready three-quart wooden dishes, divide the dough among them, set to rise, then turn them out into the oven, which must be quick. Rasp when done.

*GRAHAM BREAD

For a loaf, take two cupfuls of white bread sponge, to which add two tablespoonfuls of brown sugar, and graham flour to make a stiff batter; let it rise, after which add graham flour sufficient to knead, but not very stiff; then put it in the pan to rise and bake.

*HOW TO MAKE HOLE BREAD

Mix together yellow Indian meal and wheat meal, equal parts, salt and yeast as needed, to the consistence of a thin batter. Cover close and set before a warm fire till it works well and rises its size again. Ladle into patty-tins, or circular patties the same size on a griddle, and bake in a quick oven. When done, this bread can be torn open and the pocket filled with preserves as desired.

*ITALIAN BREAD

Make a stiff dough, with two pounds of fine flour, six of white powdered sugar, three of four eggs, a lemon peel grated, and two ounces of fresh butter. If the dough is not firm enough, add more flour and sugar. Then turn it out, and work it well with the hand, cut it into round long biscuits, and glaze them over with white of egg.

RICE & WHEAT BREAD

Simmer a pound of rice in two quarts of water till soft; when it is of a proper warmth, mix it well with four pounds of flour, and yeast, and salt as for other breads; of yeast about four large spoonfuls; knead it well; then set it to rise before the fire. Some of the flour should be reserved to make up the loaves. If the rice should require more water, it must be added, as some rice swells more than others.

SAGO BREAD

Boil two pounds of sago in three pints of fresh water until reduced to a quart, then mix with it half a pint of yeast, and pour the mixture into fourteen pounds of flour. Make into bread in the usual way.

SALT RISING BREAD

After breakfast make a starter of fresh whole milk and warm fresh water, equal parts, salt enough to season the whole sponge; stir in a handful of fine middlings or shorts. Keep the whole warm before the fire ten or twelve hours till it works and bubbles rise. After supper stir in more middlings and some white flour or Indian meal, working the sponge into a smooth mass. Cover and keep warm to rise overnight.

Next morning shape into loaves and bake. This bread takes a half day longer than other breads.

*RACHEL ZIEGLER'S SALT RISING BREAD

Mix one cupful yellow corn meal in a pint of new milk heated to a boil. Cover this starter batter well and stand in a warm place near the fire 24 hours to work. Next day, when sufficiently fermented, add starter to one and a half pints fine flour mixed thoroughly in almost two-thirds cupful lard, sugar and salt two teaspoonfuls each, dissolved in one and a half pints new milk heated to a boil. Set the whole in a lukewarm water bath about two hours till the sponge works well and bubbles rise to surface; then stir in one and one-fourth quarts more flour. Turn out on pasteboard and knead in another one and a half pints flour till smooth. Shape into loaves and when double in size bake half an hour or so in a medium oven.

STEAMED BREAD

Two cupfuls corn meal; 1 cupful graham flour; one-half cupful of New Orleans molasses; salt and teaspoonful of soda. Mix soft with sour milk, or make with sweet new milk and Gillett's baking powder.

Put in tight mold in kettle of water; steam three hours or more. This is as nice as Boston brown bread.

Use this receipt with flour instead of graham; add a cupful of beef suet, and it makes a nice pudding in the winter. Eat with syrup or cream.

*BISCUITS

Mix a quart of sweet new milk with half a cupful of melted butter; stir in a pinch of salt, two teaspoonfuls of baking powder and flour enough for a stiff batter. Have the oven at a brisk heat. Drop the batter, a spoonful in a place, on buttered pans. They will bake in fifteen minutes.

*CREAM BISCUITS

Three heaping tablespoonfuls of sour cream; put in a bowl or vessel containing a quart and fill two-thirds full of sweet new milk, two teaspoonfuls of cream of tartar, one teaspoonful of soda, a little salt; pour the cream into sufficient flour, mix soft and bake in a quick oven.

*FRENCH BISCUITS

Two cupfuls of fresh sweet butter, two cupfuls of fine white sugar, one egg (or the whites of two), half a cupful of sour milk, half a teaspoonful of soda; flour to roll; sprinkle with sugar.

137

*RYE BISCUITS

Two cupfuls of rye meal, one and a half cupfuls of flour; one-third cupful of molasses, one egg, a little salt, two cupfuls of sour milk, two even teaspoonfuls saleratus.

*SODA BISCUITS

To each quart of flour add one tablespoonful of shortening, one-half teaspoonful of salt, and three and a half heaping teaspoonfuls of Gillett's baking powder; mix baking powder thoroughly through the flour, then add other ingredients. Do not knead, and bake quickly. To use cream tartar and soda, take the same proportions without the baking powder, using instead two heaping teaspoonfuls cream tartar and one of soda. If good, they will bake in five minutes.

*TEA BISCUITS

One cupful of hot water, two of new milk, three tablespoonfuls of yeast; mix thoroughly; after it is risen, take two-thirds of a cupful of butter and a little sugar and mold it; then let it rise, and mold it into small cakes.

*BANNOCKS

One pint of corn meal, pour on it boiling water to thoroughly wet it. Let it stand a few minutes; add salt and one hen's egg and a little sweet cream, or a tablespoonful of melted sweet butter. Make into balls and fry in hot lard over a quick fire.

SPANISH BUNS

Five eggs well beaten; cut up in a cupful of warm new milk half a pound of good sweet butter, one pound of sifted flour, and a wineglassful of good yeast; stir these well together; set it to rise for an hour, in rather a warm place; when risen, sift in half a pound of white sugar, and half a grated nutmeg; add one wineglass of wine and brandy, mixed, one wineglass of rose-water, and one cupful of currants, which have been cleaned thoroughly. Mix these well, pour it into pans, and set it to rise again for half an hour. Then bake one hour. Icing is a great improvement to their appearance.

BATH BUNS

Take one pound of flour, put it in a dish, and make a hole in the middle, and pour in a dessertspoonful of good yeast; pour upon the yeast half a cupful of warm new milk, mix in one-third of the flour, and let it rise an hour. When it has risen, put in six ounces of cold fresh butter, four eggs, and a few caraway seeds; mix all together with the rest of the flour. Put it in a warm place to rise. Flatten it with the hand on a pasteboard. Sift six ounces of loaf sugar, half the size of a pea; sprinkle the particles over the dough; roll together to mix the sugar; let it rise in a warm place about twenty minutes. Make into buns, and lay on buttered tins; put sugar and nine or ten comfits on the tops, sprinkle them with water; bake in a pretty hot oven.

*BREAKFAST CAKES
One cupful of new sweet milk, one pint of flour, three eggs, piece of butter the size of a hen's egg; two teaspoonfuls cream tartar, one teaspoonful of soda, one tablespoonful of sweet butter.

BUCKWHEAT CAKES
One quart of buckwheat flour, four tablespoonfuls yeast, one tablespoonful of salt, one handful Indian meal, two tablespoonfuls molasses, not syrup. Warm water enough to make a thin batter; beat very well and set in a warm place. If the batter is the least sour in the morning, add a little soda.

*QUICK BUCKWHEAT CAKES
One quart of buckwheat flour, one-half a teacupful of corn meal or wheat flour, a little salt, and two tablespoonfuls of syrup. Wet these with cold or warm water to a thin batter, and add, lastly, four good tablespoonfuls of Gillett's baking powder.

*BROWN GRIDDLE CAKES
Take stale bread, soak in water till soft, drain off the water through a colander, beat up fine with a fork; to one quart of the crumb batter, add one quart each new sweet milk and flour, and four eggs well beaten. Mix, bake in a griddle.

*GRAHAM GEMS
One quart of sweet milk, one cupful of syrup, one teaspoonful of soda, two teaspoonfuls cream tartar, a little salt; mix cream tartar in graham flour, soda in milk, and make it as stiff with the flour as will make it drop easily from the spoon into muffin rings.

*WHEAT GEMS
Take one pint of new milk, two eggs, flour enough to make a batter not very stiff, two large spoonfuls

melted sweet butter, yeast to raise them, a little soda and salt. Bake in gem irons.

*JOHNNIE CAKE
Take one pint of corn meal, one teacupful of flour, two eggs, one pint of sweet milk, one tablespoonful of molasses, one tablespoonful of melted fresh butter, a little salt,

one teaspoonful of soda, one teaspoonful of cream of tartar; bake in square tins.

INDIAN BREAKFAST PATTIES

To one pint of Indian meal add one egg, and a little salt, pour boiling water upon it, and fry brown immediately in pork fat. Cut open and put butter between, and send to the table hot.

*MUFFINS

Take one tablespoonful of sweet butter, two tablespoonfuls of fine white sugar, two eggs—stir altogether; add one cupful of sweet milk, three teaspoonfuls of baking powder, flour to make a stiff batter. Bake twenty minutes in a quick oven.

*MUSH

Indian meal or oatmeal mush is best made in the following manner: Put fresh spring water into a kettle over the fire to boil, and put in some salt; when the water boils, stir in handful by handful corn or oatmeal, sifting a little at a time through the fingers, into the boiling water, stirring swiftly to keep it from lumping, until thick enough for use. In order to have excellent mush, the meal should be allowed to cook well, and long as possible while thin, and before the final handful is added. Though more difficult than using wetted meal, the mush better retains its nutty flavor by this method.

*FRIED MUSH

When desired to be fried for breakfast, turn into an earthen dish and set away to cool. Then cut in slices when you wish to fry; dip each piece in beaten eggs and fry on a hot griddle.

*ENGLISH PANCAKES

Make a batter of two teacupfuls of flour, four eggs, and one quart of sweet milk. Add, as a great improvement, one tablespoonful of brandy with a little nutmeg scraped in. Make the size of frying pan. Sprinkle a little granulated sugar over the pancake, roll it up, and send to the table hot.

*POP OVERS

Take three cupfuls of sweet milk and a like amount of flour, three eggs, a little salt, one tablespoonful melted butter put in the last thing; two tablespoonfuls to a puff.

ROLLS

To the quantity of light bread dough that you would take for twelve persons, add the white of one egg well beaten, two tablespoonfuls of white sugar, and two tablespoonfuls of sweet butter; work these thoroughly together; roll out about half an inch thick; cut the size desired, and spread one with melted butter and lay another upon the top of it. Bake delicately when they have risen.

FRENCH ROLLS

Take one quart of flour, add two eggs, one-half pint of new milk, a tablespoonful of yeast; knead it well; let rise till morning. Work in one ounce of sweet butter, and mold in small rolls. Bake immediately.

RUSKS

Take fresh new milk enough with one-half cupful of yeast to make a pint; make a sponge and rise, then add one and a half cupfuls of white sugar, three eggs, one-half cupful of sweet butter; spice to your taste; mold, then put in pan to rise. When baked, cover the tops with sugar dissolved in milk.

*MAUDE MUELLER'S WAFFLES

To one quart of sweet or sour milk put four eggs, two-thirds of a cupful of fresh butter, half a teaspoonful of salt, three teaspoonfuls of baking powder; flour enough to make a nice batter. If you use sour milk, leave out the baking powder, and use two teaspoonfuls of soda. Splendid.

*WAFFLES

Take one quart of new milk, two eggs; beat the whites and yolks separately; four tablespoonfuls of melted sweet butter, two teaspoonfuls Gillett's baking powder; flour to make a stiff batter. Bake well in waffle irons.

A GOOD RECEIPT FOR MAKING COMPRESSED YEAST

This yeast is obtained by straining the yeast in breweries and distilleries until a moist mass is obtained, which is then placed in a horse hair bag, and the rest of the water pressed out until the mass is nearly dry. It is then sewed up in a strong linen bag for transportation.

HOW TO KEEP YEAST

Ordinary beer yeast may be kept fresh and fit for use for several months, by placing it in a close canvas bag, and gently squeezing out the moisture in a screw press; the remaining matter becomes as stiff as clay, in which state it must be preserved in close vessels.

YEAST CAKES, OR PRESERVED YEAST

Throw a large handful of hops into two quarts of boiling water. Boil three large potatoes until they are tender. Mash them and add them to two pounds of flour.

Pour the boiling hot water over the flour through a sieve or colander, and beat it until it is quite smooth. While it is warm, add two table-spoonfuls of salt, and half a teacupful of sugar. Before it is quite cold, stir in a pint or more of good yeast. After the yeast has become quite light, stir in as much Indian meal as it will take, roll it out in cakes, and place them on a cloth in a dry place, taking care to turn them every day. At the end of a week or ten days they may be put into a bag, and should be kept in a dry place. When used, take one of these cakes, soak it in some milk-warm water, mash it smooth, and use it as any other kind of yeast.

Yeast

In reference to yeast, the use of Magic Yeast Cakes is recommended; it keeps good a year, and works quicker and better than other yeasts.

Chapter 15

Cakes, frostings, shortbreads, & other
DESSERTS

CAKES & FROSTINGS

SUGGESTIONS IN MAKING CAKES

It is very desirable that the material be of the finest quality. Sweet, fresh butter, eggs, and good flour are the first essentials. The process of putting together is also quite an important feature, and where other methods are not given herein, it would be well for the young housekeeper to observe the following directions:

Never allow the butter to oil, but soften it by putting in a moderately warm place before you commence other preparations for your cake; then put it into an earthen dish—tin, if not new, will discolor your cake as you stir it—and add your sugar; beat the butter and sugar to a cream, add the yolks of the eggs, then the milk, and lastly the beaten whites of the eggs and flour. Spices and liquors may be added after the yolks of the eggs are put in, and fruits should be put in with the flour.

The oven should be pretty hot

for small cakes, and moderate for larger. To ascertain if a large cake is sufficiently baked, pierce it with a broom—straw through the center; if done, the straw will come out free from dough; if not done, dough will adhere to the straw. Take it out of the tin about fifteen minutes after it is taken from the oven (not sooner), and do not turn it over on the top to cool.

*ALMOND CAKE

Take ten eggs, beaten separately, the yolks from the whites; beat the yolks with half a pound of white sugar; blanch a quarter of a pound of almonds by pouring hot water on them, and remove the skins; pound them in a mortar smooth; add three drops of oil of bitter almonds; and rose-water to prevent the oiling of the almonds. Stir this also into the eggs. Half a pound of sifted flour stirred very slowly into the eggs; lastly, stir in the whites, which must have been whipped to a stiff froth. Pour this into the pans, and bake immediately three-quarters of an hour.

*COCOANUT CAKE

Whip the whites of ten eggs, grate two nice cocoanuts, and add them; sift one pound of white sugar into half a pound of sifted flour; stir this well; add a little rose-water to flavor; pour into pans, and bake three-quarters of an hour.

*COMPOSITION CAKE

Five eggs, three cups of sugar, two cups of butter, five cups of flour, one wineglass of brandy; one nutmeg grated, half a pound each of raisins and currants, and three teaspoonfuls Gillett's baking powder.

*CORN STARCH CAKE

Two cups pulverized sugar, one cup butter, one cup corn starch, two cups sifted flour, seven eggs (whites beaten very light), one teaspoonful soda, two teaspoonfuls cream of tartar (or two teaspoonfuls baking powder instead of cream of tartar), flavor with lemon. In putting this together, beat butter and sugar to a light cream; dissolve corn starch in a cupful of sweet milk, leaving enough of the milk to dissolve the soda if it is used; put cream of tartar or baking powder in the flour; beat the whites of the eggs separate when the butter and sugar are ready; put all the ingredients together first, leaving the eggs and flour to the last.

*CREAM FOR CAKE

Take one half pint of cream, one tablespoonful of butter rubbed into one tablespoonful of flour. Put the cream on the fire. When it boils, stir in the butter and flour mixed; add half a teacupful sugar, two eggs very light, and flavor with vanilla. Spread between cakes, and frost or sugar top of cake to please the fancy.

*CINNAMON CAKE

Take two cups of brown sugar, one cup of butter, three-quarters cup of sweet milk, half a cup of vinegar, four eggs, large tablespoonful of cinnamon, four cups of flour, one teaspoonful of soda, two teaspoonfuls cream of tartar; mix all but vinegar and soda; then add vinegar, then soda; bake in a large tin or patty pans.

*CURRANT CAKE

Take two pounds of flour, half a pound of fresh butter rubbed into the flour, half a pound of moist sugar, a few caraway seeds, three or four tablespoonfuls of yeast, and a pint of sweet milk made a little warm. Mix all together, and let it stand an hour or two at the fire to rise; then beat it up with three eggs and a half pound of currants. Put it into a tin, and bake two hours in a moderate oven.

*COFFEE CAKE

Take three eggs, two cups of brown sugar, one cup of strong coffee, a quarter of a cup of butter, three cups of flour, one teaspoonful cream of tartar, half a teaspoonful each soda, ground cinnamon, and cloves, half a nutmeg grated, one cup of raisins, stoned; beat butter and sugar to a cream, then add eggs beaten, coffee, flour sifted, and cream of tartar, well mixed with it. Spices and raisins, then soda dissolved in sufficient warm water to absorb it. Thoroughly mix, and bake in round tins.

*CUP CAKE

Cream half a cup of butter, and four cups of sugar by beating; stir in five well beaten eggs; dissolve one teaspoonful of soda in a cup of good fresh milk or cream, and six cups of sifted flour; stir all well together, and bake in tins.

DELICATE CAKE

Mix two cups of sugar, four of flour, and half of butter, and half cup of sweet milk, the whites of seven eggs, two teaspoonfuls cream of tartar, one teaspoonful of soda, rub the cream of tartar in the flour and other ingredients, and flavor to suit the taste.

*DROP CAKE

To one pint of cream, three eggs, one pinch of salt, thicken with rye till a spoon will stand upright in it, then drop on a well buttered iron pan which must be hot in the oven.

*FRIED CAKE

Take one pint each of sour milk and sugar, two eggs, half a pint melted butter, two teaspoonfuls even full of soda; dissolve [mix] in milk flour enough to roll out into shape, and fry in hot lard.

*BELVA'S FRIED CAKES

Three eggs, one cup of sugar, one pint of new milk, salt, nutmeg, and flour enough to permit the spoon to stand upright in the mixture; add two teaspoonfuls of Gillett's baking powder and beat until very light. Drop by the dessert-spoonful into boiling lard. These will not absorb a bit of fat, and are the least pernicious of the doughnut family.

*FRUIT CAKE

Take four pounds of brown sugar, four pounds of good butter, beaten to a cream; put four pounds of sifted flour into a pan; whip 32 eggs to a fine froth, and add to the creamed butter and sugar; then take six pounds of cleaned currants, four pounds of stoned raisins, two pounds of cut citron, one pound of blanched almonds—crushed, but not pounded, to a paste—a large cup of molasses, two large spoonfuls of ground ginger, half an ounce of pounded mace, half an ounce of grated nutmeg, half an ounce of pounded and sifted cloves, and one of cinnamon. Mix these well together, then add six large wineglasses of good French brandy, and lastly, stir in the flour; beat this well, put it all into a stone jar, cover very closely, for twelve hours; then make into six loaves and bake in iron pans. These cakes will keep a year, if attention is paid to their being put in a tin case, and covered lightly in an airy place. They improve with keeping.

*LIGHT FRUIT CAKE

Take one cup butter, two cups sugar, four of flour, four eggs, one teaspoonful cream of tartar, half teaspoonful of soda, one cup sweet milk, one pound currants, half pound of citron.

*GINGER DROP CAKE

Take one cup each of sugar, molasses, lard and boiling water, one teaspoonful of soda, half a teaspoonful of cream of tartar; stir in flour until it is as thick as cake, add sugar and salt.

*GRAHAM CAKES

Take half a cup of butter, one-half cup sugar, one egg, one teacupful of sour milk, one-half teaspoonful of soda. Make a stiff batter by adding graham flour.

*GOOD GRAHAM CAKES

Two cups of sweet milk, one cup sweet cream, the white of one egg beaten to a froth, half a spoonful of salt, a dessert spoonful of baking powder; stir in the stiffened graham flour until quite thick, bake in muffin-rings or gem-tins, until well browned on top.

*JUMBLES

Stir together until of a light brown color, one pound sugar, one-half pound butter, then add eight eggs beaten to a froth, add flour enough to make them stiff enough to roll out, flavor with lemon, cut in rings half an inch thick, then bake in a quick oven.

*LEMON JELLY CAKE
Take four eggs, one cup sugar, butter the size of a hen's egg, one and a half cups flour, half cup sweet new milk, two teaspoonfuls of baking powder. Jelly—One grated lemon, one grated apple, one egg, one cup sugar; beat all together, put in a tin and stir till boils.

*MARBLE CAKE
Light Part—One and a half cups white sugar, half cup butter, half cup sweet milk, one teaspoonful cream of tartar, half teaspoonful of soda, whites of four eggs, two and a half cups flour.

Dark Part—One cup brown sugar, half cup each molasses, butter and sour milk, one teaspoon cream of tartar, one teaspoon soda, two and a half cups flour, yolks of four eggs, half teaspoon of cloves, allspice, and cinnamon, each.

*NUT CAKE
Mix each two tablespoonfuls of sweet butter and refined sugar, two eggs, one cup new milk, three cups flour, one teaspoonful cream of tartar, half teaspoonful soda, pint of nuts or almonds. Nuts may be sliced or not as suits taste.

English walnuts struck on their cheeks, rather than seams, will if properly dried not too brittle crack out in perfect halves every time.

*OAT CAKES
Mix fine and coarse oatmeal in equal proportions, add sugar, caraway seeds, a dust of salt to three pounds of meal, a heaping teaspoonful of carbonate of soda; mix all thoroughly together, then add enough boiling water to make the whole a stiff paste; roll out this paste quite thin, and sprinkle meal on a griddle. Lay the cakes on to bake, or toast them quite dry in a Dutch oven in front of the fire; they should not scorch, but gradually dry through.

*ORANGE CAKE, THE MOST DELICATE AND DELICIOUS CAKE THERE IS
Grated rind of one orange; two cups sugar; whites of four eggs and yolks of five; one cup new sweet milk; one cup butter; two large teaspoonfuls baking powder, to be sifted through with the flour; bake quick in jelly tins. Filling: Take white of the one egg that was left; beat to a froth, add a little sugar and the juice of the orange, beat together, and spread between the layers. If oranges are not to be had, lemons will do instead.

*PLAIN FRUIT CAKE
One pound each butter beaten to a cream, sifted sugar, sifted flour, twelve eggs, whites and yolks

beaten separately. Two pounds of currants, three pounds of stoned raisins chopped, one nutmeg, a little cinnamon and other spices,

half pint of wine and brandy mixed, one pound of citron cut in slices and stuck in the batter after it is in the tin. Bake slowly two or three hours.

*PLAIN CAKE

Flour, three-quarters of a pound; sugar, the same quantity; butter, four ounces; one egg and two table-spoonfuls of milk. Mix together and bake.

*PLUM CAKE

Six eggs, well beaten; one pound of sugar; the same of flour, butter and currants, four ounces of candied peel, two tablespoonfuls of mixed spices. When it is all mixed, add one teaspoonful of carbonate of soda, and one of tartaric acid. Beat it all up quickly and bake directly.

*POUND CAKE

Take four and a half cups flour, three cups each butter and sugar. Ten eggs, yolks and whites beaten separately. Mix.

PORK CAKE

Take one pound of salt pork chopped fine, boil a few minutes in half a pint of water, one cup mo-lasses, two cups sugar, three eggs, two teaspoonfuls soda, cinnamon, cloves, nutmeg to taste, one pound raisins chopped fine, flour to make a stiff batter.

*RICH SHORTBREAD

Two pounds of flour, one pound butter, and a quarter pound each of the following ingredients: can-died orange and lemon peel, sifted loaf sugar, blanched sweet almonds and caraway comfits. Cut the peel and almonds into thin slices, and mix them with one pound and a half of flour and the sugar. Melt the butter, and when cool, pour it into the flour, mixing it quickly with a spoon. Then with the hands mix it, working in the remainder of the flour; give it one roll out till it is an inch thick, cut it into the size you wish, and pinch round the edges. Prick the top with a fork, and stick in some caraway comfits; put it on white paper, and bake on tins in a slow oven.

*SEED CAKE

Take half a pound of butter and three-quarters of a pound of sugar, creamed; three eggs, beaten lightly, and two tablespoonfuls of picked and bruised caraway seed; dissolve half a teaspoonful of soda in a cup of new milk; mix these well to-gether until they are about the con-sistency of cream; then sift in two pounds of flour, mix well with a knife, and roll them out into thin cakes, about an inch thick. Bake in a quick oven.

*SPONGE CAKE

Take sixteen eggs; separate the whites from the yolks; beat them very lightly; sift into the yolks one pound of flour, adding a few drops of essence of almond or lemon, to flavor with; then add one pound and a quarter of pulverized loaf sugar; beat this well with a knife; then add the whites whipped to a stiff froth. Have ready the pans, and bake.

*SPONGE CAKE, WHITE

One and one-third coffee cups of sugar; one coffee cup flour; whites of ten eggs; beat eggs and sugar as if for frosting; add flour by degrees and bake.

*SNOW CAKE

Take one pound of arrow-root; half pound white sugar, half pound butter, the whites of six eggs, flavor with lemon, beat the butter to a cream, stir in the sugar and arrow-root, whisk the whites of the eggs to a stiff froth, beat for twenty minutes. Bake one hour.

*STRAWBERRY SHORTCAKE

First prepare the berries by picking; after they have been well washed—the best way to wash them is to hold the boxes under the faucet and let a gentle stream of water run over and through them —then drain, and pick them into an earthen bowl; now take the potato masher and bruise them and cover with a thick layer of white sugar; now set them aside till the cake is made. Take a quart of sifted flour; half a cup of sweet butter; one egg, well beaten; three teaspoonfuls of baking powder, and milk enough to make a rather stiff dough; knead well, and roll with a rolling-pin till about one inch thick; bake till a nice brown, and when done, remove it to the table, turn it out of the pan; with a light, sharp knife, cut it down lengthwise and crossways; now run the knife through it, and lay it open for a few moments, just to let the steam escape (the steam ruins the color of the berries) ; then set the bottom crust on the platter; cover thickly with berries, an inch and a half deep; lay the top crust on the fruit; dust thickly with powdered sugar, and if any berry juice is left in the bowl, pour it round the cake, not over it, and you will have a delicious shortcake.

*DELICIOUS SWISS CAKE

Beat the yolks of five eggs, and one pound of sifted loaf sugar well together; then sift in one pound of best flour, and a large spoonful of anise seed; beat these together for twenty minutes; then whip to a stiff froth the five whites, and add them; beat all well; then roll out the paste an inch thick, and cut them with a molded cutter rather small; set them aside till the next morning to bake. Rub the tins on which they are baked with yellow wax; it is necessary to warm the tins to receive the wax; then let them become cool, wipe them, and lay on the cakes. Bake of a light brown.

*WASHINGTON CAKE

One cup of sugar; a half cup of butter; a half cup of sweet milk; two eggs, two cups of flour; two teaspoonfuls of baking powder. Bake in layers as jelly cake. Jelly part: One pint of grated apples; one egg; one cup of sugar; grated rind and juice of one lemon; put in a vessel of some kind and boil; put it on the cakes hot.

*FROSTING

One pint granulated sugar, moistened thoroughly with water sufficient to dissolve it when heated; let it boil until it threads from the spoon, stirring often; while the sugar is boiling, beat the whites of two eggs till they are firm; then when thoroughly beaten, turn them into a deep dish, and when the sugar is boiled, turn it over the whites, beating all rapidly together until of the right consistency to spread over the cake. Flavor with lemon, if preferred. This is sufficient for two loaves.

*FROSTING, FOR CAKE

One cup frosting sugar, two tablespoonfuls of water boiled together; take it off the stove, and stir in the white of one egg beaten to a stiff froth; stir all together well, then frost your cake with it, and you will never want a nicer frosting than this.

*CHOCOLATE FROSTING

Whites of two eggs, one and a half cups of fine sugar, six great spoonfuls of grated chocolate, two teaspoonfuls of vanilla; spread rather thickly between layers and on top of cake. Best when freshly made. It should be made like any frosting.

ICING

The following rules should be observed where boiled icing is not used:

Put the whites of your eggs into a shallow earthen dish, and allow at least a quarter of a pound or sixteen tablespoonfuls of the finest white sugar for each egg. Take part of the sugar at first and sprinkle over the eggs; beat them for about a half hour, stirring in gradually the rest of the sugar; then add the flavor. If you use the juice of a lemon, then allow more sugar. Tartaric acid and lemon juice whitens icing. It may be shaded a pretty pink with strawberry juice or cranberry syrup, or colored yellow by putting the juice and rind of a lemon in a thick muslin bag, and squeezing it hard into the egg and sugar.

If the cake is well dredged with flour after baking, and then carefully wiped before icing is put on, it will not run, and can be spread more smoothly. Put frosting onto the cake in large spoonfuls, commencing over the center; then spread it over the cake, using a large knife, dipping it occasionally in cold water. Dry the frosting on the cake in a cool, dry place.

*ICE CREAM ICING, FOR WHITE CAKE

Two cups pulverized white sugar, boiled to a thick syrup; add three teaspoonfuls of vanilla; when cold, add the whites of two eggs well beaten and flavored with two teaspoons of citric acid.

ICING, FOR CAKES

Take ten whites of eggs whipped to a stiff froth, with twenty large spoonfuls of orange-flower water. This is to be laid smoothly on the cakes after they are baked. Then return them to the oven for fifteen minutes to harden the icing.

*ICING, BOILED

One pound pulverized sugar, pour over one tablespoonful cold water, beat whites of three eggs a little, *not* to a stiff froth; add to the sugar and water, put in a deep bowl, place in a vessel of boiling water, and heat. It will become thin and clear, afterward begin to thicken; when it becomes quite thick, remove from the fire and stir while it becomes cool till thick enough to spread with a knife. This will frost several ordinary-sized cakes.

COOKIES, MUFFINS, & SUCH

*COOKIES

Two cups light brown sugar, one cup butter, half a cup sweet milk, two eggs, one teaspoonful of soda, flour enough to roll out.

*DROP COOKIES

Whites of two eggs, one large cup of milk, one cup of sugar, one-half cup of butter, two teaspoonfuls of baking powder, flavor with vanilla, rose, or nutmeg; flour enough for thick batter, beat thoroughly, drop in buttered pans, dust granulated sugar on top, and bake with dispatch.

*COCOANUT DROPS

One pound each grated cocoanut and sugar; four well beaten eggs; four tablespoonfuls of flour, mix well, drop on pan, and bake.

*COCOANUT JUMBLES

Take one cup butter, two cups sugar, three eggs well whipped, one grated cocoanut, stirred in lightly with the flour, which must be sufficient to stiffen to the required consistency. You bake one to know when enough flour is added.

*DOUGHNUTS

One and a half cups of sugar; half a cup of sour milk, two teaspoonfuls of soda, little nutmeg, four eggs, flour enough to roll out. Fry in hot lard till golden brown.

*GINGER SNAPS

Take one cup each of sugar, molasses, butter, half a cup of sour milk, two teaspoonfuls cream of tartar, one teaspoonful of soda, one tablespoonful of ginger, flour enough to roll out, cut into size desired and bake.

*GLADYS POPOVICH'S GINGER SNAPS

Two cups of New Orleans molasses, one cup of sugar, one of butter, one teaspoonful of soda, one of cloves, one of black pepper, and two tablespoonfuls of ginger. These will keep good a month if you wish to keep them.

KISSES

Beat the whites of four eggs to a froth, stir into them half a pound powdered white sugar; flavor with lemon, continue to beat it until it will be in a heap; lay the mixture on letter paper, in the size and shape of half an egg, an inch apart, then lay the paper on hard wood and place in the oven without closing it; when they begin to look yellowish, take them out and let them cool three or four minutes, then slip a thin knife carefully under and turn them into your left hand, take another and join the two by the sides next to the paper, then lay them in a dish handling them gently. They may be baked a little harder, the soft inside taken out and jelly substituted.

MACAROONS

Blanch four ounces of almonds; and pound with four spoonfuls of orange-flower water; whisk the whites of four eggs to a froth, then mix it, and one pound of sugar, sifted with the almonds to a paste; and laying a sheet of wafer-paper on a tin, put it on in different little cakes, the shape of macaroons.

*MOLASSES COOKIES

Three cups of New Orleans molasses, one cup butter, one-half cup of lard, one heaped teaspoonful of soda, one tablespoonful of ginger, one cup hot water. Roll thick. Better after standing.

*MUFFINS

Take two cups flour, one cup milk, half cup sugar, four eggs, one-half teaspoonful each of soda and cream of tartar, one tablespoonful butter. Bake in rings.

*GRAHAM MUFFINS

Mix one pint sweet milk, sift your flour, then take half pound each graham and wheat flour, five or six spoonfuls melted butter, two and a half spoonfuls baking powder. Bake in rings in very quick oven.

*PUFFS

Two eggs, beaten very light; one cup of milk, one cup of flour, and a pinch of salt. The gems should be heated while making the puffs, which are then placed in a quick oven.

PIES & STUFF

*COCOANUT PIE

Take a teacup of cocoanut, put it into a coffee-cup, fill it up with sweet milk, and let it soak a few hours. When ready to bake the pie, take two tablespoonfuls of flour, mix with milk, and stir in three-fourths cup of milk (or water); place on the stove, and stir until it thickens. Add butter the size of a walnut, while warm. When cool, add a little salt, two eggs, saving out the white of one for the top. Sweeten to taste. Add the cocoanut, beating well. Fill the crust and

bake. When done, have extra white beaten ready to spread over the top. Return to the oven and brown lightly.

*CREAM PIE

Take eight eggs, eight ounces pounded sugar, eight ounces flour, put all together into a stewpan with two glasses of sweet milk; stir until boils; then add a quarter pound of butter, and a quarter pound of almonds, chopped fine; mix well together, make paste, roll it out half an inch thick, cut out a piece the size of a teaplate, put in a baking tin, spread out on it the cream, and lay strips of paste across each way and a plain broad piece around the edge; egg and sugar the top and bake in a quick oven.

*LEMON PIE

Grate the rind of one small lemon, or half a large one; beat the yolks of two eggs; four tablespoonfuls of sugar; beat all together; add to this one-half pint of cold water, with one and one-half tablespoonfuls of flour in it—rub smooth so there will be no lumps; beat the whites of two eggs to a stiff froth; stir this into your pie-custard before you put it in the pan. Bake with one crust, and bake slowly.

*ELVIRA'S LEMON PIE

Grate the rind of a lemon into the yolks of three fresh eggs; beat for five minutes, adding three heaping tablespoonfuls of granulated sugar; after squeezing in the juice of the lemon add half a teacupful of water; mix all thoroughly, and place in a crust the same as made for custard pie; place in oven and bake slowly. Take the whites of the three eggs, and beat to a stiff froth, adding two tablespoonfuls of pulverized sugar, and the juice of half a lemon; after the pie bakes and is cool, place the frosting on top, and put into a hot oven to brown.

*GOOD MINCE PIES

Six pounds of beef, five pounds of suet; five pounds of sugar; two ounces allspice; two ounces cloves; three-fourths ounce cinnamon; a half pint of molasses; one and a quarter pounds of seedless raisins; two pounds of currants; half pound citron chopped fine; one pound almonds, chopped fine; two oranges; one lemon-skin; and all chopped fine; two parts chopped apples to one of meat; brandy and cider to taste.

MOCK MINCE PIES

One teacup of bread; one of vinegar; one of water; one of raisins; one of sugar; one of molasses; one-half cup of butter; one teaspoonful of cloves; one of nutmeg; one of cinnamon. The quantity is sufficient for three pies. They are equally as good as those made in the usual way.

*VINEGAR PIE

Five tablespoonfuls of finest vinegar; five of sugar, two of flour, two of water, and a little nutmeg. Put in a dish, and bake.

JUMBALLS

Flour, one pound; sugar, one pound; make into a light paste with whites of six eggs beaten fine; add a half pint of cream; a half pound of butter, melted; and one pound of blanched almonds, well beaten; knead all together, with a little rosewater; cut into any form; bake in a slow oven. A little butter may be melted with a spoonful of white wine; and fine sugar thrown over the dish.

*LEMON PUFFS

Beat and sift one pound of refined sugar; put into a bowl, with the juice of two lemons, and mix them together; beat the whites of an egg to a high froth; put it into the bowl; put in three eggs with two rinds of lemon, grated; mix it well up, and throw sugar on the buttered papers; drop on the puffs in small drops, and bake them in a moderately heated oven.

*LEMON TARTS

Pare the rinds of four lemons, and boil tender in two waters, and beat fine. Add to it four ounces of blanched almonds, cut thin; four ounces of lump sugar, the juice of the lemons, and a little grated peel; simmer to a syrup. When cold, turn into a shallow tin tart dish, lined with a rich thin puff paste, and lay bars of the same over and bake carefully.

ORANGE CRUMPETS

Cream, one pint; new milk, one pint; warm it, and put in a little rennet or citric acid; when broken, stir it gently; lay it on a cloth to drain all night, and then take the rinds of three oranges, boiled, as for preserving, in three different waters; pound them very fine, and mix them with the curd, and eight eggs in a mortar, a little nutmeg, the juice of a lemon or orange, and sugar to your taste; bake them in buttered tin pans. When baked, put a little wine and sugar over them.

POMMES AU RIZ

Peel a number of apples of a good sort, take out the cores, and let them simmer in a syrup of clarified sugar, with a little lemon peel. Wash and pick some rice, and cook it in milk, moistening it therewith little by little, so that the grains may remain whole. Sweeten it to taste; add a little salt and a taste of lemon peel. Spread the rice upon a dish, mixing some apple preserves with it, and place the apples upon it, and fill up the vacancies between the apples with some of the rice. Place the dish in the oven until the surface gets brown, and garnish with spoonfuls of bright colored preserves or jelly.

PUDDINGS

AMBER PUDDING

Put a pound of butter into a saucepan, with three quarters of a pound of loaf sugar finely powdered; melt the butter, and mix well with it; then add the yolks of fifteen eggs well beaten, and as much fresh candied orange as will add color and flavor to it, being first beaten to a fine paste. Line the dish with paste for turning out; and when filled with the above, lay a crust over, as you would a pie, and bake in a slow oven. It is as good cold as hot.

*BAKED APPLE PUDDING

Pare and quarter four large apples; boil them tender with the rind of a lemon, in so little water, that when done, none may remain; beat them quite fine in a mortar; add the crumbs of a small roll, four ounces of butter melted, yolks of five and the whites of three eggs, juice of half a lemon, and sugar to taste; beat all together, and lay it in a dish with paste to turn over.

*BOILED APPLE PUDDING

Suet, five ounces; flour, eight ounces; chop the suet very fine, and roll it into the flour. Make it into a light paste with water. Roll out. Pare and core eight good sized apples; slice them; put them on the paste, and scatter upon them a half pound of sugar; draw the paste round the apples, and boil two hours or more, in a well floured cloth. Serve with melted butter sweetened.

SWISS APPLE PUDDING

Butter a deep dish; put into it a layer of bread crumbs; then a layer of finely chopped suet; a thick layer of finely chopped apples, and a thick layer of sugar. Repeat from the first layer till the dish is full, the last layer to be finger biscuits soaked in milk. Cover it till nearly baked enough; then uncover, till the top is nicely browned. Flavor with cinnamon, nutmeg, &tc., as you please. Bake from thirty to forty minutes.

APPLE & SAGO PUDDING

Boil a cup of sago in boiling water with a little cinnamon, a cup of sugar, lemon flavoring; cut the apples into thin slices, mix them with the sago; after it is well boiled add a small piece of butter; pour into a pudding dish and bake half an hour.

*APPLE PUDDING

Pare and stew three pints of apples, mash them, and add four eggs, a quarter of a pound of butter, sugar, and nutmeg, or grated lemon. Bake it on a short crust.

*APPLE POTATO PUDDING

Six potatoes boiled and mashed fine; add a little salt and a piece of butter the size of an egg; roll this out with a little flour, enough to make a good pastry crust which is for the outside of the dumpling; into this put the peeled and chopped apples; roll up like any apple dumpling; steam one hour; eat hot with liquid sauce.

ARROW-ROOT PUDDING

Take two teacupfuls of arrow-root, and mix it with half a pint of cold milk; boil another half pint of milk, flavoring it with cinnamon, nutmeg or lemon peel; stir the arrow-root and milk into the boiling milk. When cold, add the yolks of three eggs beaten into three ounces of sugar. Then add the whites beaten to a stiff froth, and bake in a buttered dish an hour. Ornament the top with sweetmeats, or citron sliced.

AUNT NELLY'S PUDDING

Take half a pound of flour, half a pound of treacle, six ounces of chopped suet, the juice and peel of one lemon, four tablespoonfuls of cream, two or three eggs. Mix and beat all together. Boil in a basin, previously well buttered, for four hours. For sauce, melted butter, a wineglassful of sherry, and two or three tablespoonfuls of apricot jam.

BLACK CAP PUDDING

Make a batter with sweet new milk, flour and eggs; butter a basin; pour in the batter, and five or six ounces of well cleaned currants. Cover it with a cloth well floured, and tie the cloth very tight. Boil nearly one hour. The currants will have settled to the bottom; therefore dish it bottom upwards. Serve with sweet sauce and a little rum.

*OSWEGO BLANC MANGE

Four tablespoonfuls or three ounces of Oswego prepared corn to one quart of milk. Dissolve the corn to some of the milk. Put into the remainder of the milk four ounces of sugar, a little salt, a piece of lemon rind, or cinnamon stick, and heat to *near* boiling. Then add the mixed corn, and boil (stirring it quite briskly) four minutes; take out the rind, and pour into a mold or cup, and keep until cold. When turned out, pour round it any kind of stewed or preserved fruits, or a sauce of milk and sugar.

*NICE BLANC MANGE

Swell four ounces of rice in water; drain and boil it to a mash in good milk, with sugar, a bit of lemon peel, and a stick of cinnamon. Take care it does not burn, and when quite soft pour it into cups, or into a shape dipped into cold water. When cold turn it out, garnish with currant jelly, or any red preserved fruit. Serve with cream or plain custard.

ARROW-ROOT BLANC MANGE

Put two tablespoonfuls of arrow-root in a quart of milk, and a pinch of salt. Scald the milk, sweeten it, and stir in the arrow-root, which must first be wet up with some of the milk. Boil up once. Orange-water, rose-water, or lemon peel may be used to flavor it. Pour into molds to cool.

BOILED BATTER PUDDING

Three eggs, one ounce of butter, one pint of milk, three tablespoonfuls of flour, a little salt. Put the flour into a basin, and add sufficient milk to moisten it; carefully rub down all the lumps with a spoon, then pour in the remainder of the milk, and stir in the butter, which should be previously melted; keep beating the mixture, add the eggs and a pinch of salt, and when the butter is quite smooth, put into a well-buttered basin, tie it down very tightly, and put it into boiling water; move the basin about for a few minutes after it is put into the water, to prevent the flour settling in any part; and boil for one hour and a quarter. This pudding may also be boiled in a floured cloth that has been wetted in hot water; it will then take a few minutes less than when boiled in a basin. Send these puddings very quickly to the table, and serve with sweet sauce, wine sauce, stewed fruit, or jam of any kind; when the latter is used, a little of it may be placed round the dish in small quantities, as a garnish.

*BREAD & BUTTER PUDDING

Butter a dish well, lay in a few slices of bread and butter, boil one pint of milk, pour out over two eggs well beaten, and then over the bread and butter, bake over half hour.

*SIMPLE BREAD PUDDING

Take the crumbs of a stale roll, pour over it one pint of boiling milk, and set it by to cool. When quite cold, beat it up very fine with two ounces of butter, sifted sugar sufficient to sweeten it; grate in half a nutmeg, and add pound of well washed currants, beat up four eggs separately, and then mix the beaten eggs with the rest, adding, if desired, a few strips of candied orange peel. All the ingredients must be beaten up together for about half an hour, as the lightness of the pudding depends upon that. Tie it up in a cloth and then boil for an hour. When it is dished, pour a little white wine sauce over it.

CHRISTMAS PLUM PUDDING

Suet, chopped small, six ounces; raisins, stoned, &tc., eight ounces; bread crumbs, six ounces; three eggs, a wineglass of brandy, a little nutmeg and cinnamon pounded as fine as possible, half a teaspoonful of salt, rather less than half pint of milk, fine sugar, four ounces; candied lemon, one ounce; citron, half an ounce; beat the eggs and spice well together; mix the milk by degrees, then the rest of the ingredients. Dip a fine, close, linen cloth into boiling water, and put in a hair sieve, flour it a little, and tie up close. Put the pudding into a saucepan containing six quarts of boiling water; keep a kettle of boiling water alongside, and fill up as it wastes. Be sure to keep it boiling for at least six hours. Serve with any sauce; or arrow root with brandy.

*CHRISTMAS PUDDING

Suet, one and a half pounds, minced small; currants, one and a half pounds; raisins, stoned, a quarter pound; sugar, one pound; ten eggs, a grated nutmeg; two ounces citron and lemon peel; one ounce of mixed spices; a teaspoonful of grated ginger; a half pound of bread crumbs, a half pound of flour, a pint of sweet milk, and a wineglassful of brandy. Beat first the eggs, add half the milk, beat all together, and gradually stir in all the milk, then the suet, fruit, &tc., and as much milk to mix it very thick. Boil in a cloth six or seven hours.

*COTTAGE PUDDING

One pint of sifted flour, three tablespoonfuls melted butter, two eggs, one cup sweet milk, two teaspoonfuls cream of tartar, one teaspoonful soda, mix and bake.

*CREAM PUDDING

Cream, one pint; the yolks of seven eggs; seven tablespoonfuls of flour; two tablespoonfuls of sugar, salt, and a small bit of soda. Rub the cream with the eggs and flour; add the rest, the milk last, just before baking, and pour the whole into the pudding dish. Serve with sauce of wine, sugar, butter, flavored as you like.

*CRUMB PUDDING

The yolks and whites of three eggs, beaten separately; one ounce of moist sugar, and sufficient bread crumbs to make it into a thick but not stiff mixture; a little powdered cinnamon. Beat all together for five minutes, and bake in a buttered tin. When baked, turn it out to the tin, pour two glasses of boiling wine over it, and serve. Cherries, either fresh or preserved, are very nice mixed in the pudding.

*DAMSON PUDDING

Four or five tablespoonfuls of flour, three eggs beaten, a pint of milk, made into batter. Stone one and a half pounds of damsons, put them and six ounces of sugar into the batter, and boil in a buttered basin for one and a half hours.

*EGG PUDDING

It is made chiefly of eggs. It is nice made thus: Beat well seven eggs; mix well with two ounces of flour; a pint and a half of milk; a little salt; flavor with nutmeg, lemon juice, and orange-flower water. Boil one and a quarter hours in a floured cloth. Serve with wine sauce sweetened.

EXCELLENT FAMILY PLUM PUDDING

Grate three-fourth pound of stale loaf, leaving out the crusts; chop very fine three-fourths pound of firm beef suet (if you wish your pudding less rich, half a pound of suet will do); mix well together with a fourth pound of flour; then add a pound of currants, well washed and well dried; half a pound of raisins, stoned, and the peel of a lemon, very finely shred and cut; four ounces of candied peel, either lemon, orange or citron, or all mingled (do not cut your peel too small or its flavor is lost); six ounces of sugar, a small teaspoonful of salt, three eggs, well beaten; mix all thoroughly together with as much milk as suffices to bring the pudding to a proper consistency, grate in a small nutmeg, and again stir the mixture vigorously. If you choose, add a small glass of brandy. Butter your mold or basin, which you must be sure to fill quite full, or the water will get in and spoil your handiwork; have your pudding cloth scrupulously clean and sweet, and of a proper thickness; tie down securely, and boil for seven or even eight hours.

*EXTRA PUDDING

Cut light bread into thin slices; form into the shape of a pudding in a dish. Then add a layer of any preserve, then a slice of bread, and repeat till the dish is full. Beat four or five eggs, and mix well with a pint of milk; then pour it over the bread and preserve, having previously dusted the same with a coating of rice flour. Boil 25 minutes.

*FIG PUDDING

Procure one pound of good figs, and chop them very fine, and also a quarter of a pound of suet, likewise chopped as fine as possible;

dust them both with a little flour as you proceed—it helps to bind the pudding together; then take one pound of fine bread crumbs, and not quite a quarter of a pound of sugar; beat two eggs in a tea-cupful of milk, and mix all well together. Boil four hours. If you choose, serve it with wine or brandy sauce, and ornament your pudding with blanched almonds. Simply cooked, however, it is better where there are children, with whom it is generally a favorite. We forgot to say, flavor with a little allspice or nutmeg, as you like; and add the spices before the milk and eggs.

GELATINE PUDDING

Half a box of gelatine dissolved in a large half pint of boiling water, when cold stir in two teacups of sugar, the juice of three lemons, the whites of four eggs beaten to a froth, put this in a mold to get stiff; and with the yolks of these four eggs, and a quart of milk make boiled custard, flavor with vanilla; when cold pour the custard round the mold in same dish.

*GOOSEBERRY PUDDING

One quart of scalded gooseberries; when cold rub them smooth with the back of a spoon. Take six table-spoonfuls of the pulp, half a pound of sugar, a quarter pound of melted butter, six eggs, the rind of two lemons, a handful of grated bread, two tablespoonfuls of brandy. Half an hour will bake this delicious pudding.

GROUND RICE PUDDING

Boil one pint of milk with a little piece of lemon peel, mix a quarter pound of rice, ground, with half a pint of milk, two ounces of sugar, one ounce butter, add these to the boiling milk. Keep stirring, take it off the fire, break in two eggs, keep stirring; butter a pie dish; pour in the mixture and bake until set.

ICE PUDDING

Put one quart of milk in a stewpan with half pound of white sugar, and stick of vanilla; boil it ten minutes; mix the yolks of ten eggs with a gill of cream, pour in the milk; then put it back again into the stewpan, and stir till it thickens (do not let it boil); strain it into a basin and leave it to cool. Take twelve pounds of ice, add two pounds of salt, mix together, cover the bottom of the pail, place the ice pot in it and build around with the ice and salt; this done, pour the cream into the pot, put on the cover, and do not cease turning it till the cream is thick; the mold should be cold; pour in the cream; three or four pieces of white paper, wetted with cold water, are placed on it before the cover is placed on. Cover with ice till wanted; dip in cold water and turn out, fruit may be put in when put in the mold.

*INDIAN PUDDING

Indian meal, a cupful; a little salt; butter, one ounce; molasses, three ounces; two teaspoonfuls of ginger, or cinnamon. Put into a quart of boiling milk. Mix a cup of cold water with it; bake in a buttered dish for fifty minutes.

*BAKED INDIAN PUDDING

Two quarts sweet milk, one pint of New Orleans molasses; one pint Indian meal; one tablespoonful of butter; nutmeg or cinnamon. Boil the milk; pour it over the meal and molasses; add salt and spice; bake three hours. This is a large family pudding.

*LEMON PUDDING

Three tablespoonfuls of powdered crackers, and eight tablespoonfuls of sugar, six eggs, one quart milk, butter the size of an egg, the juice of one lemon and grated rind. Stir it first when put in oven.

MARROW PUDDING

Pour a pint of cream boiling hot on the crumbs of a penny loaf, or French roll; cut one pound of beef marrow very thin; beat four eggs well; add a glass of brandy, with sugar and nutmeg to taste, and mix all well together. It may be either boiled or baked forty or fifty minutes; cut two ounces of citron very thin, and stick them all over it when you dish it up.

ALICE'S MARROW PUDDING

Blanch a half pound of finest almonds; put them in cold water all night; next day beat them in a mortar very fine, with orange or rose water. Take the crumbs of the penny loaf, and pour on the whole a pint of boiling cream; while it is cooling, beat the yolks of four eggs, and two whites, fifteen minutes; a

little sugar and grated nutmeg to your palate. Shred the marrow of the bones, and mix all well together, with a little candied orange, cut small; bake, &tc.

NESSELRODE PUDDING

Prepare a custard of one pint of cream, half a pint of milk, the yolks of six eggs, half a stick of vanilla, one ounce of sweet almonds, pounded, and half a pound of sugar; put them in a stewpan over a slow fire, and stir until the proper consistence, being careful not to let it boil; when cold, add a wineglass of brandy; partially freeze, and add two ounces of raisins, and half a pound of preserved fruits, cut small. Mix well, and mold. Basket shape is generally used.

*POTATO PUDDING

Take half a pound of boiled potatoes, two ounces of butter, the yolks and whites of two eggs, a quarter of a pint of cream, one spoonful of white wine, a morsel of salt, the juice and rind of a lemon; beat all to a froth; sugar to taste. A crust or not, as you like. Bake it. If wanted richer, put three ounces more butter, sweetmeats and almonds, and another egg.

*PRINCE OF WALES PUDDING

Chop four ounces of apples, the same quantity of bread crumbs, suet, and currants, well washed and picked; two ounces of candied lemon, orange, and citron, chopped fine; five ounces of pounded loaf sugar; half a nutmeg, grated. Mix all together with four eggs. Butter well and flour a tin, put in the mixture, and place a buttered paper on top, and a cloth over the paper. If you steam it the paper is sufficient. It will take two hours boiling. When you dish it, stick cut blanched almonds on it, and serve with wine sauce.

*PUDDING

One cup sugar, half cup milk, one egg, two tablespoonfuls melted butter, two cups flour, two teaspoonfuls baking powder, a little nutmeg, bake in a dish and when sent to the table, put raspberry jam under same with wine sauce.

*BAKED PUDDING

Three tablespoonfuls of Oswego Prepared Corn to one quart of milk. Prepare, and cook the same as Blanc-Mange [see above]. After it is cool, stir up with it *thoroughly* two or three eggs well beaten, and bake half an hour. It is very good.

*BOILED PUDDING

Three tablespoonfuls of Oswego Prepared Corn to one quart of milk. Dissolve the corn in some of the milk, and mix with it two or three eggs, well beaten and a little salt. Heat the remainder of the milk to near boiling, add the above preparation, and boil four minutes, stirring it briskly. To be eaten warm with a sauce. It is delicious.

*QUEEN PUDDING

One pint of bread crumbs, one quart milk, one cup sugar, yolks of four eggs, a little butter; bake half an hour, then put over the top a layer of fruit, then white of eggs beaten to a froth with sugar; to be eaten cold with cream.

*PLAIN RICE PUDDING

Wash and pick some rice; throw among it some pimento finely pounded, but not much; tie the rice in a cloth and leave plenty of room for it to swell. When done, eat it with butter and sugar, or milk. Put lemon peel to it if you please. It is very good without spice, and eaten with salt and pepper.

Another Way—Put into a very deep pan half a pound of rice washed and picked; two ounces of butter, four ounces of sugar, a few allspice pounded, and two quarts of milk. Less butter will do, or some suet. Bake in a slow oven.

RICH RICE PUDDING

Boil a half pound picked rice in water, with a bit of salt, till quite tender; drain it dry; mix it with the yolks and whites of four eggs, a quarter of a pint of cream, with two ounces of fresh butter melted in the latter; four ounces of beef suet or marrow, or veal suet taken from a fillet of veal, finely shred; three quarters pound of currants, two spoonfuls of brandy, one of peach-water, or ràtafia, nutmeg, and a grated lemon peel. When well mixed, put a paste round the edge, and fill the dish. Slice of candied orange, lemon, and citron, if approved. Bake in a moderate oven.

*RICE PUDDING WITH FRUIT

Swell the rice with a very little milk over the fire; then mix fruit of any kind with it (currants; gooseberries; scalded, pared and quartered apples; raisins; or black currants) ; put one egg into the rice to bind it; boil it well, and serve with sugar.

SAGO PUDDING

Boil four ounces of sago in water a few minutes; strain, and add milk, and boil till tender. Boil lemon peel and cinnamon in a little milk, and strain it to the sago. Put the whole into a basin; break eight eggs; mix it well together, and sweeten with moist sugar; add a glass of brandy, and some nutmeg; put puff paste round the rim of the dish, and butter the bottom. Bake three quarters of an hour.

SPANISH PUDDING

To one pint of water, put two ounces of butter, and a little salt; when it boils add as much flour as will make it the consistency of hasty pudding. Keep it well stirred, after it is taken off the fire and has stood till quite cold; beat it up with three eggs; add a little grated lemon peel and nutmeg, drop the batter with a spoon into the frying pan with boiling lard, fry quickly, put sugar over them when sent to the table.

*SUET PUDDING

Take six spoonfuls of flour, one pound of suet, shred small, four eggs, a spoonful of beaten ginger, a spoonful of salt, and a quart of milk. Mix the eggs and flour with a pint of milk very thick, and with the seasoning, mix in the rest of the milk with the suet. Boil two hours.

*TAPIOCA PUDDING

Put a quarter pound of tapioca into a saucepan of cold water; when it boils, strain it to a pint of new milk; boil till it soaks up all the milk, and put it out to cool. Beat the yolks of four eggs, and the whites of two, a tablespoonful of brandy, sugar, nutmeg, and two ounces of butter. Mix all together; put a puff paste round the dish and send it to the oven. It is very good boiled with melted butter, wine and sugar.

CUSTARDS, CHARLOTTES, & FLUMMERY

APPLE CUSTARD

Pare tart apples, core them, put them into a deep dish with a small piece of butter, and one teaspoonful of sugar, and a little nutmeg, in the opening of each apple; pour in water enough to cook them; when soft, cool them and pour over an unbaked custard so as to cover them; and bake till the custard is done.

*ARROW-ROOT CUSTARD

Arrow-root, one tablespoonful; milk, one pint; sugar one table-spoonful; and one egg. Mix the arrow-root with a little of the milk, cold; when the milk boils, stir in the arrow-root, egg and sugar, previously well beaten together. Let it scald, and pour into cups to cool. To flavor it, boil a little ground cinnamon in the milk.

BAKED CUSTARD

Boil a pint of cream with some mace and cinnamon, and when it is cold, take four yolks and two whites of eggs a little rose- and orange-flower water; salt, sugar, and nutmeg to your taste. Mix them well and bake in cups.

Or, pour into a deep dish, with or without lining or rim of paste; grate nutmeg and lemon peel over the top, and bake in a slow oven about thirty minutes.

*CHOCOLATE CREAM CUSTARD

Scrape a quarter pound of chocolate, pour on it one teacup of boiling water, and stand it by the fire until dissolved; beat eight eggs light, omitting the whites of two, and stir them by degrees into a quart of milk alternately with the chocolate and three tablespoonfuls of white sugar; put the mixture into cups and bake ten minutes.

HOW TO MAKE JELLY CUSTARD

To one cupful of any sort of jelly, add one egg, and beat well together with three teaspoonfuls of cream or milk. After mixing thoroughly, bake in a good crust.

*OATMEAL CUSTARD

Take two teaspoonfuls of the finest Scotch oatmeal, beat it up into a sufficiency of cold water in a basin to allow it to run freely. Add to it the yolk of a fresh egg, well worked up; have a pint of scalding new milk on the fire, and pour the oatmeal mixture into it, stirring it round with a spoon so as to incorporate the whole. Add sugar to your taste, and throw in a glass of sherry to the mixture, with a little grate of nutmeg. Pour it into a basin, and take it warm in bed. It will be found very grateful and soothing in cases of colds or chills. Some persons scald a little cinnamon in the milk they use for the occasion.

ORANGE CUSTARDS

Boil the rind of half a Seville orange very tender; beat it very fine in a mortar; add a spoonful of the best brandy, the juice of a Seville orange, four ounces of loaf sugar, and the yolks of four eggs; beat all together for ten minutes; then pour in gradually a pint of boiling cream; keep beating them until they are cold; put them into custard cups, and set them in an earthen dish of hot water; let them stand until they are set, take out, and stick preserved oranges on the top, and serve them hot or cold.

*RICE CUSTARDS

Boil three pints of new milk with a bit of lemon peel, cinnamon, and three bay leaves; sweeten; then mix a large spoonful of rice flour into a cup of cold milk, very smooth; mix it with the yolks of four eggs well beaten. Take a basin of the boiling milk, and mix with the cold that has the rice in it; add the remainder of the boiling milk; stir it one way till it boils; pour immediately into a pan; stir till cool, and add a large spoonful of brandy, or orange-flower water.

APPLE SNOW BALLS

Pare six apples, cut them into quarters, remove the cores, reconstruct the position of the apples; introduce into the cavities one clove and a slide of lemon peel; have six small pudding cloths at hand and cover the apples severally in an upright position with rice, tying them up tight, then place them in a large saucepan of scalding water and boil one hour; on taking them up, open the top and add a little grated nutmeg with butter and sugar.

*APPLE CHARLOTTE

Take two pounds of sound fine apples, pare and core and slice them into a pan and add one pound of loaf sugar, juice of three lemons, and the grated rind of one; let these boil until they become a thick mass. Turn into a mould and serve it cold with thick custard or cream.

CHARLOTTE RUSSE

Whip one quart rich cream to a stiff froth, and drain well on a nice hair sieve. To one scant pint of milk add six eggs beaten very light; make very sweet; flavor high with vanilla. Cook over hot water till it is a thick custard. Soak one full ounce Coxe's gelatine in a very little water, and warm over hot water. When the custard is very cold, beat in lightly the gelatine and the whipped cream. Line the bottom of your mold with buttered paper, and the sides with sponge cake or lady-fingers fastened together with the white of an egg. Fill with the cream, put in a cold place or in summer on ice. To turn out, dip the mold for a moment in hot water. In draining the whipped cream, all that drips through can be re-whipped.

RICE FLUMMERY

Boil with a pint of new milk, a bit of lemon peel, and cinnamon; mix with a little cold milk, as much rice flour as will make the whole of a good consistence, sweeten and add a spoonful of peach-water, or a bitter almond beaten; boil it, observing it does not burn; pour into a shape or a pint basin, taking out the spice. When cold, turn the flummery into a dish, and serve with cream, milk, or custard round; or put a teacupful of cream into half a pint of new milk, a glass of white wine, half a lemon squeezed and sugar.

CREAMS & SNOWS

*APPLE CREAM

One cup of thick cream, one cup of sugar, beat till very smooth; then beat the whites of two eggs and add; stew apples in water till soft; take them from the water with a fork; steam them if you prefer. Pour the cream over the apples when cold.

*GOOSEBERRY CREAM

Boil them in milk till soft; beat them, and strain the pulp through a coarse sieve. Sweeten cream with sugar to your taste; mix with the pulp; when cold, place in glasses for use.

*IMPERIAL CREAM

Boil a quart of cream with the thin rind of lemon; stir till nearly cold; have ready in a dish to serve in, the juice of three lemons strained with as much sugar as will sweeten the cream; pour it into the dish from a large teapot, holding it high, and moving it about to mix with the juice. It should be made some six to twelve hours before it is served.

RASPBERRY CREAM

Mash the fruit gently, and let it drain; then sprinkle a little sugar over—and that will produce more juice; put it through a hair sieve to take out the seeds; then put the juice to some cream, and sweeten it; after which, if you choose to lower it with milk, it will not curdle; which it would if put to the milk before the cream; but it is best made of raspberry jelly, instead of jam, when the fresh fruit cannot be obtained.

*RICE CREAM

Boil a teacupful of rice until quite soft in new milk and then sweeten it with sugar, and pile it on a dish; lay on it currant jelly or preserved fruit, beat up the whites of five eggs with a little powdered sugar and flour; add to this when beaten very stiff about a tablespoonful of rich cream and drop it over the rice.

*SNOW CREAM

To a quart of cream add the whites of three eggs, cut to a stiff froth; add four spoonfuls of sweet wine, sugar to taste, flavor with essence of lemon. Whip all to a froth, and as soon as it forms, take it off and serve in glasses.

SPANISH CREAM

Dissolve in a half pint of rose-water, one ounce of isinglass cut small; run it through a hair sieve; add the yolks of three or four eggs, beaten and mixed with half a pint of cream, and two sorrel leaves. Pour it into a deep dish, sweeten with loaf sugar powdered. Stir it till cold, and put it into molds. Lay rings round in different colored sweetmeats. Add, if you like, a little sherry, and a lump or two of sugar, rubbed well upon the rind of a lemon to extract the flavor.

WHIPPED CREAM

To one quart of good cream, put a few drops of bergamot water, a little orange-flower water, and half a pound of sugar. When it is dissolved, whip the cream to a froth, and take it up with a skimmer; drain on a sieve, and if for icing, let it settle half an hour before you put it into cups or glasses. Use that which drops into the dish under the sieve to make it froth the better; adding two whites of eggs. Colored powdered sugar may, if you like, be sprinkled on the top of each.

*ALPINE SNOW

Wash a cup of rice, cook til tender in a covered dish to keep it white; when nearly done, add a cup of rich milk, salt to taste, stir in the beaten yolks of two eggs, allow it to simmer for a moment, then place in a dish, beat the whites in two tablespoons of fine sugar. Put the rice in little heaps upon the tins, intermingling with pieces of red jelly; eat with fine sugar and cream.

COCOA SNOW

Grate the white part of a cocoanut and mix it with white sugar, serve with whipped cream, or not, as desired.

CREAM & SNOW

Make a rich boiled custard, and put it in the bottom of a dish; take the whites of eight eggs, beat with rosewater, and a spoonful of fine sugar, till it be a strong froth; put some milk and water into a stewpan; when it boils take the froth off the eggs, and lay it on the milk and water; boil up once; take off carefully and lay it on the custard.

ICE CREAM & WATER-ICE

TO MOLD ICES

Fill your mold as quickly as possible with the frozen cream, wrap it up in paper, and bury it in ice and salt, and let it remain for an hour or more to harden. For dishing, have the dish ready, dip the mold in hot water for an instant, wipe it, take off the top and bottom covers, and turn it into the dish. This must be done expeditiously.

In molding ices, it is advisable not to have the cream too stiffly frozen before putting it into the mold.

*ICE CREAM

Take two quarts of milk, one pint of cream, three eggs beaten very light, and two teaspoonfuls of arrow-root; boil in one-half pint milk; strain eggs, arrow-root, and flavor to suit; then freeze.

*GINGER ICE CREAM

Bruise six ounces of the best preserved ginger in a mortar; add the juice of one lemon, half a pound of sugar, one pint of cream. Mix well; strain through a hair sieve; freeze. One quart.

*ITALIAN ICE CREAM

Rasp two lemons on some sugar, which, with their juice, add to one pint of cream, one glass of brandy, half a pound of sugar; freeze. One quart.

*LEMON ICE CREAM

Take one pint of cream, rasp two lemons on sugar; squeeze them, and add the juice with half a pound of sugar. Mix well; freeze. One quart.

*PINE-APPLE ICE CREAM

Take one pound of pineapple, when peeled, bruise it in a marble mortar, pass it through a hair sieve; add three-quarters of a pound of powdered sugar, and one pint of cream. Freeze.

*RASPBERRY & CURRANT ICE CREAM

Take one pound of raspberries, half a pound of red currants, three quarters of a pound of sugar, and one pint of cream. Strain, color and freeze. One quart.

STRAWBERRY ICE CREAM

Take two pounds of fresh strawberries, carefully picked, and, with a wooden spoon, rub them through a hair sieve; and about a half a pound of sugar, and the juice of one lemon; color with a few drops of prepared cochineal; cream, one pint; then freeze. This will make a reputed quart. When fresh strawberries are not in season, take strawberry jam, the juice of two lemons, cream, to one quart. Color, strain, and freeze. Milk may be substituted for cream, and makes good ices. If too much sugar is used, the ices will prove watery, or perhaps will not freeze at all.

*VANILLA ICE CREAM

Pound one stick of vanilla, or sufficient to flavor it to the palate, in a mortar, with half a pound of sugar; strain through a hair sieve upon the yolks of two eggs; put it into a stewpan, with half a pint of milk; simmer over a slow fire, stirring all the time, the same as custard; when cool, add one pint of cream and the juice of one lemon; freeze. One quart.

*CHERRY WATER-ICE

One pound of cherries, bruised in a mortar with the stones; add the juice of two lemons, half a pint of water, one pint of clarified sugar, one glass of noyeau, and a little color; strain; freeze. One quart.

*LEMON WATER ICE

Take two lemons and rasp them on sugar, the juice of six lemons, the juice of one orange, one pint of clarified sugar, and half a pint of water. Mix; strain through a hair sieve; freeze. One quart.

*MELON WATER-ICE

Half a pound of ripe melon pounded in a mortar; two ounces of orange-flower water, the juice of two lemons, half a pint of water, and one pint of clarified sugar; strain; freeze. One quart.

*STRAWBERRY OR RASPBERRY WATER-ICE

One pound of scarlet strawberries or raspberries, half a pound of currants, half a pint of water, one pint of clarified sugar, and a little color; strain and freeze. One quart.

To sweeten the icebox
The atmosphere inside the icebox can be rendered wholesome, and purified from lingering smells of used or discarded foods by cleansing with a wash of water containing soda. A small basin of baking soda placed inside will keep it sweet and fresh.

Chapter 16

TWENTY CHOICE COURSE DINNER MENUS

1. Rice, Soup, Baked Pike, Mashed Potatoes, Roast of Beef, Stewed Corn, Chicken Fricassee, Celery Salad, Compote of Orange, Plain Custard, Cheese, Wafers, Coffee.

2. Mutton Soup, Fried Oysters, Stewed Potatoes, Boiled Corn Beef, Cabbage, Turnips, Pheasants, Onion Salad, Apple Pie, White Custard, Bent's Water Crackers, Cheese, Coffee.

3. Oyster Soup, Roast Mutton, Baked Potatoes, Breaded Veal Cutlets, Tomato Sauce, Baked Celery, Cabbage Salad, Apple Custard, Sponge Cake, Cheese, Coffee.

4. Macaroni Soup, Boiled Chicken with Oysters, Mutton Chops, Creamed Potatoes, Stewed Tomatoes, Pickled Beets, Peaches and Rice, Plain Cake, Cheese, Coffee.

5. Tapioca Soup, Boiled Halibut, Duchesse Potatoes, Roast Beef Tongue, Canned Peas, Baked Macaroni with Gravy, Fried Sweet Potatoes, Beet Salad, Cornstarch Pudding, Jelly Tarts, Wafers, Cheese, Coffee.

6. Vegetable Soup, Boiled Trout, Oyster Sauce, Roast Veal with Dressing, Boiled Potatoes, Stewed Tomatoes, Corn, Egg Salad, Snow Cream, Peach Pie, Sultana Biscuit, Cheese, Coffee.

7. Potato Soup, Oyster Patties, Whipped Potatoes, Roast Mutton, Spinach, Beets, Fried Parsnips, Rice Sauce, Celery Salad, Boiled Custard, Lemon Tarts, White Cake, Cheese, Coffee.

8. Veal Soup, Boiled Shad, Caper Sauce, Porterhouse Steak, Mushrooms, Pigeon Pie, Mashed Potatoes, Pickles, Rice Sponge Cakes, Canned Apricots with Cream, Cheese, Coffee.

9. Giblet Soup, Scalloped Clams, Potato Cakes, Lamb Chops, Canned Beans, Tomatoes, Sweet Potatoes, Salmon Salad, Charlotte Russe, Apricot Tarts, Cheese, Coffee.

10. Vermicelli Soup, Fried Small Fish, Mashed Potatoes, Roast Beef, Minced Cabbage, Chicken Croquettes, Beet Salad, Stewed Pears, Plain Sponge Cake, Cheese, Coffee.

11. Oxtail Soup, Fricasseed Chicken with Oysters, Breaded Mutton Chops, Turnips, Duchesse Potatoes, Chow-Chow Salad, Chocolate Pudding, Nut Cake, Cheese, Coffee.

12. Barley Soup, Boiled Trout, Cream Potatoes, Roast Loin of Veal, Stewed Mushroom, Broiled Chicken, Lettuce Salad, Fig Pudding, Wafers, Cheese, Coffee.

13. Noodle Soup, Salmon, with Oyster Sauce, Fried Potatoes, Glazed Beef, Boiled Spinach, Parsnips, with Cream Sauce, Celery, Plain Rice Pudding, with Custard Sauce, Currant Cake, Cheese, Coffee.

14. Lobster Soup, Baked Ribs of Beef, with Browned Potatoes, Boiled Duck, with Onion Sauce, Turnips, Stewed Tomatoes, Lettuce, Delmonico Pudding, Sliced Oranges, Wafers, Cheese, Coffee.

15. Chicken Broth, Baked Whitefish, Boiled Potatoes, Canned Peas, Mutton Chops, Tomatoes, Beets, Celery Salad, Apple Trifle, Lady Fingers, Cheese, Coffee.

16. Sago Soup, Boiled Leg of Mutton, Caper Sauce, Stewed Potatoes, Canned Corn, Scalloped Oysters, with Cream Sauce, Celery and Lettuce Salad, Marmalade Fritters, Apple Custard, Cheese Cakes, Coffee.

17. Vegetable Soup, Broiled Shad, Lyonnaise Potatoes, Pork Chop, with Sage Dressing, Parsnip Fritters, Macaroni and Gravy, Cauliflower Salad, Rhubarb Tarts, Silver Cake, Cheese, Coffee.

18. Chicken Soup, with Rice, Boiled Potatoes, with Cream Sauce, Roast Veal, Tomatoes, Oyster Salad, Boiled Turnips, Asparagus, Codfish, Orange Jelly, White Cake, Cheese, Coffee.

19. Macaroni Soup, Fried Shad, Tomato Sauce, Roast Mutton, Mashed Potatoes, Boiled Tongue, with Mayonnaise Dressing, Fried Parsnips, Canned Beans, Lemon Puffs, Cheese Cakes, Fruit, Coffee.

20. Scotch Broth, Baked Halibut, Boiled Potatoes, Breaded Mutton Chops, Tomato Sauce, Spinach, Bean Salad, Asparagus and Eggs, Peach Batter Pudding, with Sauce, Wafers, Cheese, Coffee.

Chapter 17

Demijohns, casks, kegs, & barrels

SPIRITUOUS LIQUORS

Brewing is the art of extracting a saccharine solution from grain, and afterward partially converting the sugar formed into alcohol. Any of the cereals—wheat, beans, peas, &tc.—may be used in brewing, but barley is the best for the manufacture of beer. Malt signifies any grain which has become sweet to the taste on account of the commencement of germination; as barley, from which ale, beer, and porter are brewed, all of which are called malt liquors. Barley steeped in water for three or four days becomes malt, when it is taken out and is allowed to sprout or germinate. It is then dried in a kiln and treated with boiling water, in order to form wort. Nearly all seeds contain a large quantity of starch, and when they begin to germinate, a peculiar nitrogenous substance called *diastase* is formed. This product, acting as a ferment, converts the starch into sugar. This process is called malting, and the subsequent partial conversion of the sugar into alcohol is called brewing. The two processes are intimately connected. In brewing, the malt undergoes six processes: The grinding; the mashing, or infusion with hot water; the boiling of the worts with hops; the cooling; the fermenting, and the clearing, storing, &tc.

DIRECTIONS FOR FAMILY BREWING

The process of brewing should form a part of the domestic economy of every family, as genuine malt liquor, when of sufficient age, but not too old, is nutritious, and peculiarly adapted to the American palate; but it is to be lamented that the knowledge of the method

of manufacturing this great and necessary article for human existence is very limited and imperfect.

The consequence of the neglect of this knowledge is, that many of the people of this great and free country are doomed to destroy their health by the consumption of the intoxicating and stupifactive compositions of the porter quacks and beer doctors, which are daily passed into their stomachs in the form of pot-house slops or wash, under the misnomers of porter, ale, intermediate beer, or that nondescript and undefinable compound, table beer.

It has been said that brewing is a difficult art; on the contrary, it is a simple and easy process, and better, more nourishing and wholesome drinks, whether porter, ale, or table beer, may be brewed, and for not much more than one-third of the price paid to the publican or brewer, by a person possessed of common sense and common industry; and this result may be obtained by following these directions,

which are distributed into the following divisions:

1. Utensils—The size or capacity of your utensils must, of course, depend on the extent of your brewing. If you brew but from one bushel of malt, a 24 gallon copper, with other utensils proportionably sized, will be best adapted for the purpose. But a 42 or 45 gallon copper is the most eligible size, and by it two bushels of malt may be brewed at a time.

The other needed utensils are: 1. A mash-tub, which may be of a capacity or guage according as you brew, from a bushel or two bushels of malt; if the former proportion, 32 gallon guage, if the latter, 60 gallons. This vessel should have a

false bottom, perforated with holes, with a spigot and faucet, for the purpose of running off the worts.

2. A wort-tub, or underback; a gyle or working-tub; two or three coppers; the necessary number of casks, a working stick, a gallon measure, a bowl dish, a hair sieve, or wicker basket to strain the hops, and a mill to crush or bruise the malt.

2. *Ingredients*—Unless your malt, hops, and water be good, your labors will be in vain, and your money thrown away; the produce will be worthless.

Malt: Malt varies much in quality; when good it presents the following appearances: Its grains are large, full of flour, and plump; they break easily across the teeth, and if drawn across a board leave a chalky trace. The shell or husk should be thin. Malt of an amber color is the best for brewing and may be had of any respectable malt-ster. Malt should be ground a day or two before wanted for use, to give a time to cool after the operation of grinding.

Hops: They, like malt, are of various qualities. When good they are of a pale olive-greenish color, of a lively fragrant smell, and, when rubbed between the hands, of a glutinous, viscid feel. If they have any browness of color on them, it is a sign that their quality has partially perished. They should be chosen free from leaves, stems, &tc., and be kept in a dry place closely packed, or they will become damp and moldy.

Water: The opinions respecting the qualities of hard and soft water for the purposes of brewing are various and conflicting. Some prefer the soft water, while others advocate the use of hard water. Water used for brewing should be as fine and free from impregnations as possible; it should be allowed sufficient time to settle and purify itself before it is used.

3. *The Brewing Preparations: Mashing, Hopping, Fermenting, and Casking*—Ascertain that all vessels are perfectly clean, for the least dirt, taint, soap or grease will distaste or spoil the whole brewing. Then you should fix your mash-tub, which should be placed a little slanting. Cause the water to boil, and lade as much of it into the mash-tub, with so much cold water as will reduce the heat to 170°F (it is absolutely necessary to use

a thermometer), as will enable you, when you have added the malt, to stir it up with ease; then gently pour in the malt, keeping the mixture constantly stirred the whole time, that every particle of the malt may be thoroughly wetted. Then cover the mash-tub closely with malt sacks or cloths. The first mash must stand two hours; then draw off a few quarts of wort into a pail, and return it into the mash-tub, that it may run off clear; when it runs clear, draw off the whole as quickly as you can.

During the time the first mash is standing on the malt, refill your copper with water and heat it to 180°F for the second mash, and when the first mash has run off, lade as much water on the malt as will make it of the same consistence as the first mash. Stir well up for a few minutes with a stirring staff, and cover the mash-tub as before directed. The second mash must stand for an hour and a half, and then be let off as quickly as possible.

The third mash requires boiling water, should be well stirred and not stand more than a hour. When you mash the third time, empty your copper of water, and, if it will hold the whole of your wort, fill it with your first and second worts, together with the hops, and likewise your third wort as soon as it has been run off; if the copper is not large enough to boil at once, *mix* your worts together, and boil

them at twice—taking care to add the hops of the first boiling to the second. Boil one hour, then strain the hops, and get the wort cool as soon as you can.

The brewer must be guided by the quantity of ale he intends to make by the wort he runs off; observing that the process of boiling and fermenting, and the absorption of wort by the hops, is attended by a waste of at least one-third. Also, in the first mashing, he will know that a bushel of malt absorbs from six to seven gallons of water.

One bushel of malt will make twelve gallons of good ale. One pound of hops produces a pleasant bitter, and is considered a good proportion to a bushel of malt; but that must be left to the palate, and less may be used if the draught is quick.

The next process, the fermentation, is the most important part of brewing, as on its management the strength, spirit, and goodness of the ale or beer entirely depends.

The proper heat of the wort for adding the yeast is 60°F; but this depends materially on the season of the year. In summer you cannot get your wort too cool; in winter you may have your wort as high as 65°, 70°, or even 75°F. Your fermenting tun should not be exposed to a current of air, as that drives off the carbonic acid gas, so necessary to be preserved in producing a good vinous fermentation.

Yeast is next mixed with the wort as follows: Take one pound of good yeast, and about two quarts of wort, stir them well together, and place them near the fire for a few minutes, till the mixture begins to ferment; then pour the whole into the fermenting tun, and give the contents a brisk rouse up with the stirring staff, then cover up the vessel. After fermenting 24 hours, take a handful of flour, the same quantity of salt, place them before the fire to get warm, and sprinkle them over the contents of the fermenting tun; give the whole a good stirring and immediately fill your barrels, which, it is very necessary, should be heated a little before the fire, and be quite dry.

If the fermentation does not begin in four or five hours, add a little more yeast, stirring well together, and follow the same method as though no fresh yeast had been required.

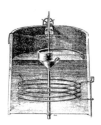

Place small tubs under the barrels, to receive the yeast, &tc., as it runs out of them, and be careful to fill up the barrels every two or three hours for a day or two. In four or five days the ale will have purged itself from the yeast. Let it stand a few days more till the vinous fermentation is completed, which is easily perceived by the yeast at the bung-hole turning brown and full of holes; when you observe this appearance, tightly bung up the barrels. In three weeks to a month, the ale will be fine, and may then be tapped.

The ale cellar should be kept as free as possible from a current of air.

Note—The following observations cannot be too strongly impressed on the mind of the brewer: The proper heat of the water in the different mashings; the length of time the water should stand on the mash; the time the wort should actually boil; the necessity of getting the wort cool as soon as possible; the proper heat of putting together the wort and yeast; and the subsequent attention thereto; but, above all, the constant care to fill up the barrels repeatedly. Attention to all these rules will ensure a fine, rich ale.

4. Directions for Managing and Preserving Malt Liquors—As malt liquors, from bad cellaring and a variety of other causes, ferment in the cask, and turn thick, sour, or are otherwise injured, you should, at different periods, watch their progress, by drawing off a little into a glass from the peg-hole. But though malt liquors are deteriorated by a variety of causes, they often fall fine of themselves, and grow mellow.

When you observe malt liquor beginning to ferment in the casks, open the bung-hole for two or three days, put into the cask two or three pounds of pulverized oyster shells, and stir the mixture well together; the liquor will soon settle, become fine, and lose its sharp taste.

When beer has become sour, or, as it is technically termed, *pricked,* the defect may be removed by introducing into the cask a portion of marble powder, reduced a little coarser than sea sand. Powdered egg and oyster shells are used for the same purpose, but not so effectually.

When beers drink hard or stale, their taste and quality may be considerably improved by introducing a proportionate quantity of the following ingredients into the casks. For a hogshead, a pound of clarified sugar, a couple of ounces of salt of tartar, and a half pound of chalk; and then well agitate the mixture for ten or fifteen minutes, for the purpose of incorporating the ingredients.

5. *Bottling*—Before proceeding to bottle ale or beer, you should ascertain whether it is in the proper state for the purpose. If its state is but slightly saccharine and has but little briskness, it is in a fit state for bottling. But if it spouts up with force, it is a sign that the liquor is still too active to be bottled with safety.

Having all your apparatus ready, fill your bottles within a couple of inches of the cork, and letting them stand uncorked for 24 hours, drive in the corks, and lay the bottles on their sides, covered with saw-dust. As the fermentation of weak malt liquors is much more violent and unmanageable than that of stronger ones, the bursting of the bottles in that state of malt liquor is much more frequent; the bins should therefore be constantly inspected, to ascertain the state of the liquor; and as soon as the bursting of one bottle announces that such is the case, you should, to prevent a like loss, immediately set them all standing up on their ends. The rule for ascertaining when beer is *up* in bottle, is when holding up the bottle to light you can perceive a rising above the beer.

6. *Methods for Cleaning Casks*—In management and preservation of malt liquors, the most anxious attention should be paid to the casks, that they are kept sweet and clean; for if the best beer that was ever brewed be put into a tainted cask, it will completely spoil it so as to be absolutely unfit for use. But slight defects may be easily remedied, either by scorching or burning a brimstone match in them. And musty, foul, or sour smells may at any time be removed by seasoning the casks with sweet grounds, or throwing brimstone on a chafing-dish of coals, placed within the cask.

ALCOHOL AS A STIMULANT

It has been demonstrated how, when sugar has undergone what appears to be a complete transformation, the beneficial portion remains, or more properly speaking, is transferred to a new substance—alcohol.

It has been shown that alcohol is the basis of all wines, beers, ales, porter, bitters, and other stimulants; it has been proved that alcohol is the life and preserve of these various liquids without which the whole fabric would fall to decay.

In the face of this, who is there bold enough to aver that alcohol, when properly employed, is not as beneficial to the system as sugar or bread?

A surfeit of either will cause excruciating pain and distress. The numerous ailments which are the direct result of overeating outnumber those which are due solely to the use of alcoholic substances.

The action of alcohol upon the nerves is that of a stimulant. It excites them according to the quantity taken, at times to an unnatural degree of activity.

This heightened action is carried to the heart, causing it to beat with greater force, thus quickening the circulation of the blood; the stimulus is thereby conveyed to the brain.

When alcohol is taken in large quantities, the effect changes. The sense of exaltation gives way to moroseness; disagreeable thoughts flash through the brain, the intelligence is weakened, images and fantastical ideas succeed each other with bewildering rapidity. The brain whirls, the victim loses his balance and falls.

If left alone, the office of the brain relaxes its functions, and a state of stupor resembling sleep follows, after which a sickly reaction takes place lasting from one to five days. This, however, is not always the case.

There are instances when from the very moment of imbibing the first potion a sensation as if of hatred seems to overpower every good feeling. The victim imagines himself at enmity with an imaginary foe, resents every offer to tranquilize his mind. To use a slang phrase, "he is full of fight"; and unless some friend knocks him down and conveys him home he is apt to commit a treacherous act or assault some inoffensive creature usually weaker than himself. Curious as it may seem, this state of inebriety gives rise to the same low cunning that is so remarkable among the insane. No amount of intoxicant will suffice to subdue the animal strength of this class of inebriates.

Neither in appearance nor demeanor can the least sign of alcoholism be discerned.

None but the habitual drinker is ever affected in the manner just described. It appears that alcohol acts with unequal intensity upon different parts of the nervous system. It makes choice of certain regions of the brain. It is proven by the unequal excitement which is produced upon different persons of diverse temperaments. In one, it stimulates energetical powers of action and thought; in another, it excites jealousy and envy; a third is surfeit, with vanity and egotism; a fourth becomes demented; a fifth, jocose and merry.

People with harsh and discordant voices imagine themselves vocalists, orators without eloquence, misers who become spendthrifts, as well as wise men who make fools of themselves, may all be considered in this category.

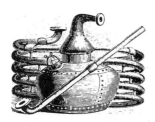

HOW TO MAKE WHISKY
Several steps are incorporated in the final product and are as follows: *Malt*—In a well-ventilated room, put a quantity of barley in a tub; pour cold water over it till the water reaches about six inches

above the grain. Allow it to remain till it becomes stale and emits a foul odor, then draw it off and replace it with fresh water. Let it stand, as before, till the grain becomes quite soft and can easily be pressed between the fingers.

Draw off the water and pile up the grain on a cement or wooden floor in separate heaps, about ten inches high. When outsides of the piles become dry and white, and the interior becomes heated, turn grain carefully so as to avoid breaking the seed.

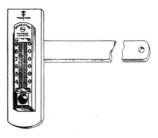

When well mixed, pile it up as before. Repeat every six hours till the germ (rootlet) has grown as long as the seed (kernel). Keep the temperature, during this entire malting process, at 60°F., at which heat the seed will start to germinate within 18 to 48 hours, and will have grown to the desired length in 8 to 12 days, when the developing rootlets wither and the grain becomes mealy. This malting process produces the enzyme *amylase*, which begins the conversion of starch in barley, and other grains, to sugar, and eventually to alcohol.

Spread the grain out on the

floor and dry carefully. When dry, separate the germ from the seed through a sieve coarse enough to pass the germ but not the seed. When done, dry the seed thoroughly. The result is *malt*. The malt is ground into coarse meal, or crushed, two days before use, to allow it to cool.

Mash—Take one bushel of malted grain; and four to seven bushels of unmalted grain, ground into coarse meal; 18 gallons of water to

each bushel of this mixed meal. Pour the meal slowly, while stirring briskly. Let stand two hours; then draw off two-thirds of the water and replace it with a like amount, the replacement water heated to 180°F. (Pure malt is sometimes used—it makes the best liquor—but this is seldom the case, especially for whiskies. The usual proportions are as given above.)

When the second water is well mixed with the grain, let stand three-quarters of an hour; then run it off separately from the first.

Repeat a third time, with water heated to 190°F, let stand one hour, then draw this off the dregs.

The first drawing is run into cooling pans and, when cool enough, is then fermented. The other two drawings are reserved for the second mashing, and take the place of the same amount of first water, thus making the subsequent drawing much stronger. This is the system usually employed in the making of good whisky.

Whisky grains
Barley, rye, corn, wheat, & oats are used in the production of good whiskies, in various proportions; such as barley and corn-meal, barley and rye-meal, barley and coarsely ground wheat (farina), and in some cases, malted oats or malted rye.

Fermentation of Grain—Mix together five bushels of ground malt and fifteen bushels of corn meal, or other grains not malted. Soak the lot in hot water (see *Mashing*), or boil it, then draw the liquor from the dregs. Run it into a wide tub, add to it one gallon of good brewer's yeast, when it has cooled down to 170°F. This will start fermentation. Keep the tub-room temperature between 65° and 85°F. (Do not let temperature rise above or fall below these limits.) Fermentation starts, bubbles rise and a rim of froth forms, first around the edge of the tub, then spreads to meet in the center of the surface, till soon all the surface is covered with creamy foam. The foam (the "making yeast" stage) thickens into little pointed brownish colored heaps on the surface and edges. As this yeast thickens, it forms a tough viscid crust, and when fermentation slackens, falls to the bottom. Prevent this by skimming the scum off as it appears. When fermentation ceases, run this liquor through the still, and at once, the distillate is whisky.

Rules to Learn Regarding Fermentation

1. The larger the quantity of mash, the better the fermentation. A good mash-tub should be very broad and shallow (some seven feet wide by one and a half feet high), with some sort of stirring device in the center, worked by hand, to keep the water and meal well mixed.

2. The temperature for fermentation *must* be between 65° and 85°F.

3. There must be a sufficient quantity of sugar (content) material present.

4. Grain mash fermentation must be started with yeast.

5. There must be water enough to dilute the pulp mass sufficiently.

6. Good ventilation is needed to carry off the gases of fermentation.

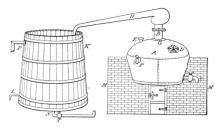

Principle of fermentation

Farina, or wheat-meal, contains the gluten, or yeasty principle, and is soluble between 160° and 212°F.

AN EXCELLENT WHISKY

Can be made by mixing five bushels of barley-malt meal, ten bushels of corn-meal, ten bushels of ground wheat (farina), and 450 gallons of water. Mash and ferment the grains; then run the fermented liquor through the still and worm.

A GOOD WHEAT WHISKY

Take five bushels ground malt, 25 bushels coarsely ground wheat-meal (farina), and 540 gallons of water. Mash, ferment, and run the liquor through the still and worm.

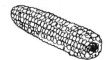

CORN WHISKY

Take five bushels coarse corn-meal, one bushel ground malt, 18 gallons of water to each bushel of mixed grains. Boil one-half the water, then mix it with the same quantity of cold water—this should bring the whole to 155°F. Draw one-half of this into the mash tub, stirring and sprinkling the meal into the water till well mixed, and resembling thin gruel. Repeat stirring at fifteen minute intervals for two hours, then allow it to settle. When clear, draw off two-thirds of it into broad shallow pans to cool rapidly, to prevent formation of acetic acid. When cooled down to 80°F, run it into a fermentation tub and add to it 2% of fresh brewer's yeast.

When fermentation is about to stop, run it into the still and follow regular distilling methods. Having drawn off two-thirds liquor from the mash, heat one-half the remainder to 180°F. Run this into a mash tub with the first; mix the whole thoroughly as before; allow it to rest 45 minutes, then run it off into the cooling pans. Repeat this the third time with the rest of the water heated to 190°F., let stand one hour, and then draw off into a separate tub.

Mix the second and third drawings together and use this mixture in place of the water in the next drawing.

RYE WHISKY

Take nine bushels malted rye, nineteen bushels of rye, not malted, but maybe coarsely ground or crushed, and 520 gallons of spring

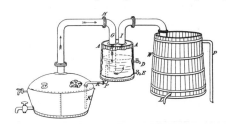

water. Heat the water to 155°F, and run one-half of it into the mash tub; then sprinkle the meal into the water slowly while stirring rapidly, to prevent lumps forming, and let stand fifteen minutes, then stir for five minutes; repeat this four times, then let the mixture settle and when clear draw off 175 gallons into the cooling pans. Heat the next water to 180°F., and run 130 gallons of it on the substance remaining in the mash tub, stirring constantly. When clear, draw off 100 gallons of wort. Ferment and distill as for any other whiskies.

A FINE WHEAT WHISKY

Take nine bushels of malted wheat grain, nineteen bushels of wheat (not malted, but coarse-ground farina), and 520 gallons of water from the spring. Throw one-half the water, heated to 160°F., into a mash tub and sprinkle the meal slowly into the water stirring constantly so as to keep the mixture smooth; let stand about two hours to become quite clear; then draw off 360 gallons of the liquor to cool as fast as possible. Then mix the dregs with the remainder of the water; let stand and draw off again. The second drawing is not fermented, but is used instead of the water for mashing the second batch. Proceed to ferment and distill as usual for whiskies.

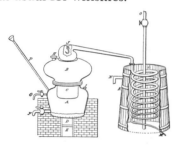

RECTIFYING OR LEACHING THE SPIRITS (Clarifying by means of ground charcoal)

Use a leach tub of ash wood some five feet high by seven feet wide, with a perforated false bottom fitted about twelve inches above the regular one. This false bottom is made to rest on four cross bars which in turn are supported by small upright posts. A coarse linen cloth is stretched across the perforated holes and the seam well calked with the same material. Twenty-five bushels of coarsely ground charcoal are packed over this cloth, and covered over with any loose bagging of any kind, and over the bagging some loose boards,

and a sufficient quantity of stones to keep them submerged.

The liquor is run into this tub, and filtered through the charcoal, and thus purified and clarified.

High wines, and new whisky, when thus purified, are known as *pure spirits,* and are used by compounders for adulterating purposes.

SUGAR WHISKY

In a 30 gallon earthen crock, earthen keg, or tub, dissolve four gallons of brewer's yeast in enough warm spring water to fill it one half full. Put to this mixture 50 pounds of moist sugar, or loaf sugar coarse ground, and stir constantly with a wooden ladle till thoroughly dissolved. Fill the tub to three inches shy of the top and cover with a flannel or muslin cloth to stay varmints and vermin. Set in a warm place, free from any air currents; and after a week the mash is fermented enough to distill. Process as for any good spirits, rerunning the tailing through the still with later batches till of sufficient proof desired.

HOW TO AGE WHISKY

Remove one head of an oaken cask, and throw in a sufficient amount of high proof spirits, which when lighted will thoroughly char the cask inside. Age as long as possible—some eight to ten years is best—before use. Then clarify through coarsely ground charcoal, as above. This will give a mellow sweet liquor, pleasant to the palate.

A LAZY MAN'S QUICK WAY TO AGE WHISKY

Put new whisky into the still, and throw upon it a couple of handfuls of fine oak chips. When the worm is closed off to stay the vapors

from boiling across, set a fire under the still long enough to build up a goodly pressure inside. Then quickly dampen the fire, and cool the still; and when the pressure is ceased, the liquor can be poured off and used as aged whisky. Great attention and caution to this method is required, to stay the still from bursting under the temporary pressure.

WHISKY AGED WITH STEAM

Turn a charred oak cask filled with new whisky on its side with the

bung-hole up, and loop a steam pipe deep into the liquor and back to the boiler through the tightly closed bung. When heated and ex-panded into the pores of the charred wood, the liquor will boil and vaporize across through another pipe barely submerged in a vessel holding a little distilled water. When the vessel is nearly full, turn off the steam, and cool the cask rapidly, when the liquor will siphon back into the cask. Add to the cask the rest of the liquor from the jar, and the whisky is now ten years old.

TO REMOVE A BAD TASTE

If a bad taste has been imparted to whisky through the indiscriminate use of essential oils or tinctures, it can be partially if not wholly removed by adding to every forty gallons of the liquor one pound of dried apples and half a pound of dried peaches.

Cut them up fine and allow them to steep in the liquor ten days; then filter the liquor. A bad taste is removed from brandy by treating it in the same manner, using one pound of ordinary raisins and half a pound of Malaga raisins, instead of the apples and peaches.

FLAVORINGS FOR BLENDED LIQUORS

For Brandy—A quarter of an ounce of oil of cognac dissolved in sixteen ounces 95 percent alcohol will flavor forty gallons of pure spirits.

For Gin—A half an ounce of oil of juniper berries will flavor forty gallons of pure spirits.

For Fruity Flavor—Five pounds of prunes, bruised in a mortar with five pounds of raisins, and steeped eight days in five gallons of spirits, will impart a fruity flavor to two hundred gallons of liquor.

For an Astringent Flavor—Five pounds of black tea boiled thirty minutes in six gallons of water, then pressed to extract the substance and mixed with five gallons of proof spirits, will supply an astringent for five barrels of liquor.

For an Artificial Bead—Sweet oil and sulphuric acid both produce a fictitious bead on liquor.

For the Bed-Bug Flavor—What is called the bed-bug flavor is produced by a few drops of strong ammonia in a barrel of liquor.

PERCENTAGE OF ALCOHOL IN LIQUORS & WINES

It has been found that liquors and wines contain alcohol in the following proportions, which, however, are subject to variations, especially in wines, some vintages being richer in saccharine substances than others, thereby producing more alcohol.

			contain		gal. Alcohol
100 gal. French brandy				53	
100 " Jamaica rum			"	53	" "
100 " Holland gin			"	53	" "
100 " Scotch whisky			"	53	" "
100 " Irish whisky			"	52	" "
100 " American whisky			"	46	" "
100 " Port wine			"	20	" "
100 " Claret wine			"	17	" "
100 " Burgundy port			"	16	" "
100 " Gooseberry wine			"	11	" "
100 " Rhine wine			"	12	" "
100 " Cider			"	9	" "
100 " White wine (Barrac)			"	10	" "
100 " Porter			"	7	" "
100 " Ale (old)			"	7	" "
100 " Ale (new)			"	4	" "
100 " Lager beer			"	3	" "

HOW TO MAKE BRANDY

Brandy can be made from berries and fruits. Nearly all berries are capable of being converted first into wine, then distilled over into brandy. Strawberries, raspberries, huckleberries, currants, cherries, &tc., are treated same as grapes.

Brandy can also be distilled direct from the fermented juice and pulp of apples, pears, peaches, grapes, currants, and other fruits, when they are converted into spir-

ituous liquors such as applejack, cherry brandy, peach brandy, &tc. Good wine grapes are, however, seldom if ever used for making brandy.

APPLEJACK OR CIDER BRANDY

Grind the apples to a pulp, express the juice, and proceed to ferment and distill the same as for grape brandy.

GRAPE (JUICE) BRANDY

Gather grapes and crush whole, including stalks and stems, into pulp, without washing. Put into fermentation tub where the liquor is drawn off into a clear tub in which it is allowed to ferment till complete at 70°F. Then the liquor is distilled same as for other brandy

or whisky. The mash, together with stems and whatever remains after the pressing, is diluted with water, and fermented separately, then run through the still into brandy. Then both liquors are mixed together.

Fruit juices are fermented the same way and require no artificial means as they contain their own ferment (yeasts), which acts spontaneously.

Heat the still hot enough to drive off the alcohol vapors (which vaporize at 173°F) but not to drive or boil off the other fermentation liquids. As soon as the surface of the still becomes heated, sound the connecting pipes between it and the worm with an iron-wire rod; if it emits a hollow sound, it is an in-

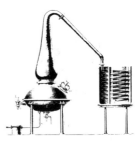

dication that all is right; if, on the contrary, a dull sound is produced by the sounding, then the still is running foul. (If so, kill the fire and cool the outside of the still with cold water till the still is clear again.)

At first, distills over an offensive gas which escapes into the air, after passing through the worm. (Water to surround and cool the worm is usually obtained from a well, a water reservoir, a stream or spring.) When that gas appears, turn on the coolant water, at 60°F, to cool the worm and condense the alcohol vapors inside it.

The first run is low wines (highly impregnated with ether and fusel oil), and should be collected in a separate tub.

As the charge progresses, the liquor becomes sweeter and higher in proof (which is measured by a hydrometer), and when made from grain is called whisky; if made from grape juice, it is called brandy.

As soon as the sweet liquor is run off (as indicated by a sudden temperature rise and a fall in proof), catch the tailings in another tub (to be used for a second charge of the still). Then distill these charges over and over again, till the desired proof is reached, as determined by the hydrometer.

One hundred gallons of grape juice produces 25 gallons of brandy.

Distilling vessels
Large wash boilers, pot-ash kettles serve well for home stills, while tin or galvanized iron pipes make good worms for condensation of the liquors.

THE ORIGIN OF GIN
In 1689 Prince William of Orange, a Dutch grandson of King Charles I, crossed the Channel to become King William III of England. Whether out of devotion to the commerce of Holland or to the health and happiness of England, he promptly began promoting a new Dutch medicinal drink called Genever.

Genever, whose name came from the French word for juniper, was the brainchild of a physician and horticultural genius named Dr. Sylvius. He believed that the juice of the juniper berry was good for what ailed the Dutch in the Seventeenth Century—probably a sort of overstuffed feeling. The distilled spirits employed to transport the juniper and other herbs down the gullet made the patients of Dr. Sylvius feel so much better that scientific study of essence of juniper seemed beside the point.

The English shortened the word genever to gin. Not only did they abbreviate the name but they also lightened the product and dried it out, little by little. By the 1830s there was a whole world of difference between full-flavored Dutch genever and delicate English gin. . . . Both of them might have medicinal properties—or they might not.

Excerpted from *The Beefeater's First 900 Years*

HOLLAND GIN: The Original Dutch Method

To 40 gallons of neutral spirits (grain alcohol at proof 100), put twelve pounds of Juniper berries. Place in an ordinary copper still, apply heat very moderately and with great caution, till the feints

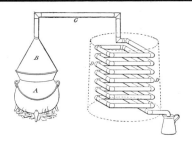

have come over. Then increase the heat till the liquor flows regularly. Keep the fire uniform throughout the operation.

GIN FROM MASH

Take 112 pounds of barley-malt, 228 pounds of rye-meal, 96 gallons of water. Heat the water to 162°F. and sprinkle the malt and meal onto the water, mixing well to avoid lumps; lower the strength of the mash down to 1.047 specific gravity (hydrometer measurement scale) by adding cold water; this will lower the temperature to 80°F. Run this liquor from the dregs into the fermentation tub, and add one-half gallon of brewer's yeast and ferment 48 hours *only*. Then run the clear liquor into the still, the low wines being kept separate from the sweet liquors. The low wines are mixed with the dregs and sediment, and run all into the still together are distilled.

When the liquor has been secured, the first and second distillates are mixed together with 15 pounds of bruised Juniper berries and a double handful of hops, this substance then undergoes another distillation.

The gin produced by this process is fully equal to any in the country and far superior to that made from grain spirits (neutral spirits) .

If found too expensive, this system can be modified to suit the occasion. If found to be too high flavored, reduce the proportion of Juniper berries, or vice versa.

A GOOD HOME STILL (devised by the Irish)

The device consists of a large three-legged iron cauldron-pot (intended as a potato or clothes boiler)

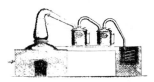

and a close-fitting cone-shaped tin cover, with a small opening at the top, connected to a long tube (C-shaped) of the same material. This tube sometimes leads through a running brook, the water of which serves to condense the vapor as it rises from the pot. Where there are no brooks, the same tin pipe is used in square coils, fitted with a water jacket made of a wash tub or barrel, and filled with water.

The fermented liquor, usually from fermented potato mash, is first put into the pot, the cover fitted on, the seams well closed, the tube which serves as the worm adjusted, a (turf) fire started, and the operation of distilling proceeds slowly. When all the fermented liquor has been distilled, it is repeated a second time. The Irish call this liquor *Poteen.*

An ingenious substitute

A strong ale hogshead is placed in a horizontal position with its bung upwards, a two inch iron pipe is screwed into the bung-hole; a two inch cock is inserted in the head of the cask at the lower edge; a one-half inch iron pipe is passed through one of the staves and connected to a steam boiler. The pipe (from the bung) is joined to a coil of pipe (the worm) of the same dimensions, placed in a molasses hogshead, which stands upright the lower head having been removed; the extreme lower end of the coil is extended through the lower portion of the stave. Live steam is used to heat the liquor. Fermented molasses constitutes the charge; the result is **Rum.**

RUM

The solution from which rum is distilled consists of the juice as well as parts of the sugar cane and in many instances the residue of sugar boiling works, principally in the West Indies, Jamaica, Barbadoes,

St. Croix, &tc. Unlike whisky, rum requires no yeast.

When a sufficient quantity of refuse is gathered together, it is put in a tub, saturated with water, and stirred well. It is let stand till fermentation sets in, which at first is very slow. (Since there is no yeast to start the first batch, thereafter yeast generated from the first batch serves to excite the next batch.)

When fermentation is complete, the liquor is distilled in the same manner as for brandy, whisky, gin, &tc.

Rum is also made from molasses, and from molasses and sugar, as well as from refuse of the sugar refining process. That made from the scummings and other waste matter alone is called sugar spirit.

RUM FROM MOLASSES

Take 40 gallons of New Orleans molasses; add to it 240 gallons of spring water heated to 100°F., mix it thoroughly.

Run this mixture into a tub made to hold 300 gallons, which is rather more broad than high.

Add to this three gallons of fresh brewer's yeast. Keep the room temperature as near as possible at 75°F.

Fermentation starts rapidly and in the course of 48 to 60 hours, the yeast will break on the surface, the scum will drop to the bottom and fermentation is complete.

Run this liquor into the still, distill according to directions and the product is rum.

HOW TO MAKE WINES

BARRELING & BOTTLING OF WINES

Wines ripen much better in large rather than small casks; if wine is ever drawn off from casks, it is necessary to fill up the void as speedily as possible with wine of the same quality, otherwise the air causes the remainder to become sour. When wines have attained their maturity in the wood, they are generally drawn off in bottles. This operation should take place in fine weather, if possible, in March or October. The bottles should be perfectly clean, and the corks sound and as elastic as pos-

sible, so that when driven beyond the contracted part of the bottle neck it might expand, and perfectly exclude the air. The mouth of the bottle might also be dipped in melted wax to assist this object, and then kept in a cool dry place or wine cellar.

CLARIFICATION OF WINES

This process is effected spontaneously by time and response, a deposit is formed at the bottom and side of the cask, which is a mixture composed of bitartrate (or cream of tartar from apothecary shops) potash, yeast, gluten, and coloring matter. This precipitate, from the susceptibility of its being mixed with the wine by agitation and change of temperature, injures the quality of it by rendering it turbid and communicating to it a new fermentation. To prevent this, the wine ought to be drawn off at different periods, all the deposits carefully separated, and put into clean casks. New made wines should be as little disturbed as possible. The removal being always injurious, because it creates a new insensible fermentation.

ERROR IN MIXING BRANDY WITH HOME-MADE WINES

It is a very common rule to mix brandy with home-made wines, as is recommended in the greater number of receipts; this practice is much to be deprecated, as it does not, as is supposed, give vinosity or flavor to the wine, or preserve it from ulterior changes. The effect, to the contrary, is to destroy the briskness of these wines—often the only good quality they possess—to render them expensive, and to diminish their wholesome character. The alcohol uncombined acts on the organs of the body in the same way as alcohol only diluted with an equivalent quantity of water. The diseases also which attend spirit-drinkers, chiefly disorders of the liver, are more commonly met with among the consumers of wine, to which brandy has been adventitiously added, though such disorders rarely if ever follow even the intemperate use of pure wine.

It has been observed that intoxication rarely, if ever, occurs among the inhabitants of wine-producing countries, a fact to be accounted for in no other way than when the alcohol forms an integral portion of some good sound wine, the free acids always present in them hinder the spirit from acting prejudicially. Tartaric acid, that one most common in good wine, has the greatest power in this respect.

However, as it is difficult to overcome prejudice, it is right to describe the mode in which brandy may be added to wine, with the least possible injury, when it is desired to make them stronger; and

then it produces a mixture certain to be discovered by an accurate palate, and in which all the evil effects are most conspicuous. To render this mixture more complete and less injurious, it should be made while the process of fermentation is still going on. The brandy may be added to the *must* at the very commencement of the process, and in this manner the union is most complete; care being taken not to add enough to check the fermentation altogether. Or else it may be done during the insensible fermentation which takes place in the cask. By these means a portion, at least, of the added spirit enters into permanent combination with the wine in consequence of its having undergone the action of the fermenting process and the injury to the quality of the wine is the least possible.

HOW TO MAKE APPLE WINE
Take pure cider made from sound ripe apples as it runs from the press; put 60 pounds of common brown sugar into fifteen gallons of cider, and let it dissolve, then put the mixture into clean barrel,

and fill the barrel up to within two gallons of being full, with clean cider; put the cask in a cool place, leaving the bung out for 48 hours; then put in the bung, with a small vent, until fermentation wholly ceases, and bung up tight; and in one year the wine will be fit for use. This wine requires no racking; the longer it stands upon the lees, the better.

HOW TO MAKE APRICOT WINE

Take sixteen pounds of the pulp of the apricot when nearly ripe, add two quarts of spring water, let the mixture stand for 24 hours and then squeeze out the juice; add to every quart of it half a pound of loaf sugar, put it into a cask and let it ferment, and when perfectly clear, bottle it. Peach wine may be made in a similar manner.

APRICOT WINE

Wipe clean and cut 24 pounds of apricots; boil them in four gallons of fresh spring water till the water has imbibed the flavor of the fruit, then strain the liquor through a hair sieve, and to each quart of it put six ounces of loaf sugar; then boil it and add twelve pounds of common sugar and two pounds of sliced beet-root. When fermented, put into the cask a half-gallon or more of good brandy, or flavorless whisky.

HOW TO MAKE BLACKBERRY WINE

Gather the blackberries when perfectly ripe, and in such a manner as to avoid bruising. Empty them, as fast as gathered, into a tub until you have a quantity sufficient to fill, with juice, the cask in which you propose to make the wine.

Have the utensils, &tc., required in the process all ready before you pick—or at least before you mash the berries. Everything must be scrupulously clean. You want a keg, a beater of seasoned hardwood, a pail, a large bowl, tureen, or other vessel into which to strain your juice, a good thick strainer—two or three folds of fine white flannel is the best material—a couple of yards of Osnaburg, a spare tube or a bucket or two, and a tub of soft spring water. Everything must be perfectly clean, and free from dirt or odor of any kind.

Crush the berries thoroughly with the beater, and then after straining the liquor, which runs freely from the pulp through the folded flannel, empty it into the cask, measuring it as you put it in. When the juice has been all drained from the pulp, you proceed to press the pulp dry. If the quantity is large, this had best be done by a regular press, but if only a few gallons are wanted, the Osnaburg answers very well. Stretch out the Osnaburg, put a gallon or a gallon and a half of the pulp into the center, fold the cloth over it on each side, and let a strong farm-hand at either end twist the cloth with all their might and strength; when the juice is well pressed out, remove and lay aside the cake of pomace, and put in more pulp. This process is apparently rough, but is both rapid and effectual. The juice so extracted is strained and measured into the cask as before mentioned. The flannel strainer and the Osnaburg may need rinsing occasionally during the work.

When all the pulp is pressed, put the hard cakes of pomace taken from the cloth into a tub, and pour upon them a little more soft spring water than you have clear juice; break up the balls and wash them thoroughly in the water, so as to obtain all the juice left in the mass, and then strain it clear; measure out as many gallons of this water as you have of clear juice, dissolve in each gallon of the water six pounds of sugar (brown or white, as you want common or first-rate wine), and when thoroughly dissolved, add the juices (first passing it again through the strainer), and mix them.

Then rinse out your cask, put it where it can stand undisturbed in a cellar; fill it perfectly full of the mixture, and lay a cloth loosely over the bung-hole. In two or three days fermentation will commence, and the impurities run over at the bung; look at it every day, and if it does not run over, with some of the mixture which you have reserved in another vessel, fill it up to the bung.

In about three weeks fermentation will have ceased, and the wine be still; fill it again, drive in the bung tight, nail a tin over it, and let it remain undisturbed until the following November, or what is better, March. Then draw it off, without shaking the cask, put it into bottles, or better demijohns, cork tightly and seal over.

For a ten-gallon cask, you will need about 4⅓ gallons of juice, a like amount of soft spring water, and 26 pounds of sugar, and in the same proportion for larger or smaller quantities. Some persons add spirit to the wine, but instead of doing good, it is only an injury.

Another process is, after pouring in the mixture for a ten-gallon cask, to beat up the whites of two or three eggs into a froth, put them into the cask, and with a long stick mix them thoroughly with the wine. In five or six days, draw the now clarified wine off by a spigot —without shaking the original cask at all—into a clean cask, bung up and tin over; to be drawn off into glass in November or March.

The more carefully your juice is strained, the better the quality of sugar, and the more scrupulously clean your utensils—particularly your kegs—the purer and better will be your wine.

The best quality, when you gather your own fruit, and make it yourself, costs you only the price of the white sugar, and when bottled will cost you in money only about twelve and a half cents a bottle.

HOW TO MAKE BLACKBERRY TARTAR

Pick ripe berries, making sure none are bruised, and when a peck is gathered, place in a large stone vessel; pour over them enough soft spring water to cover; then add two ounces of tartaric acid; mix thoroughly together. Strain through a fine hair sieve at the end of 24 hours, and put to each pint of the liquor one pound of finest sugar; put to the fire and cook at a boil for one-half hour. Take from the fire, cool a little so as not to break any glass bottles you may use, bottle and cork tightly; then place in a cool cellar till needed. Serve over chunks of ice with lemon juice and slices of lemons.

RECEIPT FOR BLACKBERRY WINE

Put to three and a half gallons of freshly picked and mashed berries, unwashed, seven quarts of soft water; and let stand two days; then strain through a horsehair sieve. To the juice add the whites of two hen's eggs whipped to a froth, fourteen pounds of common moist sugar dissolved in a gallon of spring water. Put over the fire and boil a few minutes till the whole is thoroughly mixed; skim and cool and pour the mixture into a large earthen vessel. Skim each day for the next week or so, afterwards stirring vigorously each time; then pour into demijohns, but do not cork. Cover the bottles with cloth and leave till fermentation wholly ceases and the wine be still; then pour off, bottle, cork tightly.

CHERRY WINE

Take Morella cherries, picked off from their stalks, mash them in a mortar to detach the pulp without bruising the stones, and suffer the mass to stand 24 hours. Press the pulp through a coarse hair sieve, and to every six gallons add from 16 to 18 pounds of loaf sugar. Allow it to ferment, and as soon as the wine be clear, draw it from the lees.

Damson wine may be made in a similar manner.

HOW TO MAKE ARTIFICIAL APPLE CIDER

Imitation cider consists of 25 gallons of sweet soft water, 25 pounds of New Orleans sugar; one pint of yeast; two pounds of tartaric acid. Put all the ingredients into a clean cask, and stir them up well after standing 24 hours with the bung out. Add three gallons of spirits, then bung the cask up tight, and let it stand 48 hours, after which time it will be ready for use.

Champagne cider can be prepared by taking ten gallons of cider, old and clear. Put this in a strong, ironbound cask pitched inside (like beer casks); add two and one-half pints of clarified white plain syrup; then dissolve in it five ounces of tartaric acid; keep the bung ready in hand, then add seven and a half ounces of potassium bicarbonate; bung it up as quickly and as well as possible.

HOW TO KEEP SWEET CIDER FROM TURNING TO VINEGAR

The casks into which cider is put, whenever racked off, should always have been thoroughly *scalded* and *dried;* and, as before observed, never be filled with but a few gallons. Should this precautions be neglected, a second fermentation will surely and quickly succeed, and the delicious beverage made will be converted into a spurious sort of vinegar. No power of art can procure for it its former richness and purity.

There is a practice call *stumming*—it signifies the fumigating the cask with burning sulphur, and sometimes found advantageous. In it a piece of canvas cloth, twelve inches by two, is dipped into melted brimstone; when dry, light it, and suspend it through the bung-hole of the cask (in which are a few gallons of cider), until it

is burnt out. Stop the cask for an hour or two; then roll the cask until the cider and sulphurous acid

are incorporated; after this, fill the cask. The combustion of brimstone checks the improper fermentation; but, if a few cloves, or a small quantity of cinnamon or ginger, be strewed over the liquid sulphur, the combustion will impart their flavors to the whole cask of cider. This process should never take place until the vinous fermentation has ceased.

THE HAND CIDER-MILL

It consists of two wooden cylinders, indented; each being about ten inches in diameter, and enclosed in a manner very similar to that of other mills. Each cylinder is fed from the top, and the mill is turned by hand. This mill performs its duties well; by its operation, the rind, kernel, and stalk, are bruised, and the fleshy parts are reduced to a perfect pulp. The cylinders can be moved from a nearer to a greater distance; and therefore, the advance of the business is regular and progressive, from the moment the skin is first cut until the cylinders are so close together that the smallest kernel cannot pass through unbruised. Occasionally, indeed, a pair of finer toothed instruments are used, working beneath the former ones; the effect is more effectual.

But though there is much saving of time in the latter process, there is considerable expenditure of labor. The horse-mill cannot be made to produce equal fineness without great difficulty; for, however careful the person employed to agitate the fruit while grinding, and of keeping it to the runner, may be, a considerable proportion must be conveyed to press without having been well-ground. Two disadvantages belong to the hand-mill in its present state—loss of time and increased manual labor (for it is difficult, with the assistance of three men, to grind a hogshead a day); but with a horse-mill, from two to three hogsheads may be made by a man and woman, or younger person, and one horse. However, on a farm, a hand-mill is capable of great improvement, as relates to time, by attaching to it a large horizontal wheel and a horse. This has been occasionally done, and with advantage.

RED & BLACK CURRANT WINE

Take equal proportions of red and black currants, mash the berries, and having squeezed out the juice, dilute it with a similar proportion of water, and to every two quarts of the diluted juice add two pounds of sugar. Put it into a cask and place it in a warm place to ferment. When it has ceased fermenting, bung it close, and when clear, draw it off from its lees, and bottle it.

BRISK CURRANT WINE

Gather the currants when they have attained their full growth, but before they have shown much tendency to ripen; separate the berries from their stalks; mash the fruit, and proceed in the same manner as for making brisk gooseberry wine.

BLACK CURRANT CORDIAL

To every four quarts of black currants, picked from the stems and lightly bruised, add one gallon of the best whisky; let it remain four months, shaking the jar occasionally, then drain off the liquor and strain. Add three pounds of loaf sugar and a quarter of a pound of best cloves, slightly bruised; bottle well and seal.

CURRANT WINE

Take one quart of currant juice, three pounds of common sugar, sufficient spring water to make a gallon.

HOW TO MAKE CURRANT WINE

The currants should be fully ripe when picked; put them into a large tub, in which they should remain a day or two; then crush with the hands, unless you have a small patent wine press, in which they should not be pressed too much, or the stems will be bruised, and impart a disagreeable taste to the juice. If the hands are used, put the crushed fruit, after the juice is poured off, in a cloth or sack and press out the remaining juice. Put the juice back into the tub after cleansing it, where it should remain about three days, until the first stages of fermentation are over, and removing once or twice a day the scum copiously arising to the top.

Then put the juice in a vessel—a demi-john, keg, or barrel—of a size to suit the quantity made, and to each quart add three pounds of the best yellow sugar, and soft water sufficient to make a gallon. Thus ten quarts of juice and thirty pounds of sugar will give you ten gallons of wine, and so on in proportion. Those who do not like sweet wine can reduce the quantity of sugar to two and a half, or who wish it very sweet, raise it to three and a half pounds per gallon.

The vessel must be full, and the bung or stopper left off until fermentation ceases, which will be in twelve to fifteen days. Meanwhile, the cask must be filled up daily with currant juice left over, as fermentation throws out the impure matter. When fermentation ceases, rack the wine off carefully, either from the spigot or by a syphon, and keep running all the time. Cleanse the cask thoroughly with boiling water, then return the wine, bung up tightly, and let it stand four or five months, when it will be fit to drink, and can be bottled if desired.

All the vessels, casks, &tc., should be perfectly sweet, and the whole operation should be done with an eye to cleanliness. In such event, every drop of brandy or other spirituous liquors added will detract from the flavor of the wine and will not, in the least degree, increase its keeping qualities. Currant wine made in this way will keep for an age.

DANDELION WINE

Take one gallon yellow flower heads, best freshly gathered on a sunny April day, midday before the bees gorge themselves on the pollen; throw the flowers into a large tub and immediately pour over them two gallons of fresh boiling spring water; let the mixture stand closely covered 48 hours, stirring occasionally with a stick. Then put it to the fire and boil fifteen minutes with the peels chopped fine of two oranges and two lemons. Strain through a hair sieve onto five pounds of lump sugar; and add the juice and pulp of the oranges and lemons. Pour the mixture into a cask of sufficient size to hold the quantity of wine; cool and add one-half pint of yeast; cover the bunghole over with a flannel cloth while the mixture works, filling the cask daily with additional mixture as fermentation casts out the impure articles. When it clears and the wine be still, rack into clean bottles and stopper tightly. Let stand in a cool place, or ale cellar, till December or, even better, till late the next spring.

EXCELLENT ELDERBERRY WINE

To every five quarts of bruised berries, add two quarts of soft spring water; strain the juice through a fine hair sieve, and add to every quart of the diluted juice one pound of loaf sugar. Boil the mixture for a quarter of an hour, and suffer it to ferment. For flavoring the wine, ginger, allspice, or any aromatic may be used inclosed in a bag, and suspended in the cask; then removed when the desired flavor is produced.

ELDERBERRY WINE

Take two quarts of blossoms, cut from their fleshy stalks finely, and place in an earthen tub; cover over with eighteen pounds of yellow sugar boiled in six gallons of spring water. When cool, add one pint of brewer's yeast and four teaspoonfuls of lemon juice. Let stand a week to ten days, then strain through a fine sieve or cloth, and throw into a cask with six pounds of raisins. Shake vigorously for four or five days, then put in a steady place where it can stand at rest till December or better even later. Then bottle.

FINE GINGER WINE

Dissolve twelve pounds of sugar in eighteen quarts of water; add to this six ounces of bruised ginger, and the peel of four lemons; boil it an hour, and when nearly cold put to it a tablespoonful of yeast, with the juice of four lemons and a pound of raisins stoned; then put in the cask, stirring it every day for a fortnight, and then add a quart of brandy and an ounce of isinglass; stop it down, and in two months it will be fit to bottle. The spile should remain loose for two or three days after the bung is made firm, so as to allow the disengaged carbonic acid gas to escape.

HOW TO MAKE GOOSEBERRY WINE

Pick and bruise the gooseberries, and to every pound put a quart of cold spring water, and let it stand three days, stirring it twice or thrice a day. Add to every gallon of juice three pounds of loaf sugar; fill the barrel, and when it is done working, add to every twenty quarts of liquor, one quart of good brandy, and a little isinglass. The gooseberries must be picked when they are just changing color. The liquor ought to stand in the barrel at least six months. Taste it occasionally, and bottle when the sweetness has gone off.

BRISK GOOSEBERRY WINE

Bruise unripe gooseberries, and let them stand twelve hours, squeeze out the juice and strain it, to separate the seeds, and add to every six pints of this liquor three pounds of loaf sugar; suffer it to ferment, and when perfectly bright, which will be in about three months, bottle it off.

METHOD OF MAKING GOOSEBERRY WINE

Take 100 pounds of unripe gooseberries, free them from their stalks, and bruise in a wooden tub; add to this eight gallons of spring water, and after remaining for twelve hours, put it into a coarse canvas bag and squeeze out the liquor.

Pour upon the residue two gallons of water, macerate for twelve hours, then press, and add it to that previously obtained. Put the whole of the juice into a tub, and add from 60 to 80 pounds of white loaf sugar, and three pounds of crude bitartrate of potash. Then mix the whole, and make the total bulk of the liquor to the amount of 21 gallons, cover it over and let stand in a moderately warm place. When it begins to ferment, which will take place in a day or two, care should be taken to skim off the yeast, as it appears on the surface, and to repeat this operation from time to time till no more yeast becomes separated. This process completed, the liquor must be drawn from the dregs into a cask which must be completely filled with the wine.

In consequence of the slow fermentation in the cask, a small quantity of yeast will continue to be separated, and overflow the bung-hole—hence the quantity of the liquor diminished; this loss must be compensated for by adding more liquor, so as to keep the cask constantly full.

When the slow fermentation has nearly ceased, the bung may be put loosely in place, and the vent-hole fitted with a peg, so that the carbonic acid which becomes developed, might escape. When no more froth appears, the vent peg must be withdrawn, and the spile then made firm, and the cask left at rest for six months; the wine should now be drawn off from its lees into another cask; if it is not now fine, it might be rendered so by the addition of isinglass dis-

solved in water, which will render it clear in a few days, afterwards, it may be bottled and stored in a cool cellar.

GRAPE WINE
Crush two pecks of freshly picked and stemmed grapes; pour over the mass in a large earthen vessel one gallon of boiling soft water; let stand undisturbed for a day and a half; then strain through a hair sieve and add six pounds of white sugar; stir till dissolved. Pour into jugs and let stand open till fermentation ceases, keeping bottles even full. When the wine be still, cork and store for six months to a year when it will be fit for use.

HOW TO MAKE GRAPE WINE
Take two quarts of grape juice, two quarts of water, four pounds of sugar. Extract the juice from the grape in any simple way; if only a few quarts are desired, it can be

done with a strainer and a pair of squeezers, if a larger quantity is desired, put the grapes into cheese press made particularly clean, putting on sufficient weight to express the juice of a full hoop of grapes, being careful that none but perfect grapes are used, perfectly ripe and free from blemish.

After the first pressing, put a little water to the pulp and press a second time, using the juice with the second pressing with the water to be mixed with the clear grape juice. If only a few quarts are made, place the wine, as soon as mixed, into bottles, fill them even full and allow to stand in a warm place until it ferments, which will take about 36 hours usually; then remove all the scum, cool and put into a dark, cool place. But if a few gallons are desired, place in a keg—but the keg must be even full; and after fermentation has ceased and the scum removed, draw off and bottle, and cork tight.

WINE FROM THE LEAVES & TENDRILS OF THE VINE

Take about 40 to 50 pounds of young leaves, plucked with their stems; pour seven or eight gallons of boiling water on them and let it macerate for 24 hours. Pour off the liquor; press the leaves well so as to obtain all the juice that is possible, add another gallon of water to the leaves, and press again. From 25 to 30 pounds of loaf sugar may be added as thought proper, and the whole quantity made up to ten gallons and a half, and follow the

instructions as recommended for gooseberry wine.

WINE FROM MATURE FRUITS

Wine from mature fruits may be made in the same manner as that given for gooseberry wine, and it may be made either sweet or dry. If sweet wine be desired, the quantity of the fruits should not exceed 80 pounds, if a dry wine be wished, it may extend to 120 pounds. If the strength of the wine be wished to be increased, the sugar might be increased to 80 pounds.

MULBERRY WINE

Take mulberries when nearly ripe and bruise them in a tub, and to every two quarts of the bruised berries, add a like quantity of spring water; let the mixture stand for 24 hours, strain it through a coarse sieve, and having added to every two gallons of the diluted juice six to eight pounds of loaf sugar, allow it to ferment, and when fine, bottle it.

ORANGE WINE

Take the outer rind of 50 Seville oranges, so thinly pared that no white appears in it; pour on it six gallons of boiling spring water, let stand for eight to ten hours, and having strained off the liquor, whilst slightly warm, add to it the juice of the pulp, and about sixteen pounds of lump sugar, and a tablespoonful or two of yeast; suffer it to ferment in the cask for about five days, or till the fermentation has apparently ceased, and when the wine is perfectly transparent, draw it off from its lees, and bottle it.

HOW TO MAKE RATIFIA

To two gallons of the best brandy put two quarts of finest sweet sherry, a like amount of Madiera wine, of orange-flower and rose-water a quart each, dissolved in six pounds of loaf sugar. Throw into an earthen crock together with six quarts of apricot kernels; stir shortly, and set in a sunny place to rest for four or five weeks. Bottle, cork tight, and set away for use in a cool ale cellar.

RAISIN WINE

Take 48 pounds of raisins picked from their stalks, pour over them twelve gallons of boiling soft water, and add twelve pounds of sugar; let them mascerate ten to fourteen days, stirring it every day, then pour off the liquor, squeeze out the raisins, and add to it a pound and a half of bitartrate of potash. Put the liquor into a cask, reserving a sufficient quantity for filling up the cask, and draw off the wine when the fermentation has ceased.

RAISIN WINE POSSESSING THE FLAVOR OF FRONTIGNAC

Take twelve pounds of raisins and boil in twelve gallons of spring water, and when perfectly soft, separate the pulp from the stones. Add the pulp to the water in which the raisins were boiled, pour this mixture over 24 pounds of white sugar, and allow it to ferment with the addition of a half pint of yeast; when the fermentation has nearly ceased, add half a peck of elder flowers, confined in a bag, which should be suspended in the cask, and removed when the wine has acquired the desired flavor. When the wine has become clear, draw it off into bottles.

RASPBERRY WINE

To five quarts of mashed raspberries, add four quarts of water; let the mixture stand 24 hours, strain the mass through a coarse hair sieve, and to every gallon add from two to three pounds of lump sugar, and allow it to ferment.

HOW TO MAKE CHINESE RICE WINE

Put in a large earthen jar, two pounds of stoned raisins, three pounds of dried rice grains, five pounds of lump sugar, two oranges sliced thin, a half pint of yeast, dissolved in two gallons of tepid spring water. Mix together the whole till dissolved; cover and let rest from four to five weeks; stir with a large wooden ladle or spoon daily the first week, then every other day the next, and leave undisturbed thereafter. Strain through a fine hair strainer, let stand for six months to a year before use.

HOW TO MAKE STRAWBERRY TARTAR

Pick, cull, and clean 24 pounds of fully ripened strawberries; put into a large stone vessel and cover with one gallon of spring water in which is dissolved ten ounces of tartaric acid; set aside for two days. Strain carefully without bruising the berries; and to each pint of juice add one and a half pounds of pulverized sugar. Stir till the mixture is thoroughly dissolved, and set aside a few days more before bottling with a light cork. Should a bit of fermentation be noted, remove the corks till it be still; then cork tightly and store in a cool place till needed.

Oh—Good Lord

The Horse and Mule live thirty years,
Yet nothing know of wine and beers.

Most Goats and Sheep at twenty die,
And have never tasted Scotch or Rye.

A Cow drinks water by the ton,
And so at eighteen is nearly done.

A Dog in milk and water soaks,
And then in twelve short years he croaks.

Your modest, sober, bone-dry Hen
Lays eggs for Nogs, then dies at ten.

All Animals are strictly dry,
They sinless live and swiftly die.

But sinful, Ginful, Beer-soaked men
Survive some three score years and ten.

While some of us, though mighty few,
Stay sozzled till we're ninety-two.

Origin Unknown

Part Two

—•—

FOLK REMEDIES

A WORD OF CAUTION

100 years ago, people afflicted with *affections* and *infirmities* entrusted themselves to faith . . . and to catch-as-catch-can cures, dredged from folklore wisdom and found in home pantries and medicine chests.

In those horse-and-buggy days, village apothecaries offered drugs and chemicals for *cures,* which our forefathers then concocted in their own kitchens and administered to the ailing with tablespoon and prayer.

Today, it is hard to tell whether ancestral potence or potions actually invigorated growth of the family tree. Today you, like your forebears, take these nostrums

solely at your own risk. When in doubt, ye of little faith should consult a physician, who in Grandmother's day most likely prescribed and compounded such remedies for himself.

NOTE: Neither the author nor the publisher suggests that you use any of these century-old medications or remedies. All of them are authentic, but some could be harmful. They are presented here for your enjoyment of things past.

Chapter 18

How to meet them

ACCIDENTS & INJURIES

As accidents are constantly liable to occur; the importance of knowing how best to meet the various emergencies that may arise can hardly be over-estimated. In all cases, and under all circumstances, the best help to assist a party in this trying moment is *presence of mind*.

HARVEST BUG BITES
The best remedy is the use of benzine, which immediately kills the insect. A small drop of tincture of iodine has the same effect.

BITES & STINGS OF INSECTS
Such as bees, wasps, hornets, &tc., although generally painful, and

ofttimes causing much disturbance, yet are rarely attended with fatal results. The pain and swelling may generally be promptly arrested by bathing freely with a strong solution of equal parts of common salt and baking soda, in warm water; or by the application of spirits of hartshorn; or of volatile liniment (one part of spirits of hartshorn and two of olive oil). In the absence of the other articles, warm oil may be used; or the application of a cut raw onion to the swelling; or if these are not at hand, apply a paste made from fresh clay-earth. If the sting of the insect is left in the wound, as is frequently the case, it should always be extracted. If there is faintness, give some stimulant—as a tablespoonful of brandy and water, or brandy and ammonia.

MAD DOG BITES

1. Take immediately warm vinegar or tepid water; wash the wound clean therewith and then dry it; pour upon the wound, then, ten or twelve drops of muriatic acid; mineral acids destroy the poison of the saliva, by which means the evil effects of the latter are neutralized.

2. Many think that the only sure preventative of evil following the bite of a rabid dog is to suck the wound immediately, before the poison has had time to circulate with the blood. If the person bit cannot get to the wound to suck it, he must persuade or pay another to do it for him. There is no fear of any harm following this, for the poison entering by the stomach cannot hurt a person. A spoonful of the poison might be swallowed with impunity, but the person who sucks the place should have no wound on the lip or tongue, or it might be dangerous. The precaution alluded to is a most important one, and should never be omitted prior to an excision and the application of lunar caustic in every part, especially the interior and deep-seated portions. No injury need be anticipated if this treatment is adopted promptly and effectively. The poison of hydrophobia remains latent on an average of six weeks; the parts heal over, but there is a pimple or wound, more or less irritable; it then becomes painful; and the germ, whatever it is, ripe for dissemination into the system, and then all hope is gone. Nevertheless, between the time of the bite and the activity of the wound previous to dissemination, the caustic of nitrate of silver is sure preventive; after that it is as useless as all the other means. The best mode of application of nitrate of silver is by introducing it solidly into the wound.

SERPENT BITES

The poison inserted by the stings and bites of many venomous reptiles is so rapidly absorbed, and of so fatal a description, as frequently to occasion death before any remedy or antidote can be applied; and they are rendered yet more dangerous from the fact that these wounds are inflicted in parts of the country and world where precautionary measures are seldom thought of, and generally at times when people are least prepared to meet them.

1. In absence of any remedies, the first best plan to adopt on being bitten by any of the poisonous snakes is to do as recommended above in Mad Dog Bites—viz., to wash off the place immediately; if possible get the mouth to the spot, and forcibly suck out all the poison, first applying a ligature above the wound as tightly as can be borne.

2. A remedy promulgated by the Smithsonian Institute is to take 30 grains iodine potassium, 30 grains iodine, 1 ounce water to be applied externally to the wound by saturating lint or batting—the same to be kept moist with the antidote until the cure be effected, which will be in one hour, and sometimes instantly.

3. Also is recommended carbolic acid, diluted and administered internally every few minutes until recovery is certain.

4. Also, if a proper amount of dilute ammonia water be injected into the circulation of the patient suffering from snake-bite, the curative effect is usually sudden and startling, so that, in many cases, men have thus been brought back, as it were, by magic, from the very shadow of death.

HOW TO STOP BLOOD

Take the fine dust of tea, or the scrapings of the inside of tanned leather. Bind it upon the wound closely, and blood will soon cease to flow.

BLEEDING AT THE NOSE

1. Roll up a piece of paper and press it under the upper lip.

2. In obstinate cases, blow a little gum Arabic up the nostrils through a quill, which will immediately stop the discharge; powdered alum is also good.

3. Pressure by the finger over the small artery near the ala (wing) of the nose, on the side where the blood is flowing, is said to arrest the hemorrhage immediately.

BLEEDING FROM THE LUNGS

A case has been related in which inhalation of very dry persulphate of iron, reduced to a palpable powder, entirely arrested bleeding from the lungs, after all the usual remedies—lead, opium, &tc.—had failed. A small quantity was administered by drawing into the lungs every hour during part of the night and following day.

BLEEDING FROM THE BOWELS

The most common cause of this, when not a complication of some disease, is hemorrhoids or piles. Should serious hemorrhage occur, rest and quiet, and cold water poured slowly across the lower portion of the belly, or cloths wet with cold water, or better, with ice water applied over the belly and thighs, and to the lower end of the bowels, will ordinarily arrest it. In some cases it may be necessary, to use injections of cold water, or even put small pieces of ice in the rectum.

BLEEDING FROM THE MOUTH

This is generally caused by some injury to the cheeks, gums, or teeth, or tongue, but it sometimes occurs without any direct cause of this kind, and no small alarm may be caused by mistaking it for bleeding from the lungs. Except when an artery of some size is injured, bleeding from the mouth can generally be controlled by gargling and washing the mouth with cold water, salt and water, or alum and water, or some persulphate of iron may be applied to the bleeding surface. Sometimes obstinate or even alarming bleeding may follow the pulling of a tooth. The best remedy for this is to plug the cavity with lint or cotton wet with the solution of persulphate of iron, and apply a compress which may be kept in place by closing the teeth on it.

BLEEDING FROM THE STOMACH (Vomiting blood)

Hemorrhage from the stomach is seldom so serious as to endanger life; but as it may be a symptom of some dangerous infection, it is always best to consult a physician concerning it. In the meantime, as in all other varieties of hemorrhage, perfect quiet should be preserved. A little salt, or vinegar, or lemon juice, should be taken at intervals, in a small glass of fresh cool water, or ice-water, as ice may be swallowed in small pieces, and cloths wet with ice-water, or pounded ice applied over the stomach.

BLEEDING FROM VARICOSE VEINS

Serious and even fatal hemorrhage may occur from the bursting of a large varicose or "broken" vein. Should such an accident occur, the bleeding may be best controlled, until proper medical aid can be procured, by a tight bandage; or a "stick tourniquet," remembering that the blood comes toward the heart in the veins, and from it in the arteries. The best thing to prevent the rupture of varicose or broken veins is to support the limb by wearing elastic stockings, or a carefully applied bandage.

BURNS & SCALDS

There is no class of accidents that cause such an amount of agony, and none which are followed with more disastrous results.

_1._ By putting the burned part under cold water, milk, cold tea, or other bland fluid, instantaneous and perfect relief from all pain will be experienced. On withdrawal, the burn should be perfectly covered with half an inch or more of common wheaten flour, put on with a dredging-box or in any other way, and allowed to remain until a cure is effected, when the dry, caked flour will fall off, or can be softened with water, disclosing a beautiful, new and healthy skin, in all cases where the burns have been superficial.

_2._ Dissolve white lead in flaxseed oil to the consistency of milk, and apply over the entire burn or scald every five minutes. It can be applied with a soft feather. This is said to give relief sooner, and to be more permanent in its effects, than any other application.

_3._ Make a solution of alum (4 to 8 oz. to a quart of hot water), cooled to tepid or cold. Bathe the burn or scald with a linen rag, wetted with this mixture, then bind the wet rag on it with a strip of linen, and moisten the bandages with the alum water frequently, without removing it during two or three days. Or, dip a cotton cloth in this alum solution and apply immediately on the burn. As soon as it becomes hot or dry, replace it by another, and continue doing so as often as the cloth dries, which at first will be every few minutes. The pain will immediately cease, and after 24 hours of this treatment the burn will be healed; especially if commenced before blisters are formed. The astringent and drying qualities of the alum will entirely prevent their formation.

4. Glycerine, 5 oz.; white of eggs, 4 oz.; tincture of arnica, 3 oz. Mix the glycerine and white of eggs thoroughly in a mortar, and gradually add the arnica. Apply freely on linen rags night and morning, washing previously with warm castile soapsuds.

5. Take one drachm of finely powdered alum and mix thoroughly with the whites of two eggs and one teacup of fresh lard; spread on a cloth, and apply to the parts burnt. It gives almost instant relief from pain, and, by excluding the air, prevents excessive inflammatory action. The application should be changed at least once a day.

6. A tepid bath, containing a couple of pinches of sulphate of iron, gives immediate relief to young children who have been extensively burned. In the case of a child four years old, with a bath repeated twice a day—twenty minutes each bath—the suppuration deceased, lost its odor, and the little sufferer was soon convalescent.

7. For severe scalding, carbolic acid has recently been used with marked benefit. It is to be mixed with 30 parts of the ordinary oil of lime water to one part of the acid. Linen rags saturated in the carbolic emulsion are to be spread on the scalded parts, and kept moist by frequently smearing with the feather dipped in the liquid. Two advantages of this mode of treatment are, the exclusion of air, and the rapid healing by a natural restorative action without the formation of pus, thus preserving unmarred and personal appearance of the patient—a matter of no small importance to some people.

8. The immediate relief from pain in severe burns and scalds may be had by the application of a poultice of tea leaves, with attention paid to the changing of the poultice each time that it becomes dried.

CHOKING

In case of choking, a violent slap with the open hand between the shoulder blades of the sufferer will often effect a dislodgment., In case the accident occurs with a child, and the slapping process does not afford instant relief, it should be grasped by the feet, and placed head downwards, and the slapping between the shoulders renewed; but in case this induced violent suffocative paroxysms, it must not be repeated. If the substance, whatever it may be, has entered the windpipe, and the coughing and inverting the body fail to dislodge it, it is probable that nothing but cutting open the windpipe will be of any avail; and for this the services of a surgeon should always be procured. If food has stuck in the throat or gullet, the forefinger should be immediately introduced; and if lodged at the entrance of the gullet, the substance may be reached and extracted possibly with the forefinger alone, or may be seized with a pair of pincers, if at hand, or a curling tongs, or anything of that kind. This procedure may be facilitated by directing the person to put the tongue well out, in which position it may be retained by the individual himself, or by a bystander, by grasping it, covered with a handkerchief or towel. Should this fail, an effort should be made to excite retching or vomiting by passing the finger to the root of the tongue, in hopes that the offending substance may in this way be dislodged; or it may possibly be effected by suddenly and unexpectedly dashing in the face a basin of cold water, the shock suddenly relaxing the muscle spasm present, and the involuntary gasp at the same time may move it up or down. If this cannot be done, as each instant's delay is of vital importance to a choking man, seize a fork, a spoon, a penholder, pencil, quill, or anything suitable at hand, and endeavor to push the article down the throat. If it be low down the gullet, and other means fail, its dislodgement may sometimes be effected by dashing cold water on the spine, or vomiting may be induced by an emetic of sulphate of zinc—20 grains in a couple of tablespoonfuls of warm water—or of common salt and mustard in like manner, or it may be pushed into the stomach by extemporizing a probang, by fastening a small sponge to the end of a stiff strip of whalebone, extricated with discretion from a lady's corset. If this cannot be done, a surgical operation will be necessary. Fish bones or other sharp substances, when they cannot be removed by the finger or forceps, may sometimes be dislodged by swallowing some pulpy mass, such as masticated bread, &tc. Irregularly shaped substances—a plate with artificial teeth, for instance—can ordinarily be removed only by surgical interference.

COLIC

Use a hot fomentation over the abdomen, and a small quantity of ginger, peppermint, or common

tea. If not relieved in a few minutes, then give an injection of a quart of warm water with 20 to 30 drops of laudanum, and repeat it if necessary. A half teaspoonful of sweetened water, with or without a few drops of spirits of lavender or essence of peppermint, will often give prompt relief.

CONVULSIONS

In small children convulsions frequently happen from teething, sometimes from worms or from some irritating substance within the stomach or bowels, and sometimes from some affection of the brain.

When a child has convulsions, place it immediately in a warm or hot bath, and sponge its head with hot water. Then apply a hot mustard plaster to the wrists, ankles and soles of the feet; or, in case a plaster

cannot be got, apply a cloth wrung out of hot mustard water. Allow these to remain until the skin reddens, and use care that the same do not blister. After the fit has subsided, use great care against its return by attention to the cause which gave rise to it.

Convulsions in adults may be treated in accordance with the manner which gave rise to them. During the attack, great care should be taken that the party does not injure himself, and the best preventive is a cork or soft piece of wood, or other suitable substance, placed between the teeth to prevent biting the tongue or cheeks; tight clothing must be removed or loosened—this is especially true in the case of ladies' corsets; mustard poultices should be applied to the extremities and over the abdomen; abundance of fresh air should be secured by opening windows and doors, and preventing unnecessary crowding of persons around; cold water may be dashed on the face and chest; and if there be plethora, with full pounding pulse, with evidence of cerebral or other internal congestion, the abstraction of a few ounces of blood may be beneficial.

CRAMPS

Such spasmodic or involuntary contractions of the muscles generally of the extremities, are accompanied by great pain. The muscles of the legs and feet are the most commonly affected with cramp, especially after great exertion. The best treatment is immediately to stand upright, and to well rub the part with the hand. The application of strong stimulants (as spirits of ammonia), or of anodines (as opiate liniments) has been recommended. When cramps occur in the stomach, a teaspoonful of sal volatile in water, or a drachm glassful of good brandy, should be swallowed immediately. When cramp comes on during cold bathing, the limb should be thrown out as suddenly and violently as possible, which will generally remove it, care being also taken not to become flurried nor frightened, as presence of mind is very essential to personal safety on such occasions. A common cause of cramp is indigestion, and the use of acescent liquors; these should be avoided.

CUTS

In case the flow of blood is trifling, stop the bleeding by bringing the edges of the wound together. If the flow of blood is great, of a bright vermillion color, and flows in spurts or with a jerk, an artery is severed, and at once should pressure be made on the parts by the finger (between the cut and the heart), until a compress is arranged by a tight ligature above the wounded part. Then the finger may be taken off, and if the blood still flows, tighten the handkerchief or other article that forms the ligature, until it ceases. If at this point the attendance of a physician or surgeon cannot be secured, take strong silk thread, or wax together three or four threads, and cut them into lengths about a foot long. Wash the parts with warm water, and then with a sharp hook or small pair of pincers in your hand, fix your eye steadfastly upon the wound, and directing the ligature to be slightly released, you will see the mouth of the artery from which the blood springs. At once seize it, draw it out a little, while an assistant passes a ligature round it, and ties it up tight with a double knot. In this way, take up in succession every bleeding vessel you can see or get hold of. If the wound is too high up in a limb to apply the ligature, do not lose your presence of mind. If it is the thigh, press firmly on the groins; if in the arm, with the hand-end or ring of a common door-key make pressure above the collar bone, and about its middle, against its first rib, which lies under it. The pressure should be continued until assistance is procured and the vessel tied up. If the wound is on the face, or other place where pressure cannot effectually be made, place a piece of ice directly over the wound, allowing it to remain there until the blood coagulates, when it may be removed, and a compress and bandage be applied.

After the bleeding is arrested, the surrounding blood should be cleared away, as well as any extraneous matter; then bring the sides of the wound into contact throughout the whole depth, in order that they may grow together as quickly as possible, retaining them in their position by strips of adhesive plaster. If the wound be deep and extensive, the wound itself and the adjacent parts must be supported by proper bandages. The position of the patient should be such as will relax the skin and muscles of the wounded part. Rest, low and unstimulating diet, will complete the requirements necessary to a speedy recovery.

HOW TO DISTINGUISH DEATH

As many instances occur of parties being buried alive, they being to all appearance dead, the great importance of knowing how to distinguish real from imaginary death need not be explained. The appearances which mostly accompany death are an entire stoppage of breathing, of the heart's action; the eyelids are partly closed, the eyes glassy, and the pupils usually dilated; the jaws clenched, the fingers partially contracted, and the lips and nostrils more or less covered with frothy mucus, with increasing pallor and coldness of surface, and the muscles soon become rigid and the limbs fixed in their position. But as these same conditions may also exist in certain other cases of suspended animation, great care should be observed, whenever there is the least doubt concerning it, to prevent the unnecessary crowding of the room in which the corpse is, or of parties crowding around the body; nor should the body be allowed to remain lying on the back without the tongue being so secured as to prevent the glottis or orifice of the windpipe being closed by it; nor should the face be closedly covered; nor rough usage of any kind be allowed. In case there is great doubt, the body should not be allowed to be inclosed in the coffin, and under no circumstances should burial be allowed until there are unmistakable signs of decomposition.

Of the numerous methods proposed as signs for real death, the following are selected:

1. So long as breathing continues, the surface of a mirror held to the mouth and nostrils will become dimmed with moisture.

2. If a strong thread or cord be tied around the finger of a living person, the portion beyond the cord or thread will become red and swollen—if dead, no change is produced.

3. If the hand of a living person is held before a strong light, a portion of the margin or edges of the fingers is translucent—if dead, every part of it is opaque.

4. A coal of fire, a piece of hot iron, or the flame of a candle, applied to the skin, if life remains, will blister—if dead, it will merely sear.

5. A bright steel needle introduced and allowed to remain for half an hour in living flesh will be still bright, when removed—if dead, it will be tarnished by oxydation.

6. A few drops of a solution of atropia (2 grains to ½ oz. of water) introduced into the eye, if the person is alive, will cause the pupils to dilate—if dead, no effect will be produced.

7. If the pupils are already dilated, and the person is alive, a few drops of tincture of the calabar bean will cause them to contract— if dead, no effect will be produced.

DISLOCATIONS

These injuries can mostly be easily recognized:

1. By the deformity that the dislocation gives rise to by comparing the alteration in shape with the other side of the body.

2. Loss of some of the regular movements of the joints.

3. In case of dislocation, surgical aid should be procured at once. While waiting the arrival of a physician, the injured portion should be placed in a position most comfortable to the patient, and frequent cold bathing or cloths wrung out of cold water, applied to the parts affected, so as to relieve suffering and prevent inflammation.

FOREIGN BODIES IN EARS

Great care should be taken in removing foreign bodies from the ear, as serious injury may be inflicted. Most foreign bodies, especially those of small size, can be easily removed by the use of a syringe with warm water, and in most cases no other means should be used. Should the first efforts fail, repeat the operation. A syringe throwing a moderately small and continuous stream is the best adapted for the purpose, and the removal may generally be facilitated by inclining the ear downward while using the syringe. Severe inflammation may be excited, and serious injury done, by rash attempts to seize a foreign body in the ear, with a forceps or tweezers, or by trying to pick it out with a pin or needle, or with an ear scoop. Should it be necessary from any cause to use instruments, great care should be observed, and but very little force exerted. It has lately been recommended, when foreign bodies cannot be removed by syringing the ear, to introduce a small brush or swab of frayed linen or muslin cloth, or a bit of sponge moistened with a solution of glue, and keep it in contact with the foreign body until the glue adheres, when the body may be easily removed.

INSECTS IN THE EAR

Insects in the ear may be easily killed by pouring oil in the ear, after which remove by syringing. (*See* Foreign Bodies in Ears.)

TO REMOVE HARDENED WAX

Hardened ear wax may be softened by dropping into the ear some oil or glycerine, and then syringing. (*See* Foreign Bodies in Ears).

FOREIGN BODIES IN EYES

To remove small particles from the eye, unless they have penetrated the globe, or become fixed to the conjunctiva, do as follows: Grasp the upper lid between the thumb and forefinger, lift it from the eyeball, and having drawn it down as far as possible outside the lower lid, let it slide slowly back to its place, resting upon the lower lid as it goes back; and then wipe the edges of the lids with a soft handkerchief to remove the foreign substance. This may be repeated a number of times, if necessary, without injury. Should this means fail, evert the lids and remove the foreign substance by touching it lightly with the fold of a handkerchief, or with the point of a roll of paper made like a candle-lighter; or, if necessary, with a small pair of forceps. A drop of sweet oil instilled in the eye, while perfectly harmless, provokes a flow of tears that will frequently wash away any light substance.

Bits of metal, sharp pieces of sand, &tc., sometimes penetrate the globe of the eye, and, unless removed, may excite so much inflammation as to destroy the eye. They should be removed by a competent surgeon.

FAINTING

Lay a person who has fainted in a current of air, or in such a position that the air from an open window or door will have full play upon the face. Do not allow parties to crowd closely around, but give the sufferer plenty of room. Recovery will take place in a few minutes. The clothes also may be opened, and cold water sprinkled upon the face, hands, and chest; and some pungent substance, as smelling salts, camphor, aromatic vinegar, &tc., may be applied to the nostrils; and as soon as able to swallow, a little fresh water, or spirits and water, may be given. Persons who faint easily should avoid crowded rooms and places where the air is close.

FITS

See Convulsions.

CLOTHING ON FIRE

If a woman's clothes catch on fire, let her instantly roll herself over and over on the ground. In case anyone be present, let him throw her down and do the like, and then wrap her up in a table-cloth, rug, coat, or the first woolen article that can be found.

FRACTURES

As only general rules for treating the various fractures can be given, those suffering from such are advised to immediately apply to the nearest surgeon, and not rely upon an inexperienced party.

FROST-BITE

Place the party suffering in a room without fire, and rub the frozen or frosted parts with snow, or pour ice-water over them until sensation begins to return. As soon as a stinging pain is felt, and a change of color appears, then cease the rubbing, and apply cloths wet with ice-water, and subsequently, if active inflammation follows and suppuration results, a solution of carbolic acid in water, one part to thirty, should be applied. If mortification sets in, amputation is generally necessary. Where persons suffer from the constitutional effects of cold, hot stimulants should be given internally, and the body rubbed briskly with the hands and warm flannel.

LOCK JAW
It is said that the application of warm lye, made of ashes as strong as possible, to a wounded part, will prevent a locked jaw; if a foot or hand, immerse in it; if another part of the body, bathe with flannels wrung out of the warm lye.

SCALDS
See Burns and Scalds.

SPRAINS
The portions most frequently implicated are the wrist and ankle; no matter which portion it may be, however, rest and quietness is a very important part of the treatment, and, when possible, in an elevated position. If the wrist is sprained it should be carried in a sling; if the ankle, it should be supported on a couch or stool. Cold lotions should be freely applied, and irrigation by pouring water from a pitcher or tea-kettle resorted to several times a day to prevent inflammation. Later, frictions with opodeldoc, or with some other stimulating liniment, and supporting the parts by pressure made with a flannel roller (or a laced stocking when the ankle is involved) will be useful to restore tone; or strips of adhesive plaster properly applied will be useful for the same purpose. Recovery from severe sprains is always tedious. It is an old saying that "a bad sprain is worse than a broken bone."

SPRAINED ANKLE
Wash the ankle frequently with cold salt and water, which is far better than warm vinegar or decoctions of herbs. Keep the foot as cold as possible to prevent inflammation, and sit with it elevated on a cushion. Live on a very low diet, and take every day some cooling medicine. By obeying these directions only, a sprained ankle has been cured in a few days.

STINGS OF BEES & WASPS
See Bites & Stings of Insects.

SUFFOCATION FROM NOXIOUS GASES, FOUL AIR, FIRE DAMP, &tc.
Remove victim to fresh air and dash cold water over his head, neck and chest; carefully apply hartshorn or smelling salts to the nostrils, and when the breathing is feeble or has ceased, resort to artificial respiration. Keep up the

warmth of the body, and as soon as the patient can swallow, give stimulants in small quantities.

SUNSTROKE

This is caused by long exposure in great heat, especially when accompanied with great fatigue and exhaustion. Though generally happening from exposure to the sun's rays, yet precisely similar effects may be and are produced from any undue exposure to great and exhaustive heat, such as workmen are exposed to in foundries, gas factories, bakeries, and other similar employments. Its first symptoms are pain in the head and dizziness, quickly followed by loss of consciousness, and resulting in complete prostration; sometimes, however, the attack is sudden, as in apoplexy. The head is generally burning hot, and the face dark and swollen, the breathing labored and snoring, and the feet and hands cold. Remove the patient at once to a cool and shady place, and lay him down with his head a little raised; apply ice or iced water to the head and face; loosen all clothes around the neck or waist; bathe the chest with cold water; apply mustard plasters, or cloths wetted with turpentine, to the calves and soles of the feet, and as soon as the patient can swallow, give weak brandy or whisky and water.

POISONS, THEIR SYMPTOMS & ANTIDOTES

When a person has taken poison, the first thing to do is to compel the patient to vomit, and for that purpose give any emetic that can be most readily and quickly obtained, and which is prompt and energetic,

but safe in its action. For this purpose there is, perhaps, nothing better than a large teaspoonful of ground mustard in a tumbler of warm water, and it has the advantage of being almost always at hand. If the dry mustard is not to be had, use mixed mustard from the mustard pot. Its operation may generally be facilitated by the addition of a like quantity of common table salt. If the mustard is not at hand, give two or three teaspoonfuls of powdered alum in syrup or molasses, and give freely of warm water to drink, or give ten to twenty grains of sulphate of zinc (white vitriol), or twenty to thirty grains of ipecac, with one or two grains of tartar emetic, in a large cup of warm water, and repeat every ten minutes until three or four doses are given, unless free vomiting is sooner produced. After vomiting has taken place, large draughts of warm water should be given the patient, so that the vomiting will continue until the poisonous substances have been thoroughly evacuated, and then suitable antidotes should be given.

If vomiting cannot be produced, the stomach pump should be used. When it is known what particular kind of poison has been swallowed, then the proper antidote for that poison should be given, but when this cannot be ascertained, as is often the case, give freely of equal parts of calcined magnesia, pulverized charcoal, and sesquioxide of

iron, in sufficient quantity of water. This is a very harmless mixture, and is likely to be of great benefit, as the ingredients, though very simple, are antidotes for the most common and active poisons.

In case this mixture cannot be obtained, the stomach should be soothed and protected by the free administration of demulcent, mucilaginous or oleaginous drinks, such as the whites of eggs, milk, mucilage of gum arabic, or slippery elm bark, flaxseed tea, starch, wheat, flour, or arrow-root mixed in water, linseed or olive oil, or melted butter or lard.

Subsequently, the bowels should be moved by some gentle laxative, such as a tablespoonful or two of castor oil, or a teaspoonful of calcined magnesia; and pain or other evidence of inflammation must be relieved by the administration of a few drops of laudanum, and the repeated application of hot poultices, fomentations and mustard plasters.

The following are the names of the articles that may give rise to poisoning, most commonly used, and their antidote:

MINERAL ACIDS: Sulphuric Acid (Oil of Vitriol), Nitric Acid (Aqua Fortis), Muriatic Acid (Spirits of Salts)

Symptoms—Acid, burning taste in the mouth, acute pain in the throat, stomach and bowels; frequent vomiting, generally bloody, mouth and lips excoriated, shriveled, white or yellow; hiccough, copious stools, more or less bloody, with great tenderness in the abdomen; difficulty breathing, irregular pulse, excessive thirst, while drink increases the pain and rarely remains in the stomach; frequent but vain efforts to urinate; cold sweats, altered countenance, convulsions generally preceding death, nitric acid causes yellow stains; sulphuric acid, black ones.

Treatment—Mix calcined magnesia in milk or water to the consistence of cream, and give freely to drink, a glassful every couple of minutes, if it can be swallowed. Common soap (hard or soft), chalk, whiting, or even mortar from the wall mixed with water, may be given, until magnesia can be obtained. Promote vomiting by tickling the throat, if necessary; and when the poison is got rid of, give flaxseed or elm tea, gruel or other mild drinks. The inflammation which always follows wants good treatment to save the patient's life.

VEGETABLE ACIDS: Acetic, Citric, Oxalic, Tartaric

Symptoms—Intense burning pain of the mouth, throat, and stomach; vomiting blood which is highly acid, violent purging, collapse, stupor, and death.

Oxalic Acid is frequently taken in mistake for Epsom salts, to which in shops it often bears a strong resemblance.

Treatment—Give chalk or magnesia in a large quantity of water, or large draughts of lime water. If these are not at hand, scrape the wall or ceiling, and give the scrapings, mixed with water.

PRUSSIC OR HYDROCYANIC ACID (Laurel Water, Cyanide of Potassium, Bitter Almond Oil)

Symptoms—In large doses, almost invariably instantaneously fatal; when not immediately fatal, sudden loss of sense and control of the voluntary muscles; the odor of the poison is generally perceptible on the breath.

Treatment—Chlorine, in the form of chlorine water, in doses of from one to four fluid drachms, diluted. Weak solution of chloride lime of soda; water of ammonia (spirits of hartshorn) largely diluted may be given, and the vapor of it cautiously inhaled. Cold affusion, and chloroform in half to teaspoonful doses in glycerine or mucilage, repeated every few minutes, until the symptoms are ameliorated. Artificial respiration.

ACONITE (Monkshood, Wolfsbane)

Symptoms—Numbness and tingling in the mouth and throat, and afterwards in other portions of the body, with sore throat, pain over the stomach, and vomiting; dimness of vision, dizziness, great prostration, loss of sensibility and delirium.

Treatment—An emetic and then brandy in tablespoonful doses, in ice-water, every half hour; spirits of ammonia in half teaspoonful doses in like manner; the cold douche over the head and chest, warmth to the extremities, &tc.

ALKALIES & THEIR SALTS: Concentrated Lye, Woodash Lye, Caustic Potash, Ammonia, Hartshorn

Symptoms—Caustic, acrid taste, excessive heat in the throat, stomach and intestines; vomiting of bloody matter, cold sweats, hiccough, purging of bloody stools.

Treatment—The common vegetable acids. Common vinegar, being always at hand, is most frequently used. The fixed oils, as castor, flaxseed, almond, and olive oils form soaps with the alkalies and thus also destroy their caustic affects. They should be given in large quantity.

ALCOHOL, BRANDY, & OTHER SPIRITUOUS LIQUORS

Symptoms—Confusion of thought, inability to walk or stand, dizziness, stupor, highly flushed or pale face, noisy breathing.

Treatment—After emptying the stomach, pour cold water on the head and back of the neck, rub or slap the wrists and palms, and the ankles and soles of the feet, and give strong, hot coffee, or aromatic spirits of hartshorn, in teaspoonful doses in water. The warmth of the body must be sustained.

ANTIMONY & ITS PREPARATIONS: Tartar Emetic, Antimonial Wine, Kerme's Mineral

Symptoms—Faintness and nausea, soon followed by painful and continued vomiting, severe diarrhoea, constriction and burning sensation in the throat, cramps, or spasmodic twitchings, with symptoms of nervous derangement, and great prostration of strength, often terminating in death.

Treatment—If vomiting has not been produced, it should be effected by tickling the fauces, and administering copious draughts of warm water. Astringent infusions, such as of gall, oak bark, and Peruvian bark, act as antidotes, and should be given promptly. Powdered yellow bark may be used until the infusion is prepared, or very strong green tea should be given promptly. To stop the vomiting, should it continue, blister over the stomach by applying a cloth wet with strong spirits of hartshorn, and then sprinkle on one-eighth to one-fourth of a grain of morphia.

ARSENIC & ITS PREPARATIONS: Ratsbane, Fowler's Solution, &tc.

Symptoms—Generally within an hour pain and heat are felt in the stomach, soon followed by vomiting, with a burning dryness in the throat and great thirst; the matters vomited are generally colored, either green or yellow, or brownish, and sometimes bloody. Diarrhoea or dysentery ensues, while the pulse is becoming small and rapid, yet irregular. Breathing is much oppressed; difficulty in vomiting may occur, while cramps, convulsions, and even paralysis often precede death, which sometimes takes place within five or six hours after arsenic has been taken.

Treatment—Give a prompt emetic and then hydrate of peroxide of iron (recently prepared) in table-spoonful doses every ten or fifteen minutes until the urgent symptoms are relieved. In the absence of this, or while it is being prepared, give large draughts of new milk and raw eggs, limewater and oil, melted butter, magnesia in a large quantity of water, or even if nothing else is at hand, flour and water, always, however, giving an emetic the first thing, or causing vomiting by tickling the throat with a feather, &tc. The inflammation of the stomach which follows must be treated by blisters, hot fomentations, mucilaginous drinks, &tc.

BELLADONNA, OR DEADLY NIGHT SHADE

Symptoms—Dryness of the throat and mouth, great thirst, difficulty in swallowing, nausea, dimness,

confusion or loss of vision, great enlargement of the pupils, dizziness, delirium and coma.

Treatment—There is no known antidote. Give a prompt emetic and then reliance must be placed on continual stimulation with brandy, whisky, &tc., and to necessary artificial respiration. Opium and its preparations, as morphia, laudanum, &tc., are thought by some to counteract the effects of belladonna, and may be given in small and repeated doses, as also strong black coffee and green tea.

BLUE VITRIOL, OR BLUE STONE

See Copper.

CANTHARIDES (Spanish or Blistering Fly) & MODERN POTATO BUG

Symptoms—Sickening odor of the breath, sour taste, with burning heat in the throat, stomach, and bowels; frequent vomiting, often bloody; copious bloody stools, great pain in the stomach, with burning sensation in the bladder and difficulty in urinating, followed with terrible convulsions, delirium and death.

Treatment—Excite vomiting by drinking plentifully of sweet oil or other wholesome oils, sugar and water, milk, or slippery elm bark tea; give injections of castor oil and starch, or warm milk. The inflammatory symptoms which generally follow must be treated by a medical man. Camphorated oil or camphorated spirits should be rubbed over the bowels, the stomach, and the thighs.

CAUSTIC POTASH
See Alkalies.

COBALT, OR FLY POWDER
Symptoms—Heat and pain in the throat and stomach, violent retching and vomiting, cold and clammy skin, small and feeble pulse, hurried and difficult breathing, diarrhoea, &tc.

Treatment—An emetic, followed by the free administration of milk, eggs, wheat flour and water, and mucilaginous drinks.

COPPER (Blue Vitriol, Verdigris or Pickles or Food Cooked in Soul Copper Vessels)
Symptoms—General inflammation of the alimentary canal, suppression of urine; hiccough, a disagreeable metallic taste, vomiting, violent colic, excessive thirst, sense of tightness of the throat, anxiety; faintness, giddiness, and cramps and convulsions generally precede death.

Treatment—Large doses of simple syrup as warm as can be swallowed, until the stomach rejects the amount it contains. The whites of eggs and large quantities of milk. Hydrated peroxide of iron.

CREOSOTE & CARBOLIC ACID
Symptoms—Burning pain; acrid, pungent taste; thirst; vomiting; purging; &tc.

Treatment—An emetic, and the free administration of albumen, as the whites of eggs, or in the ab-sence of these, milk, or flour and water.

CORROSIVE SUBLIMATE
See Mercury.

DEADLY NIGHT-SHADE
See Belladonna.

FOX-GLOVE, OR DIGITALIS
Symptoms—Loss of strength, feeble and fluttering pulse, faintness, nausea, and vomiting and stupor; cold perspiration, dilated pupils, sighing, irregular breathing, and sometimes convulsions.

Treatment—After vomiting, give brandy and ammonia in frequently repeated doses, apply warmth to the extremities, and if necessary resort to artificial respiration.

GASES: Carbonic Acid, Chlorine, Cyanogen, Hydrosulphuric Acid, &tc.
Symptoms—Great drowsiness, difficult respiration, features swollen, face blue as in strangulation.

Treatment—Artificial respiration, cold douche, frictions with stimulating substances to the surface of the body. Inhalation of steam containing preparations of ammonia. Cupping from nape of neck. Internal use of chloroform.

HELLEBORE, OR INDIAN POKE

Symptoms—Violent vomiting and purging, bloody stools, great anxi-

ety, tremors, vertigo, fainting, sinking of the pulse, cold sweats and convulsions.

Treatment—Excite speedy vomiting by large draughts of warm water, or molasses and water, by tickling the throat with the finger or a feather, use emetics; give oily and mucilaginous drinks, oily purgatives, clysters, acids, strong coffee, camphor and opium.

HEMLOCK (CONIUM)

Symptoms—Dryness of the throat, tremors, dizziness, difficulty in swallowing, prostration and faint-ness, limbs powerless or paralyzed, pupils dilated, pulse rapid and feeble; insensibility and convulsions sometimes precede death.

Treatment—Empty the stomach, and give brandy in tablespoonful doses with half teaspoonful of spirits of ammonia, frequently repeated, and if much pain and vomiting, give bromide of ammonia in five grain doses every half hour. Artificial respiration may be required.

HENBANE, OR HYOSCYAMUS

Symptoms—Muscular twitching, inability to articulate plainly, dimness of vision and stupor; later, vomiting and purging, small, intermittent pulse, convulsive movement of the extremities and coma.

Treatment—Similar to Opium Poisoning, which see.

IODINE

Symptoms—Burning pain in throat, lacerating pain in the stomach, fruitless efforts to vomit, excessive tenderness of the epigastrium.

Treatment—Free emesis, prompt administration of starch, wheat flour, or arrow-root, beat up in water.

LEAD: Acetate of Lead, Sugar of Lead, Dry White Lead, Red Lead, Litharge, or Pickles, Wine or Vinegar, Sweetened by Lead

Symptoms—When taken in large doses, a saccharine but astringent metallic taste exists, with constriction in the throat, pain in the region of the stomach, painful, obstinate, and frequently bloody vomiting, hiccough, convulsions or spasms, and death. When taken in small but long-continued doses, it produces colic, called painter's colic; there is great pain, obstinate constipation, and in extreme cases paralitical symptoms, especially wrist-drop, with a blue line along the edge of the gums.

Treatment—To counteract the poison, give alum in water, one and a half ounces to a quart; or, better still, Epsom salts or Glauber salts, an ounce of either in a quart of water; or dilute sulphuric acid, a teaspoonful to a quart of water. If a large quantity of sugar of lead has been recently taken, empty the stomach by an emetic of sulphate of zinc (one drachm in a quart of water), giving one-fourth to commence, and repeating smaller doses until free vomiting is produced; castor oil should be given to clear the bowels, and injections of oil and starch freely administrated. If the body is cold, use the warm bath.

MEADOW SAFFRON
See Belladonna.

LAUDANUM
See Opium.

LOBELIA, OR INDIAN POKE
Symptoms—Exaggerated vomiting, and purging, pains in the bowels,

contraction of the pupils, delirium, coma, and convulsions.

Treatment—Use mustard over the stomach, and brandy and ammonia.

MERCURY & CORROSIVE SUBLIMATE (bug poisons frequently contain this poison), RED PRECIPITATE, CHINESE OR ENGLISH VERMILLION

Symptoms—Acrid, metallic taste in the mouth, immediate constriction and burning in the throat, with anxiety and tearing pains in both stomach and bowels, sickness, and vomiting of various colored fluids, and sometimes bloody and profuse diarrhoea, with difficulty and pain in urinating; pulse quick, small and hard; faint sensations, great debility, difficulty with breathing, cramps, cold sweats, syncope and convulsions.

Treatment—If vomiting does not already exist, emetics must be given immediately—albumen of eggs in continuous large doses, and infusion of catechu afterwards, sweet milk, mixtures of flour and water in successive cupfuls, and to check excessive salivation put a half ounce of chlorate of potash in a tumbler of water, and use freely as a gargle, and swallow a tablespoonful every hour or two.

LUNAR CAUSTIC
See Nitrate of Silver.

MONKSHOOD
See Aconite.

MORPHINE
See Opium.

NITRATE OF SILVER
(Lunar Caustic)

Symptoms—Intense pain and vomiting and purging of blood; with mucus and shreds of mucus membranes; and if these stand they become dark.

Treatment—Give freely of a solution of common salt in water, which decomposes the poison, and afterwards flaxseed or elm bark tea, and after à while a dose of castor oil.

NUX VOMICA
See Strychnine.

OPIUM & ALL ITS PREPARATIONS: Morphine, Laudanum, Paregoric, &tc.

Symptoms—Giddiness, drowsiness, increasing of stupor, and insensibility; pulse usually, at first, quick and irregular, with breathing hurried, and afterwards pulse slow and feeble, and respiration slow and noisy; the pupils are contracted and the eyes and face congested, and later, as death approaches, the extremities become cold, the surface is covered with cold, clammy perspiration, and the sphincters relax. The effects of opium and its preparations, in poisonous doses, appear in from one half to two hours from its administration.

Treatment—Empty the stomach immediately with an emetic or with a stomach pump. Then give very strong coffee without milk; put mustard plasters on the wrists and ankles; use the cold douche to the head and chest, and if the patient is cold and sinking give brandy, or whisky and ammonia. Belladonna is thought by many to counteract the poisonous effects of opium, and may be given in doses of half to a teaspoonful of the tincture, or two grains of the extract, every twenty minutes, until some effect is observed in causing the pupils to expand. Use warmth and friction, and if possible prevent sleep for some hours, for which purpose the patient should be walked about between two persons, and if necessary a bunch of switches may be freely used. Finally, as a last resort, use artificial respiration, and a persistence in it will sometimes be rewarded with success in apparently hopeless cases. Galvanism should also be tried.

OXALIC ACID
See Acids.

PHOSPHORUS (found in Lucifer Matches and some Rat Poisons)

Symptoms—Symptoms of irritant poisoning; pain in the stomach and bowels; vomiting; diarrhoea; tenderness and tension of the abdomen.

Treatment—An emetic is to be promptly given; copious draughts containing magnesia in suspension; mucilaginous drinks. General treatment for inflammatory symptoms.

POISONOUS FISH

Symptoms—In an hour or two—often in much shorter time—after the fish has been eaten, a weight at the stomach comes on, with slight vertigo and headache; sense of heat about the head and eyes; considerable thirst, and often an eruption of the skin.

Treatment—After full vomiting, an active purgative should be given to remove any of the noxious matter from the intestines. Vinegar and water may be drunk after the above remedies have operated, and the body may be sponged with the same. Water made very sweet with sugar, with aromatic spirits of ammonia added, may be drunk freely as a corrective. A solution of chlorate of potash, or of alkali, the latter weak, may be given to obviate the effect of the poison. If spasms ensue after evacuation, laudanum in considerable doses is necessary. If inflammation should occur, combat in the usual way.

POISONOUS MUSHROOMS

Symptoms—Nausea, heat and pain in the stomach and bowels; vomiting and purging, thirst, convulsions and fainting, pulse small and frequent, dilated pupils and stupor, cold sweats and death.

Treatment—The stomach and bowels are to be cleared by an emetic of ground mustard or sulphate of zinc, followed by frequent

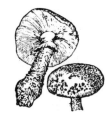

doses of Glauber or Epsom salts, and large stimulating clysters. After the poison is evacuated, either may be given with small quantities of brandy and water. But if inflammatory symptoms manifest themselves, such stimuli should be avoided, and these symptoms appropriately treated.

POTASH
See Alkalies.

PRUSSIC ACID, HYDROCYANIC ACID
See Acids.

POISON IVY
Symptoms—Contact with, and with many persons a near approach to the vine, gives rise to violent erysipelatous inflammation, especially

of the face and hands, attended with itching, redness, burning and swelling, with watery blisters.

Treatment—Give saline laxatives, and apply weak lead and laudanum, or limewater and sweet oil, or bathe the parts freely with spirits of nitre. Anointing with oil will prevent poisoning from it.

SALTPETRE (Nitrate of Potash or Sodium)

Only poisonous in large quantities.
Symptoms—Nausea, painful vomiting, purging, convulsions, faintness, feeble pulse, cold feet and hands, with tearing pains in stomach and bowels.

Treatment—Treat just as directed for Arsenic, for there is no antidote known, and emptying the stomach and bowels with mild drinks must be relied on.

SAVINE

Symptoms—Sharp pains in the bowels, hot skin, rapid pulse, violent vomiting and sometimes purging, with great prostration.

Treatment—Mustard and hot fomentations over the stomach and bowels, and ice only allowed in the stomach until the inflammation ceases. If prostration comes on, food and stimulants must be given by injection.

STRAMONIUM, THORN-APPLE, OR JAMESTOWN WEED (Jimson Weed)

Symptoms—Vertigo, headache, perversion of vision, slight delirium, sense of suffocation, disposition to sleep, bowels relaxed and all excretions augmented.

Treatment—The same as for Belladonna.

STRYCHNINE & NUX VOMICA

Symptoms—Muscular twitching, and constriction of the throat, difficult breathing and oppression of the chest; violent muscular spasms then occur, continuous in character like lock-jaw, with the body bent backwards, sometimes like a bow.

Treatment—Provide, if obtainable, one ounce or more of bone charcoal mixed with water, and follow with an active emetic; then give chloroform in teaspoonful doses, in flour and water or glycerine, every few minutes while the spasms last, and afterwards brandy and stimulants, and warmth of the extremities if necessary. Recoveries have followed the free and prompt administration of oils or melted butter or lard. In all cases empty the stomach if possible.

SULPHATE OF ZINC (White Vitriol)

See Zinc.

TIN: Chloride of Tin, Solution of Tin (Used by Dyers), Oxide of Tin or Putty Powder

Symptoms—Vomiting, pains in the stomach, anxiety, restlessness, frequent pulse, delirium, &tc.

Treatment—Empty the stomach, and give whites of eggs in water, milk in large quantities, or flour beaten up in water, with magnesia or chalk.

TARTAR EMETIC
See Antimony.

TOBACCO
Symptoms—Vertigo, stupor, fainting, nausea, vomiting, sudden nervous debility, cold sweat, tremors, and at times fatal prostration.

Treatment—After the stomach is empty, apply mustard to the abdomen and to the extremities, and give strong coffee, with brandy and other stimulants, with warmth to the extremities.

ZINC: Oxide of Zinc, Sulphate of Zinc, White Vitriol, Acetate of Zinc
Symptoms—Violent vomiting, astringent taste, burning pain in the stomach, pale countenance, cold extremities, dull eyes, fluttering pulse. Death seldom ensues, in consequence of the emetic effect.

Treatment—The vomiting may be relieved by copious draughts of warm water. Carbonate of soda, administered in solution, will decompose the sulphate of zinc. Milk and albumen will also act as antidotes. General principles to be observed in the subsequent treatment.

WOORARA
Symptoms—When taken into the stomach it is inert; when absorbed through a wound it causes sudden stupor and insensibility, frothing at the mouth and speedy death.

Treatment—Suck the wound immediately, or cut it out and tie a cord around the limb between the wound and the heart. Apply iodine, or iodide of potassium, and give internally; also try artificial respiration.

Chapter 19

How to cure infirmities

THE FAMILY PHYSICIAN

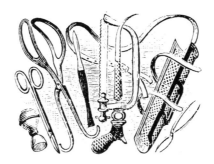

HUMAN LONGEVITY

Or 100,000 male and female children, in the first month they are reduced to 90,396, or nearly one-tenth. In the second, to 87,936. In the third, to 86,175. In the fourth, to 84,720. In the fifth, to 83,571. In the sixth, to 82,526, and at the end of the first year, to 77,528—the deaths being 2 to 9. The next four years reduce the figure to 62,448, indicating 37,552 deaths before the completion of the fifth year.

At 25 years the 100,000 are half, or 49,995; at 52, one-third. At 58, a fourth, or 25,000; at 67, a fifth; at 76, a tenth; at 81, a twentieth, or 5,000; and ten attain the age of 100 years.

Children die in large propor-

tions because their diseases cannot be explained, and because their organs are not habituated to the functions of life. The mean of life varies in different countries from 40 to 45. A generation from father to son is about 30 years; of men in general five-sixths die before 70, and fifteen-sixteenths before 80.

After 80, it is more endurance than enjoyment. The nerves are blunted, the senses fail, the muscles are rigid, the softer tubes become hard, the memory fails, the brain ossifies, the affections are buried, and hope ceases. The remaining one-sixteenth die at 80; except one-thirty-third, at 90. The remainder die from inability to live, at or before 100.

At the age of 36 the lean man usually becomes fatter and the fat man leaner. Again, between the years of 43 and 50 his appetite fails, his complexion fades, and his tongue is apt to be furred on the least exertion of body or mind. At this period his muscles become flabby, his joints weak; his spirits droop, and his sleep is imperfect and unrefreshing. After suffering under these complaints a year, or perhaps two, he starts afresh with renewed vigor, and goes on to 61 or 62, when a similar change takes place, but with aggravated symptoms. When these grand periods have been successfully passed, the gravity of incumbent years is more strongly marked, and he begins to boast of his age.

BIRTHS

On the average men have their first-born at 30, and women at 28. The greatest number of deliveries take place between 25 and 35. The greatest number of deliveries take place in the winter months, and in February; and the smallest in July, i.e., to February, as 4 to 5 in towns and 3 to 4 in the country. The night births are to the day as 5 to 4.

HUMAN STRENGTH

In experiments on human strength it has been found that men of five feet, weighing 126 lbs., could lift vertically 156 lbs. 8 inches; 217 lbs. 1.2 inches. Others, 6.1 feet, weighing 183 lbs., could lift 156 lbs. 13 inches, and 217 lbs. 6 inches. Others 6 feet 3 inches tall, weighing 185 lbs., could lift 156 lbs. 16 inches and 217 lbs. 9 inches. By a variety of experiments, it has been determined that the mean human strength is 30 lbs., with a velocity of 2.5 feet per second; or it is equal to the raising half a hogshead 10 feet in a minute.

RULES FOR THE PRESERVATION OF HEALTH

Pure atmospheric air is composed of nitrogen, oxygen, and a very small proportion of carbonic acid gas. Air, once breathed, has lost the chief part of its oxygen, and acquired a proportionate increase of carbonic acid gas. Therefore, good health requires that we breathe the same air only once.

The solid part of our bodies is continually wasting and requires to be repaired by fresh substance. Therefore, food, which is to repair the loss, should be taken with due regard to the exercise and waste of the body.

The fluid part of our bodies also

wastes constantly; there is but one fluid in animals, which is water. Therefore, water only is necessary, and no artifice can produce a better drink.

The fluid of our bodies is to the solid in proportion as nine to one. Therefore, a similar proportion should prevail in the total amount of food taken.

Light exercises an important influence upon the growth and vigor of animals and plants. Therefore, our dwellings should freely admit the sun's rays.

Decomposing animal and vegetable substances yield various noxious gases, which enter the lungs and corrupt the blood. Therefore, all impurities should be kept away from our abodes, and every precaution be observed to secure a pure atmosphere.

Warmth is essential to all the bodily functions. Therefore, an equal bodily temperature should be maintained by exercise, by clothing, or by fire.

Exercise warms, invigorates, and purifies the body; clothing preserves the warmth the body generates; fire imparts warmth externally. Therefore, to obtain and preserve warmth, exercise and clothing are preferable to fire.

Fire consumes the oxygen of the air, and produces noxious gases. Therefore, the air is less pure in the presence of candles, gas or coal fire, than otherwise, and the deterioration should be repaired by increased ventilation.

The skin is a highly-organized membrane, full of minute pores, cells, blood vessels, and nerves; it imbibes moisture or throws it off according to the state of the atmosphere or the temperature of the body. It also "breathes," like the lungs, though less actively. All the internal organs sympathize with the skin. Therefore, it should be repeatedly cleansed.

Late hours and anxious pursuits exhaust the nervous system and produce disease and premature death. Therefore, the hours of labor and study should be short.

Mental and bodily exercise are equally essential to the general health and happiness. Therefore, labor and study should succeed each other.

Man will live most happily upon simple solids and fluids, of which a sufficient but temperate quantity should be taken. Therefore, over-indulgence in strong drinks, tobacco, snuff, opium, and all mere indulgences, should be avoided.

Sudden alternations of heat and cold are dangerous (especially to the young and the aged). Therefore, clothing, in quantity and quality, should be adapted to the alternations of night and day, and of the seasons. And therefore, also, drinking cold water when the body is hot, and hot tea and soups when cold are productive of many evils.

Never visit a sick person (especially if the complaint be of a contagious nature) with an empty stomach, as this disposes the system more readily to receive the contagion. And in attending the sick person, place yourself where the air passes from the door or window to the bed of the diseased; not between the diseased person and any fire that is in the room as the heat of the fire will draw the infectious vapors in that direction.

FOOD DIGESTION TABLE
Showing the time required for the ordinary articles of food.

Soups—Chicken, 3 hours; mutton, 3½ hours; oysters, 3½ hours; vegetable, 4 hours.

Fish—Bass, broiled, 3 hours; codfish, boiled, 2 hours; oysters, raw, 3 hours; oysters, roasted, 3¼ hours; oysters, stewed, 3½ hours; salmon (fresh), boiled, 1¾ hours; trout, fried, 1½ hours.

Meats—Beef, roasted, 3 hours; beefsteak, broiled, 3 hours; beef (corned), boiled, 4¼ hours; lamb, roast, 2½ hours; lamb, boiled, 3 hours; meat, hashed, 2½ hours; mutton, broiled, 3 hours; mutton, roast, 3¼ hours; pig's feet, soused, 1 hour; pork, roast, 5¼ hours; pork, boiled, 4½ hours; pork,

broiled, 3¼ hours; sausage, fried, 4 hours; veal, broiled, 4 hours; veal, roast, 4¼ hours.

Poultry & Game—Chicken, fricasseed, 3¾ hours; duck (tame), roasted, 4 hours; duck (wild), roasted, 4¾ hours; fowls (domestic), roasted or boiled, 4 hours; goose (wild), roasted, 2½ hours; goose (tame), roasted, 2¼ hours; turkey, boiled or roasted, 2½ hours; venison, broiled or roasted, 1½ hours.

Vegetables—Asparagus, boiled, 2½ hours; beans (lima), boiled, 2½ hours; beans (string), boiled, 3 hours; beans, baked (with pork), 4½ hours; beets (young), boiled, 3¾ hours; beets (old), boiled, 4 hours; cabbage, raw, 2 hours; cabbage, boiled, 4½ hours; cauliflower, boiled, 2½ hours; corn (green), boiled, 4 hours; onions, boiled, 3 hours; parsnips, boiled, 3 hours; potatoes, boiled or baked, 3½ hours; rice, boiled, 1 hour; spinach, boiled, 2½ hours; tomatoes, raw or stewed, 2½ hours; turnips, boiled, 3½ hours.

Bread, Eggs, Milk, &tc.—Bread, corn, 3½ hours; bread, wheat, 3½ hours; cheese, 3½ hours; custard, 2¾ hours; eggs, raw, 2 hours; eggs, soft-boiled, 3 hours; eggs, hard-boiled or fried, 3½ hours; gelatine, 2½ hours; tapioca, 2 hours.

SUPERSTITIONS REGARDING BABIES
It is believed by many that if a child cries at its birth and lifts up only one hand, it is born to command.

It is thought very unlucky not to weigh the baby before it is dressed. When first dressed, the clothes should not be put on over the head, but drawn on over the feet, for luck. When first taken from the room in which it was born, it must be carried upstairs before going down, so that it will rise in the world. In any case, it must be carried upstairs or up the street, the first time taken out. It is also considered in England and Scotland unlucky to cut the baby's nails or hair before it is twelve months old. The saying:

Born on Monday, fair of face;
Born on Tuesday, full of God's
grace;
Born on Wednesday, the best to be
had;
Born on Thursday, merry and glad;
Born on Friday, worthily given;
Born on Saturday, work hard for a
living;
Born on Sunday, shall never know
want,

is known with various changes all over the Christian world; one deviation from the original makes Friday's child "free in giving." Thursday has one very lucky hour just before sunrise.

The child that is born on the
Sabbath day
Is bonny and good and gay,

while

He who is born on New Year's
morn
Will have his own way as sure as
you're born.

And

He who is born on Easter morn
Shall never know care, or want, or
harm.

TERMS USED IN MEDICINE

Antihelminthes are medicines which have the power of destroying or expelling worms from the intestinal canal.

Anticorbutics are medicines which prevent or cure the scurvy.

Antipasmodics are medicines given to relieve spasms, or irregular and painful action of the muscles or muscular fibers, as in Epilepsy, St. Vitus' Dance, &tc.

Aromatics are medicines which have a grateful smell and agreeable pungent taste.

Astringents are those remedies which, when applied to the body, render the solids dense and firmer.

Carminatives are those medicines which dispell flatulency of the stomach and bowels.

Cathartics are medicines which accelerate the action of the bowels, or increase the discharge of stool.

Demulcents are medicines suited to prevent the action of acrid and stimulating matters upon the mucous membranes of the throat, lungs, &tc.

Diaphoretics are medicines that promote or cause perspirable discharge by the skin.

Diuretics are medicines which increase the flow of urine by their action upon the kidneys.

Emetics are those medicines which promote vomiting.

Emmenagogues are medicines which promote the menstrual discharge.

Emollients are those remedies which, when applied to the solids of the body, render them soft and flexible.

Epispastics are those which cause blisters when applied to the surface.

Errhines are substances which, when applied to the lining membrane of the nostrils, occasion a discharge of mucous fluid.

Escharotics are substances used to destroy a portion of the surface of the body, forming sloughs.

Expectorants are medicines capable of facilitating the excretion of mucous from the chest.

Narcotics are those substances having the property of diminishing the action of the nervous and vascular systems and of inducing sleep.

Rubefacients are remedies which excite the vessels of the skin and increase its heat and redness.

Sedatives are medicines which have the power of allaying the actions of the systems generally, or of lessening the exercise of some particular function.

Sialogogues are medicines which increase the flow of saliva.

Stimulants are medicines capable of exciting the vital energy, whether as exerted in sensation or motion.

Tonics are those medicines which increase the tone or healthy action, or strength of the living system.

RECEIPTS FOR CURATIVES

The following receipts will be found of great value, especially in emergencies.

HOW TO CURE AGING

Steep the young leaves of periwinkle or creeping myrtle in fresh

spring water until the latter has imbibed all the essence; a teacupful taken each day will slow the aging process; it quickens the mind, and purifies the blood, and prevents anxieties. Some find it quite beneficial to add a wineglassful of brandy.

AGUE IN THE BREAST

Take one part of gum camphor, two parts yellow bees-wax, three parts clean lard; let all melt slowly, in any vessel (earthen is best), on stove. Use either cold or warm; spread very thinly on cotton or linen cloth, covering those with flannel. No matter if the breast is broken, it will cure if persevered in. Do not, no matter how painful, cease from drawing milk from the breast that is affected.

CURE FOR AGUE & FEVER

Take of cloves and cream of tartar each one-half ounce, and one ounce of Peruvian bark. Mix in a small quantity of tea, and take it on well days, in such quantities as the stomach will bear.

AGUE, MIXTURE

1. Mix 20 grains quinine with one pint diluted gin or port wine, and add ten grains subcarbonate of iron. Dose: a wineglass each hour until the ague is broken, and then two or three times a day until the whole has been used.

2. Take Peruvian bark, two ounces; wild cherry tree bark, one ounce; cinnamon, one drachm; powdered capsicum, one teaspoonful; sulphur, one ounce; port wine, two quarts. Let it stand a day or two. Dose: a wineglassful every two or three hours until the disease is broken, and then two or three times a day until all is taken.

APOPLEXY

Occurs only in the corpulent or obese, and in the gross or high-livers. To treat, raise the head to a nearly upright position; unloosen all tight clothes, strings, &tc., and apply cold water to the head and warm water and warm clothes to the feet. Have the room cool and well ventilated. Give nothing by the mouth until the breathing is relieved, and then only draughts of cold water.

ASTHMA

Take hyssop water and poppy water, of each ten ounces; oxymel of squills, six ounces; syrup of maiden hair, two ounces. Take one spoonful when you find any difficulty in breathing.

HOW TO CURE BAD BREATH

Bad or foul breath will be removed by taking a teaspoonful of the following mixture after each meal: One ounce liquor of potassa, one ounce chloride of soda, one and a half ounces phosphate of soda, and three ounces of water.

Another Way—Chlorate of potash, three drachms; rose-water, four ounces. Dose: a tablespoonful four or five times daily.

RECEIPT FOR "SOZODONT"

Take of potassium carbonate, one-half ounce; honey, four ounces; alcohol, two ounces; water, ten ounces; oil of wintergreen and oil of rose, to flavor, sufficient. This makes an excellent rinse for the mouth.

BILIOUS COMPLAINTS

Take the root and branch of dandelion, and steep it in soft water a sufficient time to extract all the essence; then strain the liquor and simmer until it becomes quite thick. Dose: from one to three glasses a day may be taken with good effect.

BLISTERS

On the feet, occasioned by walking, are cured by drawing a needleful of worsted thread through them; clip it off at both ends and leave it till the skin peels off.

RAISING BLOOD

Make a tea of white oak bark, and drink freely during the day; or take half a pound of yellow dock root, boil in new milk, say one quart; drink one gill three times a day, and take one pill of white pine pitch every day.

BOILS

Make a poultice of ginger and flour, and lay it on the boil. This will soon draw it to a head.

SWELLED BOWELS IN CHILDREN

Bathe the stomach of the child with catnip steeped, mixed with fresh butter and sugar.

HOW TO CURE BUNIONS

A bunion is a swelling on the ball of the great toe, and is the result of pressure and irritation by friction. The treatment for corns applies also to bunions; but in consequence of the greater extension of the disease, the cure is more tedious. When a bunion is forming, it may be stopped by poulticing and by carefully opening it with a lancet.

HOW TO CURE CANCER

Boil down the inner bark of red and white oak to the consistence of molasses; apply as a plaster, shifting it once a week; or, burn red-oak bark to ashes; sprinkle it on the sore till it is eaten out; then apply a plaster of tar; or, take garget berries and leaves of stramonium; simmer them together in equal parts of neatsfoot oil and the tops of hemlock; mix well together, and apply it to the parts affected; at the same time make a tea of wintergreen (root and branch); put a handful into two quarts of water; add two ounces of sulphur and drink of this tea freely during the day.

CASTOR OIL MIXTURE
Castor oil, one dessertspoonful; magnesia, the like amount. Rub together into a paste. By this combination, the taste of the oil is almost entirely concealed, and children will take it without opposition.

HOW TO DISGUISE CASTOR OIL
Rub up two drops of oil of cinnamon with an ounce of glycerine and add an ounce of castor oil. Children will take it as a luxury and ask for more.

CASTOR OIL EMULSIONS
Take castor oil and syrup, each one ounce; the yolks of an egg, and orange-flower water, one-half ounce. Mix. This makes a very pleasant emulsion, which is readily taken by adults and children alike.

HOW TO MAKE CAMPHOR ICE
To make camphor ice in small quantities for home use: Melt together over a water-bath white wax and spermaceti, each one ounce; camphor, two ounces; in sweet almond oil, one pound; then titurate until the mixture has become homogeneous, and allow one pound of rosewater to flow in slowly during the operation.

HOW TO CURE CATARRH
Take the bark of sassafras root, dry and pound it; use it as a snuff, taking two or three pinches a day.

HOW TO CURE CHILBLAINS
Sulphurous acid is recommended in this affliction. It should be applied with a camel's hair brush, or by means of a spray producer. One application of this effects a cure. The acid should be used pure. A good wash for hands or feet affected with chilblains is sulphurous acid, three parts; glycerine, one part; and water, one part. The acid will be found particularly useful in the irritating, tormenting stage of chilblains.

Another Way—Make a strong lye by boiling wood ashes in water. Put your feet in a small tub, and cover them with the lye as hot as you can bear it. Gradually add more lye, hotter and hotter. Keep them in half an hour, bathing and rubbing them continually, and being very careful to keep the lye hot.

Another Way—Wash the parts in strong alum water; apply as hot as can be borne.

HOW TO CURE BROKEN CHILBLAINS
Mix together four fluid ounces collodion; one and a half fluid ounces

of Venice turpentine; and one fluid ounce castor oil.

CHILBLAINS & CHAPPED HANDS

When chilblains manifest themselves the best remedy not only for preventing their ulcerating, but overcoming the tingling, itching pain, and stimulating the circulation of the part of healthy action, is the liniment of belladonna, two drachms; the liniment of aconite, one drachm; carbolic acid, ten drops; collodion flexile, one ounce; painted with a camel's hair pencil over their surface. When the chilblains vesicate, ulcerate or slough, it is better to omit the aconite and apply the other components of the liniment without it. The collodion flexile forms a coating or protecting film, which excludes the air, while the sedative liniments allay the irritation, generally of no trivial nature.

For chapped hands is advised the free use of glycerine and good oil, in the proportion of two parts of the former to four of the latter; after this has been well rubbed into the hands and allowed to remain for a little while, and the hands subsequently washed with Castile soap and water, recommended also is belladonna and collodion flexile to be painted on, and the protective film allowed to remain permanently.

These complaints not infrequently invade persons of languid circulation and relaxed habit, who should be put on a generous regi-

men, and treated with ferruginous tonics. Obstinate cases are occasionally met with which no local application will remedy, unless some disordered state of the system is removed, or the general condition of the patient's health improved.

Chapped lips are also benefited by the stimulating form of application advocated, but the aconite must not be allowed to get on the lips, or a disagreeable tingling results.

HOW TO CURE ITCHING CHILBLAINS

Take hydrochloric acid, one part; and water, eight parts; mix. Apply on going to bed. This must not be used if the skin is broken.

Another Way—Sal Ammoniac, two ounces; rum, one pint; camphor, two drachms. The affected part is wetted night and morning, and when dry is touched with a little simple ointment of any kind—cold cream or pomatum.

Another Way—Oil of turpentine, four ounces; camphor, six drachms; oil of cajeput, two drachms. Apply with friction.

CHILBLAIN BALM

Boil together ten fluid ounces olive oil, two fluid ounces Venice turpentine, and one ounce yellow wax; strain, and while still warm add, constantly stirring, two and a half drachms balsam of Peru and ten grains camphor.

CHILBLAIN LOTION

Dissolve one ounce of muriate of ammonia in a half pint cider vinegar, and apply frequently. One-half pint of alcohol may be added to this lotion with good results.

CHILBLAIN OINTMENT

Take mutton tallow and lard, of each three-fourths a pound avoirdupois; melt in an iron vessel, and add hydrated oxide of iron, two ounces, stirring continually with an iron spoon until the mass is of a uniform black color; when nearly cool add Venice turpentine, two ounces; Armenian bole, one ounce; oil of bergamot, one drachm; rub up the bole with a little olive oil before putting it in. Apply several times daily by putting it upon lint or linen. It heals the worst cases in a few days.

RUSSIAN REMEDY FOR CHILBLAIN

Slices of the rind of fully ripened cucumbers, dried with the soft parts attached. Previous to use, they are softened by soaking them in warm water, and are then bound on the sore parts with the inner side next to them, and left on all night. This treatment is said to be adopted for both broken and unbroken chilblains.

SIGNS OF DISEASE IN CHILDREN

In the case of a baby not yet able to talk, it must cry when it is ill. The colic makes a baby cry loud, long and passionately, and shed tears—stopping for a moment then beginning again.

If the chest is affected, it gives one sharp cry, breaking off immediately, as if crying hurt.

If the head is affected, it cries in sharp, piercing shrieks, with low moans and wails between. Or there may be quiet dozing, and startings between.

If the complaint is one of insufficient humors from birth, the baby will seldom cry spontaneously; it must be made to cry, when it will sound usually hoarse, of low tone and intensity.

If a healthy baby, its cry varies in intensity as it draws in and lets out its breath; when upset or angry, its volume becomes louder than when merely uncomfortable.

It is easy enough to perceive, where a child is attacked by disease, that there has been some change taken place; for either its skin will be dry and hot, its appetite gone; it is stupidly sleepy, or fretful or crying; it is thirsty, or pale and languid, or in some way betrays that something is wrong.

When a child vomits, or has diarrhoea, or is costive and feverish, it is owing to some derangement, and needs attention. But these various symptoms may continue for a day or two before the nature of the disease can be determined.

A warm bath, warm drinks, &tc., can do no harm, and may help to determine the cause. On coming out of the bath, and being well rubbed with the hand, the skin will show symptoms of rash, if it is a skin disease which has commenced.

By the appearance of the rash, the nature of the disease can be learned. Measles are in patches, dark red, and come out first about the face. If scarlet fever is impending, the skin will look a deep pink all over the body, though most so about the neck and face. Chicken-pox shows fever, but not so much running at the nose, and appearance of cold, as in measles, nor is there as much of a cough. Besides, the spots are smaller, and do not run much together, and are more diffused over the whole surface of the skin; and enlarge into blisters in a day or two.

HOW TO CURE CHOLERA

Take laudanum, tincture cayenne, compound tincture rhubarb, peppermint and camphor, of each equal parts. Dose: ten to thirty drops. In plain terms, take equal parts of tincture of opium, red pepper, rhubarb, peppermint and camphor, and mix them for use. In case of diarrhoea, take a dose of ten to twenty drops in three or four teaspoonfuls of water. No one who has this by him, and takes it in time, will ever have the cholera.

CHOLERA REMEDY, HARTSHORN'S

Take of chloroform, tincture of opium, spirits of camphor, and spirits of aromatic ammonia, each one and one-half fluid drachms; creosote, three drops; oil of cinnamon, eight drops; brandy, two fluid drachms. Dilute a teaspoonful with a wineglass of water, and give two teaspoonfuls every five minutes, followed by a lump of ice.

HOW TO CURE COLDS

Take three cents' worth of liquorice, three of rock candy, three of gum Arabic, and put them into a quart of water; simmer them till thoroughly dissolved, then add three cents' worth of paregoric, and a like quantity of antimonial wine.

REMEDY FOR CHEST COLD

Melt together a piece of camphor in a small quantity of olive oil; apply warm to the skin of the chest. Then cover over with a piece of wool flannel and leave overnight.

BILIOUS COLIC

Mix two tablespoonfuls of Indian meal in half a pint of cold water; drink it at two draughts.

HOW TO CURE CONSUMPTION

Take one tablespoonful of tar, and the yolks of three hen's eggs, beat them well together. Dose: one tablespoonful morning, noon and night.

CAUSTIC FOR CORNS

Tincture of iodine, four drachms; iodide of iron, twelve grains; chloride of antimony, four drachms; mix and apply with a camel's hair brush, after paring the corn. It is said to cure in three times.

HOW TO CURE CORNS

1. Take equal parts of mercurial and galbanum ointments; mix them well together, spread on a piece of soft leather, and apply it to the corns morning and evening. In a few days benefit will be derived.

2. Take two ounces of gum ammoniac, two ounces of yellow wax, and six ounces of verdigris; melt them together, and spread the composition on soft leather; cut away as much of the corn as you can, then apply the plaster, and renew it every fortnight till the corn is away.

3. Get four ounces of white diachylon plaster, four ounces of shoemaker's wax, and 6o drops of muriatic acid or spirits of salt. Boil them for a few minutes in an earthen pipkin, and when cold roll the mass between the hands, and apply it on a piece of white leather.

4. Soak the feet well in warm water, then with a sharp instrument pare off as much of the corn as can be done without pain, and bind up the part with a piece of linen or muslin thoroughly saturated with sperm oil, or, which is better, the oil which floats upon the surface of the herring or mackerel. After three or four days the dressing may be removed by scraping, when the new skin will be found of a soft and healthy texture, and less liable to the formation of a new corn than before.

5. The corn itself may be completely destroyed by rubbing it often with a little caustic solution of potash till the soft skin is formed.

6. Scrape to a pulp sufficient Spanish garlic and bind on the corn over night, after first soaking it well in warm water, and scrape off as much as possible of the hardened portion in the morning. Repeat the application as required.

7. Boil tobacco down to an extract; then mix with it a quantity of white pine pitch, and apply it to the corn; renew it once a week until the corn disappears.

Corns may be prevented by wearing easy shoes. Bathe the feet frequently in lukewarm water, with a little salt or potash dissolved in it.

HOW TO RELIEVE CORNS

Bind them up at night in a cloth wetted with tincture of arnica, to relieve the pain, and during the day occasionally moisten the stocking over the corn with arnica if the shoe is not large enough to allow the corn being bound up with a piece of linen rag.

REMEDIES FOR CORNS

The pain occasioned by corns may be greatly alleviated by the following preparations:

1. Into a one-ounce vial put two drachms of muriatic acid and six drachms of rose-water. With this mixture wet the corns night and morning for three days. Soak the feet every evening in warm water without soap. Put one-third of the acid into the water, and with a little picking the corn will be dissolved.

2. Take a lemon, cut off a small piece, then nick it so as to let in the toe with the corn; tie this on at night so that it cannot move, and in the morning you will find that, with a blunt knife, you may remove a considerable portion of the corn. Make two or three applications, and great relief will be the result.

HOW TO CURE SOLVENT CORNS

Expose salt of tartar (pearlash) in a wide-mouth vial in a damp place until it forms an oil-like liquid, and apply to the corn.

HOW TO CURE SOFT CORNS

Scrape a piece of common chalk, and put a pinch to the soft corn, and bind a piece of linen rag upon it.

HOW TO CURE TENDER CORNS

A strong solution of tannic acid is said to be an excellent application to tender feet as well as a preventive of the offensive odor attendant upon their profuse perspiration. To persons living far out in the country is recommended a strong decoction of oak bark as a substitute.

GOOD COUGH MIXTURES

1. Two ounces ammonia mixture; five ounces camphor mixture; one drachm tincture of digitalis (foxglove) ; one-half ounce each of sweet spirits of nitre and syrup of poppies; two drachms solution of sulphate of morphia. A tablespoonful of this mixture is to be taken four times a day.

2. Tincture of blood-root, one ounce; sulphate of morphia, one and a half grains; tincture of digitalis, one-half ounce; wine of antimony, one-half ounce; oil of wintergreen, ten drops. Mix. Dose: from twenty to forty drops twice or three times a day. Excellent for a hard, dry cough.

3. Common sweet cider, boiled down to one-half, makes a most excellent syrup for colds or coughs for children; is pleasant to the taste, and will keep for a year in a cool cellar. In recovering from an illness, the system has a craving for some pleasant drink. This is found in cider which is placed on the fire as soon as made, and allowed to come to a boil, then cooled, put in casks, and kept in a cool cellar.

4. Roast a large lemon very carefully without burning; when it is thoroughly hot, cut and squeeze into a cup upon three ounces of sugar candy, finely powdered; take a spoonful whenever your cough troubles you. It is as good as it is pleasant.

5. Pare off the yellow rind of the lemon, slice the lemon and put a layer of lemon and a thick layer of sugar in a deep plate; cover close with a saucer, and set in a warm place. This is an excellent remedy for a cold.

6. Put one quart hoarhound to one quart of water, and boil it down to a pint; add two or three sticks of liquorice and a tablespoonful of essence of lemon.

7. Syrup of onions (*see* page 259).

8. The following mixture makes cough candy or troches: Tincture of squills, two ounces; camphorated tincture of opium and tincture of tolu, of each take one-fourth ounce; wine of ipecac, one-half ounce; oil of Gaultheria, four drops; sassafras, three drops; and of anise seed oil, two drops. This mixture is to be placed in five pounds of candy which is just ready to take from the fire; continue the boiling a little longer, so as to form into sticks.

CROUP, REMEDY FOR IN ONE MINUTE

This remedy is simple alum. Take a knife or grater, and shave or grate off in small particles about a teaspoonful of alum; mix it with about twice its quantity of sugar, to make it palatable, and administer as quickly as possible. Its effect will be truly magical, as almost instantaneous relief will be afforded.

CURE FOR DEAFNESS

1. Take ant's eggs and onion juice. Mix them and drop into the ear.

2. Drop into the ear, at night, six or eight drops of hot sweet oil.

CURE FOR CHRONIC DIARRHOEA

Pulverize together subnitrate of bismuth, one drachm; cinchona, yellow, powdered, one-half drachm; charcoal, vegetable, one drachm; make twenty powders of this mixture and take two or three of them a day during intervals between meals.

BLACKBERRY CORDIAL (for diarrhoea)

To one quart blackberry juice add one pound of white sugar, one tablespoonful each cloves, allspice, cinnamon and nutmeg. Boil together fifteen minutes, and add a wineglass of whisky, brandy or rum. Bottle while hot, cork tight and seal. Used in diarrhoea and dysentery. Dose: a wineglassful for an adult, half that quantity for a child. It can be taken two or three times a day if the case is severe.

REMEDIES FOR DIARRHOEA

Take one teaspoonful of salt, the same of good vinegar, and a tablespoonful of water; mix and drink.

It acts like a charm on the system, and even one dose will generally cure obstinate cases of diarrhoea, or the first stages of cholera. If the first dose does not bring complete relief, repeat the dose, as it is quite harmless.

Another Way—The best rhubarb root, pulverized, one ounce; peppermint leaf, one ounce; capsicum, one-eighth ounce; cover with boiling water and steep thoroughly, strain, and add bicarbonate of potash and essence of cinnamon, of each one-half ounce; with brandy (or good whisky) ; equal in amount to the whole, and loaf sugar, four ounces. Dose: for an adult, one or two tablespoonfuls; for a child, one or two teaspoonfuls, from three to six times per day, until relief is obtained.

Another Way—To half a bushel of blackberries, well mashed, add a quarter of a pound of allspice, two ounces of cinnamon, two ounces of cloves; pulverize well, mix and boil slowly until properly done; then strain or squeeze the juice through homespun or flannel, and add to each pint of the juice a pound of leaf sugar, boil again for some time; take it off, and while cooling, add half a gallon of the best Cognac brandy.

HOW TO CURE DIPHTHERIA
Lemon juice, as a local application in diphtheria, is often preferred to chlorate of potash, nitrate of silver, and perchloride of lime water. It is used by dipping a little plug of cottonwool, twisted around a wire, in the juice, and pressing it against the diseased surface four or five times daily.

CURE FOR DROPSY
Take the leaves of a currant bush and make into tea, drink it.

A CERTAIN CURE FOR DRUNKENNESS
Take of sulphate of iron, five grains; magnesia, ten grains; peppermint water, eleven drachms; spirits of nutmeg, one drachm. Administer twice a day. It acts as a tonic and stimulant, and so partially supplies the place of the accustomed liquor, and prevents the absolute physical and moral prostration that follows the sudden breaking off from the use of stimulating drink.

CURE FOR DRUNKENNESS
The following singular means of curing habitual drunkenness is employed with great success: It consists in confining the drunkard in a room, and in furnishing him at discretion with his favorite spirit diluted with two-thirds of water; as much wine, beer and coffee as he desires, but continuing one-third of spirit; all the food—the bread, meat, and the legumes—are steeped in spirit and water. The poor devil is continually drunk and dort. On the fifth day of this regime, he has an extreme disgust for spirit; he earnestly requests other diet; but his desire must not be yielded to, until the poor wretch no longer desires to eat or drink; he is then certainly cured of his penchant for

drunkenness. He acquires such a disgust for brandy and other spirits that he is ready to vomit at the very sight of it.

Spontaneous combustion
Noted scientists have proven the unsoundness of spontaneous combustion. Yet there are a proven nineteen instances of something akin, or the rapid ignition of the human body by contact with flame as a consequence of the saturation of its tissues by alcohol.

CURES FOR DYSENTERY

1. Take equal parts of tincture of rhubarb, tincture of capsicum, tincture of camphor, essence of ginger, and laudanum. Mix; shake well and take from ten to twenty drops every thirty minutes until relief is obtained. This is the dose for an adult. Half the amount for a child under twelve years of age.

2. Take some butter off the churn, immediately after being churned, just as it is, without being salted or washed; clarify it over the fire like honey. Skim off all the milky particles when melted over a clear fire. Let the patient (if an adult) take two tablespoonfuls of the clarified remainder, twice or three times within a day. This has never failed to effect a cure, and in many cases it has been almost instantaneous.

3. In diseases of this kind, the Indians used the roots and leaves of the blackberry bush, a decoction of which in hot water, well boiled down, is taken in doses of a gill before each meal, and before retiring to bed. It is an almost infallible cure.

4. Beat one egg in a teacup; add one tablespoonful of loaf sugar and half a teaspoonful of ground spice; fill the cup with sweet milk. Give the patient one tablespoonful once in ten minutes until relieved.

5. Take one tablespoonful of common salt, and mix it with two tablespoonfuls of vinegar and pour upon it half a pint of water, either hot or cold (only let it be taken cool). A wineglassful of this mixture in the above proportions, taken every half hour, will be found quite efficacious in curing dysentery. If the stomach be nauseated, a wineglassful taken every hour will suffice. For a child, the quantity should be a teaspoonful of salt and one of vinegar in a teacupful of water.

CURE FOR DYSPEPSIA

1. Take the bark of white poplar root, boil it thick, and add a little spirit, and then lay it on the stomach.

2. Take wintergreen and black cherry-tree bark and yellow dock; put into two quarts of water; boil down to three pints; take two or three glasses daily.

3. Eat onions. This remedy is said to be infallible.

4. Take two parts of well-dried and pounded pods of red pepper, mixed with one part of ground mustard, and sift it over everything you eat or drink.

5. Take an effervescing solution of citrate of magnesia, made as follows: Dissolve citric acid 400 grains in water 2,000 grains, add carbonate of magnesia 200 grains; stir until dissolved. Filter into a 12-ounce bottle containing syrup of citric acid 1,200 grains. Add boiled and filtered water to fill the bottle, drop in bicarbonate of potash (in crystals) 30 grains, and immediately cork. Shake until bicarbonate of potash is dissolved. The syrup of citric acid is made from citric acid eight parts, water eight parts, spirit of lemon four parts, syrup 890 parts.

6. Sal volatile combined with camphor is a splendid remedy.

7. Take a little cold water in which has been dissolved a teaspoonful of salt.

HOW TO CURE EARACHE

Take a small piece of cotton batting or cotton wool, make a depression in the center with the finger, then fill it up with as much ground pepper as will rest on a five-cent piece; gather it into a ball and tie it up; dip the ball into sweet oil and insert it into the ear, covering the latter with cotton wool, and use a bandage or cap to retain it in its place. Almost instant relief will be experienced; and the application is so gentle that an infant will not get injured by it, but experience relief as well as adults.

Another Way—Roast a piece of lean mutton, squeeze out the juice and drop it into the ear as hot as it can be borne.

EGGS AS CURATIVES

Eggs are not only food but also medicine. The white is the most efficacious of remedies for burns, and the oil extractable from the yolk is regarded by the Russians as an almost miraculous salve for cuts, bruises, and scratches. A raw egg, if swallowed in time, will effectually detach a fish bone fastened in the throat; and the whites of two eggs will render the deadly corrosive sublimate as harmless as a dose of calomel. They strengthen the consumptive, invigorate the feeble, and render the most susceptible all but proof against jaundice in its more malignant phase.

CURE FOR INFLAMED EYES

Pour boiling water on alder flowers, and steep them like tea; when cold, put three or four drops of laudanum into a small glass of the alder tea, and let the mixture run into the eyes two or three times a day; and the eyes will become perfectly strong in a couple of weeks.

EYES, GRANULAR INFLAMMATION

A prominent oculist says that the contagious Egyptian or granular inflammation of the eyes is spreading throughout the country, and that he has been able in many—and indeed in a majority—of cases, to trace the disease to what are commonly called rolling towels. Towels of this kind are generally found in country hotels and the dwellings of the working classes, and, being thus used by nearly everyone, are made the carriers of one of the most troublesome diseases of the eye. This being the case, it is urgently recommended that the use of these rolling towels be discarded, and thus one of the special vehicles for the spread of a most dangerous disorder of the eyes—one by which thousands of working men are annually deprived of their means of support—will no longer exist.

CURE FOR STY IN EYE

Bathe frequently with warm water. When the sty bursts, use an ointment composed of one part of citron ointment and four of spermaceti, well rubbed together, and smear along the edge of the eye-lid.

CURE FOR WEEPING EYES

Wash the eyes with chamomile tea night and morning.

HOW TO CURE ERYSIPELAS

Dissolve five ounces of salt in one pint of good brandy, and take two tablespoonfuls three times a day.

CURE FOR FELONS

1. Stir one-half teaspoonful of water into an ounce of Venice turpentine until the mixture appears like granulated honey. Wrap a good coating of it around the finger with a cloth. If the felon is only recent, the pain will be removed in six hours.

2. As soon as the part begins to swell, wrap it with a cloth saturated thoroughly with the tincture of lobelia. An old physician says that he has known this to cure scores of cases, and that it never fails if applied in season.

CURE FOR FEVER SORES

Take of hoarhound, balm, sarsaparilla, loaf sugar, aloes, gum camphor, honey, spikenard, spirits of turpentine, each two ounces. Dose: one tablespoonful three mornings, missing three; and for a wash, make a strong tea of sumach, washing the affected parts frequently, and keeping the bandages well wet.

CURE FOR FITS

Take of tincture of foxglove, ten drops at each time twice a day, and increase one drop at each time as long as the stomach will bear it, or it causes a nauseous feeling.

HOW TO CURE GOITER

Make a decoction in an iron pot of one bushel of skunk cabbage stalks and roots, cut in small pieces, in a gallon of soft water; boil the whole till reduced to one-half and strain. Then add three-fourths pound, each mutton tallow and clarified lard, and one-half pound tar; mix well with an iron spoon; when cool, add three ounces spirits of turpentine, and two ounces of olive oil; pour into an earthen jar and let stand overnight. Apply this salve to throat and cover with a linen. Repeat this daily till the affliction leaves.

GRAVEL

1. Make a strong tea of the low herb called heart's ease, and drink freely.

2. Make of Jacob's ladder a strong tea, and drink freely.

3. Make of bean leaves a strong tea, and drink freely.

GLYCERINE OINTMENT FOR CHAPPED HANDS

Melt together spermaceti, two

drachms; white wax, one-half drachm; oil of sweet almonds, two ounces; and then add glycerine, one ounce and stir brisky till cool.

An admirable application for chapped hands.

CHAPPED HANDS
See Chilblains and Chapped Hands; Glycerine Ointment for Chapped Hands.

HEADACHE DROPS
For the cure of nervous, sun, and sick headaches, take two quarts of alcohol, three ounces of Castile soap, one ounce camphor, and two ounces ammonia. Bathe forehead and temples.

SICK HEADACHE
Ergot is recommended, especially for the nervous or sick headache. It will take care of a larger proportion of cases than any other remedy. The theory of its action is that it lessens the quantity of blood to the brain by contracting the muscular fibers of the arterial walls. Ten or twenty drops given repeatedly every half hour till relief is obtained, or four or five doses are used. In other forms of disease, where opium alone is contraindicated, its bad effects are moderated by combining it with ergot.

CURE FOR NERVOUS HEADACHE
Alcohol dilut., four ounces; olei cinnamon, four minims; potassa bromide, five drachms; extract of hyoscyamus fluid, one and one-half drachms; fiat lotio. One or two teaspoonfuls, if required.

SICK HEADACHE PREVENTATIVE
Take a spoonful of powdered charcoal in molasses every morning, and wash it down with a little tea, or drink half a glass of raw rum or gin, and drink freely of mayweed tea.

HOW TO CURE SCURF IN THE HEAD
A simple and effective remedy. Into a pint of water drop a lump of fresh quicklime, the size of a walnut; let it stand all night, then pour the water off clear from the sediment or deposit; add one-quarter pint of the best vinegar, and wash the head with the mixture. Perfectly harmless; only wet the roots of the hair.

HEARTBURN
See Dyspepsia.

OINTMENT FOR HEMORRHOIDS
Sulphate of morphia, three grains; extract of stramonia, thirty grains; olive oil, one drachm; carbonate of lead, sixty grains; lard, three drachms.

OINTMENT FOR PILES

Tannin, two drachms; water, two fluid drachms; triturate together, and add lard, one and a half drachms. An excellent application for piles.

HOW TO CURE HICCOUGH

A convulsive motion of the diaphragm and parts adjacent. The common causes are flatuency, indigestion, acidity, and worms. It may usually be removed by the exhibition of warm carminatives, cordials, cold water, weak spirits, camphor julep, or spirits of sal volatile. A sudden fright or surprise will often produce the like effect. An instance is recorded of a delicate young lady who was troubled with hiccough for some months, and who was reduced to a state of extreme debility from the loss of sleep occasioned thereby, who was cured by a fright, after medicines and topical applications had failed. A pinch of snuff, a glass of cold soda-water, or an ice-cream, will also frequently remove this complaint.

CURE FOR HIVES

The disease is caused by a perversion of the digestive functions, accompanied by a disturbance of the circulation. It is not attended with danger, and is of importance only from the annoyance which it causes. Relief may be obtained in most instances by the use of cream of tartar daily to such extent as to move the bowels slightly. Make a strong solution, sweeten it pleasantly, and take a teaspoonful, say after each meal, until the effect above mentioned is produced, and continue the treatment until the hives cease to be troublesome.

HIVE SYRUP

Put one ounce each of squills and seneca snake-root into one pint of water; boil down to one-half and strain. Then add one-half pound of clarified honey containing twelve grains tartrate of antimony. Dose for a child: ten drops to one teaspoonful, according to age. An excellent remedy for croup.

HOW TO CURE HOARSENESS

1. Make a strong tea of horseradish and yellow dock root, sweetened with honey, and drink freely.

2. Beat a fresh egg and thicken it with fine white sugar. Eat of it freely and the hoarseness will soon be relieved.

3. Take one drachm of freshly scraped horseradish root, to be infused with four ounces of water in a close vessel for three hours, and made into a syrup, with double its quantity of vinegar. A teaspoonful has often proved effectual.

HOW TO CURE HUMORS

Take equal parts of saffron and seneca snake-root, make a strong tea, drink one half pint a day, and this will drive out all humors from the system.

HOW TO CURE HYSTERIA

Take the leaves of motherwort and thoroughwort, and the bark of poplar root; equal parts. Mix them in molasses, and take four spoonfuls of them when the first symptoms of disorder are felt, and they will effectually check it.

HOW TO CURE BARBER'S ITCH
Moisten parts effected with saliva (spittle) and rub it over thoroughly three times a day with the ashes of a good Havana cigar. This is a simple remedy, yet it has cured the most obstinate cases.

ITCH OINTMENT
1. Take one pound of lard, one pound of suet, eight ounces sugar of lead, two ounces of vermillion. Mix. Scent with a little bergamot.

2. Take one ounce bichloride of mercury, one pound of lard, one pound of suet, one and a half ounces of hydrochloric acid. Melt and mix well, and when perfectly cold, stir in essence of lemon, four drachms; essence of bergamot, one drachm.

3. Take one ounce powdered chloride of lime, one pound of lard. Mix well, then add two drachms essence of lemon.

4. Take one part bichloride of mercury; fifteen parts of lard. Mix well together.

5. Take one part of white precipitate; twelve parts of lard. Mix.

A portion of either of these ointments must be well rubbed on the parts affected, night and morning.

6. White precipitate, fifteen grains; saltpetre, one-half drachm; flowers of sulphur, one drachm; mix well with lard, two ounces. Long celebrated for cure of itch.

SULPHUR OINTMENT FOR ITCH
Flowers of sulphur, eight ounces; oil of bergamot, two drachms, lard, one pound. Rub freely three times a day.

HOW TO CURE THE SEVEN-YEAR ITCH
1. Use plenty of Castile soap and water, and then apply freely iodide of sulphur ointment; or take any given quantity of simple sulphur ointment and color it to a light brown or chocolate color with subcarbonate of iron, and then perfume it. Apply this freely, and if the case should be a severe one, administer mild alteratives in conjunction with the outward application.

2. The sulphur bath is a good remedy for itch or any other kind of skin disease. Leprosy (the most obstinate of all) has been completely cured by it, and the common itch only requires two or three applications to completely eradicate it from the system.

3. Benzine, it is said, will effect

a complete cure for scabies in the course of half to three-quarters of an hour, after which the patient should take a warm bath from twenty to thirty minutes.

HOW TO CURE JAUNDICE

1. Take the whites of two hen's eggs, beat them up well in a gill of water; take of this a little every morning; it will soon do good. It also creates an appetite, and strengthens the stomach.

2. Take of black cherry-tree bark, two ounces; blood root and gold thread, each half an ounce; put in a pint of brandy. Dose: from a teaspoonful to a tablespoonful morning and night.

HOW TO CURE STIFFENED JOINTS

Take the bark of white oak and sweet apple trees, equal parts; boil them down to a thick substance, and then add the same quantity of goose-grease or oil, simmer all together, and then rub it on the parts effected.

HOW TO CURE KIDNEY DISEASE

Take equal parts of the oil of red cedar and the oil of spearmint. Dose: one tablespoonful three times daily.

HOW TO CURE LAME BACK

Take the berries of red cedar and allow them to simmer in neatsfoot oil, and use as an ointment.

HOW TO CURE CHAPPED LIPS

1. Take two ounces of white wax, one ounce of spermaceti, four ounces of oil of almonds, two ounces of honey, one-fourth ounce of essence of bergamot, or any other scent. Melt the wax and spermaceti; then add the honey, and melt all together, and when hot add the almond oil by degrees, stirring till cold.

2. Take oil of almonds, three ounces; spermaceti, half an ounce; virgin rice, one-half ounce. Melt these together over a slow fire, mixing with them a little powder of alkane root to color it. Keep stirring till cold, and then add a few drops of the oil of rhodium.

3. Take oil of almonds, spermaceti, white wax, and white sugar candy, equal parts. These form a good white lip salve.

GLYCERINE CREAM FOR CHAPPED LIPS

Take of spermaceti, four drachms; white wax, one drachm; oil of almonds, two troy ounces; glycerine, one troy ounce. Melt the spermaceti, wax and oil together, and when cooling stir in glycerine and perfume.

HOW TO CURE SORE LIPS

Wash the lips with strong tea, made from the bark of the white oak.

A GOOD SPRING WHITE LINIMENT

Take half a pint of spirits of turpentine, and the same quantity of good vinegar, the unbeaten whites of two hen's eggs, and one ounce of ammonia water. Mix well together in a stone or earthen jar, shaking the mixture till it emulsifies to a cream-like consistence. Store in a cool place. A good recipe to make each spring.

A WONDERFUL LINIMENT

Two ounces of oil of spike, two ounces of origanum, two ounces of hemlock; two ounces of wormwood, four ounces of sweet oil, two ounces of spirits of ammonia, two ounces gum camphor, two ounces of spirits of turpentine. Add one quart of strong alcohol. Mix well together and bottle tight. This is an unequaled horse liniment and of the best ever made for human ailments such as rheumatism, sprains, &tc.

LIVER COMPLAINT

Make a strong tea of the syrup of burdock, wormwood and dandelion, equal parts, and drink freely.

HOW TO REMOVE MOTH PATCHES

Wash the patches with solution of common bicarbonate of soda and water several times during the day for two days, or till the patches are removed, which will usually be in 48 hours. After the process wash with some nice toilet soap, and the skin will be left nice, smooth and clear of patches.

MUMPS

This disease, most common among children, begins with soreness and stiffness in the sides of the neck. Soon a swelling of the parotid glands takes place, which is painful and continues to increase for four or five days, sometimes making it difficult to swallow, or open the mouth. The swelling sometimes comes on one side at a time, but commonly upon both. There is often heat, and sometimes fever, with a dry skin, quick pulse, furred tongue, constipated bowels, and scanty and high-colored urine. The disease is contagious. The treatment is very simple—a mild diet, gentle laxative, occasional hot fomentations, and wearing a piece of flannel round the throat.

HOW TO PREVENT INGROWING NAILS

If the nail of your toe be hard, and apt to grow round, and into the corners of your toe, take a piece of broken glass and scrape the top very thin; do this whenever you cut your nails, and by constant use it makes the corners fly up and grow flat, so that it is impossible they should give you any pain.

EGG GRUEL (for nausea)

Boil eggs from one to three hours until hard enough to grate; then boil new milk and thicken with the eggs, and add a little salt. Excellent in case of nausea.

A SURE CURE FOR NEURALGIA

Fill a tight-top thimble with cotton wool, and drop on it a few drops of strong spirits of hartshorn. The open mouth of the thimble is then applied over the seat of the pain for a minute or two, until the skin is blistered. The skin is then rubbed off, and upon the denuded surface is applied a small quantity of morphia, one-fourth grain. This affords almost instant relief. A second application of the morphia, if required, is to be preceded by first rubbing off the new formation that has sprung up over the former blistered surface.

Another Way—The following application, highly recommended, will relieve facial or any other neuralgia almost instantaneously: Albumen of egg, one drachm; rhigolene, four ounces; oil of peppermint, two ounces; collodion and chloroform, each one ounce. Mix well. Agitate occasionally for 24 hours, and by gelatinization a beautiful and semi-solidified opodeldoc-looking compound results, which will retain its consistency and hold the ingredients intimately blended for months. Apply by smart friction with the hand, or gently with a soft brush, or mop along the course of the nerve involved.

Another Way—Mix one and one-half drachms iodide of potash, fifteen grains of quinine and one ounce ginger syrup, and two and a half ounces water. Dose: a tablespoonful every three hours.

NEURALGIA OF THE STOMACH

Take of distilled water of cherry laurel, five parts; muriate of morphia, one-tenth part. Mix and dissolve. Dose: one drop on a lump of sugar immediately before meals.

OINTMENT FOR SORE NIPPLES

Glycerine, rose water and tannin, equal parts, rubbed together into an ointment, is very highly recommended for sore and cracked nipples.

REMEDIES FOR PAINS

1. Steep marigold in good cider vinegar and frequently wash the affected parts. This will afford speedy relief.

2. Take half a pound of tar and the same quantity of tobacco, and boil them down separately to a thick substance; then simmer them together. Spread a plaster and apply it to the affected parts, and it will afford immediate relief.

INSTANTANEOUS PAIN KILLER

Another, and even more instant, cure of pain is made as follows: Take equal parts of aqua-ammonia, sulphuric ether, and alcohol, and apply over the pain.

PAINTER'S COLIC

Make of tartaric acid a syrup similar to that of lemon syrup; add a sufficient quantity of water, and drink two or three glasses a day.

PILES

See Hemorrhoids.

HOW TO CURE PIMPLES

Take a teaspoonful of the tincture of gum guaiacum and one teaspoonful of vinegar; mix well and apply to the affected parts.

HOW TO MAKE COURT PLASTER

Isinglass, 125 grains; alcohol one and three-fourths ounce; glycerine, twelve minims; water and tincture of benzoin, each sufficient quantity. Dissolve the isinglass in enough water to make the solution weigh four fluid ounces. Spread half of the latter with a brush upon successive layers of taffeta, waiting after each application until the layer is dry. Mix the second half of the isinglass solution with the alcohol and glycerine, and apply in the same manner. Then reverse the taffeta, coat it on the back with tincture of benzoin, and allow it to become perfectly dry. There are many other formulas, but this is official. The above quantities are sufficient to make a piece of court plaster fifteen inches square.

POOR MAN'S PLASTER

Melt together beeswax, one ounce; tar, three ounces; resin, three ounces, and spread on paper or muslin.

STRENGTHENING PLASTER

Litharge plasters, 24 parts; white resin, six parts; yellow wax and olive oil, of each three parts, and red oxide of iron, eight parts. Let the oxide be rubbed with the oil, and the other ingredients added melted, and mix with the whole well together. The plaster, after being spread over the leather, should be cut into strips two inches wide and strapped firmly around the joint.

BREAD & MILK POULTICE

Take stale bread in crumbs, pour boiling sweet milk, or milk and water over it, and simmer till soft, stirring it well; then take it from the fire, and gradually stir in a little glycerine or sweet oil, so as to render the poultice pliable when applied.

FLAXSEED (LINSEED) POULTICE

Take of linseed, powdered, four ounces; hot water sufficient, mix and stir well with a spoon, until of suitable consistence. A little oil should be added and some smeared over the surface as well, to prevent its getting hard. A very excellent poultice, suitable for many purposes.

SPICE POULTICE

Powdered cinnamon, cloves, and cayenne pepper, of each two ounces; rye meal, or flour, spirits and honey, of each sufficient to make of suitable consistence.

QUINSY

This is an inflammation of the tonsils, or common inflammatory sore throat; commences with a slight feverish attack, with considerable pain and swelling of the tonsils, causing some difficulty in swallowing; as the attack advances these symptoms become more intense, there is headache, thirst, a painful sense of tension, and acute darting pains in the ears. The attack is generally brought on by exposure to cold, and lasts from five to seven days, when it subsides naturally, or an abscess may form in tonsils and burst, or the tonsils may remain enlarged, the inflammation subsiding.

Treatment—The patient should remain in a warm room, the diet chiefly milk and good broths, some cooling laxative and diaphoretic medicine may be given; but the greatest relief will be found in the frequent inhalation of the steam of hot water through an inhaler, or in the old-fashioned way, through the spout of a teapot.

REMEDIES FOR RHEUMATISM

1. Bathe the parts affected with water in which potatoes have been boiled, as hot as can be borne, just before going to bed; by morning it will be much relieved, if not removed. One application of this simple remedy has cured the most obstinate of rheumatic pains.

2. Half an ounce of pulverized saltpetre put in half a pint of sweet oil; bathe the parts affected, and a sound cure will be speedily effected.

3. Rheumatism has frequently been cured by a persistent use of lemon juice, either undiluted or in the form of lemonade. Suck half a lemon every morning before breakfast, and occasionally during the day, and partake of lemonade when thirsty in preference to any other drink. If severely afflicted, a physician should be consulted, but, in all cases, lemon juice will hasten the cure.

4. By the valerian bath, made simply by taking one pound of valerian root, boiling it gently for about fifteen minutes in one gallon of water, straining and adding the strained liquid to about twenty gallons of water in an ordinary bath. The temperature should be about 98°, and the time of immersion from twenty to thirty minutes. Pains must be taken to dry the patient perfectly upon getting out of the bath. If the inflammation remains refractory in any of the joints, linseed meal poultices should be made with a strong decoction of valerian root and applied.

RHEUMATIC LINIMENT

Take of olive oil, spirits of camphor, and chloroform, two ounces each; sassafras oil, one drachm. Add the oil of sassafras to the olive oil, then the spirits of camphor, and shake well before putting in the chloroform; shake when used, and keep it corked, as the chloroform evaporates very fast if it is left open. Apply three or four times daily, rubbing in well, and always toward the body.

RHEUMATIC PLASTER

Take one-fourth pound of resin and like quantity of sulphur; melt by a slow fire, and add one ounce of cayenne pepper and one-fourth of an ounce of camphor gum; stir well till mixed, and temper with neatsfoot oil.

HOW TO CURE RING-WORMS

1. To one part sulphuric acid, add sixteen to twenty parts of water. Use a brush and feather, and apply it to the parts night and morning. A few dressings will generally cure. If the solution is too strong and causes pain, dilute it with water, and if the irritation is excessive, rub on a little oil or other softening application, but always avoid the use of soap.

2. Or, wash the head with soft soap every morning, and apply the following lotion every night; one-half drachm of subcarbonate of soda dissolved in one gill of vinegar.

SALT RHEUM

1. Make a strong tea of elm root bark; drink the tea freely, and wash the affected part in the same.

2. Take one ounce of blue flag root, steep it in half a pint of gin; take a teaspoonful three times a day—morning, noon, and night—and also wash with the same.

3. Take one ounce of oil of tar, one drachm of oil of checker-berry; mix. Take from five to twenty drops morning and night as the stomach will bear.

HEALING SALVE

Sweet oil, three quarts; resin, three ounces; beeswax, three ounces. Melt together; then add powdered red lead, two pounds; heat all these together and when nearly cold add a piece of camphor gum as large as a nutmeg. Good for burns, &tc.

BLEEDING OF THE STOMACH

Take a teaspoonful of camomile tea every ten minutes until the bleeding stops.

SICKNESS OF THE STOMACH

Drink three or four times a day of the steep made from the bark of white poplar roots.

How to make a steam bath
The most nourishing steam bath that can be applied to a person who is unable to sweat and can take but little food in the stomach: Produce the sweating by burning alcohol under the chair in which the person sits, with blanket covering to hold the heat. Use caution and but little alcohol. Fire it in a shallow iron pan or old saucer.

SUNBURN & TAN

1. Take two drachms of borax, one drachm of Roman alum, one drachm of camphor, half an ounce of sugar candy, a pound of ox-gall. Mix, and stir well for ten minutes or so, and repeat this stirring three or four times a day for a fortnight, till it appears clear and transparent. Strain through blotting paper, and bottle for use.

2. Milk of almonds made thus: Take of blanched bitter almonds half an ounce; soft water half a pint; make an emulsion by beating the almonds and water together, strain through a muslin cloth, and it is made.

3. A preparation composed of equal parts of olive oil and lime water is also an excellent remedy for sunburn.

TO PRODUCE SWEAT

Take of nitre, one-half drachm; snake's head (herb), saffron, camphor, snake-root seneca, bark of sassafras root, each one ounce; ipecac, and opium, each one-half ounce; put the above in three quarts of Holland gin, and take a tablespoonful in catnip tea every few minutes, til the sweat is produced.

SYRUP OF ONIONS

Take a quarter bushel of dry onions, cleaned, pared, and sliced thin; add sufficient soft water to boil till water imbibes their essence; strain through a hair sieve; then boil over a slow fire till half that amount; add one-half pound of loaf sugar, mix till dissolved; cool and bottle for use. A tablespoonful three times daily is an excellent remedy for coughs and colds.

TEETHING

Young children whilst cutting their first set of teeth often suffer severe constitutional disturbance. At first there is restlessness and peevishness, with slight fever, but not infrequently these are followed by convulsive fits, as they are commonly called, which depends on the brain becoming irritated; and sometimes under this condition the child is either cut off suddenly, or the foundation of serious mischief to the brain is laid.

The remedy, or rather the safeguard, against these frightful consequences is trifling, safe, and almost certain, and consists merely in lancing the gum covering the tooth which is making its way through. When teething is about, it may be known by the spittle constantly driveling from the mouth and wetting the frock. The child has its fingers in its mouth, and bites hard any substance it can get hold of.

If the gums be carefully looked at, the part where the tooth is pressing up is swollen and redder than usual; and if the finger be pressed on it the child shrinks and cries, showing that the gum is tender.

When these symptoms occur, the gum should be lanced, and sometimes the tooth comes through the next day, if near the surface; but if not so far advanced, the cut heals and a scar forms, which is thought by some objectionable, as rendering the passage of the tooth more difficult.

This, however, is untrue, for the scar will give way much more easily than the uncut gum; if the tooth does not come through after two or three days, the lancing may be repeated; and this is more especially needed if the child be fractious, and seems in much pain.

Lancing the gums is further advantageous, because it empties the inflamed part of its blood, and so relieves the pain and inflammation. The relief children experience in the course of two or three hours from the operation is often very remarkable, as they almost immediately become lively and cheerful.

TETTER

After a slight feverish attack, lasting two or three days, clusters of small, transparent pimples, filled sometimes with a colorless, sometimes with a brownish lymph, appear on the cheeks or forehead, or on the extremities, and at times on the body. The pimples are about the size of peas, and break after a few days, when a brown or yellow crust is formed over them, which falls off about the tenth day, leaving the skin red and irritable. The eruption is attended with heat, itching, tingling, fever, and restlessness, especially at night. Ringworm is a curious form of tetter, in which the inflamed patches assume the form of a ring.

Treatment—Consists of a light diet, and gentle laxatives. If the person be advanced in age, and feeble, a tonic will be desirable. For a wash, white vitriol, one drachm; rosewater, three ounces, mixed; or an ointment made of alder-flower ointment, one ounce; oxide of zinc, one drachm.

HOW TO CURE SORE THROAT

"One who has tried it" communicates the following sensible item about curing sore throat: Take one ounce of camphorated oil and five cents' worth of chloride of potash. Whenever any soreness appears in the throat, put the potash in half a tumbler of water, and with it gargle the throat thoroughly; then rub the neck thoroughly with the camphorated oil at night before going to bed, and also pin around the throat a small strip of woolen flannel. This is a simple, cheap and sure remedy.

SORE THROAT LINIMENT

Gum camphor, two ounces; Castile soap, shaved fine, one drachm; oil of turpentine and oil of origanum, each one-half ounce; opium, one-fourth of an ounce; alcohol, one pint. In a week or ten days they will be fit for use. Bathe the parts freely two or three times daily until relief is obtained.

TONIC POWDER FOR GOOD CONDITION

Ground ginger, one pound; antimony sulphide, one pound; powdered sulphur, one pound; saltpetre. Mix altogether and administer in a gruel or mash, in such quantities as may be required.

REMEDIES FOR TOOTHACHE

1. One drachm of alum, reduced to an impalpable powder; three drachms of nitrous spirits of ether. Mix and apply them to the tooth on cotton.

2. Mix a little salt and alum equal portions, grind it fine, wet a little lock of cotton, fill it with the powder and put it in your tooth.

3. To one drachm of collodion

add two drachms of Calvert's carbolic acid. A gelatinous mass is precipitated, a small portion of which inserted in the cavity of an aching tooth, invariably gives immediate relief.

4. Saturate a small bit of clean cotton wool with a strong solution of ammonia, and apply it immediately to the affected tooth. The pleasing contrast immediately produced in some cases causes fits of laughter, although a moment previous extreme suffering and anguish prevailed.

5. Sometimes a sound tooth aches from sympathy of the nerves of the face with other nerves. But when toothache proceeds from a decayed tooth either have it taken out, or put hot fomentations upon the face, and hot drinks into the mouth, such as tincture of cayenne.

FREE PASSAGE OF URINE
The leaves of the currant bush made into a tea, and taken as a common drink.

SCALDING OF THE URINE
Take equal parts of the oil of red cedar and the oil of spearmint. Mix together well, and take two tablespoonfuls twice a day.

URINARY OBSTRUCTIONS
Steep pumpkin seeds in gin, and drink about three glasses a day; or administer half a drachm of uva ursi every morning, and a dose of spearmint.

VENEREAL COMPLAINTS
Take equal parts of the oil of red cedar, combined with sarsaparilla, yellow dock and burdock made into a syrup; add to a pint of this an ounce of gum guiacum. Dose: from a tablespoonful to a wineglass, as best as you can bear.

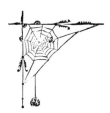

TO CURE WARTS
Warts are formed by the small arteries, veins, and nerves united together, taking on a disposition to grow by extending themselves upward, carrying the scarf-skin along with them, which, thickening, forms a wart. Corns are a similar growth, brought about by the friction of tight boots and shoes.

1. Take a piece of diachylon plaster, cut a hole in the centre the size of the wart, and stick it on, the wart protruding through. Then touch it daily with aquafortis, or nitrate of silver. They may be removed by tying a string tightly around them.

2. Take a blacksmith's punch, heat it red hot and burn the warts with the end of it. When the burn gets well, the warts will be gone forever.

3. Scrape down enough dry cobwebs to make a ball large enough to, or a little more than, cover the wart and not touch the flesh around the same; lay it on top of the wart, ignite it and let it be, until it is all burnt up. The wart will turn white, and in a few days come out.

4. Pass a pin through the wart; apply one end of the pin to the flame of a lamp; hold it there until the wart fries under the action of the heat. A wart so treated will leave.

5. Dissolve as much common washing soda as the water will take up; wash the warts with this for a minute or two, and let them dry without wiping. Keep the water in a bottle and repeat the washing often, and it will take away the largest warts.

6. They may be cured surely by paring them down until the blood comes slightly and then rubbing them with lunar caustic. It is needless to say this hurts a little, but it is a sure cure. The hydrochlorate of lime applied in the same way will cure after several applications and some patience; so will strong good vinegar, and so it is said will milk-weed.

The cures founded upon superstitious practices, such as muttering some phrases over the excrescence, stealing a piece of beef, rubbing the wart therewith and then burying it under the leaves to await decay, &tc., are all the remnants of a past state of ignorance and are of no use whatever. Warts are generally only temporary and disappear as their possessors grow up.

HOW TO REMOVE WARTS FROM THE HAND

Take salicylic acid, thirty grains; extract of cannabis, indic., ten grains; collodion, one-half ounce. Mix well and apply with perseverance. Sooner or later the warts will go.

HOW TO REMOVE WARTS PAINLESSLY

Touch the wart with a little nitrate of silver, or with nitric acid, or with aromatic vinegar. The silver salt will produce a black, and the nitric acid a yellow stain, either of which will wear off in a short while. The vinegar scarcely discolors the skin.

HOW TO CURE WHOOPING-COUGH

Take a quart of spring water, put in a large handful of chin-cups that grow upon moss, a large handful of unset hyssop; boil it to a pint, strain it off, and sweeten it with sugar-candy. Let the child, as often as it coughs, take two spoonfuls at a time.

HOW TO CURE WHITE SWELLING

1. Draw a blister on the inside of the leg below the knee; keep it running with ointment made of hen manure, by simmering it in hog's lard with onions.

2. Rub the knee with the following kind of ointment: bits of pep-

permint, oil of sassafras, checker-
berry, juniper, one drachm each;
simmer in one-half pint neatsfoot
oil, and rub on the knee three times
a day.

HOW TO CURE WOUNDS

Catnip steeped, mixed with fresh
butter and sugar. May be taken internally and externally.

HOW TO CURE WORMS IN CHILDREN

1. Take one ounce of powdered
snakehead (herb) , and one drachm
each of aloes and prickly ash bark;
powder these, and to one-half teaspoonful of this powder add a teaspoonful of boiling water and a
teaspoonful of molasses. Take this
as a dose, night or morning, more
or less, as the symptoms may require.

2. Take tobacco leaves, pound
them up with honey, and lay them
on the belly of the child or grown
person, at the same time administering a dose of some good physic.

3. Take garden parsley, make it
into tea and let the patient drink
freely of it.

4. Take the scales that will fall
around the blacksmith's anvil,
powder them fine, and put them in
sweetened rum. Shake when you
take them, and give a teaspoonful
three times a day.

Chapter 20

How to be handsome
COSMETIQUES

Where is the woman who would not be beautiful? If such there be —but no, she does not exist. From that memorable day when the Queen of Sheba made a formal call on the late lamented King Solomon until the recent advent of Jersey Lily, the power of beauty has controlled the fate of dynasties and the lives of men.

How to be beautiful, and consequently powerful, is a question of far greater importance to the feminine mind than pre-destination or any other abstract subject. If women are to govern, control, manage, influence, and retain the adoration of husbands, fathers, brothers, lovers or even cousins, they must look their prettiest at all times.

All women cannot have good features, but they can look well, and it is possible to a great extent to correct deformity and develop

much of the figure. The first step to good looks is good health, and the first element of health is cleanliness. Keep clean—wash freely, bathe regularly. All the skin wants is leave to act, and it takes care of itself.

In the matter of baths, it is not strongly advocated she plunge into ice-water; it takes a woman with clear grit and a strong constitution to endure it. If a hot bath be used, let it come before retiring, as there is less danger of taking cold afterwards; and, besides, the body is weakened by the ablution and needs immediate rest. It is well to use a flesh-brush, and afterwards rinse off the soap suds by briskly rubbing the body with a pair of coarse toilet gloves.

The most important part of the bath is the drying. Every part of the body should be rubbed to a glowing redness, using a coarse crash towel at the finish. If sufficient friction cannot be given, a small amount of bay rum applied with the palm of the hand will be found efficacious.

Value of a sun bath
A sun bath is of more worth than much warming by the fire.

Ladies who have ample leisure and who lead methodical lives, take a plunge or sponge bath three times a week, and a vapor or sun bath every day. To facilitate this very beneficial practice, a south or east apartment is desirable. The lady denudes herself, takes a seat near the window, and takes in the warm rays of the sun. The effect is both beneficial and delightful.

If, however, she be of a restless disposition, she may dance, instead of basking, in the sunlight. Or, if she be not fond of dancing, she may improve the shining hours by taking down her hair and brushing it, using sulphur water, pulverized borax dissolved in alcohol, or some similar dressing. It would be surprising to many ladies to see her carefully wiping the separate locks on a clean, white towel until the dust of the previous day is entirely removed. With such care it is not necessary to wash the head, and the hair under this treatment is invariably good.

One of the most useful articles of the toilet is a bottle of ammonia, and any lady who has once learned its value will never be without it. A few drops in the water takes the place of the usual amount of soap, and cleans out the pores of the skin as well as a bleach will do. Wash the face with a flesh-brush, and rub the lips well to tone their color.

It is well to bathe the eyes before putting in the spirits, and if it is desirable to increase their brightness, this may be done by dashing soapsuds into them. Always rub the eyes, in washing, toward the nose. If the eyebrows are inclined to spread irregularly, pinch the hairs together where thickest. If they show a tendency to meet, this contact may be avoided by pulling out the hairs every morning before the toilet.

The dash of Orientalism in costume and lace now turns a lady's attention to her eyelashes, which are worthless if not long and drooping. Indeed, so prevalent is the desire for this beautiful feature that hair-dressers and ladies' artists have scores of customers under treatment for invigorating their stunted eyelashes and eyebrows.

To obtain these fringed curtains, anoint the roots with a balsam made of two drachms of nitric oxide of mercury mixed with one of leaf lard. After an application, wash the roots with a camel's hair brush dipped in warm milk. Tiny scissors are used, with which the lashes are carefully but slightly trimmed every other day. When obtained, refrain from rubbing or even touching the lids with the fingernails. There is more beauty in a pair of well-kept eyebrows and full, sweeping eyelashes than people are aware of, and a very unattractive and lusterless eye assumes new beauty when it looks out from beneath elongated fringes.

Many ladies have a habit of rubbing the corners of their eyes to remove the dust that will frequently accumulate there. Unless this operation is done with little friction it will be found that the growth of hair is very spare, and in that case it will become necessary to pencil the barren corners.

Instead of putting cologne water on the handkerchief, which has come to be considered a vulgarism among ladies of correct tastes, the perfume is spent on the eyebrows and lobes of the ears.

If commenced in youth, thick lips may be reduced by compression, and thin linear ones are easily modified by suction. This draws the blood to the surface, and produces at first a temporary and, later, a permanent inflation. It is a mistaken belief that biting the lips reddens them. The skin of the lips is very thin, rendering them extremely susceptible to organic derangement, and if the atmosphere does not cause chaps or parchment, the result of such harsh treatment will develop into swelling or the formation of scars. Above all things, keep a sweet breath.

Everybody can not have beautiful hands, but there is no plausible reason for their being ill kept. Red hands may be overcome by soaking the feet in hot water as often as possible. If the skin is hard and dry, use tar or oatmeal soap, saturate them with glycerine, and wear gloves in bed. Never bathe them in hot water, and wash them no oftener than is necessary. There are dozens of women with soft, white hands who do not put them in water once a month. Rubber gloves are worn in making the toilet, and they are cared for by an ointment of glycerine and rubbed dry with chamois-skin or cotton flannel.

HOW TO SOFTEN HANDS
After cleansing the hands with soap, rub them well with oatmeal while wet.

HOW TO REMOVE TAR FROM HANDS
Rub the hands with the outside of fresh orange or lemon peel and dry immediately. The volatile oils dissolve the tar so that it can be rubbed off.

HOW TO REMOVE STAINS FROM HANDS
Damp the hands first in water, then rub them with tartaric acid, or salt of lemons, as you would with soap; rinse them and rub dry.

Glycerine
Glycerine does not agree with a dry skin; it softens but does not moisten.

HOW TO WHITEN HANDS
1. Stir one-fourth pound of Castile soap, and place it in jars near the fire; pour over it one-half pint of alcohol; when the soap is dissolved and mixed with the spirit, add one ounce of glycerine, in the same amount of oil of almonds, with a few drops of essence of violets, or attar of roses; then pour into molds to cool for use.

2. A wineglass of eau-de-cologne, and one of lemon juice, two cakes of broken Windsor soap, mixed well together, when hard, will form an excellent substance.

SHEEP SHEARERS' HAND LOTION
Workers who handle wool and shear sheep are envied by many ladies for their wonderfully soft

hands. Their secret lies in the oil, lanolin, which is found in abundance in the wool of the sheep. Soak gum of tragacanth, one tablespoonful, in one pint of warm water, keeping it closed tight and warm for 24 hours, shaking frequently to hasten dissolution. When all is dissolved, add a quart of warm water, close tight, and soak 24 hours longer, with frequent shaking. Add bay rum, four ounces, and glycerine, four ounces; a little rosewater or perfume may be added to ones desire. Bottle and keep in a cool dry place.

GLYCERINE LOTION

For softening the skin of the face and hands, especially during the commencement of cold weather, and also for allaying the irritation caused by the razor: Titurate, four and a half grains of cochineal with one and a half fluid ounces of boiling water, adding gradually; then add two and a half fluid ounces of alcohol. Also make an emulsion of eight drops of attar of roses with thirty grains of gum arabic and eight fluid ounces of water; then add three fluid ounces of glycerine, and ten fluid drachms of quince mucilage. Mix the two liquids.

HOW TO TAKE CARE OF THE NAILS

The nails should be kept clean by the daily use of the nail brush and soap and water. After wiping the

hands, but while they are still soft from the action of the water, gently push back the skin which is apt to grow over the nails, which will not only preserve them neatly rounded, but will prevent the skin from cracking around their roots (nail springs), and becoming sore. The points of the nails should be pared at least once a week; biting them should be avoided.

FINGERNAILS AS AN INDICATION OF CHARACTER

A white mark on the nail bespeaks misfortune.

Pale or lead-colored nails indicate melancholy people.

Broad nails indicate a gentle, timid, and bashful nature.

Lovers of knowledge and liberal sentiments have round nails.

People with narrow nails are ambitious and quarrelsome.

Small nails indicate littleness of mind, obstinacy and conceit.

Choleric, martial men delighting in war, have red spotted nails.

Nails growing into the flesh at the points or sides indicate luxurious tastes.

People with very pale nails are subject to much infirmity of the flesh and persecution by neighbors and friends.

HOW TO WHITEN NAILS

The best wash for whitening the nails is two drachms of diluted sulphuric acid, one drachm of tincture of myrrh, added to four ounces of spring water; first cleanse the hands, and then apply the wash.

The gentlewoman of means never bathes her hands in hot water, and washes them no oftener than is necessary. The same treatment is not unfrequently applied to the face with the most successful results. If such methods are used, it would be just as well to keep the knowledge of it from the gentlemen. There is one instance of a beautiful young lady who has not washed her face for three years, yet it is always clean, rosy, sweet and kissable. With some of her other secrets she gave it to her lover for safe keeping. Unfortunately, it proved to be her last gift to that gentleman, who declared in a subsequent note that "I can not reconcile my heart and my manhood to a woman who can get along without washing her face."

TO REMOVE TAN

Tan may be removed from the face by mixing magnesia in soft water to the consistency of paste, which should then be spread on the face and allowed to remain a minute or two. Then wash off with Castile soap suds, and rinse with soft water.

TO CLEAR A TANNED SKIN

Wash with a solution of carbonate of soda and a little lemon juice; then with Fuller's earth-water, or the juice of unripe grapes.

HOW TO REMOVE FRECKLES

Freckles, so persistently regular in their annual return, have annoyed the fair sex from time immemorial, and various means have been devised to eradicate them, although thus far with no decidedly satisfactory results. The innumerable remedies in use for the removal of these vexatious intruders, are either simple and harmless washes, such as parsley or horseradish water, solutions of borax, &tc., or injurious nostrums, consisting principally of lead and mercury salts.

If the exact cause of freckles were known, a remedy for them might be found. A chemist in Moravia, observing the bleaching effect of mercurial preparations, inferred that the growth of a local parasitical fungus was the cause of the discoloration of the skin, which extended and ripened its spores in the warmer season.

Knowing that sulpho-carbolate of zinc is a deadly enemy to all parasitic vegetation (itself not being otherwise injurious), he applied this salt for the purpose of removing the freckles. The compound consists of two parts of sulpho-carbolate of zinc, twenty-five parts of distilled glycerine, twenty-five parts of rose-water, and five parts of scented alcohol, and is to be applied twice daily for from half an hour to an hour, then washed off with cold water.

Protection against the sun by veiling and other means is recommended, and in addition, for persons of pale complexion, some mild preparation of iron.

HOW TO MAKE A CLEANSING POULTICE FOR THE FACE

An excellent poultice to draw out disorders and cleanse the pores of the face skin may be made from clay-earth mixed with soft spring water to the consistence of paste, which is spread over the face, at leisure, and left two hours; then rinse with cold water.

COMPLEXION WASH

Put in a vial one drachm of benzoin gum in powder, one drachm

nutmeg oil, six drops of orange-blossom tea, or apple-blossoms put in a half pint of rain water and boiled down to one teaspoonful

and strained, one pint of sherry wine. Bathe the face morning and night; will remove all flesh worms and freckles and give a beautiful complexion. Or, put one ounce of powdered gum of benzoin in a pint of whisky; to use, put in water in wash-bowl till it is milky, allowing it to dry without wiping. This is perfectly harmless.

PEARL WATER FOR THE FACE

Put half a pound best Windsor soap scraped fine into half a gallon of boiling water; stir it well until it cools, add a pint of spirits of wine and half an ounce of oil of rosemary; stir well. This is a good cosmetique, and will remove freckles.

WASH FOR A BLOTCHED FACE

Rose water, three ounces; sulphate of zinc, one drachm; mix. Wet the face with it, gently dry it and then touch it over with cold cream, which also gently dry off.

WRINKLES IN THE SKIN

White wax, one ounce; strained honey, two ounces; juice of lily bulbs, two ounces. The foregoing

melted and stirred together will remove wrinkles.

FACE POWDER

Take of wheat starch, one pound; powdered orris-root, three ounces; oil of lemon, thirty drops; oil of bergamot and oil of cloves, each fifteen drops. Rub together thoroughly.

HOW TO SOFTEN & CLEAN THE FACE WITHOUT SOAP

Wet the face with warm water, and steep the pores in it for a few minutes, then gently rub yellow corn-meal onto the face with the fingers or a flesh-brush until the skin is flushed by the friction thereof; rinse with cold water and lightly rub dry.

FLESHWORMS

These specks, when they exist in any number, are a cause of much unsightliness. They are minute corks, if such a term may be used, of coagulated lymph, which closes the orifices of some of the pores or exhalent vessels of the skin. On the skin immediately adjacent to them being pressed with the finger nails, these bits of coagulated lymph will come from it in vermicular form. They are vulgarly called "flesh-worms," many persons fancying them to be living creatures. These may be got rid of and prevented from returning, by washing with tepid water, by proper friction with a towel, and by the application of a little cold cream. The longer these little piles are permitted to remain in the skin the more firmly they become fixed; and after a time, when they lose their moisture they are converted into long bony spines as dense as bristles, and having much of that character. They are known by the name of spotted achne.

With regard to local treatment, the following lotions are calculated to be serviceable:

1. Distilled rose-water, one pint; sulphate of zinc, 20 to 60 grains.

2. Sulphate of copper, twenty grains, rose-water, four ounces; water, twelve ounces. Mix and apply to skin.

3. Oil of sweet almonds, one ounce; fluid potash, one drachm; shake well together and then add rose-water, one ounce, pure water, six ounces. Mix.

The mode of using these remedies is to rub the pimples for some minutes with a rough towel, and then dab them with the lotion.

4. Wash the face twice a day with warm water, and rub dry with a coarse towel. Then with a soft towel rub in a lotion made of two ounces of white brandy, one ounce of cologne, and one-half ounce of liquor potassa.

CARE OF THE TEETH

The mouth has a temperature of 98°, warmer than is ever experienced in the shade in the latitude of New England. It is well known that if beef, for example, be exposed in the shade during the warmest of our summer days, it will very soon decompose. If we eat beef for dinner, the particles invariably find their way into the spaces between the teeth. Now, if these particles of beef are not removed, they will frequently remain till they are softened by decomposition. In most mouths this process of decomposition is in constant progress. Ought we to be surprised that the gums and teeth against which these decomposing or putrefying masses lie should be subjects of disease?

How shall our teeth be preserved? The answer is very simple —keep them clean. How shall they be kept clean? Answer—by a toothpick, rinsing with water, and the daily use of a brush.

The toothpick should be a quill, not because the metalic picks injure the enamel, but because the quill pick is so flexible it fits into all the irregularities between the teeth.

Always after using the toothpick the mouth should be thoroughly rinsed. If warm water be not at hand, cold may be used, although warm is much better. Closing the lips, and with a motion familiar to all, everything may be thoroughly rinsed from the mouth.

Every morning, on rising, and every evening, on going to bed, the toothbrush should be used, and the teeth, both inside and outside, thoroughly brushed.

Much has been said *pro* and *con,* upon the use of soap with the toothbrush. Highly favored for both morning and evening is the use of soap by most intelligent people. Castile or other good soap will answer this purpose. (Whatever is good for the hands and face is good for the teeth.) The slightly unpleasant taste which soap has when we begin to use it will soon be unnoticed.

WASH FOR TEETH & GUMS

The teeth should be washed both night and morning, a moderately small and soft brush being used; after the morning ablution, pour on a second toothbrush, slightly dampened, a little of the following lotion: carbolic acid, twenty drops; spirits of wine, two drachms; distilled water, six ounces. After using this lotion a short time the gums become firmer and less tender, and impurity of the breath (which is most commonly caused by bad teeth) , will be removed. It is a great mistake to use hard toothbrushes, or to brush the teeth until the gums bleed.

TOOTH POWDERS

Many persons, while laudably devoted to the preservation of their teeth, do them harm by too much officiousness. They daily apply to them some dentifrice powder, which they rub so hard as not only to injure the enamel by excessive friction, but to hurt the gums even more than by the abuse of the toothpick.

The quality of some of the dentifrice powders advertised in the newspapers is extremely suspicious, and there is reason to think that they are not altogether free from a corrosive ingredient. One of the safest and best compositions for the purpose is a mixture of two parts of prepared chalk, one of Peruvian bark, and one of hard soap, all finely powdered, which is calculated not only to clean the teeth without hurting them, but to preserve the firmness of the gums.

Besides the advantage of sound teeth for their use in mastication, a proper attention to their treatment conduces not a little to the sweetness of the breath. This is, indeed, often affected by other causes existing in the lungs, the stomach, and sometimes even in the bowels, but a rotten state of the teeth, both from the putrid smell emitted by carious bones and the impurities lodged in their cavities, never fails of aggravating an unpleasant breath wherever there is a tendency of that kind.

PEARL DENTIFRICE

Prepared chalk, one-half pound; powdered myrrh, two ounces; camphor, two drachms; orris-root powdered, two ounces. Moisten the camphor with alcohol and mix all together.

WASH FOR THE HAIR

Castile soap, finely shaved, one teaspoonful; spirits of hartshorn, one drachm; alcohol, five ounces, cologne water, and bay rum, in equal quantities enough to make eight ounces. This should be poured on the head, followed by warm water (soft water) ; the result will be, on washing, a copious lather and a smarting sensation to the person operated on. Rub this well into the hair. Finally, rinse with warm water, and afterwards with cold water. If the head is very much clogged with dirt, the hair will come out plentifully but the scalp will become white and perfectly clean.

HOW TO CLEAN THE HAIR

From the too frequent use of oils in the hair, many ladies destroy the tone and color of their tresses. The Hindoos have a way of remedying this. They take a hand basin filled with cold water, and have ready a small quantity of pea flour. The hair is in the first place submitted to the operation of being washed in cold water, a handful of the pea flour is then applied to the head and rubbed into the hair for ten minutes at least, the servant adding fresh water at short intervals, until it becomes a perfect lather. The whole head is then washed quite clean with copious supplies of the aqueous fluid, combed, and afterwards rubbed dry by means of coarse towels. The hard and soft brush is then resorted to, when the hair will be found to be wholly free from all encumbering oils and other impurities, and assumes a glossy softness, equal to the most delicate silk. This process tends to preserve the tone and natural color

of the hair, which is so frequently destroyed by the too constant use of caustic cosmetiques.

OIL TO MAKE THE HAIR CURL

Olive oil, one pound; oil of organum, one drachm; oil of rosemary, one and one-half drachms.

BANDOLINE

To one quart of rose water add an ounce and a half of gum tragacanth; let it stand forty-eight hours, frequently straining it, then strain through a coarse linen cloth; let it stand two days, and again strain; add to it a drachm of oil of roses; used by ladies dressing their hair, to make it lie in any position.

CURE FOR DANDRUFF

1. Good mild soap is one of the safest remedies, and is sufficient in ordinary cases; carbonate of potash or soda is too alkaline for the skin. Every application removes a portion of the cuticle, as you may observe by smoothness of the skin of your hands after washing them with it.

2. Borax is recommended; but this is also soda combined with a weak acid, boracic acid, and may by protracted use also injuriously act on the scalp. Soap is also soda or potash combined with the weak, fatty acids; and when the soap contains an excess of the alkalies or is sharp, it is as injurious as the carbonate of potash. All that injures the scalp injures the growth of the hair.

3. One of the best applications from the vegetable kingdom is the mucilaginous decoction of the root of the burdock, called *bardane* in French.

4. In the mineral kingdom, the best remedy is a solution of the flowers of sulphur in water, which may be made by the addition of a very small portion of sulphide of potassium, say ten or twenty grains to the pint. This solution is shaken up with the sulphur, and the clear liquid remaining on the top is used. This receipt is founded on the fact that sulphur is a poison for inferior vegetable or animal growth, like dandruff, itch, &tc., and is not at all a poison for the superior animal like man.

A GOOD RECIPE TO PREVENT HAIR COMING OUT

Scald black tea, two ounces, to one gallon of boiling water; strain and add three ounces glycerine, tincture of cantharides one-half ounce, bay rum one quart. Mix well and perfume. This is a good preparation for frequent use in its effect both on the scalp and hair, but neither will be kept in good condition without care and attention to general health.

PREPARATION FOR THE CURE OF BALDNESS

Rum, one pint; alcohol, one ounce; distilled water, one ounce; tincture of cantharides, a half drachm; carbonate of potash, a half drachm; carbonate of ammonia, one drachm. Mix the liquids after having dissolved the salts, and filter. After the skin of the head has been wetted with this preparation, it should be washed with water.

HAIR RESTORATIVE

Take castor oil, six fluid ounces; alcohol, 26 fluid ounces. Dissolve. Then add tincture of cantharides (made with strong alcohol), one fluid ounce; essence of jessamine (or other perfumes), one and a half fluid ounces.

Part Three

—•—

CARE
OF THE
HOUSE & FARM

Chapter 21

Absolutely indispensable information &

HOUSEHOLD HINTS

of their volume (more or less) of mud, so that if 36 cubic miles of water (the estimated quantity) flow daily into the sea, 0.36 cubic miles of soil are daily displaced.

WATER

Water is the absolute master, former and secondary agent of the power of motion in everything terrestrial. It is the irresistible power which elaborates everything, and the waters contain more organized beings than the land.

Rivers hold in suspension 100th

River water contains about 30 grs. of solid matter in every cubic foot. Fresh water springs of great size abound under the sea. Perhaps the most remarkable springs exist in California, where they are noted for producing sulphuric acid, ink, and other remarkable products.

The top surface of ice on a pond, the amount of water let in and out being the same day by day, is not

necessarily on a level with the water surface. Ice is slightly elastic, and when fast to the shore the central portion rises and falls with slight variations in water level, the proportion above and below water level being as is the weight of ice to the weight of water it displaces.

Hard and soft water do not freeze at the same rate. Soft water freezes quicker and keeps better, for packing, than hard water.

In freezing, water purifies itself by clearing itself from chemicals, but does not clear itself from any mechanical mixtures such as mud and clay.

TO PURIFY WATER

To purify water in glass vessels and aquariums, it is recommended to add to every 100 grams of water four drops of a solution consisting of one gram of salicylic acid in 300 grams of water. In this manner, water may be kept fresh for three months without being renewed.

TEST FOR HARD OR SOFT WATER

Dissolve a small quantity of good soap in alcohol. Let a few drops fall into a glass of water. It it turns milky, it be hard; if not, it be soft.

TEST FOR EARTHY MATTERS OR ALKALI IN WATER

Take litmus paper dipped in vinegar, and if on immersion, the paper returns to its true shade, the water does not contain earthy matter or alkali. If a few drops of syrup be added to a water containing an earthy matter, it will turn green.

TEST FOR CARBONIC ACID IN WATER

Take equal parts of water and clear lime water. If combined or free carbonic acid be present, a precipitate is seen, to which, if a few drops of muriatic acid be added, an effervescence commences.

TEST FOR MAGNESIA IN WATER

Boil the water to a twentieth part of its weight, and then drop a few grains of neutral carbonate of ammonia into a glass of it, and a few drops of phosphate of soda. If magnesia be present, it will fall to the bottom.

TESTS FOR IRON IN WATER

1. Boil a little nutgall and add to the water. If it turns gray or slate color, black iron is present.

2. Dissolve a little prussiate of potash, and, if iron is present, it will turn blue.

TEST FOR LIME IN WATER

Into a glass of water put two drops of oxalic acid and blow upon it. If it gets milky, lime is present.

TEST FOR ACID IN WATER

Take a piece of litmus paper and place in the water. If it turns red, the water contains acid. If it precipitates on adding lime water, it is carbonic acid. If a blue sugar paper is turned red, it is a mineral acid.

HOW TO KEEP RAIN-WATER SWEET

The best way to keep rain-water sweet in a cistern, is first to collect it in a tank, and filter it into the cistern below the ground surface. This will remove the organic matters, and prevent fermentation. Care should also be taken to prevent surface drainage into it.

THE EXPANSIVE POWER OF WATER

It is a well known, but not less remarkable, fact that if the tip of an exceedingly small tube be dipped into water, the water will rise spontaneously in the tube throughout its whole length. This may be shown in a variety of ways; for instance, when a piece of sponge, or sugar, or cotton is just allowed to touch water, these substances being all composed of numberless little

tubes, draw up the water, and the whole of the piece becomes wet. It is said to *suck up* or *imbibe* the moisture. We see the same wonderful action going on in nature in the rising of the sap through the small tubes or pores of the wood, whereby the leaves and upper portions of the plant derive nourishment from the ground.

This strange action is called "capillary," from the resemblance the minute tubes bear to a hair, the Latin for which is *capillus*. It is, moreover, singular that the absorption of the water takes place with great force. If a dry sponge be enclosed tightly in a vessel, it will expand when wetted, with sufficient force to burst it, unless very strong.

HOW TO PROTECT THE EMBANKMENTS AROUND FARMYARD PONDS

Farmers often have trouble with the loose soil of newly-made embankments, around freshly dug farmlot watering ponds for livestock, so apt to slip or be washed away before they can be covered with vegetation. The best way to prevent this is to sow the banks with the double poppy. Several months elapse before grasses and clover develop their feeble roots, but the double poppy germinates in a few days, and in a fortnight has grown sufficiently to afford some protection to the slopes. While at the end of three or four months the roots, which are ten or twelve inches in length, are found to have interlaced so as to retain the earth far more firmly than those of any grass or grain. Although the double poppy is an annual, it sows itself after the first year.

HOW TO PREPARE SOAPS & WASHING PREPARATIONS

HOW TO CLARIFY TALLOW

Dissolve one pound of alum in one quart of water, add to this 100 lbs of tallow in a jacket kettle (a kettle set in a larger one, and the intervening space filled with water; this prevents burning the tallow). Boil three-quarters of an hour and skim. Then add one pound of salt dissolved in a quart of water. Boil and skim. When well clarified, the tallow should be nearly the color of water.

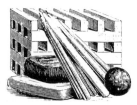

HOW TO HARDEN TALLOW

The following receipt is used with success: To one pound of tallow take one-fourth pound of common rosin; melt them together, and mold them the usual way. This will give a candle of superior lighting power, and as hard as a wax candle; a vast improvement upon the common tallow candle in all respects except color.

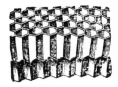

HOW BEESWAX IS REFINED & MADE NICE & YELLOW

Pure white wax is obtained from the ordinary beeswax by exposure to the influence of the sun and weather. The wax is sliced into thin flakes and laid on sacking or coarse cloth, stretched on frames, resting on posts to raise them from the ground. The wax is turned over frequently and occasionally sprinkled with soft water if there be not dew and rain sufficient to moisten.

If, on breaking the flakes, the wax still appears yellow inside, it is necessary to melt it again and flake and expose it a second time, or even oftener, before it becomes thoroughly bleached, the time required being mainly dependent upon the weather.

HOW TO MAKE HARD SOAP

After the raw soda, or barilla is ground or pounded, it is placed in a vat in alternate layers with unslacked lime, the bottom layer being lime. Water is allowed to infiltrate through those layers, and lye is secured as it trickles through a hole in the bottom of the vat. The lime absorbs the carbonic acid of the soda, making the lye caustic or fit for the soap kettle; and the quantity of lime applied must be in proportion to the quantity of carbonic acid in the soda. To every twenty pounds of tallow add one gallon of weak lye, and boil until the lye is spent. The mass must be

then cooled for one hour, the spent lye drawn off, and another gallon of strong lye be added; the mixture again boiled until the second dose of lye is spent, and the same process must be repeated for several days, until the mixture, if properly managed, is converted into white tallow soap, which should be allowed to cool gradually and settle, when it is poured into molds, and when solid it is cut into the bars which are found in our markets. Twenty pounds of tallow ought to make thirty pounds of first-quality hard soap, allowing three pounds of soda-ash for every twenty pounds of tallow. The balance of the weight is made up by the large quantity of water which enters into combination with the grease and alkali in the course of saponification.

When yellow, or resin, soap is required, the hard soap has to be made in the usual manner, and at the last charge of lye, or when the soapy mass ceases to absorb any more lye, one-third the weight of pounded resin is introduced, the mixture constantly stirred, and the boil kept up vigorously until the resin has become incorporated with the soap. The whole must stand until it settles, and the soap then dipped out. Resin soap, when well made, should be of fine bright color.

HOW TO MAKE SOFT SOAP

The principle difference between hard and soft soap is, that three parts of fat afford, in general, fully five parts hard soda-soap; but three parts of fat or oil will afford six or seven parts of potash-soap of a moderate consistence. From its cheapness, strength, and superior solubility, potash soap is preferred for many purposes, particularly for the scouring of woolens.

The lyes prepared for making soft soaps should be made very strong, and of two densities, as the process of making potash or soft soap differs materially from that of making soda or hard soap. A portion of the fat or oil being placed in the boiling pan, and heated to near the boling point of water, a certain portion of the weaker lye is introduced, and the fire kept up so as to bring the mixture to the boiling point; then some more oil and lye are introduced alternately, until the pan is filled. The boiling is continued gently, strong lye being added until the saponification is complete. The fire should then be removed, and some good soap, previously made, added while cooling down, to prevent any change by evaporation. One pound of oil requires about one-third of a pound of American potash, and will make one and three-quarters to two pounds of well-boiled soap, containing about 40 percent of water. Sixty pounds of lard will make 100 pounds of first-class soft soap, by using one and a half cans of concentrated lye, which is made from salt, and is really a soda-lye.

WASHING PREPARATION

Take a quarter of a pound of soap, and a quarter of a pound of soda, and a quarter of a pound of quicklime. Cut up the soap and dissolve it in one quart of boiling water; pour one quart of boiling water over the soda, and three quarts of boiling water upon the quicklime.

The lime must be quick and fresh; if it is good it will bubble up on pouring the hot water upon it. Each must be prepared in separate vessels, the lime must settle so as to leave the water on top perfectly clear; then strain it carefully (not disturbing the settlings) into the washboiler with the soda and soap; let it scald long enough to dissolve the soap, then add six gallons of soap water. The clothes must be put to soak over night, after rubbing soap upon the dirtiest parts of them. After having the above in readiness, wring out the clothes which have been put to soak, put them on to boil, and let each lot boil half an hour; the same water will answer for the whole washing. After boiling each lot half an hour drain them from the boiling water, put them in a tub and pour upon them two or three pailfuls of clear, hot water; after this they will want very little rubbing, then rinse through two waters, blueing the last. When dried they will be a beautiful white. After washing the cleanest part of the white clothes, take two pails of the suds in which they have been washed, put it over the fire and scald, and this will wash all the flannels and colored clothes without any extra soap. The white flannels, after being well washed in the suds, will require to be scalded by turning on a tea-kettle of boiling water.

RECEIPT TO MAKE GOOD SHAVING SOAP

Either 66 pounds of tallow or 34 pounds of cocoanut oil, or 33 pounds of tallow and the same quantity of palm oil and 34 pounds of cocoanut oil, treated by the cold process, with 120 pounds caustic soda lye of 27° Baumé, will make 214 pounds of shaving soap.

SOAPINE & PEARLINE

These compounds consist of partly effloresced sal soda mixed with half its weight of soda ash. Some makers add a little yellow soap, coarsely powdered, to disguise the appearance, and others a little carbonate of ammonia or borax.

HOW TO MAKE STARCH ENAMEL FOR STIFFENING COLLARS, CUFFS, &tc.

Use a little gum arabic thoroughly dissolved in the starch.

HANGING OUT CLOTHES IN WINDS

When there is want to place clothes, hung on their hangers, out of doors for drying during high windy days, a piece of loggers' chain, tied on each end to the clothesline poles, will keep the hangers from sliding together or falling to the ground. The hooks of the hangers may be inserted into the chain loops which secure them thoroughly.

HOW TO HANDLE CLOTH

HOW TO KEEP RABBIT'S-WOOL CLOTH FROM SHEDDING

Cloth made from carded wool of the long-haired Angora rabbit may be kept from dropping this hair by the application of extreme cold. Garments made of this cloth, such as sweaters, jackets, and the like, should be rolled tight, placed inside an earthen jar or other vessel of suitable size; then put into the

icebox or icechest for three or four hours. This process is said to prevent for all times the shedding of the cloth.

HOW TO CLEANSE FEATHER BEDS

When feather beds become soiled and heavy they may be made clean and light by being treated in the following manner: Rub them over with a stiff brush, dipped in hot soap-suds. When clean lay them on a shed, or any other clean place where the rain will fall on them. When thoroughly soaked let them dry in a hot sun for six or seven successive days, shaking them up well and turning them over each day. They should be covered over with a thick cloth during the night;

if exposed to the night air they will become damp and mildew. This way of washing the bed-ticking and feathers makes them very fresh and light, and is much easier than the old-fashioned way of emptying the beds and washing the feathers separately, while it answers quite as well. Care must be taken to dry the bed perfectly before sleeping on it. Hair mattresses that have become hard and dirty can be made nearly as good as new by ripping them, washing the ticking, and picking the hair free from bunches and keeping it in a dry, airy place several days. Whenever the ticking gets dry, fill it lightly with the hair, and tack it together.

HOW TO CLEAN BED-TICKS

Apply Poland starch, by rubbing it on thick with a cloth. Place it in the sun. When dry, rub it if necessary. The soiled part will be clean as new.

HOW TO KEEP BLANKETS SOFT

A little ammonia and borax in the water, when washing blankets, keeps them soft and prevents shrinking.

Another Way—If quilts are folded or rolled tightly after washing, then beaten with the rolling-pin or potato masher, it lightens up the cotton and makes them seem soft and new.

To bleach white clothes, hang them dripping in the sun, rewetting several times before drying. They bleach more and faster than when dried from a damp wet.

CARPETS

HOW TO WASH CARPETS

Shake and beat it well; lay it upon the floor and tack it firmly; then with a clean flannel wash it over with a quart of bullock's gall mixed with three quarts of soft, cold water. Any particular dirty spot should be rubbed with pure gall.

HOW TO CLEAN CARPETS

Before proceeding to sweep a carpet a few handfuls of waste tea-leaves should be sprinkled over it. A stiff hair broom or brush should be employed, unless the carpet is

very dirty, when a whisk or carpet-broom should be used first, followed by another made of hair, to take off the loose dust. The frequent use of a stiff carpet-broom soon wears off the beauty of the best carpet. An ordinary clothes brush is best adapted for superior carpets. When carpets are very dirty, they should be cleaned by shaking and beating.

Beat it with a stick in the usual manner until all the dust is removed, then take out the stains, if any, with lemon or sorrel juice. When thoroughly dry, rub it all over with the crumb of a hot wheaten loaf, and if the weather is very fine, let hang out in the open air for a night or two. This treatment will revive the colors and make the carpet appear equal to new.

HOW TO CLEAN CARPETS ON THE FLOOR TO MAKE THEM LOOK BRIGHT

To a pailful of water add three pints of oxgall; wash the carpet with this until a lather is produced, which is then washed off with clean spring water.

HOW TO REMOVE SPOTS ON CARPETS

A few drops of carbonate of ammonia, and a small quantity of warm rain water, will prove a safe and easy antacid, &tc., and will change, if carefully applied, discolored spots upon carpets, and indeed, all spots, whether produced by acids or alkalies. If one has the misfortune to have a carpet injured by whitewash, this will immediately restore it.

HOW TO REMOVE INK SPOTS FROM CARPETS

As soon as the ink has been spilled, take up as much as you can with a sponge, and then pour on cold water repeatedly, still taking up the liquid; next rub the place with a little wet oxalic acid or salt of sorrel, and wash it off immediately with cold water, and then rub on some hartshorn.

STAIN REMOVERS & CLEANSERS

RECEIPT FOR MAKING INSTANTANEOUS INK & STAIN EXTRACTOR

Take of chloride of lime, one pound, thoroughly pulverized, and four quarts of soft water. The foregoing must be thoroughly mixed and shaken when first put together. It is required to stand 24 hours to

dissolve the chloride of lime; then strain through a cotton cloth, after which add a teaspoonful of acetic acid to every ounce of the chloride of lime water.

HOW TO REMOVE STAIN FROM CLOTH

Tartaric acid, or salt of lemons, will quickly remove stains from white muslin or linen. Put less than half a teaspoonful of salt or acid into a tablespoonful of water; wet the stain with it, and lay it in the sun for an hour; wet it once or twice with cold water during the time; if this does not quite remove it, repeat the acid water, and lay it in the sun.

HOW TO REMOVE WAX FROM ARTICLES

When possible place the article in a large flat pan, then pour over it sufficient cider vinegar to cover. Let stand one hour, then rub as hard as possible with a soft flannel until all the wax is softened and dissolved in the vinegar; then throw out the vinegar.

HOW TO REMOVE WINE FROM ARTICLES

Salt is the best ingredient to be found in the kitchen to remove wine, or the like, from tablecloths or carpets upon which spilled. Pour on the discolored spot of wine, enough salt to thoroughly cover and imbibe all the liquor, then repeat if necessary, after brushing off all the salt first saturated. In this manner the cloth or carpet will be restored to its new condition.

HOW TO REMOVE PAINT SPOTS FROM WOOD

To take spots of paint off wood, lay a thick coating of lime and soda mixed together over it, letting it stand 24 hours; then wash off with warm water, and the spot will be gone.

HOW TO TAKE VARNISH SPOTS OUT OF CLOTH

Use chloroform or benzine, and as the last resource, spirits of turpentine, followed after drying by benzine.

RECEIPT FOR ONE OF THE VERY BEST SCOURING PASTES

Oxalic acid, one part; iron peroxide, fifteen parts; powdered rottenstone, twenty parts; palm oil, sixty parts; petrolatum, four parts. Pulverize the oxalic acid, and add rouge and rottenstone, mixing thoroughly and sifting to remove all grit; then add gradually the palm oil and petrolatum, incorporating thoroughly. Add oil of myrbane or oil of lavender to suit. By substituting your red ashes made from stove coal for the abrasives, an inferior representative of the foregoing paste will be produced.

A "PASTE" METAL POLISH FOR CLEANING & POLISHING BRASS

Oxalic acid, one part; iron peroxide, fifteen parts; palm oil twenty parts; petrolatum, six parts; powdered rottenstone thirty parts. See that the solids are thoroughly pulverized and sifted, then add and thoroughly mix oil and petrolatum.

TO REMOVE SPOTS ON BRASS

Sulphuric acid will remove spots from brass that will not yield to oxalic acid. It may be applied with a brush, but great care must be taken that no drop of the acid shall come in contact with the clothes or skin, as it is ruinous to garments and cuticle. Bath brick or rottenstone may be used for polishing.

HOW TO CLEAN THE BUILDINGS & PERSONAL ITEMS

HOW TO CLEAN YOUR CELLAR

When you give your cellar its spring cleaning, add a little copperas water and salt to the whitewash.

HOW TO CLEAN THE FIREPLACE

To remove the soot and grit which sticks to the inside of the chimney corner, throw several large handfuls, or more, of common bay salt into the fire, at your pleasure. This will render the hearth nearly free of soot and make the fire burn more brightly.

HOW TO CLEAN BRICKS TO USE AGAIN

Take of oil of olive, benzine, and cider vinegar, equal parts; brush or pour it onto the surface of the bricks; but do not ever apply an excess as to cover the mortar between. Let dry, when the bricks will appear like new.

HOW TO CLEAN WALLPAPER

Make of equal parts of cornstarch and soft water a smooth paste; rub it on the spots; when it is dry, brush it off with a stiff brush. You will never see where the spots were.

A RECEIPT FOR MAKING GOOD SHOE DRESSING

Take of gum shellac, one-half pound; alcohol, three quarts; dissolve, and add camphor, one and a half ounces; and of lampblack, two

ounces. The foregoing will be found to give an excellent gloss, and is especially adapted to any leather, the surface of which is roughened by wear.

HOW TO DRY LEATHER SOFT

Fill the dampened shoes or boots with sufficient paper to fill them out to shape; then apply saddle soap and rub thoroughly into the pores of the leather till it will hold no more. Put them in a cool dry place to dry for 24 hours or more, when you will find the leather very soft and supple.

HOW TO KEEP SPECTACLES FROM STEAMING UP
Rub over both sides of the spectacle lenses a thin film of soft soap, then polish it very clear, this will prevent the lenses, cold from the winter air, from clouding up in the warm house.

HOW TO BRIGHTEN WAXED FRUITS
A few drops of good corn whisky, placed on a cotton flannel, and rubbed briskly over ornamental waxed fruits will clean them like new and leave on a fine shine.

HOW TO OXIDIZE SILVER
For this purpose a pint of sulphide of potassium, made by intimately mixing and heating together two parts of thoroughly dried potash and one part of sulphur powder, is used. Dissolve two or three drachms of this compound in one and three-fourths pints of water, and bring the liquid to a temperature of 155° to 175° F., when it is ready for use. Silver objects, previously freed from dust and grease with soda lye and thorough rinsing in water, plunged into this bath are instantly covered with an iridescent film of silver sulphide, which in a few seconds more becomes blue black. The objects are then removed, rinsed off in plenty of fresh water, scratch brushed, and if necessary polished.

PAPER FIXATIVES, GLASS POLISH, FIRE GRENADES, & FRICTION MATCHES

HOW TO TOUGHEN PAPER
A recipe for rendering paper as tough as wood or leather consists

of mixing chloride of zinc with the pulp in the course of manufacture. It has been found that the greater the degree of concentration of zinc, the greater will be the toughness of the paper. It can be used for making boxes and for roofing.

HOW TO KEEP & UTILIZE BOOKS

Books exposed to the atmosphere keep in better condition than if confined in a bookcase.

A poor book had best be burned to give place to a better, or even to an empty shelf, for the fire destroys its poisons, and puts it out of the way of doing harm.

Better to economize in the purchasing of furniture or carpets than to scrimp in the buying of good books or papers.

Our sitting rooms need never be empty of guests nor our libraries of society, if the company of good books is admitted to them.

HOW TO FASTEN PENCIL MARKS SO THEY WON'T BLUR

Immerse paper containing the marks to be preserved in a bath of cold water, then flow or immerse in milk a moment; hang up to dry. Those having often had recourse to this method, in preserving pencil and crayon drawings, will warrant it a sure cure.

HOW TO TRANSFER NEWSPAPER PRINTS TO GLASS

First coat the glass with dammar varnish, or else with Canada balsam, mixed with an equal volume of oil of turpentine, and let it dry until it is very sticky, which takes half a day or more. The printed paper to be transferred should be well soaked in soft water, and carefully laid upon the prepared glass, after removing surplus water with blotting paper, and pressed upon it so that no air bubbles or drops of water are seen underneath. This should dry a whole day before it is touched; then with wetted fingers begin to rub off the paper at the back. If this be skillfully done, almost the whole of the paper can be removed, leaving simply the ink upon the varnish. When the paper has been removed, another coat of varnish will serve to make the whole more transparent. This recipe is sold at from $3 to $5 by itinerants.

HOW TO POLISH PLATE GLASS

To polish plate glass and remove slight scratches, rub the surface gently, first with a clean pad of fine cotton wool, and afterwards with a similar pad covered over with cotton velvet, which has been charged with fine rouge. The surface will acquire a polish of great brilliancy, quite free from any scratches.

HOW TO FROST GLASS

Take two ounces of spirits of salts, two ounces of oil of vitriol, one ounce of sulphate of copper, one ounce of gum arabic; mixed together and dabbed on with a brush.

Another Way—Dab your squares regularly over with putty; when dry go over them again. The imitation will be executed.

Another Way—Mix Epsom salts with porter and apply it with a brush.

Another Way—Grind and mix white lead in three-quarters of boiled oil, and one-quarter of spirits of turpentine, and, to give the mixture a very drying quality, add sufficient quantities of burnt white vitriol and sugar of lead. The color must be made exceedingly thin, and put on the panes of glass with a large paint-brush in as even a manner as possible. When a number of panes are thus painted, take a dry duster, quite new, and dab the ends of the bristles on the glass in quick succession til you give it a uniform appearance; repeat this operation till the work appears very soft, and it will then appear like ground glass. When the windows require fresh painting, get the old coat off first by using strong pearlash water.

HOW TO MAKE HAND FIRE GRENADES

Fill ordinary quart wine bottles with a saturated solution of common salt, and place them where they will do the most good in case of need. They will be found nearly as serviceable as the expensive hand grenades you buy. Should a fire break out, throw them with force sufficient to break them into the fire. The salt will form a coating on whatever object the water touches, and make it nearly incombustible, and it will prove effectual in many

cases, where a fire is just starting, when the delay in procuring water might be fatal.

A GOOD & CHEAP PREPARATION TO PUT ON FRICTION MATCHES

The igniting composition varies with different makers. The following recipe may be taken as fairly representative, the first being the best:

1. Phosphorus by weight, one-half part; potassium chlorate, four parts; glue, two parts; whiting, one part; finely powdered glass, four parts; water, eleven parts.

2. Phosphorus by weight, two parts; potassium chlorate, five parts; glue, three parts; red lead, one and one-half parts; water, twelve parts.

3. A German mixture for matches: Potassium chlorate, 7.8 parts; lead hyposulphite, 2.6 parts; gum arabic, one part. Mix well together, then dip match sticks on one end into mixture and let dry.

GLUES, CEMENTS, & PASTES

GLUE FROM FRUIT SAP GUMS

The sap gum balls from the bark of apricot and other fruit trees, when

powdered and dissolved in cider vinegar to the consistence of glue, make an excellent mucilage for household use.

RECIPE FOR GLUE SIZE

A coating of good glue size is made by dissolving half a pound of glue in a gallon of water, then applying it to the wall to be papered.

To keep glue sweet
Put a little carbolic acid in your glue or paste pot. It will keep the contents sweet for a long time.

HOW TO MAKE LIQUID GLUE

Take a wide-mouthed bottle, and dissolve in it eight ounces of best glue in half a pint of water, by setting it in a vessel of water, and heating until dissolved. Then add slowly two and a half ounces of strong nitric acid at 36° Baumé, stirring all the while. Effervescence takes place, with generation of fumes. When all the acid has been added, the liquid is allowed to cool. Keep it well corked, and it will be ready for use at any time.

FLOUR PASTE, FOR ALL PURPOSES

Mix one pound of rye flour in luke-warm water, to which has been added one teaspoonful of pulverized alum; stir until free of lumps. Boil in the regular way, or slowly pour on boiling water, stirring all the time until the paste becomes stiff. When cold, add a full quarter pound of common strained honey, mix well. Observe the precaution to use only regular bee honey, and not a patent mixture.

A LIQUID CEMENT FOR CEMENTING LEATHER,
That Will Not Be Affected by the Action of Water
A good cement for splicing leather is gutta percha dissolved in carbon disulphide, until it is of the thick-

ness of treacle; the parts to be cemented must first be well thinned down, then pour a small quantity of the cement on both ends, spreading it well so as to fill the pores of the leather; warm the parts over a fire for about half a minute, apply

then quickly together, and hammer well. The bottle containing the cement should be tightly corked, and kept in a cool place. This cement is excellent for mending harnesses.

CEMENT TO MEND IRON POTS & PANS

Take two parts of sulphur, and one part, by weight, of fine black lead; put the sulphur in an old iron pan, holding it over the fire until it begins to melt, then add the lead; stir well until all is mixed and melted; then pour out on an iron plate or smooth stone. A sufficient quantity of this compound being placed upon the crack of an iron pot to be mended, can be soldered by a

hot iron in the same way a tinsmith solders his sheets. If there is a small hole in the pot, drive a copper rivet in it, and then solder over it with this cement.

A CEMENT TO STICK WHITE METAL TOPS ON GLASS BOTTLES

One of the best cap cements consists of resin, five ounces; beeswax, one ounce; red ocher or Venetian red in powder, one ounce. Dry the earth thoroughly on a stove at a temperature of 212°F. Melt the wax and resin together, and stir in the powder by degrees. Stir until cold, less the earthy matter settle to the bottom.

A RECEIPT FOR MAKING BLACK CEMENT (used for filling letters cut out in brass)

Mix asphaltum, brown japan, and lampblack into a puttylike mass; fill in the spaces, and finally clean the edges with turpentine.

CELLULOID CEMENT

A good cement for celluloid made from one part shellac dissolved in one part of spirit of camphor and three to four parts of ninety percent alcohol. The cement should be applied warm, and the broken parts securely held together until the solvent has entirely evaporated.

A CEMENT

Recommended as something which can hardly be picked to pieces, it is made as follows: Mix equal parts of lime and brown sugar together with water, and be sure the lime is thoroughly air-slacked. The mortar is equal to Portland cement, and is of extraordinary strength.

A CHEAP CONCRETE

A kind of concrete made without cement is composed of 8 parts of sand, gravel, and pebbles; one part burnt and powdered common earth, one part pulverized clinkers and cinders, and one and a half parts of unslacked hydraulic lime. These materials are thoroughly incorporated while dry into a homogeneous mixture, which is then wetted up and well beaten. The result of this is a hard and solid mass, which sets almost immediately, becoming exceedingly strong after a few days. It may be made still stronger by the addition of a small proportion—say, one part—of cement.

METAL PAINT, WOOD STAINS, & WOOD-RELATED ITEMS

SOAPSTONE PAINT FOR IRON

Both in China and Japan soapstone has long been largely used for protecting structures built of soft stone and other materials specially liable to atmospheric influences. It has been found that powdered

soapstone in the form of paint has preserved obelisks, formed of stone for hundreds of years, which would, unprotected, have long ago crumbled away. Seeing what a preservative quality this material has, it is

specially of interest to shipowners to learn that nothing takes hold of the fibre of iron and steel so easily and firmly as soapstone. For the inside painting of steel and iron ships it is found to be excellent. It has no anti-fouling quality, but is anti-corrosive.

HOW TO STAIN WOOD

The following are receipts for staining wood, which are used in large establishments with great success:

Light Walnut—Dissolve three ounces of permanganate of potash in six pints of water, and paint the wood twice with the solution. After the solution has been left on the wood for from five to ten minutes, the wood is rinsed, dried, oiled, and finally polished.

Light Mahogany—One ounce finely cut alkanet root, two ounces pow-

dered aloe, and two ounces powdered dragon's blood are digested with 26 ounces of strong spirits of wine in a corked bottle, and left in a moderately warm place for four days. The solution is then filtered off, and the clear filtrate is ready for use. The wood which is to be stained is first passed through nitric acid, then dried, painted over with the alcoholic extract, dried, oiled, then polished.

Dark Walnut—Three ounces of permanganate of potash are dissolved in six pints of water, and the wood is painted twice with this solution. After five minutes, the wood is washed and grained with acetate of iron (the ordinary iron liquor of the dyer) at 20°Tw. Dry, oil, and polish as usual.

Gray—One ounce nitrate of silver is dissolved in 45 ounces of water, and the wood painted twice with the solution, afterwards the wood is submitted to the action of hydrochloric acid, and finally washed with ammonia. It is then dried in a dark place, then oiled and polished. This is said to give remarkably good results on beech, pitch pine and poplar.

Black—Seven ounces of logwood are boiled with three pints of water, filtered, and the filtrate mixed with a solution containing one ounce of sulphate of copper (blue copperas). The mixture is left to clear, and the clear liquid is decanted while still hot. The wood is placed in this liquor for 24 hours; it is then

exposed to the air for 24 hours, and afterwards passed through a hot bath of nitrate of iron at 6° Tw. If the black, after this treat-

ment, should not be sufficiently developed, the wood has to be passed again through the first logwood bath.

STAINING & POLISHING MAHOGANY

Your best plan will be to scrape off all the old polish, scrape well with glass paper, then oil with linseed oil both old and new parts; to stain the new pieces, get half an ounce of bichromate of potash, and pour a pint of boiling water over it; when cold bottle it. This, used with care, will stain the new or light parts as dark as you please, if done as follows: Wipe off the oil clean, and apply the solution with a piece

of rag, held firmly in the hand, and just moisten with the stain. Great care is required to prevent the stain running over the old part, for any place touched with it will show the mark through the polish when finished. You can vary the color by giving two or more coats if required. Then repolish your job altogether in the usual way. Should you wish to brighten up the old mahogany, use polish dyed with Bismarck brown as follows: Get three pennysworth of Bismarck brown, and put it into a bottle with enough naphtha or methylated spirits to dissolve it. Pour a few drops of this into your polish, and you will find that it gives a nice rich red color to the work—but don't dye the polish too much, just tint it.

Green walnut husks at harvest when freshly crushed and applied will stain furniture scratches to render them invisible to all but the sharpest eye.

FIREPROOF WHITEWASH

A fireproof whitewash can be readily made by adding one part silicate of soda (or potash) to every five parts of whitewash. The addition of a solution of alum to whitewash is recommended as a means to prevent the rubbing off of the wash.

THE STRENGTH OF WET WOOD

Wood, which is a more unyielding material, acts with tremendous force when wetted, and advantage has been taken of this fact in splitting blocks of granite. After a mass of granite has been rent from a mountain by blasting, it is measured in every direction to see how best to divide it into smaller blocks. These are traced out by straight lines on the surface, and a series of holes are drilled at short intervals along this line. Wedges of dry wood are then tightly driven into the holes and wetted, and the combined action of the swelling wood splits the block in the direction required, and without any destructive violence. The same process is then carried out upon the other faces, and the roughly-shapen block finished with the hammer and chisel.

TO MEASURE INCH BOARDS (BOARD FEET)

Multiply the length of the board in feet by its breadth in inches, and divide the product by 12; the quotient will be the number of square feet in the boards.

TO FIND THE QUANTITY OF LUMBER IN A LOG

Multiply the diameter in inches at the small end by one-half the number of inches, and this product by the length of the log in feet, which last product divide by 12.

Example: How many board feet of lumber can be made from a log 30 inches in diameter and 14 feet long?

$$30 \times 15 = 450 \times 14 = 6300/12 = 525 \text{ board feet. Ans.}$$

WOOD MEASURE

Wood is measured, and bought and sold by the cord, and fractions of a cord. A cord of wood is a pile 8 feet long, 4 feet wide, and 4 feet high, and therefore contains 128 cubic feet. When the wood is cut 4 feet long and corded in a pile 4 feet high and 8 feet long, this will be a cord. Hence, divide by 128 to find the number of cords.

Example: How many cords of wood in a pile 4 feet wide, 5 feet high, and 28 feet 6 inches long?

$$4 \times 5 = 20 \times 28 \text{ ft. } 6 \text{ in.}$$
$$(\text{or } 28\frac{1}{2} \text{ ft.}) =$$
$$570 \text{ cubic feet}/128 =$$
$$4\frac{1}{2} \text{ cords nearly. Ans.}$$

GROWTH, QUALITY, & WHEN TO SECURE TIMBER

Timber grown in the northern states and Canada is hardy and more merchantable, but northern climate is inimical to mahogany, box, lignumvitae, and other dense tropical woods which require a warm climate. Trees grown in wet localities, with the exception of cedar, willow, poplar, &tc., are not firm and durable as those grown on dry and elevated positions, where the soil is largely composed of loam, intersperced with sand, gravel and stones. Those found in deep forests are usually straighter, less knotty, and more merchantable than trees exposed to the ravages of storms, &tc., bordering on clearings, or on hillsides and exposed places. While sheltered positions are most favorable for growth of timber, the quality of hardness is imparted by exposure.

A TEST FOR SOUNDNESS OF TIMBER

The soundness of timber may be ascertained by placing the ear close to one end of the log, while another person delivers a succession of smart blows with a hammer or mallet upon the opposite end, when a continuance of the vibrations will indicate to an experienced ear even the degree of soundness. If only a dull thud meets the ear, the listener may be certain that unsoundness exists.

QUANTITY OF CHARCOAL FROM DIFFERENT WOODS

100 parts of oak make 23 of charcoal; beech 21, deal 19, apple 23.7, elm 23, ash 25, birch 24, maple 22.8, willow 18, poplar 20, red pine 22.1, white pine 23. The charcoal used in gunpowder is made from willow, alder, and a few other woods. The charred timber found in the ruins of Herculaneum has undergone no change in 1,800 years.

FUEL VALUES OF SOME COMMON WOODS

Shagbark hickory, 30.8 million BTUs (British Thermal Units of heat) per cord; white oak, 30.8; sugar maple, 29.7; American beech, 28; red oak, 27.3; yellow birch, 26.6; white ash, 25.9; American elm, 23.8; red maple, 23.8; paper birch, 23.8; black cherry, 23.1; Douglas fir, 21.4; Eastern white pine 15.8.

RELATIVE TOUGHNESS OF WOODS

Ash, 100; beech, 85; cedar of Lebanon, 84; larch, 83; sycamore and common walnut, each, 68; occidental plane, 66; oak, hornbeam, and Spanish mahogany, each, 62; teak and acacia, each, 58; and young chestnut, 52.

RELATIVE HARDNESS OF WOODS

Taking shell bark hickory as the highest standard of our forest trees, and calling it 100, other trees will compare with it for hardness as follows:

Shell Bark Hickory, 100
Pignut Hickory, 96
White Oak, 84
White Ash, 77
Dogwood, 75
Scrub Oak, 73
White Hazel, 72
Apple Tree, 70
Red Oak, 69
White Beech, 65
Black Walnut, 65
Black Birch, 62
Yellow Oak, 60
Hard Maple, 58
White Elm, 56
Red Cedar, 56
Wild Cherry, 55
Yellow Pine, 54
Chestnut, 52
Yellow Poplar, 51
Butternut, 43
White Birch, 43
White Pine, 30

HOW TO PRESERVE POSTS

Wood can be made to last longer than iron in the ground, if prepared according to the following receipt: Take boiled linseed oil and stir in pulverized coal to the consistency of paint. Put a coat of this over the timber, and there is not a man alive who will live to see it rot.

Timber intended for posts is rendered almost proof against rot by thorough seasoning, charring and immersion in hot coal tar.

PILE DRIVING IN SANDY SOIL

The greatest force will not effect a penetration exceeding fifteen feet.

ARTIFICIAL WOOD

You can produce an artificial fire and waterproof wood in the following manner. More or less finely divided wood shavings—straw, tan, &tc.—singly or mixed are moistened with a weak solution of zinc chloride of about 1.026 specific gravity, and allowed to dry. They are then treated with a basic solution of magnesium chloride of 1.725 to 1.793 specific gravity, and pressed into moulds. The materials remain ten to twelve hours under pressure, during which time they harden while becoming heated. After being dried for several days in a warm, airy place, they are placed for ten or twelve hours into a strong solution of zinc chloride of about 1.205 specific gravity, and finally dried again. The product is stated to be workable like hardwood, and to be capable of taking a fine polish after being tooled. It is fireproof and impermeable by water, and weak acid or alkaline solutions, and not affected by the humidity of the atmosphere, being well suited to decorative purposes, as it will not warp and fly like wood, but retains its form.

Chapter 22

Tools, machines, maintenance & repair

WORKSHOP FORMULAS

USEFUL WORKSHOP HINTS

Leather Belts—Clean and oil leather belts without taking them off their pulleys. If taken off they will shrink. Then a piece must be put into them, and removed again after the belt has run a few days.

Decay of Stone—The decay of stone, either in buildings or monuments, may be arrested by heating and treating with paraffin mixed with a little creosote. A common "paint burner" may be used to heat the stone.

Engine Vibration Test—Set an engine upon three or four movable points, as upon three cannon balls. Connect with steam and exhaust by means of rubber hose. If the engine will run up to speed without moving itself back and forth, then that engine will run a long time with little repair. If it shakes itself around the room, then buy another engine.

Winter Care for Steam Pipes—When you begin to fix up the mill for cold weather, don't forget to put a steam trap in each and every steam pipe which can be opened into the atmosphere for heating purposes.

Leading Steam Joint—For leading steam joints, mix the red lead or litharge with common commercial glycerine, instead of linseed oil.

Bearing Oil—Look well to the bearing of your shafting engines and machines. Sometimes 25, 30, 40,

and even 50 percent of your power is consumed through lack of good oil.

Water Wheels—When you buy a water wheel, be sure to buy one small enough to run at full gate while the stream is low during the summer months. If you want more power than the small wheel will give, then put in two or more wheels of various sizes.

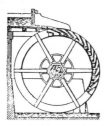

To Trim Rubber—When it becomes necessary to trim a piece of rubber, it will be found that the knife will cut much more readily if dipped in water.

Forging Chisels—When forging a chisel or other cutting tool, don't upset the end of the tool. If necessary, cut it off, but don't try to force it back into a good cutting edge.

To Clean Boilers—In tubular boilers, the handholes should be often opened, and all the collections removed from over the fire. When

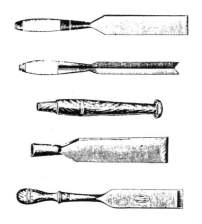

boilers are fed in front, and are blown off through the same pipe, the collection of mud or sediment in the rear end should be often removed.

THE SHARPENING OF TOOLS

Instead of oil, which thickens and smears the stone, a mixture of glycerine and spirit is recom-

mended. The proportions of the composition vary according to the class of tool to be sharpened. One with a relatively large surface is best sharpened with a clear fluid, three parts of glycerine being mixed with one part of spirit. A graver having a small cutting edge only requires a small pressure on the stone, and in such case the glycerine should be mixed with only two or three drops of spirit.

HOW TO ETCH STEEL

The following is one of the best processes employed by cutters and others in etching names and designs on steel: Take copper sulphate, sulphate of alum, and sodium chloride, of each two drachms, and strong acetic acid one and one-half ounces, mixed together. Smear the metal with yellow soap, and write with a quill pen without a split.

HOW TO MAKE AN EMERY FILE TOOL

An ingenious device for stretching emery cloth for use in the workshop consists of a couple of strips of wood about 14 inches long, hinged longitudinally, and of round, half-round, triangular, or any other shape in cross section. On the inside faces of the wood strips are pointed studs, fitting into holes on the opposite side. The strip of emery cloth is laid onto one set of the studs, and the file, as it is called, closed, which fixes the strip on one side. It is then similarly fixed on the other side, and thus constitutes what is called an emery file—which is a handy and convenient arrangement for workshop use.

HOW TO MAKE ARTIFICIAL WHETSTONE

Gelatine of good quality is dissolved in its own weight of water, the operation being conducted in a dark room. To the solution is added one and one-half percent bichromate of potash, which has previously been dissolved in a little water. A quantity of very fine emery, equal to nine times the weight of the gelatine, is intimately mixed with the gelatine solution. Pulverized flint may be substituted for emery. The mass is molded into any desired shape, and is then consolidated by heavy pressure. It is dried by exposure to strong sunlight for several hours.

HOW TO MEND A BROKEN FILE

There is no tool so easily broken as a file that a machinist has worked with, and is about the first thing that snaps when a kit of tools gets upset upon the cross-beam of a machine or a tool board from the bed of an engine lathe. It cannot even be passed from one workman to another without being broken; if the file is a new one or still good

for anything, if an apprentice has got anything to do with it, they are never worth mending, however great may be their first cost, unless the plaster of Paris and lime treatment can make a perfect weld without injuring the steel, or disturbing the form of the teeth. Steel that is left as hard as a file is very brittle, and soft solder can hold as much on a steady pull if it has a new surface to work from. Take a file, as soon as it is broken, and wet the break with zinc dissolved in muriatic acid, and then tin over with the soldering iron. This must be done immediately as soon as the file is broken, as the break begins to oxydize when exposed to the air, and in an hour or two will gather sufficient to make it impossible for the parts to adhere. Heat the file as warm as it will bear without disturbing its temper as soon as well tinned, and press the two pieces firmly together, squeezing out nearly all the solder, and hold in place until the file cools. This can be done with very little to trim off, and every portion of the break fitting accurately in place. Bring both pieces in line with each other, and, for a file, it is as strong in one place as in another, and is all that could be asked for under the very best of welding treatment.

HOW TO PROPERLY LACE A QUARTER-TURN BELT

In order to have equal strain on both sides of the belt, begin on the outside of the belt at the middle, pass one end of the lacing through one end of the belt and bring it out through the corresponding hole of the other end of the belt, laying it diagonally off to the left. Now pass

the other end of the lacing through the hole last used, and carry it over the first strand of the lacing on the inside of the belt, passing it through the first hole used, and lay it diagonally off to the right. Now proceed to pass the lacing through the holes of the belt in a zigzag course, leaving all the strands inside the belt parallel with the belt, and all the strands outside the belt oblique. Pass the lace twice through the holes nearest the edge of the belt, then return the lace in the reverse order toward the center of the belt, so as to cross all the oblique strands, and make all the inside strands double. Finally pass the end of the lacing through the first hole used, then outward through an awl hole, then hammering it down to cause it to hold. The left side is to be laced in a similar way.

HOW TO SPLICE A BELT TO MAKE IT RUN LIKE AN ENDLESS BELT

Use the toughest yellow glue prepared in the ordinary way, while hot, stirring in thoroughly about

20 percent of its weight of tannic acid, or extract of tan bark. Apply to the splice and quickly clamp to-

gether. The splice should be made of scarfed edges extending 3 to 6 inches back, according to the thickness of belt. The surface is to be perfectly clean and free from oil.

In tanning, four pounds of oak bark make one pound of leather.

RECEIPT FOR AXEL GREASE

1. One gallon water; one-third pound soda; ten pounds palm oil. Mix by heat, and stir till nearly cold.

2. One gallon each of water and rape oil; one-third pound soda; one-fourth pound palm oil.

3. One gallon water; three pounds tallow; six pounds palm oil, one-third pound soda. Heat to 210°F. and stir until cool.

4. Eight pounds tallow; ten pounds palm oil, one pound plumbago. Makes a good lubricator for wagon wheels.

RECIPES FOR PLUMBERS

Soldering Mixture—Chloride of zinc, so much used in soldering iron, has, besides its corrosive qualities, the drawback of being unwholesome when used for soldering the iron tins employed to can fruit, vegetables and other foods. A soldering mixture has been found

which is free from these defects. It is made by mixing one pound of lactic acid with one pound of glycerine and eight pounds of water.

Acid-proof Wooden Tanks—A wooden tank may be rendered capable of withstanding the effects of nitric and sulphuric acids by the following method: Cover the inside with paraffin; go over the inside with a sadiron heated to the temperature used in ironing the clothes. Melt the paraffin under the iron so as to drive it into the wood as much as possible, then with a cooler iron melt on a coat thick enough to completely cover the wood.

To Brass Small Articles—To one quart of water add half an ounce each of sulphate of copper and protochloride of tin. Stir the article

in the solution till the desired color is obtained. Use the sulphate of copper alone for a copper color.

To Bronze Tin—Tin and tin alloys, after careful cleansing from oxide and grease, are handsomely and permanently bronzed if brushed over with a solution of one part of sulphate of copper (bluestone) and one part of sulphate of iron (copperas) in twenty parts of water. When this has dried, the surface should be brushed with a solution of one part of acetate of copper (verdigris) in acetic acid. After several applications and dryings of the last named, the surface is polished with a soft brush and bloodstone powder. The raised portions

are then rubbed off with soft leather moistened with wax in turpentine, followed by rubbing with dry leather.

HOW TO PROTECT WATER PIPES AGAINST FREEZING

A device has been brought forward for protecting water pipes against freezing, the arrangement being based upon the fact that water in motion will remain liquid at a lower temperature than water. at rest. One end of a copper rod, placed outside the building, is secured to a bracket, and the other end is attached to one arm of a weighted elbow lever; to the other arm of the lever is secured a rod which passes into the building and operates a valve in the water pipe. By means of turn buckles the length of the copper rod can be ad-

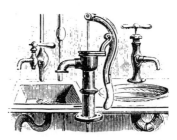

justed so that before the temperature reaches the point at which there would be danger of the water in the pipes freezing, the valve will be opened to allow a flow of water; beyond this point the valve opening will increase and the flow become more rapid as the cold becomes more intense, and as the temperature rises the valve is closed. This plan sets up a current in the pipes, which replaces the water as it grows cold by the warmer water from the main.

HOW TO DRILL HOLES FOR WATER PIPES THROUGH PLATE GLASS

The quickest and best way to drill holes for water pipes through plate glass is by using a hardened (file temper) drill, with spirits of turpentine and camphor to make the

drill bite. A broken file in a breast brace will do good work if a power drill is not obtainable.

USEFUL RECIPE FOR A CAULKING COMPOUND

For stopping the joints between slates or shingles, &tc. and chimneys, doors, windows, &tc., a mixture of stiff white-lead paint, with sand enough to prevent it from running, is very good, especially if protected by a covering of strips of lead or copper, tin, &tc., nailed to the mortar joints of the chimney, after being bent so as to enter said joints, which should be scraped out for an inch in depth, and afterwards refilled.

Mortar protected in the same way, or even unprotected, is often used for this purpose, but it is not equal to the paint and sand. Mortar a few days old (to allow refractory particles of lime to slack), mixed

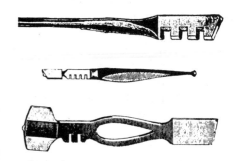

with blacksmith's cinders and molasses, is much used for this purpose, and becomes very hard and effective.

Chapter 23

Useful facts for the house & yard

FLORA, FAUNA & WEATHER

HOW TO PRESERVE ROSEBUDS

A method employed in Germany to keep rosebuds fresh into the winter, consists in first covering the end of the recently cut stem with wax, and then placing each one in a closed paper cup or cone, so that the leaves do not touch the paper. The cup is then coated with glue, to exclude air, dust, and

moisture, and when dry it is stood up in a cool place. When wanted for use, the bud is taken out of the cup and placed in water, after cut-

ting off the end, when the rose will bloom in a few hours.

HOW TO PRESERVE NATURAL FLOWERS

(A good preparation by which you can take a natural flower, and dip it in, that will preserve it)
Dip the flowers in melted paraffin, withdrawing them quickly. The liquid should only be just hot enough to maintain its fluidity and the flowers should be dipped one at a time, held by the stalk, and moved about for an instant to get rid of air bubbles. Fresh cut specimens free from moisture make excellent specimens in this way.

Another Way—Put some fresh cut flowers, partly opened in bloom, which have had their stalks removed and a small wire attached to the flower base for support, in to a vessel, either earthen or tin, which has placed on its bottom a one inch layer of gel of silica powdered. Sprinkle in the interstices between the blossoms more gel of silica, being careful not to bruise or disrupt the petals, until they are wholly covered. Cover the vessel tight and seal with hot wax. After two or three days, it may be opened, and the silica powder gently sifted off. The blossoms will feel crisp and still show their original colors. If stored too long, they will be brittle and break easily. Their wire "stems" can then be incorporated into bouquets by covering them with green ribbon.

HOW TO STOP FLOWER VASE MARKS ON TABLETOPS
Glue a canning rubber to the bottom of a vessel of flowers to keep it from marring a tabletop.

HOW TO PREVENT BUGS IN THE GARDEN
A wise farmer will plant strong aromatic vegetables, such as chives, garlic, onions, or shallots, in the rows of the other vegetables, and also among the flowers, to prevent troublesome bugs and worms from completely destroying the plants.

HOW TO KEEP SNAILS DOWN
Sprinkling salt on the top and bottom of the garden wall is said to keep snails from climbing up or down.

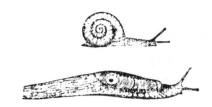

HOW TO LURE HUMMINGBIRDS TO THE GARDEN
To lure these tiny creatures into the yard, so as to enjoy their colorful presence, plant in the garden flowers whose nectar attracts the

little birds. Fuchsia, lily-vines, morning glories, and other nectar-producing plants will produce excellent results.

RANK OF MELODY AMONG SONG BIRDS

The melodiousness of singing birds ranks as follows: The nightingale first, then the linnet, titlark, sky-lark and woodlark. The mocking-bird has the greatest powers of imitation; the robin and goldfinch are superior in vigorous notes.

CRICKETS AS NIGHT WATCHMEN

Welcome into your garden the common cricket which, it is said, will warn of intruders at night by ceasing its chirping. When the intruder has passed on, the cricket will resume its singing.

HOW CRICKETS TELL TEMPERATURE

Of a summer's night, one can tell the temperature by listening to the song of the crickets. To the number of chirps counted during a quarter of a minute add forty. This number is said to be the temperature. The finest temperature tellers are the white tree crickets.

SIGNS OF STORMS APPROACHING

A ring around the sun or moon stands for an approaching storm, its near or distant approach being indicated by its larger or smaller circumference.

When the sun rises brightly and immediately afterwards becomes veiled with clouds, the farmer distrusts the day. Rains which begin early in the morning often stop by nine in place of "eleven," the hour specified in the old saw, "If it rains before seven, it will cease by eleven."

On a still, quiet day, with scarcely the least wind afloat, the farmer can tell the direction of impending storm by cattle sniffing the air in the direction whence it is coming. They are said to smell the moisture added by the storm to the air.

Lack of dew in summer is a rain sign.

Sharp white frosts in autumn and winter precede damp weather, and it is said one can stake his reputation as a prophet on the fact that three successive white frosts are an infallible sign of rain.

Spiders do not spin their webs out of door before rain.

Previous to rain, flies sting sharper, bees remain in their hives or fly but short distances, and almost all animals appear uneasy.

HOW TO PRESERVE ORGANIC OBJECTS IN THEIR ORIGINAL FORMS

For a few weeks preservation of flowers, butterflies, &tc., is recommended a mixture composed of two and a half ounces of chloride of sodium, two and three-fourths drachms of saltpetre, and one pint of water, to which is to be added three percent of boric acid.

Chapter 24

How to destroy, dissuade, expel

HOUSEHOLD PESTS

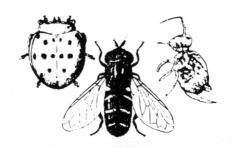

HOW TO DESTROY ANTS
Ants that frequent houses or gardens may be destroyed by taking flowers of brimstone (sulphur), half a pound, and potash, four ounces; set them in an iron or earthen pan over the fire till dissolved and united; afterward beat them to a powder, and infuse a

little of this powder in water; and wherever you sprinkle it the ants will die or fly the place.
Another Way—Old rags dipped in coal oil or kerosene will stop the passage of ants.

HOW TO DESTROY BLACK ANTS
A few leaves of green wormwood, scattered among the haunts of these

troublesome insects, is said to be effectual in dislodging them.
HOW TO DESTROY RED ANTS
The best way to get rid of ants, is to set a quantity of cracked walnuts or shell-barks on plates, and put them in the closet or places where the ants congregate. They are very fond of these and will collect on them in myriads. When

they have collected on them make a general *auto-da-fé*, by turning nuts and ants together into the fire, and then replenish the plates with fresh nuts. After they have become so thinned off as to cease collecting on plates, powder some camphor and put in the holes and crevices, whereupon the remainder of them will speedily depart. It may help the process of getting them to assemble on shell-barks, to remove all edibles out of their way for some time.

HOW TO DESTROY BLACK BEES

Place two or three shallow dishes —the large kind of flower-pot saucer will do—half filled with water, on the floors where they assemble, with strips of cardboard running from the edge of the vessel to the floor, at a gentle inclination; these the unwelcomed guests will eagerly ascend, and so find a watery grave.

HOW TO DESTROY BEDBUGS

1. When they have made a lodgement in the wall, fill all the apertures with a mixture of soft soap and Scotch snuff. Take the bedstead to pieces, and treat that in the same way.

2. A strong decoction of red pepper applied to bedsteads will either kill the bugs or drive them away.

3. Put the bedstead into a close room and set fire to the following composition, placed in an iron pot upon the hearth, having previously closed up the chimney, then shut the door, let them remain a day: Sulphur, nine parts; saltpetre, powdered, one part. Mix. Be sure to open the door of the room five or six hours before you venture to go into it a second time.

4. Rub the bedstead well with lampoil; this alone is good, but to make it more effectual, get ten cents worth of quicksilver and add to it. Put it into all the cracks around the bed, and they will soon disappear. The bedstead should first be scalded and wiped dry, then put on with a feather.

5. Corrosive sublimate, one ounce; muriatic acid, two ounces; water, four ounces; dissolve, then add turpentine, one pint; decoction of tobacco, one pint. Mix. For the decoction of tobacco boil one ounce of tobacco in a half pint of water. This mixture must be applied with a paint brush. This wash is deadly poison.

6. Rub the bedstead in the joints with equal parts of spirits of turpentine and kerosene oil, and the cracks of the surbase in room where there are many. Filling up all the cracks with hard soap is an excellent remedy.

March and April are the months when bedsteads should be examined to kill all the eggs.

7. Mix together two ounces spirits of turpentine, one ounce corrosive sublimate and one pint alcohol.

8. Distilled vinegar, or diluted good vinegar, one pint; camphor one-half ounce; dissolve.

9. White arsenic, two ounces; lard, thirteen ounces; corrosive sublimate, one-fourth ounce; venetian red, one-fourth ounce (Deadly poison).

10. Strong mercurial ointment, one ounce; soft soap, one ounce; oil of turpentine, a pint.

11. Gasoline and coal oil are both excellent adjuncts, with cleanliness, in ridding a bed or house of these pests.

12. Set in the middle of the room a dish containing four ounces of brimstone. Light it, and close the room as tight as possible, stopping the keyhole of the door with paper to keep the fumes of the brimstone in the room. Let it remain for three or four hours, then open the windows and let it air thoroughly. The brimstone will be found to have also bleached the paint, if it was a yellowish white.

13. Benzine and gasoline will kill bedbugs as fast as they can reach them.

14. A weak solution of zinc chloride is also said to be an effectual banisher of these pests.

HOW TO DESTROY CATERPILLARS

Boil together a quantity of rue, wormwood, and any cheap tobacco (equal parts) in common water. The liquid should be very strong. Sprinkle it on the leaves and young branches every morning and evening during the time the fruit is ripening.

HOW TO DESTROY COCKROACHES & BEETLES

1. Strew the roots of black hellebore, at night, in the places infested by these vermin, and they will be found in the morning dead or dying. Black hellebore grows in marshy grounds, and may be had at the herb shops.

2. Put about a quart of water sweetened with molasses in a tin wash basin or smooth glazed china bowl. Set it at evening in a place frequented by the bugs. Around the base put an old piece of carpet,

that the bugs will have easy access to the top. They will go down in the water, and stay till you come.

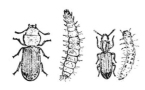

3. Take pulverized borax, four parts; flour, one part; mix intimately and distribute the mixture in cupboards which are frequented by the roaches; or blow it, by means of a bellows, into the holes or cracks that are infested by them.

4. By scattering a handful of fresh cucumber parings about the house.

5. Take carbonic acid and powdered camphor in equal parts; put them in a bottle; they will become fluid. With a painter's brush of the size called a sash tool, put the mixture on the cracks or places where the roaches hide; they will come out at once. Then kill.

6. Mix up a quantity of fresh-burned plaster of Paris (gypsum, such as is used for making molds and ornaments), with wheat flour

and a little sugar, and distribute on shallow plates and box boards, and place in the corners of the kitchen and pantry, where they frequent. In the darkness they will feast themselves on it. Whether it interferes with their digestion or not, is difficult to ascertain, but after three or four nights renewal of the preparation, no cockroaches will be found on the premises.

7. Sprinkle boric acid, powdered, around the places where they frequent and it will be found effectual every time. Cockroaches soon learn to avoid the stronger poisons, but are not frightened by the slowly acting boric acid which they crawl through at will, until it is too late.

HOW TO DESTROY CRICKETS

Sprinkle a little quicklime near to the cracks through which they enter the room. The lime may be laid down overnight, and swept away in the morning. In a few days they will most likely all be destroyed. But care must be taken that the children do not meddle with the lime, as a very small portion of it, getting into the eye, would prove exceedingly hurtful. In case of such an accident, the best thing to do would be to wash the eye with vinegar and water.

HOW TO GET RID OF FLEAS

Much of the largest number of fleas are brought into the family circle by pet dogs and cats. The oil of pennyroyal will drive these insects off; but a cheaper method, where the herb flourishes, is to throw your cats and dogs into a decoction of it once a week. When the herb cannot be got, the oil can be procured. In this case, saturate strings with it and tie them around the necks of the dogs and cats. These applications should be repeated

every twelve or fifteen days. Mint freshly cut, and hung round a bedstead, or on the furniture, will prevent annoyance from bed insects; a few drops of oil of lavender will be more efficacious.

HOW TO DESTROY FLIES

1. Take an infusion of quassis, one pint; brown sugar, four ounces;

ground pepper, two ounces. To be well mixed together, and put in small shallow dishes where required.

2. Black pepper (powdered), one drachm; brown sugar, one drachm; milk or cream, two drachms. Mix, and place it on a plate or saucer where the flies are most troublesome.

3. Pour a little simple oxymel (an article to be obtained at the druggists') into a common tumbler glass, and place in the glass a piece of cap paper, made into the shape of an upper part of a funnel, with a hole at the bottom to admit flies.

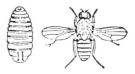

Attracted by the smell, they readily enter the trap in swarms, and by the thousands soon collected prove that they have not the wit nor disposition to return.

4. Take some jars, mugs, or tumblers, fill them half full with soapy water; cover them as jam-pots are covered, with a piece of paper, either tied down or tucked under the rim. Let this paper be rubbed inside with wet sugar, molasses, honey, or jam, or anything sweet; cut a small hole in the center, large enough for a fly to enter. The flies settle on the top, attracted by the smell of the bait; they then crawl through the hole to feed upon the sweets beneath. Meanwhile the warmth of the weather causes the soapy water to ferment, and produces a gas which overpowers the flies, and they drop down into the vessel. Thousands may be destroyed this way, and the traps last a long time.

5. It may be well worth knowing that water in which three or four onions have been boiled, applied with a gilding brush to the frames of pictures, chimney glasses and window sills, will prevent flies from lighting on them and will not injure the frames.

HOW TO MAKE FLY PAPER

Melt resin, and add thereto whilst soft, sufficient sweet oil, lard, or lamp oil to make it, when cold, about the consistency of honey. Spread on writing paper, and place in a convenient spot. It will soon be filled with ants, flies, and other vermin.

HOW TO EXPEL INSECTS

All insects dread pennyroyal; the smell of it destroys some, and drives others away. At the time that fresh pennyroyal cannot be gathered, get oil of pennyroyal;

pour some into a saucer, and steep in it small pieces of wadding or raw cotton, and place them in corners, closet shelves, bureau drawers, boxes, &tc., and the cockroaches, ants, and other insects will soon disappear. It is also well to place some between the mattresses, and around the bed. It is also a splendid thing for brushing off that terrible little insect, the seed tick.

HOW TO KILL LICE

All kinds of lice and their nits may be got rid of by washing with

a simple decoction of stavesacre (Delphinium staphisagria), or with a lotion made with the bruised seed in vinegar, or with the tincture, or by rubbing in a salve made with the seeds and four times their weight of lard very carefully beaten together. The acetic solution and the tincture are the cleanliest and most agreeable preparations, but all are equally efficacious in destroying both the creatures and their eggs, and even in relieving the intolerable itching which their casual presence leaves behind on many sensitive skins. The alkaloid delphinia may also be employed, but possesses no advantage except in the preparation of an ointment, when for any reason that form of application would be preferred.

HOW TO DESTROY MICE

1. Use tartar emetic mingled with some favorite food. The mice will leave the premises.

2. Take one part calomel, five parts of wheat flour, one part sugar, and one-tenth of a part of ultramarine. Mix together in a fine powder and place it in a dish. This is a most efficient poison for mice.

3. Anyone desirous of keeping seeds from the depredations of mice can do so by mixing pieces of camphor gum in with the seeds. Camphor placed in drawers or trunks will prevent mice from doing them injury. The little animal objects to the odor and keeps a good distance from it. He will seek food elsewhere.

HOW TO DRIVE AWAY MOSQUITOES

1. A camphor bag hung up in an open casement will prove an effectual barrier to their entrance. Cam-

phorated spirits applied as perfume to the face and hands will prove an effectual preventive; but when bitten by them, aromatic vinegar is the best antidote.

2. A small amount of the oil of pennyroyal sprinkled around the room will drive away the mosquitoes. This is an excellent recipe.

3. Take of gum camphor a piece half the size of an egg, and evaporate it by placing it in a tin vessel and holding it over a lamp or candle, taking care that it does not ignite. The smoke will soon fill the room and expel the mosquitoes.

HOW TO PRESERVE CLOTHING FROM MOTHS

1. Procure shavings of cedar wood and enclose in muslin bags, which should be distributed freely among clothes.

2. Procure shavings of camphor wood, and enclose in bags.

3. Sprinkle pimento (allspice) berries among the clothes.

4. Sprinkle clothes with the seeds of the musk plant.

5. An ounce of gum camphor and one of the powdered shell of red pepper are macerated in eight ounces of strong alcohol for several days, then strained. With this tincture the furs or clothes are sprinkled over, and rolled up in sheets.

6. Carefully shake and brush woolens early in the spring, so as to be certain that no eggs are in them; then sew them up in cotton or linen wrappers, putting a piece of camphor gum, tied up in a bit of muslin, into each bundle, or into the chests and closets where the ar-

ticles are to lie. No moth will approach while the smell of the camphor continues. When the gum is evaporated, it must be renewed. Enclose them in a moth-proof box with camphor—no matter whether made of white paper or white pine —before any eggs are laid on them by early spring moths. The notion of having a trunk made of some particular kind of wood for this purpose is nonsense. Furs or woolens, put away in spring time, before moth eggs are laid, into boxes, trunks, drawers, or closets even, where moths cannot enter, will be safe from the ravages of moth-worms, provided none were in them that were laid late in the autumn, for they are not of spontaneous production.

7. A twist of fresh tobacco, left to dry in a closet, will dispel moths most effectually.

8. Moths or any summer flying insects may be enticed to their destruction by a bright tin pan half filled with kerosene and set in a dark corner of the room. Attracted by the bright tin, the moth will meet his death in the kerosene.

HOW TO KILL MOTHS IN CARPETS

Wring a coarse crash towel out of clear water, spread it smoothly on the carpet, iron it dry with a good hot sadiron, repeating the operation on all parts of the carpet suspected of being infected with

moths. No need to press hard, and neither the pile nor color of the carpet will be injured, and the moths will be destroyed by the heat and steam.

HOW TO DESTROY RATS

1. When a house is infested by rats which refuse to be caught by cheese and other baits, a few drops of the highly-scented oil of rhodium poured on the bottom of the

cage will be an attraction which they cannot refuse.

2. Place on the floor near where their holes are suppose to be a thin layer of moist caustic potash. When the rats travel on this, it

will cause their feet to become sore, which they lick, and their tongues become likewise sore. The consequence is, that they shun this locality, and seem to inform all the neighboring rats about it, and the result is that they soon abandon a house that has such mean floors.

3. Cut some cork as thin as wafers, and fry, roast, or stew them in grease, and place the same in their track; or a dried sponge fried or dipped in molasses or honey, with a small quantity of bird lime or oil of rhodium, will fasten to their fur and cause them to depart.

4. If a live rat be caught, and a small bell be fastened around his neck and allowed to escape, all of his brother rats as well as himself will very soon go to some other neighbor's house.

5. If a live rat be caught and smeared over with tar or train oil, and afterwards allowed to escape in the holes of other rats, he will cause all soon to take their departure.

6. Take a pan, about twelve inches deep, and half fill it with water; then sprinkle some bran on the water and set the pan in a place where the rats most frequent. In the morning you will find several rats in the pan.

7. Take flour, three parts; sugar, one-half part; sulphur, two parts; and phosphorous, two parts. Mix well and smear on meat and place near where the rats are most troublesome.

8. Squills are an excellent poison for rats. The powder should be mixed with some fatty substance, and spread upon slices of bread. The pulp of onion is also very good. Rats are very fond of either.

9. Take two ounces of carbonate of barytes, and mix with one pound of suet or tallow, place a portion of this within their holes and about their haunts. It is greedily eaten, produces great thirst, and death ensues after drinking. This is a very effectual poison, because it is both tasteless and odorless.

10. Take one ounce of finely powdered arsenic, one ounce of lard; mix these into a paste with meal, and put about the haunts of rats.

11. Make a paste of one ounce of flour, one-half gill of water, one drachm of phosphorous. Or, one ounce of flour, two ounces of powdered cheese crumbs, and one-half drachm of phosphorous; add to each of these mixtures a few drops of oil of rhodium, and spread this on thin pieces of bread like butter; the rats will eat of this greedily, and it is sure poison.

12. Mix some ground plaster of Paris with some sugar and Indian meal. Set it on a plate, and leave beside each plate a saucer of water. When the rats have eaten the mixture, they will drink the water and die. To attract them towards it, sprinkle on the edge of the plates a little of the oil of rhodium.

13. Another method of getting rid of rats is to strew pounded potash on their holes. The potash gets into their coats and irritates the skin, and the rats desert the place.

14. The Dutch method: This is said to be used successfully in Holland. A number of rats are left together to themselves in a large trap or cage, with no food whatsoever; their craving hunger will at last cause them to fight, and the weakest will be eaten by the others. After a short time the fight is renewed, and the next weakest is the victim, and so it goes on till one strong rat is left. When this one has eaten the last remains of the others, it is set loose. The animal now has acquired such a taste for rat-flesh that he is the terror of ratdom, going round seeking what rat he may devour. In an incredibly short time, the premises are abandoned by all other rats, which will not come back before the cannibal rat has left or has died.

15. Catch a rat and smear him over with a mixture of phosphorous and lard, and then let him loose. The house will soon be emptied of these pests.

WAYS TO EXPEL SKUNKS

1. When one is so unfortunate as to have the house cellar occupied by a family of skunks, the intruders can be compelled to leave when naphthalene powders are sprinkled close around the base of the house, with only one narrow passageway left open for their departure. They will not return while the powders remain.

2. A dish of flowers of sulphur can be ignited and slipped by long pole or stick under the house or into the cellar, where the fumes will soon cause the animals to de-

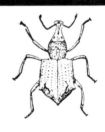

part. Thereafter, ventilate the house and cellar with fresh air for several days.

3. Dogs and cats which to their dismay and agony have encountered the odorous, burning spray of a skunk can be treated with large amounts of tomato juice, rubbed well into their coats, repeated for two or three days, then rinsed with clear water.

4. Milk, vinegar and weak solutions of hyposulphite of soda are also effective bath solutions, but persistent skunk odor repels all effectual treatment.

5. The best way to rid skin and clothing of odor is washing in a solution of one cupful ammonia water to a bucketful of fresh water. But it may prove harmful to skin and eyes of affected animals, when got into their eyes, nose or mouth.

HOW TO RID DRINKING WATER OF VERMIN

Go to the river or pond, and with a small net (a piece of old mosquito bar will do) collect a dozen or more of the small fishes known as minnows, and put them in your

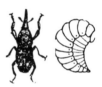

cistern, and in a short time you will have clear water, the wiggle-tails and reddish-colored bugs or lice being gobbled up by the fishes. When no minnows are to be got, nearly same results may be got with small frogs placed in the cistern.

HOW TO EXPEL WEAVILS

A muslin bag filled with either whole or pounded cloves, and placed on the pantry shelf will successfully keep the cereals, grains, and flour free of troublesome little weavils.

Part Four

REMEDIES
FOR
FARM ANIMALS

ANOTHER WORD OF CAUTION

Veterinary medicine has changed greatly during this last century. Bloodletting and leeching are no longer fashionable for either man or his beasts.

While some *cures* are offered here only as insight into livestock medications available to our forefathers, others are still sound today.

Many *cures* have survived scientific changes for the single reason that the afflicted animals survived despite the *cures*. Happily—but sadly for the involved beasts— other *cures* expired with those ailing animals.

Again, the reader takes these notrums solely at his own risk. When in doubt, a veterinarian should be consulted.

NOTE: Neither the author nor the publisher suggests that you use any of these century-old medications or remedies. All of them are authentic, but some could be harmful. They are presented here for your enjoyment of things past, and not as advice for the present.

Chapter 25

Nostrums & home remedies
MEDICINES FOR HORSES

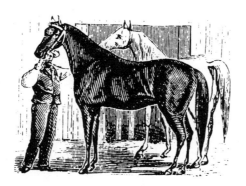

DURABILITY OF A HORSE

A horse will travel 400 yards in 4½ minutes at a walk, 400 yards in 2 minutes at a trot, and 400 yards in 1 minute at a gallop.

The usual work of a horse is taken at 22,500 lbs., raised 1 foot per minute, for 8 hours per day.

A horse will carry 250 lbs., 25 miles per day of 8 hours.

An average draught-horse will draw 1,600 lbs. 23 miles per day on a level road, weight of the wagon included.

The average weight of a horse is 1,000 lbs.; his strength is equal to that of 5 men.

In a horse mill, moving a 3 ft. per second, track 25 ft. in diameter, he exerts with the machine the power of 4½ horses.

The greatest amount a horse can pull in a horizontal line is 900 lbs; but he can only do this momentarily; in continued exertion, probably only half of this is the limit.

He attains his growth in 5 years, will live 25, average 16 years.

A horse will live 25 days on

water, without solid food; 17 days without eating or drinking; but only 5 days on solid food, without drinking.

A cart drawn by horses over an ordinary road will travel 1.1 miles per hour of trip.

A 4-horse team will haul from 25 to 30 cubic feet of lime stone at each load. The time expended in loading, unloading, &tc., including delays, averages 35 minutes per trip. The cost of loading and unloading a cart, using a horse tram at the quarry, and unloading by hand, when labor is $1.25 per day, and the horse is 75¢, is 25¢ per perch (24.75 cubic feet).

The work done by an animal is greatest when the velocity with which he moves is one-eighth of the greatest with which he can move when not impeded, and the force then exerted .45 of the utmost force the animal can exert at a dead pull.

TERMS USED IN ANIMAL MEDICINE, including some also used in the medical treatment of humans

ALTERATIVES

This term is not very scientific, but it is in very general use, and easily explains its own meaning, though the *modus operandi* of the drugs employed to carry it out is not so clear. The object is to replace unhealthy action by a healthy one, without resorting to any of the distinctly defined remedies, such as tonics, stomachics, &tc. As a general rule, this class of remedies produces its effect by acting slowly but steadily on the depurgatory organs, as the liver, kidneys and skin. The following may be found useful:

1. Disordered States of the Skin—Emetic tartar 5 ounces, powdered ginger 3 ounces, opium 1 ounce; syrup enough to form 16 balls; one to be given every night.

2. A Simple Cooling—Barbadoes aloes 1 ounce, Castile soap 1½ ounces, ginger ½ ounce; syrup enough to form 6 balls; one to be given every morning.

3. Also, Barbadoes aloes 1½ drachms, emetic tartar 2 drachms, Castile soap 2 drachms; mix.

*4. Alterative Ball for General Use—*Black sulphuret of antimony 2 to 4 drachms, sulphur 2 drachms, nitre 2 drachms; linseed meal and water enough to form a ball.

*5. For Generally Defective Secretions—*Flowers of sulphur 6 ounces, emetic tartar 5 to 8 drachms, corrosive sublimate 10 grains; linseed meal mixed with hot water enough to form 6 balls, one of which may be given two or three times a week.

*6. In Debility of Stomach—*Calomel 1 scruple, aloes 1 drachm, cascarilla bark, in powder, 1 drachm, gentian root, in powder, 1 drachm, ginger, in powder, 1 drachm, Castile soap 3 drachms; syrup enough to make a ball, which may be given twice a week, or every other night.

ANAESTHETICS

Anaesthetics produce insensibility to all external impressions, and therefore to pain. They resemble narcotics in their action, and, when taken into the stomach, may be considered purely as such. The most certain and safe way of administering them is by inhalation, and chloroform is the drug now universally employed. The *modus operandi* of the various kinds has never yet been satisfactorily explained; and when the comparison is made, as it often is, to the action of intoxicating fluids, we are no nearer to it than before. With alcoholic fluids, however, the disorder of the mental functions is greater in proportion to the insensibility to pain; and if they are taken in sufficient quantities to produce the latter effect, they are dangerous to life itself. The action of anaesthetics on the horse is very similar to that on man.

ANODYNES

Sometimes called narcotics, when taken into the stomach pass at once into the blood, and there act in a special manner on the nervous centers. At first, they exalt the nervous force; but they soon depress it, the second stage coming on sooner according to the increase of the dose. They are given either to soothe the general nervous system, or to stop diarrhoea; or sometimes to relieve spasm, as in colic or tetanus. Opium is the chief anodyne used in veterinary medicine, and it may be employed in very large doses:

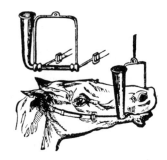

*1. Anodyne Drench for Colic—*Linseed oil 1 pint, oil of turpentine 1 to 2 ounces, laudanum 1 to 2 ounces; mix, and give every hour till relief is afforded.

2. Anodyne Ball for Colic—(Only useful in mild cases.) Powdered opium ½ to 2 drachms, camphor 2 drachms, ginger 1½ drachms; make into a ball with liquorice powder and treacle, and give every hour while the pain lasts. It should be kept in a bottle or bladder.

3. Anodyne Ball (ordinary)— Opium ½ to 1 drachm, Castile soap 2 tp 4 drachms, ginger 1 to 2 drachms, powdered anise seed ½ to 1 ounce, oil of caraway seeds ½ drachm; syrup enough to form a ball, to be dissolved in half pint of warm ale, and given as a drench.

4. Anodyne Drench in Superpurgation, or Ordinary Diarrhoea —Gum arabic 2 ounces, boiling water 1 pint; dissolve and then add oil of peppermint 25 drops, laudanum ½ to 1 ounce; mix and give night and morning if necessary.

5. In Chronic Diarrhoea—Powdered chalk and gum arabic, of each 1 ounce, laudanum ½ ounce, peppermint water 10 ounces; mix, and give night and morning.

ANTACIDS

As the term implies, these remedies are used to neutralize acids, whether taken into the stomach to an improper extent, or formed therein as products of diseases.

They are often classed as alternatives, when used for the latter purpose. They include the alkalies and alkaline earths, but are not much used in veterinary medicine.

ANTHELMINTICS

Drugs which are used to destroy worms receive this name in medical literature, when the author is wedded to the Greek language. The admirers of Latin call them *vermifuges,* and in English they receive the humble name of worm medicines. Their action is partly by producing a disagreeable or fatal impression on the worm itself, and partly by irritating the mucous lining of the bowels, and thus causing them to expel their contents. Failing, the following may be useful:

1. Worm Ball—Assafœtida 2 drachms, calomel 1½ drachms, powdered sarin 1½ drachms, oil of male fern 30 drops; treacle enough to make a ball, which should be given at night, and followed by a purge next morning.

2. Mild Drench for Worms— Linseed oil 1 pint, spirit of turpentine 2 drachms; mix and give every morning.

ANTISPASMODICS

These are medicines which are intended to counteract excessive muscular action, called spasm or, in the limbs, cramps. This deranged condition depends upon a variety of causes, which are generally of an irritating nature, and its successful treatment will often depend upon the employment of remedies calculated to remove the cause, rather than directly to relieve the effect. It therefore follows that, in many cases, the medicines most successful in removing spasm, will be derived from widely separate divisions of the *materia medica*—such as aperients, anodynes, alteratives, stimulants, and tonics. It is useless to attempt to give many formulas for their exhibition; but there are one or two medicines which exercise a peculiar control over spasm, and we shall give them without attempting to analyze their mode of operation.

1. In Colic—Spirit of turpentine 3½ ounces, laudanum 1½ ounces, Barbadoes aloes 1 ounce; powder the aloes, and dissolve in warm water; then add the other ingredients, and give as a drench.

2. Clyster in Colic—Spirit of turpentine 6 ounces, aloes 2 drachms; dissolve in three quarts of warm water, and stir the turpentine well into it.

3. Antispasmodic Drench—Gin 4 to 6 ounces, tincture of capsicum 2 drachms, laudanum 3 drachms, warm water 1½ pints; mix and give as a drench, where there is no inflammation.

APERIENTS

Aperients, or purges, are those medicines which quicken or increase the evacuation from the bowels, varying, however, a good deal in their mode of operation. Some merely act by exciting the muscular coat of the bowels to contract; others cause an immense watery discharge, which, as it were, washes out the bowels; whilst a third set combines the action of the two. The various purges also act upon different parts of the canal, some stimulating the small intestines, whilst others pass through them without affecting them, and only act upon the large bowels; and others, again, act upon the whole canal. There is a third point of difference in purges, depending upon their influencing the liver in addition, which mercurial purgatives certainly do, as well as rhubarb and some others, and which effect is partly due to their absorption into the circulation, so that they may be made to act, by injecting into the veins, as strongly as by actual swallowing, and their subsequent passage into the bowels. Purgatives are likewise classed, according to the degree of their effect, into laxatives acting mildly, and drastic purges, or cathartics, acting very severely.

1. Ordinary Physic Balls—Barbadoes aloes 3 to 8 drachms, hard soap 4 drachms, ginger 1 drachm. Dissolve in as small a quantity of boiling water as will suffice; then slowly evaporate to the proper consistence, by which means griping is avoided.

2. A Warmer Physic Ball—Barbadoes aloes 3 to 8 drachms, carbonate of soda ½ drachm, aromatic powder 1 drachm, oil of caraway 12 drops. Dissolve as above, and then add the oil.

3. Gently Laxative Ball—Barbadoes aloes 3 to 5 drachms, rhubarb powder 1 to 2 drachms, ginger 2 drachms, oil of caraway 15 drops. Mix and form into a ball as in No. 1.

4. Stomachic Laxative Balls for Washy Horses—Barbadoes aloes 3 drachms, rhubarb 2 drachms, ginger 1 drachm, cascarilla powder 1 drachm, oil of caraway 15 drops, carbonate of soda 1½ drachms. Dissolve the aloes as in No. 1, and then add the other ingredients.

5. Purging Balls With Calomel—Barbadoes aloes 3 to 6 drachms, colomel ½ to 1 drachm, rhubarb 1 to 2 drachms, ginger ½ to 1 drachm, Castile soap 2 drachms. Mix as in No. 1.

6. Laxative Drench—Barbadoes aloes 3 to 4 drachms, canella alba 1 to 2 drachms, salts of tarter 1 drachm, mint water 8 ounces. Mix.

7. Another Laxative Drench—Castor oil 3 to 6 ounces, Barbadoes aloes 3 to 5 drachms, carbonate of soda 2 drachms, mint water 8 ounces. Mix by dissolving the aloes in the mint water by the aid of heat, and then adding the other ingredients.

8. Mild Opening Drench—Castor oil 4 ounces, Epsom salts 3 to 5 ounces, gruel 2 pints. Mix.

9. A Very Mild Laxative—Castor oil 4 ounces, linseed oil 4 ounces, warm water or gruel 1 pint. Mix.

10. Used in the Staggers—Barbadoes aloes 4 to 6 drachms, common salt 6 ounces, flour of mustard, 1 ounce, water 2 pints. Mix.

11. A Gently Cooling Drench in Slight Attacks of Cold—Epsom salts 6 to 8 ounces, whey 2 pints. Mix.

12. Purgative Clyster—Common salt 4 to 8 ounces, water 8 to 16 pints.

ASTRINGENTS

These appear to produce contraction on all living animal tissues with which they come into contact, whether in the interior or on the exterior of the body, and whether immediately applied or by absorption into the circulation. But great doubt exists as to the exact mode in which they act; and, as in many other cases, we are obliged to content ourselves with their effects, and to prescribe them empirically. They are divided into astringents administered by the mouth, and those applied locally to external ulcerated or wounded surfaces:

1. For Bloody Urine—Powdered catechu ½ ounce, alum ½ ounce, cascarilla bark in powder 1 to 2 drachms, liquorice powder and treacle enough to form a ball, to be given twice a day.

2. For Diabetes—Opium a half drachm, ginger powdered two drachms, oak bark powdered an ounce, alum as much as the tea will dissolve, camomile tea one pint. Mix for a drench.

3. External Astringent Powders for Ulcerated Surfaces—Powdered alum 4 ounces, Armenian bole 1 ounce.

Another—White vitriol 4 ounces, oxide of zinc 1 ounce. Mix.

4. Astringent Lotion—Goulard extract 2 to 3 drachms, water ½ pint. Mix.

Another—Sulphate of copper 1 to 2 drachms, water 1½ pint. Mix.

5. An Astringent Ointment for Sore Heels—Acetate of lead 1 drachm, lard 1 ounce. Mix.

6. Another for the Same—Nitrate of silver powdered ½ drachm, Goulard extract 1 drachm, lard 1 ounce. Mix and use a very small portion every night.

BLISTERS OR VESICANTS

Blisters are applications which inflame the skin, and produce a secretion of serum between the cutis and cuticle, by which the latter is raised in the form of small bladders; but in consequence of the presence of hair, these are very imperfectly seen in the horse. They consist of two kinds—one used for the sake of counter-irritation, by which the original disease is lessened, in consequence of the establishment of this irritation at a short distance from it; the other, commonly called "sweating" in veterinary surgery, by which a discharge is obtained from the vessels of the part itself, which are in that way relieved and unloaded; there is also a subsequent process of absorption in consequence of the peculiar stimulus applied.

1. A Mild Blistering Ointment (Counter-Irritant)—Hog's lard 4 ounces, Venice turpentine 1 ounce, powdered cantharides 6 drachms; mix and spread.

2. Stronger Blistering Ointment (Counter-Irritant)—Spirits of turpentine 1 ounce, sulphuric acid, by measure, 2 drachms; mix carefully in an open place; and add hog's lard 4 ounces, powdered cantharides 1 ounce; mix and spread.

3. Very Strong Blister Ointment (Counter-Irritant)—Strong mercurial ointment 4 ounces, oil of origanum ½ ounce, finely powdered euphorbium 3 drachms, powdered cantharides ½ ounce; mix and spread.

4. Rapidly Acting Blister Ointment (Counter-Irritant)—Best flour of mustard 8 ounces, made into a paste with water; add oil of turpentine 2 ounces, strong liquor of ammonia 1 ounce; this is to be well rubbed into the chest, belly, or back, in case of acute inflammation.

5. Sweating Blister—Strong mercurial ointment 2 ounces origanum oil 2 drachms, corrosive sublimate 2 drachms, cantharides powdered 3 drachms; mix and rub in with the hand.

6. Strong Sweating Blister, for Splints, Ring-Bones, Spavins, &tc.—Biniodide of mercury 1 to 1½ drachms, lard 1 ounce; to be well rubbed into the legs after cutting the hair short; and followed by the daily use of arnica in shape of a wash, as follows, which is to be painted on with a brush: tincture of arnica 1 ounce, water 12 to 15 ounces; mix.

7. A Liquid Sweating Blister—Cantharides 1 ounce, spirit of turpentine 2 ounces, methylated spirit of wine 1 pint; mix and digest for a fortnight, then strain.

Another—Powdered cantharides 1 ounce, commercial pyroligneous acid 1 pint; mix and digest for a fortnight; then strain.

CAUSTICS OR CAUTERIES

Caustics are substances which burn away the living tissues of the body, by the decomposition of their elements. They are of two kinds—first, the actual cautery, consisting in the application of the burning iron, and called firing; and, secondly, the potential cautery, by means of the powers of mineral caustics, such as fused potassa, lunar-caustic, corrosive sublimate, &tc. Firings are better left to the hand of the veterinary physician, while the following are the ordinary chemical applications used as potential cauteries:

1. Fused Potass—It is difficult to manage, because it runs about in all directions, and little used in veterinary medicine.

2. Lunar Caustic, or Nitrate of Silver—It is very valuable to the veterinary surgeon, and constantly used to apply to profuse granulations.

3. Sulphate of Copper—It is almost equally useful, but not so strong as lunar caustic; it may be well rubbed in to all high granulations, as in broken knees and similar growths.

4. Corrosive Sublimate in powder—It acts most energetically upon warty growths, but should be used with great care and discretion. It may safely be applied to small surfaces, but should not without a regular practitioner to larger ones.

5. Yellow Orpiment—It is not so strong as Corrosive Sublimate, and may be used with more freedom. It will generally remove warty growths, by picking off their heads and rubbing it in.

6. Muriate of Antimony—This also is called Butter of Antimony; a strong but rather unmanageable caustic, and used either by itself or mixed with more or less water.

7. Chloride of Zinc—It is a most powerful caustic. It may be used in old sinuses in solution, 7 drachms in a pint of water.

Milder Caustics—Verdigris—either in powder or mixed with lard as an ointment, in the proportion of 1 to 3. *Red precipitate*—ditto, ditto. *Burnt alum*—used dry. *Powdered white sugar.*

Mild Liquid Caustics—Solution of nitrate of silver—5 to 15 grains to the ounce of distilled water. *Solution of blue vitriol*—of about double the above strength. *Chloride of zinc*—1 to 3 grains to the ounce of water.

CHARGES

These are adhesive plasters which are spread while hot on the legs, and at once covered with short tow, so as to form a strong and unyielding support while the horse is at grass.

1. Ordinary Charge—Burgundy pitch 4 ounces, Barbadoes tar 6 ounces, beeswax 2 ounces, red lead 4 ounces. The first three are to be melted together and afterwards the lead is to be added. The mixture is to be kept constantly stirred until sufficiently cold to be applied. If too stiff (which will depend upon the weather) it may be softened by the addition of a little lard or oil.

2. Arnica Charge—Canada balsam 2 ounces, powdered arnica leaves 1 ounce. The balsam is to be melted and worked up with the leaves, adding spirits of turpentine if necessary. When thoroughly mixed, to be well rubbed into the whole leg, in a thin layer, and to be covered over with Charge No. 1, which will set on its outside and act as a bandage, while the arnica is a restorative to the weakened vessels. This is an excellent application.

CLYSTERS OR ENEMATA

Clysters are intended either to relieve obstruction or spasm of the bowels, and are of great service when properly applied. They may be made of warm water or gruel, of which some quarts will be required in colic. They should be thrown up with the proper syringe, provided with valves and flexible tube.

For the turpentine clyster in colic, *see* Antispasmodics.

For Aperient clysters, *see* Aperients.

Anodyne Clyster in Diarrhoea— Starch made as for washing 1 quart, powdered opium 2 drachms. The opium is to be boiled in water and added to the starch.

CORDIALS

These are medicines which act as temporary stimulants to the whole system, and especially to the stomach. They augment the strength and spirits when depressed, as after over-exertion in work:

1. Cordial Balls—Powdered caraway seeds 6 drachms, ginger 2 drachms, oil of cloves 20 drops, treacle enough to make into a ball.

Another—Powdered anise seeds 6 drachms, powdered cardamons 2 drachms, powdered cassia 1 drachm, oil of caraway 20 drops. Mix with treacle into ball.

2. Cordial Drench—A quart of good ale warmed with plenty of grated ginger.

3. Cordial and Expectorant— Powdered anise seeds ½ ounce, powdered squill 1 drachm, powdered myrrh 1½ drachms, balsam of Peru enough to form a ball.

Another—Liquorice powder ½ ounce, gum ammoniacum 3 drachms, balsam of tolu 1½ drachms, powdered squill 1 drachm, linseed meal and boiling water enough to form into a mass.

DEMULCENTS

These are used for the purpose of soothing irritations of the bowels, kidneys, or bladder—in the two last cases by their effect upon the secretion of urine.

1. A Demulcent Drench—Gum Arabic ½ ounce, water 1 pint. Dissolve and give as a drench night and morning, or mixed with a mash.

Another—Linseed 4 ounces, water 1 quart. Simmer till a strong and thick decoction is obtained, and give as above.

2. Marshmallow Drench—Marshmallows a double handful, water 1 quart. Simmer as in the second part of No. 1 and use in the same way.

DIAPHORETICS

These have a special action on the skin, increasing the perspiration sometimes to an enormous extent.

1. Ordinary Diaphoretic Drench—Solution of acetate of ammonia 3 to 4 ounces, laudanum 1 ounce. Mix and give at night.

Another—Solution of acetate of ammonia 2 ounces, spirits of nitric ether 2 ounces. Mix and give as above.

2. In Hide-Bound—Emetic tartar 1½ drachms, camphor ½ drachm, ginger 2 drachms, opium ½ drachm, oil of caraway 15 drops, linseed meal and boiling water to form a ball, which is to be given twice or thrice a week.

3. In Hide-Bound (but not so efficacious)—Antimonial powder 2 drachms, ginger 1 drachm, powdered caraway seeds 6 drachms, oil of anise seed 20 drops. Mix as above.

These remedies require moderate exercise in clothing to bring out their effects, after which the horse should be wisped till quite dry.

DIGESTIVES

These are applications which promote suppuration, and the healing of wounds or ulcers.

Digestive Ointment—Red precipitate 2 ounces, Venice turpentine 3 ounces, beeswax 1 ounce, hog's lard 4 ounces; melt the last three ingredients over a slow fire, and when nearly cold stir in the powder.

DIURETICS

These are medicines which promote the secretion and discharge of urine, the effect being produced in a different manner by different medicines; some acting directly upon the kidneys by sympathy with the stomach, while others are taken up by the blood vessels, and in their elimination from the blood, cause an extra secretion of the urine. In either case, their effect is to diminish the watery part of the blood, and thus promote the absorption of fluid effused into any of the cavities, or into the cellular membranes in the various forms of dropsy.

1. Stimulating Diuretic Ball—Powdered resin 3 drachms, sal prunella 3 drachms, Castile soap 3 drachms, oil of juniper 1 drachm; mix.

2. A More Cooling Diuretic Ball—Powdered nitre ½ to 1 ounce, camphor 1 drachm, juniper berries 1 drachm, soap 3 drachms; mix, adding linseed meal enough to form a ball.

3. Diuretic Powder for a Mash—

Nitre ½ to ¾ ounce, resin ½ to ¾ ounce, mix.

4. Another More Active Powder —Nitre 6 drachms, camphor 1½ drachms; mix.

EMBROCATIONS

These are liniments which are stimulating or sedative external applications, intended to reduce the pain and inflammation of internal parts, when rubbed into the skin with the hand.

1. A Mustard Embrocation—Best flour of mustard 6 ounces, liquor of ammonia 1½ ounces, oil of turpentine 1½ ounces; mix with sufficient water to form a thin paste.

2. A Stimulating Embrocation— Camphor ½ ounce, oil of turpentine 1½ ounces, spirit of wine 1½ ounces; mix.

3. A Sweating Embrocation for Windgalls, &tc.—Strong mercurial ointment 2 ounces, camphor ½ ounce, oil of rosemary 2 drachms, oil of turpentine 1 ounce; mix.

4. Another, but Much Stronger— Strong mercurial ointment 2 ounces, oil of bay 1 ounce, oil of origanum ½ ounce, powdered cantharides ½ ounce; mix.

5. A Most Active Sweating Embrocation—Biniodide of mercury ½ to 1 drachm powdered arnica leaves 1 drachm, soap liniment 2 ounces; mix.

6. A Wonderful Liniment for Both Horse and Man—Oil of spike 2 ounces, origanum 2 ounces, hemlock 2 ounces, wormwood 2 ounces, sweet oil 4 ounces, spirit of ammonia 2 ounces, gum camphor 2 ounces, spirits of turpentine 2 ounces. Add one quart of strong alcohol. Mix well together and bottle tight. Excellent for rheumatism, sprains, &tc.

EMULSIONS

When oily matters have their globules broken down by friction with mucilaginous substances, such as gum arabic or yolk of egg, they are called emulsions, and are specially useful in soothing irritation of the mucous membrane, of the trachea and bronchi.

1. Simple Emulsion—Linseed oil 2 ounces, honey 3 ounces, soft water 1 pint, subcarbonate of potass 1 drachm; dissolve the honey and potass in the water; then add the linseed oil by degrees in a large mortar, when it should assume a milky appearance. It may be given night and morning.

2. Another More Active Emulsion—Simple emulsion No. 1, 7 ounces, camphor 1 drachm, opium in powder ½ drachm, oil of anise seed 30 drops; rub the last three ingredients together in a mortar with some white sugar; then add the emulsion by degrees.

HORSE EXPECTORANTS

These medicines excite or promote a discharge of mucus from the lining membrane of the bronchial tubes, thereby relieving inflammation and allaying cough.

1. Expectorant Ball in Ordinary Cough Without Inflammation— Gum ammoniacum ½ ounce, powdered squill 1 drachm, Castile soap 2 drachms; honey enough to form a ball.

2. *For an Old Standing Cough (Stomach)* —Assafœtida 3 drachms, galbanum 1 drachm, carbonate of ammonia ½ drachm, ginger 1½ drachms; honey enough to form a ball.

3. *Strong Expectorant Ball*—Emetic tarter ½ drachm, calomel 15 grains, digitalis ½ drachm, powdered squill ½ drachm, linseed meal and water enough to form a ball, which is not to be repeated without great care.

FEBRIFUGES

Generally called fever medicines, are given to allay the arterial and nervous excitements which accompany febrile action. They do this partly by their agency on the heart and arteries through the nervous system, and partly by increasing the secretions of the skin and kidneys.

1. *Fever Ball*—Nitre 4 drachms, camphor 1½ drachms, calomel and opium, of each 1 scruple, linseed meal, as above.

Another—Emetic tartar 1½ to 2 drachms, compound powder of tragacanth 2 drachms; linseed meal and water enough to form a ball.

Another—Nitre 3 drachms, camphor 2 drachms; mix as above.

2. *Cooling Powder for Mash*—Nitre 6 drachms to 1 ounce; may be given in a bran mash.

3. *A Cooling Drench*—Nitre 1 ounce, sweet spirits of nitre 2 ounces, tincture of digitalis 2 drachms, whey 1 pint.

LOTIONS OR WASHES

Consist of liquids applied to the external parts, either to cool them or to produce a healthy action in the vessels.

1. *Cooling Solution for External Inflammation*—Goulard extract 1 ounce, vinegar 2 ounces, spirits of wine or gin 3 ounces, water 1½ pints; mix, and apply with a calico bandage.

2. *Another, Useful for Inflamed Legs, or for Galled Shoulders or Back*—Sal ammoniac 1 ounce, vinegar 4 ounces, spirits of wine 2 ounces, tincture of arnica 2 drachms, water ½ pint; mix.

3. *Lotion for Foul Ulcers*—Sulphate of copper 1 ounce, nitric acid ½ ounce, water 8 to 12 ounces; mix.

4. *Lotion for the Eyes*—Sulphate of zinc 20 to 25 grains, water 6 ounces; mix.

5. *Very Strong One, and Only to Be Dropped In*—Nitrate of silver 5 to 8 grains, distilled water 1 ounce; mix and use with a camel-hair brush.

NARCOTICS

A distinction is sometimes made between anodynes and narcotics, but in veterinary medicine there is no necessity for separating them. (*See* Anodynes.)

REFRIGERANTS

These medicines lower the animal body heat by contact with the skin, the ordinary ones being cold air, cold water, ice, and evaporative lotions. (*See* Lotions.)

SEDATIVES

These medicines depress the action of the circulatory and nervous systems, without effecting the mental functions. They are very strong and powerful in their effects; and

digitalis, which is the drug commonly used for this purpose, has a special quality known by the name of *cumulative;* that is to say, if repeated, small doses are given at intervals for a certain time, the effect is produced almost equal to that which would follow the exhibition of the whole quantity at once. Besides digitalis, aconite is also sometimes used to lower the action of the heart, and by many it is supposed to be equal in potency to that drug, without the danger which always attends its use.

STIMULANTS

By this term is understood those substances which excite the action of the whole nervous and vascular systems; almost all medicines are stimulants to some part or other, as, for instance, aperients, which stimulate the lining of the bowels, but to the general system are lowering. On the other hand, stimulants, so called *par excellence,* excite and raise the action of the brain and heart.

An Excellent Stimulant—Old ale 1 quart, carbonate of ammonia ½ to 2 drachms, tincture of ginger 4 drachms; mix and give as a drench.

(For other stimulants, *see* Cordials.)

STOMACHICS

Stomachics are medicines given to improve the tone of the stomach, when impaired by bad management or disease.

Stomachics Ball—Powdered gentian ½ ounce, powdered ginger 1½ drachms, carbonate of soda 1 drachm; treacle to form a ball.

Another—Cascarilla powdered 1 ounce, myrrh 1½ drachms, Castile soap 1 drachm; mix with syrup or treacle into a ball.

Another—Powdered colombo ½ to 1 ounce, powdered cassia 1 drachm, powdered rhubarb 2 drachms; mix with syrup or treacle into a ball.

STYPTICS

Styptics are remedies which have a tendency to stop the flow of blood either from internal or external surfaces. They are used either by the mouth, or to the part itself in the shape of lotions, &tc.; or the actual cautery, which is always the best in external bleeding, may be employed. Sometimes, however, the part cannot be reached with the heated iron, and is yet within the influence of an injection, as in bleeding from the nostrils, for which the following may be employed:

Matico leaves—½ ounce, boiling water 1 pint, infuse, and when cold strain and inject into the nostrils.

(For internal styptics, *see* Astringents.)

TONICS

Augment the vigor of the whole body permanently, whilst stimulants only act for a short time. They are chiefly used after low fever.

Tonic Ball—Sulphate of iron ½ ounce, extract of camomile 1 ounce; mix and form into ball.

Horses in Norway have a very sensible way of taking their food, which perhaps might be beneficially followed in this country. They have a bucket of water put down beside their allowance of hay. It is interesting to see with what relish they take a sip of the one and a mouthful of the other alternately, sometimes only moistening their mouths, as a rational being would do while eating a dinner of such dry food. A broken-winded horse is scarcely ever seen in Norway, and the question is if the mode of feeding has not something to do with the preservation of the animal's respiratory organs.

Chapter 26

Home remedies & other information of interest

MEDICINES FOR CATTLE, SHEEP, & SWINE

MEDICINES FOR CATTLE

1. Drink, Alterative—Take flowers of sulphur 2 ounces, black sulphuret of antimony 1 ounce, Æthiop's mineral ½ ounce, nitre 2 ounces; mix and divide into four powders, give one every second morning in a little thick gruel.

Turning into a salt marsh would be an excellent auxiliary.

2. Drink, Anodyne—Take powdered opium ½ drachm, sweet spirit of nitre 2 ounces; rub them well together, adding the fluid by

small quantities at a time, and give the mixture in a pint of warm gruel.

3. Drink, Astringent—Take prepared chalk 2 ounces, oak bark powdered 1 ounce, catechu powdered ½ ounce, opium powdered 2 scruples, ginger powdered 2 drachms; mix, and give in a quart of warm gruel.

4. Drink, Astringent, with Mutton Suet—Take mutton suet 1 pound, new milk 2 quarts; boil them together till the suet is dissolved; then add opium powdered ½ drachm, ginger 1 drachm; having previously well mixed them with a spoonful or two of the fluid.

5. Astringent, Mild—Take oak bark powdered ½ ounce, catechu powdered 2 drachms, opium powdered ½ scruple; mix together in a pint of gruel or warm water.

6. An Astringent Powder—Take blue vitrol powdered ½ ounce, powdered alum ½ ounce, prepared chalk 2 ounces, Armenian bole 1 ounce; mix.

7. Astringent, for Stimulating—Take oil of juniper 2 to 4 drachms, tincture of opium 1 ounce, oil of turpentine 1 ounce; mix, and give in a pint of linseed tea once or twice a day.

8. Embrocation for Bite of Serpents—Take hartshorn and olive oil equal quantities. Shake them well together and rub the wound and the neighboring parts well with the liniment morning and night.

9. Drink for Inflammation of the Bladder—Take antimonial powder 2 drachms, powdered opium 1 scruple; rub well together with a small portion of very thick gruel, and repeat the dose morning and night.

10. Ointment, for Blister—Take lard 12 ounces, resin 4 ounces, melt them together, and when they are getting cold add oil of turpentine 4 ounces, powdered cantharides 5 ounces; stirring the whole together.

11. Bull Burnt (venereal disease), Lotion for—Take Goulard's extract 1 ounce, spirit of wine 2 ounces, water ½ pint; mix.

12. Camphorated Oil Mix—Take camphor 2 ounces, and break into small pieces; put it into a pint of spermaceti, or common olive oil, and let the bottle, being closely corked and shaken every day, stand in a warm place until the camphor is dissolved.

13. Drink, Cordial—Take caraway powder 1 ounce, gentian powdered ½ ounce, essence of peppermint 20 drops; mix.

14. Drink, Good Cordial—Take caraway seeds in powder ½ ounce, anise seeds in powder ½ ounce, ginger ½ ounce; mix with a pint of good ale, made hot.

15. Drink, Cough & Fever—Take emetic tartar 1 drachm, powdered digitalis ½ drachm, nitre 3 drachms; mix and give in a quart of tolerably thick gruel.

16. Cow-Pox, Lotion for—Take sal ammoniac ¼ ounce, white wine vinegar ½ pint, camphorated spirit of wine 2 ounces, Goulard's extract 1 ounce; mix and keep it in a bottle for use.

17. Lotion, A Discutient—Take bay salt 4 ounces, vinegar 1 pint, water 1 quart, oil of origanum 1 drachm; add the oil to salt first; rub them well down with a little water; then gradually add the balance of the water and vinegar.

18. Lotion, A Disinfectant—Take solution of chloride of lime, in powdered ¼ ounce, water 1 pint; mix.

19. Drink, Diuretic—Take powdered nitre 1 ounce, powdered resin 2 ounces, ginger 2 drachms; mix well together in a little treacle, and give them in a warm gruel.

20. Eye Lotion, A Sedative—Take dried leaves of foxglove powdered 1½ ounces; infuse them in a pint of Cape or dry raisin wine for a fortnight, and keep the infusion for use.

21. Eye Lotion, A Sedative—Take the extract of Goulard 2 drachms, spiritous tincture of digitalis (made in the same manner as the vinous in receipt 20) 2 drachms, tincture of opium 2 drachms, water 1 pint; this should also be introduced into the eye. Two or three drops at a time will suffice.

22. Lotion for the Eye, Strengthening—Take white vitriol 1 scruple, spirit of wine 1 drachm, water 1 pint; mix them together, and use the lotion in the same manner as Nos. 20 and 21.

23. Drink, an Expectorant—Take liquorice root 2 ounces; bruise and boil in a quart of water until the fluid is reduced to a pint, then gradually and carefully add powdered squills 2 drachms, powdered gum guaiacum 1 drachm, tincture of balsam of tolu ½ ounce, honey 2 ounces; give it morning and night.

24. Fumigation of Barn—Take common salt 2 pounds, oil of vitriol 1 pound; mix.

25. Liniment—Take alum and white vitriol, of each ½ ounce, treacle 1 gill; dissolve in a pint of warm water.

26. Anodyne Drink, for Lock Jaw—Take camphor 1 drachm, rub it down in an ounce of spirit of wine; to this add: powdered opium 1 drachm; and give the mixture in a small quantity of thick gruel.

27. Physic Drink, for Lock Jaw, Strong—Take Barbadoes aloes 1½ ounce, kernel of croton nut powder 10 grains; dissolve in as small quantity of boiling water as possible, and give them when the liquid is sufficiently cool.

28. Fine Mange Ointment—Take flowers of sulphur 1 pound, strong mercurial ointment 2 ounces, common turpentine ½ pound, lard 1½ pounds; melt the turpentine and lard together; stir well in the sulphur when these begin to cool; and afterwards rub down the mercurial ointment on a marble slab with the other ingredients.

29. Murrain, Drink for—Take sweet spirit of nitre ½ ounce, laudanum ½ ounce, chloride of lime, in powder 2 ounces, prepared chalk 1 ounce; rub them well together, and give them with a pint of warm gruel.

30. Drink, Tonic, for Murrain—Take columbia root 2 drachms, canella bark 2 drachms, ginger 1 drachm, sweet spirit of nitre ½ ounce; rub them together, and give in a pint of thick gruel.

31. Ointment, Good Healing & Cleansing—Take lard 2 pounds,

resin ½ pound; melt them together, and when nearly cold, stir in calamine, very finely powdered, half a pound.

32. Ointment, Iodine—Take iodate of potash 1 drachm, lard 7 drachms; rub them well together.

33. Drink, Laxative—Take Epsom salts ½ pound, sulphur 2 to 4 ounces, nitre ½ ounce, ginger 2 drachms, spirit of nitrous ether 1 ounce; dissolve in warm water or gruel, and repeat once a day for several days.

34. Drink, Purging—Take Epsom salts 1 pound, powdered caraway seeds ½ ounce; dissolve in a quart of warm gruel and give.

35. Drink, Purging—Take emetic tartar ½ drachm, nitre 2 drachms, powdered gentian root 1 drachm, powdered camomile flowers 1 drachm, powdered ginger ½ drachm; pour upon them a pint of boiling ale, and give the infusion when nearly cold.

36. Drink, Purgative, Strong—Take Epsom or Glauber salts 12 ounces, flowers of sulphur 4 ounces, powdered ginger 4 drachms, spirit of nitrous ether 1 ounce; to be dissolved in warm water.

37. Drink, Physic, Strong—Take Epsom or Glauber salts ½ pound, kernel of croton nut 10 grains; take off the shell of the croton nut, and weigh the proper quantity of the kernel, rub it down to a fine powder, gradually mix it with half a pint of thick gruel, and give it and immediately afterwards give the salts, dissolved in a pint and a half of thinner gruel.

38. Drink, Sulphur, Purging— Take sulphur 8 ounces, ginger ½ ounce; mix with a quart of warm gruel. The drink should be repeated every third day if the bowels appear to require it.

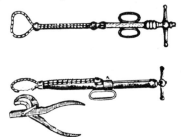

*39. Drink, Rheumatic—*Take nitre 2 drachms, tartarized antimony 1 drachm, spirit of nitrous ether 1 ounce, anise seed powder 1 ounce; mix with a pint of very thick gruel, and repeat the dose morning and night, except when it is necessary to give the sulphur purging drink, No. 38.

40. Drink, Cordial, Rheumatic —Take rhododendron leaves 4 drachms, boil them in a quart of water until it is diminished to a pint; strain the decoction, and to half of the liquid, warm, add gum guaiacum finely powdered 2 drachms, powdered caraway seeds

2 drachms, powdered anise seeds 2 drachms; mixed with half a pint of warm ale.

41. Embrocation, Rheumatic— Take neatsfoot oil 4 ounces, camphorated oil, spirit of turpentine, laudanum, each 1 ounce, oil of origanum 1 drachm; mix.

*42. Drink, Stimulating—*Take digitalis 1 scruple, emetic tartar ½ drachm, nitre 3 drachms, powdered squills 1 drachm, opium 1 scruple; mix, and give in a pint of gruel.

*43. Drink, Stimulating—*Take Epsom or Glauber salts 1 pound, ginger ½ ounce, carbonate of ammonia ½ ounce, pour one quart of boiling water upon the ingredients; stir them well, and give when milk warm.

44. Drink, Stimulant, Warm— Take ginger powdered ½ ounce, caraway seeds 6 drachms, allspice ½ ounce; mix in a quart of warm water or mild ale.

45. Stimulating Drink, Mild— Take ginger 1 drachm, gentian 1 drachm, spirit of nitrous ether 1 ounce; mix, and give in a pint of gruel.

46. Charge for Old Strains & *Lameness—*Take burgundy pitch 4 ounces, common pitch 4 ounces, yellow wax 2 ounces, Barbadoes tar 6 ounces; melt them together in a ladle, and apply the mixture to the parts when thoroughly warm and liquid.

47. An Embrocation for Strains, Strong—Take bay salt 4 ounces, oil of origanum 1 drachm; rub them well together, until the salt is reduced to a powder; then add: vinegar ½ pint, spirit of wine 2 ounces, water 1 quart.

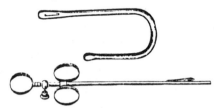

48. Embrocation for Strains, Strongest—Take spirits of turpentine ½ ounce, oil of origanum ½ ounce, olive oil 1½ pints, cantharides 1 ounce; mix them together; shake them often and keep in a bottle for use.

49. Ointment for Sore Teats—Take elder ointment 6 ounces, beeswax 2 ounces; mix them together, and add an ounce each of sugar of lead and alum in fine powder, and stir them together until cold.

50. Ointment, Mercurial Garget—Take soft soap 1 pound, mercurial ointment 2 ounces, camphor rubbed down with a little spirit of wine 1 ounce; rub them well together.

51. Tonic Powder, Alterative—Take flowers of sulphur 4 ounces, black sulphuret of antimony 1 ounce, Æthiop's mineral ½ ounce, nitre 2 ounces, powdered gentian 2 ounces, powdered ginger 1 ounce; mix and divide into six powders, and give one daily.

52. Drink, Tonic—Take gentian root powdered ½ ounce, ginger powdered 1 drachm, Epsom salts 2 ounces; mix the whole with a pint of warm gruel, and give it morning and night.

53. Drink, Tonic—Take gentian 2 drachms, tartrate of iron 1 drachm; mix, and give in a pint of gruel.

54. Drink, Tonic, Mildest—Take gentian 2 drachms, emetic tartar ½ drachm, nitre ½ ounce, spirit of nitrous ether ½ ounce; mix, give in gruel.

55. Tonic, Strong—Take powdered ginger 1 drachm, powdered caraway seeds 1 drachm, gentian powdered 4 drachms, spirit of nitrous ether 1 ounce; to be mixed slowly with gruel.

56. Vermin, Excellent Lotion for—Take corrosive sublimate 2 drachms, rub it down in 2 ounces of spirits of wine, and add a pint of water.

57. Vermin, A Mercurial Ointment for—Take strong mercurial ointment 1 ounce, lard 7 ounces; mix them well together, and rub the ointment well on wherever the lice appear.

58. Whey, Alum—Take alum ½ ounce, water 2 quarts; boil them together for 10 minutes and drain.

59. Drink, Turpentine, Good for Worms—Take oil of turpentine 2 ounces, sweet spirit of nitre 1 ounce, laudanum ½ ounce, linseed oil 4 ounces; mix, and give in a pint of gruel.

60. Drink for the Yellows—Take of calomel and opium, a scruple; mix and suspend in a little thick gruel.

MEDICINES FOR CALVES

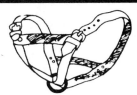

1. Drink, Aperient for—Take Epsom salts, from 1 to 2 ounces, according to the age and size of the calf, and dissolve in half a pint of gruel; then add ginger, 1 scruple; essence of peppermint 3 drops; mix.

2. Diarrhoea in—Take prepared chalk 2 drachms, powdered opium 10 grains, powdered catechu ½ drachm, ginger ½ drachm, essence of peppermint 5 drops; mix and give twice a day in half pint of gruel.

3. Hoove in (Bloat)—Take oil of turpentine 1 ounce, linseed oil 3 to 4 ounces, ginger powdered 1 drachm; mix. To be repeated at the interval of a week, as often as may be required.

4. Purging, to Stop—Take Dover's powder 2 scruples, starch or arrow-root in powder 1 ounce, compound cinnamon powder 1 drachm, powdered kino ½ drachm; boil the starch or arrow-root in a pint of water until it becomes well thickened, and then gradually stir in the other ingredients.

MEDICINES FOR SHEEP

1. Astringent Drink—Take compound chalk powder with opium 1 drachm, gentian 1 scruple, essence

of peppermint 3 drops; mix with a little thin starch, and give morning and night.

2. Astringent, Powder for—Take prepared chalk ¼ ounce, ginger ½ drachm, catechu powdered ½ drachm, powdered opium 2 grains; give this in a little gruel twice daily, until the purging abates.

3. Physic for Blown—Take Glauber salts 1 ounce, and dissolve in peppermint water 4 ounces; to this add tincture of ginger 1 drachm; tincture of gentian 1 drachm; boiling water one ounce. This should be given every six hours until the bowels are open, and half the quantity on each of the next four mornings.

4. Lotion for Cloudiness on the Eyes—Take corrosive sublimate 4 grains; rub it down with spirits of wine ¼ ounce; and add one pint of water.

5. Cooling Fever Drink—Take of powdered digitalis 1 scruple, emetic tartar 10 grains, nitre 2 drachms; mix with thick gruel, and let it be given twice a day.

6. Fly, Powder for—Take white lead 2 pounds, red lead 1 pound, and mix them together.

7. Ointment for Sore Heads—Take black pitch 2 pounds, tar 1 pound, flowers of sulphur 1 pound; melt them in an iron pot over a very slow fire, stirring together the ingredients as they begin to melt, but carefully watching the compound, and removing the pot from the fire the moment the ingredients are well mixed, and before they begin to boil, for they would then rapidly swell to an extraordinary extent, and the whole mass would run over into the fire.

8. Arsenical Wash for Lice—Take arsenic 2 pounds, soft soap 4 pounds, dissolve in 30 gallons of water.

9. Mercurial Wash for Lice—Take corrosive sublimate 1 ounce, spirits of wine 2 ounces. Rub the corrosive sublimate in the spirit until it is dissolved, and then add cream of tartar 1 ounce, bay salt 4 ounces. Dissolve the whole in two quarts of water, and apply a little of it with a small piece of sponge whenever the lice appear.

10. Laxative Medicine—Take Epsom salts 1 ounce, ginger 1 scruple, gentian 1 drachm, warm water 2 ounces, linseed oil 1 ounce; the above may be given either alone or with gruel, to a full grown sheep; and from one-fourth to one-half to a lamb, according to its age.

11. Mild Laxative—Take linseed oil 2 ounces, powdered opium 2 grains; to be mixed with linseed tea, linseed and oatmeal gruel should be given several times a day, and the second day the astringent powder for sheep should be given.

12. Purging Drink—Take Epsom salts 2 ounces, powdered caraway ¼ ounce; warm thin gruel sufficient to dissolve the salts.

13. Mixture for the Rot—Take common salt 8 ounces, powdered gentian 2 ounces, ginger 1 ounce, tincture of colombo 4 ounces; put the whole into a quart bottle so as to fill the bottle.

14. Second Mixture for the Rot—Take of the receipt, Mixture for the Rot (which see), one quart. To this add, spirits of turpentine 3 ounces. Shake them well together when first mixed, and whenever the medicine is given, and two tablespoonfuls are the usual dose.

15. Caustic, Astringent Powder for Foot Rot—Take verdigris, Armenian bole, and sugar of lead, equal parts. Rub them well together, until they are reduced to a fine powder.

16. Mercurial Ointment for Scab—Take crude quicksilver 1 pound, Venice turpentine ½ pound, spirits of turpentine 2 ounces, mix.

17. Mild ointment for Scab—Take flower of sulphur 1 pound, Venice turpentine 4 ounces, rancid lard 2 pounds, strong mercurial ointment 4 ounces; rub them well together.

18. Powerful Ointment for Scab—Take white hellebore 3 ounces, bichloride of mercury 2 ounces, fish oil 12 pounds, resin 6 ounces, tallow ½ pound; the first two ingredients to be mixed with a portion of the oil; and then melt the other ingredients and add.

19. Smearing Mixture for Scab—Take a gallon of common tar, and 12 pounds of any sweet grease. Melt them together, stirring them well while they are cooling.

20. Strengthening Drink—Take prepared chalk 1 ounce, catechu ½ drachm, opium 20 grains, spirit of nitrous ether 2 drachms, gentian 1 drachm; to be dissolved in gruel, and given twice a day till the purging ceases; after which the last two ingredients, with a drachm of nitre and 10 grains of tartarized antimony, should be given in gruel once a day.

21. General Tonic Drink—Take gentian 2 drachms, colombo 1 drachm, ginger ½ drachm; give in four ounces of warm gruel.

22. Tonic Drink—Take gentian root powdered 1 drachm, caraway powder ½ drachm, tincture of caraway 10 drops; give in a quarter of a pint of thick gruel.

23. Tonic Drink for Debility—Take gentian and powdered caraway seeds, of each 1 ounce; colombo and ginger, of each ½ ounce. Pour a quart of boiling water upon them, and let the infusion stand three days, stirring it well every day. Then pour off the clear liquid, and bottle it for use. Give a tablespoonful daily in a little gruel, mixed with an equal quantity of good ale.

and give in a little warm swill, or milk, or mash.

MEDICINES FOR SWINE

1. Alterative, Powder for—Take flowers of sulphur ¼ ounce, Æthiop's mineral 3 grains, nitre

and cream of tartar ½ drachm; mix and give daily in a little thickened gruel or wash.

2. Fever Medicines for—Take digitalis 3 grains, antimonial powder 6 grains, nitre ½ drachm; mix

OTHER INTERESTING FACTS

GESTATION PERIODS OF VARIOUS ANIMALS

The Horse—The gestation period of the horse and ass is eleven months each.

The Cow—The cow, like the human being, has a gestation period of nine months.

Sheep—The ewe has a gestation period of five months. Twins are not the least unusual.

Swine—The sow has a gestation period of sixteen weeks.

Other domesticated or familiar animals—Plains buffalo, twelve months; dog, nine weeks; cat, eight

weeks; she-wolf, from ninety to ninety-five days. The goose sits thirty days; swans, forty-two; hens, twenty-one; ducks, thirty; peahen and turkey hen, twenty-eight; canaries, fourteen; pigeons, fourteen; and parrots, forty.

LONGEVITY OF DOMESTICATED & FAMILIAR ANIMALS

Beaver, 50 years; deer, 20; wolf, 20; fox, 14 to 16; chamois, 25; monkey and baboon, 16 to 18; hare, 8; squirrel, 7; rabbit, 7; swine, 25; stag, under 50; horse, 30; ass, 30; sheep, under 10; cow, 20; ox, 30; swan, parrot and raven, 200; eagle, 100; goose, 80; hen and pigeon, 10 to 16; hawk, 36 to 40; crane, 24; blackbird, 10 to 12; peacock, 20; pelican, 40 to 50; thrush, 8 to 10; wren, 2 to 3; nightingale, 15; blackcap, 15; linnet, 14 to 23; goldfinch, 20 to 24; redbreast, 10 to 12; skylark, 10 to 30; titlark, 5 to 6; chaffinch, 20 to 24; starling, 10 to 12; crocodile, 100; tortoise, 100 to 200; and whale, estimated 1,000.

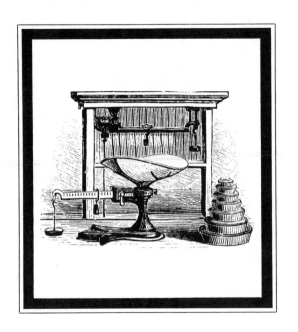

Part Five

WEIGHTS & MEASURES

Chapter 27

Seeds, feeds, corn in the crib, & other

TABLES

LIQUID OR WINE MEASURE

Used in measuring liquids such as molasses, milk, and various liquids. A minim is about 1 drop.

60 minims = 1 drachm (dram).
8 drachms = 1 ounce.
1 teaspoonful = 120 drops of water, or 60 drops of thick fluid.
1 teaspoonful = 5 cubic centimeters.
2 teaspoonfuls = a dessertspoonful.
3 teaspoonfuls = 1 tablespoonful.
1 tablespoonful = 15 cubic centimeters or ½ oz.
2 tablespoonfuls = 1 ounce.

1 ounce = 30 cubic centimeters.
8 ounces = 1 cupful.
16 tablespoonfuls = 1 cupful.
1 gill = ½ cupful.
2 gills = 1 cupful.
4 gills = 1 pint–pt.
2 cupfuls = 1 pint–pt.
2 pints = 1 quart–qt.
8 gills = 1 quart–qt.
4 quarts = 1 gallon–gal.
31½ gal. = 1 barrel–bbl.
2 bbl. = 1 hogshead–hhd.
Also,
36 gallons = 1 barrel of ale or beer.
54 gallons = 1 hogshead of ale or beer.
42 gallons = 1 tierce.
2 hogsheads = 1 pipe or but.
2 pipes = 1 tun.
231 cubic inches = 1 gallon.

DRY MEASURE
Used in measuring grain, fruit & vegetables.
2 pints (pt.) = 1 quart–qt.
8 qt. = 1 peck–pk.
4 pk. = 1 bushel–bu.

AVOIRDUPOIS WEIGHT
Used in weighing hay, grain, groceries, and coarse articles.
437½ grains = 1 ounce–oz.
16 ounces = 1 pound–lb.
25 lb. = 1 quarter–qr.
4 qr. = 1 hundred weight–cwt.
20 cwt. = 1 ton (short).
2240 lb. = 1 long ton.

The long ton is used in the United States custom houses and in England.

TROY WEIGHT
For weighing gold, silver, and jewels.
24 grans (gr.) = 1 pennyweight–pwt.
20 pwt. = 1 ounce–oz.
12 oz. = 1 pound–lb.

APOTHECARIES' WEIGHT
Used by druggists in compounding medicines, although drugs are bought at wholesale by avoirdupois weight.
20 grains (gr. xx) = 1 scruple–℈
3 scruples (℈ iij) = 1 drachm–ʒ
8 drachms (ʒ viij) = 1 ounce–℥
12 ounces (℥ xij) = 1 pound–lb.

CLOTH MEASURE
2¼ inches = 1 nail–na.
4 na = 1 quarter–qr.
4 qr. = 1 yard–yd.
5 qr. = 1 Ell English–E.E.

MISCELLANEOUS TABLE
12 units = 1 dozen.
12 dozen = 1 gross.
12 gross = 1 great gross.
20 things = 1 score.
100 pounds = 1 quintal of fish.
196 pounds = 1 barrel of flour.
200 pounds = 1 barrel of pork or beef.
600 pounds = 1 barrel of rice.
56 pounds = 1 firkin of butter.
14 pounds = 1 stone of iron or lead.
21½ pound = 1 pig.
8 pigs = 1 fother.
3 inches = 1 palm.
4 inches = 1 hand.

9 inches = 1 span.
18 inches = 1 cubit.
22 inches (nearly) = 1 sacred cubit.
2½ feet = 1 military pace.
3 feet = 1 common pace.

HOW TO MEASURE CORN IN THE CRIB
Common sense rules to follow:

Rule: 1st—Measure the length, breadth and height of the crib inside the rail; multiply them together and divide by two, the result is the number of bushels of *shelled* corn.

Rule: 2d—Level the corn so that it is of equal depth throughout, multiply the length, breadth and depth together, and this product by four, and cut off one figure to the right of the product; the other will represent the number of bushels of *shelled* corn.

Rule: 3d—Multiply the length by height, and then by width, add two ciphers to the result and divide by 124; this gives the number of bushels of *ear* corn.

HOW TO MEASURE GRAIN IN A BIN
By the United States standard, 2150.42 cubic inches makes a bushel. As a cubic foot contains 1728 cubic inches, a bushel is to a cubic foot nearly as 2150 is to 1728; or for all practical purposes as 5 to 4. Therefore, to convert cubic feet into bushels, it is only necessary to multiply by 4/5 or 80%.

Example: How many bushels of wheat in a bin 12 feet long, 8 feet wide, and 4 feet deep?

$12 \times 8 = 96 \times 4 = 384$ cubic feet;
$384 \times 4/5$ (or $\times .8$) $= 307\frac{1}{5}$
bushels. Ans.

In order to find the number of bushels which a bin of a given size will hold, find the contents of the bin in cubic feet, then diminish the contents by one-fifth and the result will be the contents in bushels.

CAPACITY OF BOXES
Taking *inside* dimensions, the following capacities can be found:

A box 24 inches $\times$ 16 inches $\times$ 28 inches deep will contain a barrel.
A box 16 inches $\times$ 15½ inches $\times$ 8 inches deep will contain a bushel.
A box 13½ inches $\times$ 13½ inches $\times$ 11¼ inches deep will contain a bushel.
A box 12 inches $\times$ 11½ inches $\times$ 9 inches deep will contain a half-bushel.
A box 10 inches $\times$ 10 inches $\times$ 10¾ inches deep will contain a half-bushel.
A box 8⅕ inches $\times$ 8 inches $\times$ 8 inches deep will contain a peck.
A box 8 inches $\times$ 8 inches $\times$ 4⅛ inches deep will contain a gallon.
A box 7 inches $\times$ 7 inches $\times$ 4½ inches deep will contain a half-gallon.
A box 3 inches $\times$ 3 inches $\times$ 4⅕ inches deep will contain a quart.
A box 3 inches $\times$ 3 inches $\times$ 3⅔ inches deep will contain a pint.

A wagon-box or bed 10 feet long, 4 feet wide, and 15 inches deep, has a capacity of 40 bushels.

MEASURING HAY
Of course, the only accurate method of finding the amount of hay in a given bulk is to weigh it. This, in many cases, is impossible, owing to its bulk and character, and it then becomes necessary to have some other method of arriving at the quantity, which can only be done approximately. Some kinds of hay are light, while others are heavy, but for all ordinary purposes of estimating the amount of hay in mows and stacks the following rules will be found sufficient:

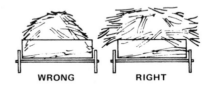

WRONG   RIGHT

When loaded on wagons or stored in barns, 20 cubic yards of hay make a ton.

When well settled in mows and stacks, 15 cubic yards make a ton. This is for medium sized mows or stacks; if the hay is piled to a great hight, it will be much more compact and near the bottom will be much heavier per cubic yard.

To find the number of tons in long square stacks—Multiply the length in yards by the width in yards and that by *half* the hight in yards, and divide by 15.

Example: How many tons in a rick of hay 20 yards long, 5 yards wide and 8 yards high?

$$20 \times 5 = 100 \times 8 \div 2 =$$
$$400 \div 15 = 26\frac{2}{3} \text{ tons. Ans.}$$

To find the number of tons in circular stacks—Multiply the square of the distance round the stack in yards by the hight in yards and divide by 25. This will give the number of cubic yards in the stack; then divide by 15 for the number of tons.

Example: How many tons of hay in a circular stack whose measurement around the base is 20 yards and hight 8 yards?

$$20 \times 20 = 400 \times 8 =$$
$$3200 \div 25 = 128 \div 15 =$$
$$8\frac{8}{15} \text{ tons. Ans.}$$

Common clover and timothy hay packed under ordinary circumstances will measure 500 cubic feet to the ton. In calculating the weight of hay in bulk, very often many things have to be taken into consideration and hence it is difficult to acertain it precisely.

Weights of various units of hay —A ton of hay, 2000 pounds; a bale, 300 pounds; a truss (of new hay), 60 pounds; a truss (of old hay), 56 pounds; a truss of straw, 40 pounds; a load of hay, 36 trusses.

TO FIND THE WEIGHT OF CATTLE BY MEASUREMENT

Multiply the girth in inches by the distance along the back from the tail to the fore part of the shoulder blade, and divide by 144 for the superficial feet. Then multiply the superficial feet by the number of pounds allowed for cattle of different girths and the product will be the number of pounds of beef, veal or pork in the animal.

Cattle having a girth of from 5 to 7 feet, allow 23 pounds to the superficial foot.

Cattle having a girth of from 7 to 9 feet, allow 31 pounds per superficial foot.

Small cattle and calves having a girth of from 3 to 5 feet, allow 16 pounds to the superficial foot.

Pigs and sheep having a girth of less than 3 feet, allow 11 pounds to the superficial foot.

Example: What is the weight of beef in a steer whose girth is 80 inches and length is 68 inches?

80 inches in girth $\times$ 68 inches in length =

5440 $\div$ 144 = 37¾ square feet $\times$ 23 = 8681¼ pounds. Ans.

When the animal is but half fattened, a deduction of one pound in every 20 is made; and if very fat, one pound for every 20 must be added.

QUANTITY OF SEED NEEDED TO SOW AN ACRE

Wheat, 1½ to 2 bushels; rye, 1½ to 2 bu.; oats, 3 bu.; barley, 2 bu.; buckwheat, ½ bu.; corn, broadcast, 4 bu.; corn in drills, 2 to 3 bu.; corn in hills, 4 to 8 quarts; broom corn, ½ bu.; potatoes, 10 to 15 bu.; rutabagas, ¾ pounds; millet, ¼ bu.; clover, white, 4 quarts; clover, red, 8 quarts; timothy, 6 quarts; orchard grass, 2 quarts; red top, 1 to 2 pecks; blue grass, 2 bu.; mixed lawn grass, ½ bu.; tobacco, 2 oz.

HARVEST WHEAT GRAIN YIELDS

A quarter of wheat, comprising 8 bushels, yields 14 bushels 2½

pecks, divided into seven distinct kinds of flour: Fine flour, 5 bushels 3 pecks; bran, 3 bushels; twentypenny, 3 bushels; seconds, 2 pecks; pollard, 2 bushels; fine middlings, 1 peck; coarse middlings, 1 peck.

LONG, OR LINEAR MEASURE

Used to compute distances in any direction.

12 inches (in.) = 1 foot–ft.
3 feet = 1 yard–yd.
5½ yards = 1 rod–rd.
40 rods = 1 furlong–fur.
8 furlongs = 1 mile–mi.
Also,

3 barley corns = 1 inch, used by shoemakers.
4 inches = 1 hand, used to measure horses.
6 feet = 1 fathom, used to measure depths at sea.

1.15 statute miles = 1 geographic mile, used to measure distance at sea.
3 geographic miles = 1 league.

60 geographic miles
69½ statute miles $\Big\}$ = 1 degree.
360 degrees = circumference of the earth.

SURVEYOR'S MEASURE

7.92 inches = 1 link–l.
251. inches = 1 rod–rd.
4 rd. or 66 ft. = 1 chain–ch.
10 sq. chains — 1 acre–a.
640 acres = 1 sq. mile–sq. mi.
36 sq. mi. = 1 township.

SQUARE MEASURE

Used in measuring surfaces.

144 sq. inches = 1 sq. foot–sq. ft.
9 sq. ft. = 1 sq. yard–sq. yd.
30¼ sq. yd. = 1 sq. rod–sq. rd.
40 sq. rd. = 1 rood–R.
4 sq. R. = 1 acre–a.
640 sq. a. = 1 sq. mile–sq. mi.

CUBIC MEASURE

Used in measuring solids of all kinds.

1728 cu. in. = 1 cubic foot–cu. ft.
27 cu. ft. = 1 cubic yard–cu. yd.
16 cu. ft. = 1 cord foot–crd. ft.
8 crd ft. or
128 cu. ft. $\Big\}$ = 1 cord of wood–C.

2150.4 cu. in. = 1 bushel*–bu.
268.8 cu. in. = 1 gallon–gal.

* English Winchester bushel

CIRCULAR MEASURE

Used to determine localities by estimating latitude and longitude, and measure difference of time. All circles, of whatever size, are supposed to be divided into the same number of parts—as quadrants, degrees, &tc.

60 seconds = 1 minute–′
60′ = 1 degree–°
.30° = 1 sign–S.
12 S. or 360° = 1 circle–C.

HOW TO FIND HOW MUCH TIN VESSELS WILL HOLD

For the Contents of a Cylinder— Square the diameter, then multiply the product by 0.7854. Again, multiply by the height (all in inches). Divide the product by 231 for gallons.

For the Frustum of a Cone— Add together the squares of the diameters of the large and small ends; to this add the product of the diameter of the two ends. Multiply this sum by 0.7854. Multiply this product by the height (all in inches). Then divide by 231 for the number of gallons.

HOW TO FIND THE CAPACITY OF A CISTERN OR WELL

Cylindrical vessels of uniform width— The gallon is, by United States standard, 231 cubic inches, and in order to find the number of cubic inches in a cask, we square the diameter in inches, and multiply by the decimal .7854 to find the surface of the base, then multiply this by the depth in inches. Now since multiplying by .7854 and afterwards dividing by 231 is equivalent to multiplying only by 34, it will be seen that we have the following rule:

Multiply the square of the diameter in inches by the depth in inches, and this product by 34, and point off four figures; the result will be the capacity in gallons and decimals of a gallon.

Example: A can measures 15 inches in diameter and is 2 feet 2 inches deep. How many gallons of oil will it contain?

$15 \times 15 = 225 \times 34 = 7650 \times 26 = 19.89$ (or 19 89/100) gallons. Ans.

If the can be not full, stand it on the end, and multiply by the height of the liquid instead of the length of the can, for the actual contents.

Cisterns wider at one end than the other—Add the width at the top and the width of the base together and take half, to find the average diameter; then square this diameter, multiply by 34, and this result again by the depth, and the result will be in gallons and decimals

of gallons as in the previous rule.

In calculating the capacity of cisterns, &tc., $31\frac{1}{2}$ gallons are estimated to one barrel, and 63 gallons to one hogshead.

HOW TO MEASURE ROUND TANKS

Square the diameter of the tank, and multiply by 0.7854, which gives the area; then mutiply by depth of tank, and the cubic contents will be found. Allow $6\frac{1}{4}$ gallons for each cubic foot.

SUSTAINING POWER OF ICE

The sustaining power of ice at various degrees of thickness is given as follows:

At the thickness of two inches, ice will support a man.

At a thickness of four inches, ice will support a man on horseback.

At a thickness of six inches, ice will support teams with moderate loads.

At a thickness of eight inches, ice will support heavy loads.

At a thickness of ten inches, ice will support 1,000 pounds to the square foot.

HEAT & COLD

Degrees of heat above zero at which substances melt—lead, 594°; tin, 421°; arsenic, 365°; sulphur, 226°; beeswax, 151°; gutta percha, 145°;

tallow, 97°; lard, 95°; pitch, 91°; ice, 33°.

Degrees of heat above zero at which substances boil—Ether, 98°; alcohol, 173°; water, 212°; petroleum, 306°; linseed oil, 640°; blood heat, 98°; eggs hatch, 104°.

MOTHER SHIPTON'S PROPHECY

The lines known as "Mother Shipton's Prophecy" were first published in England in 1485, before the discovery of America, and, of course, before any of the discoveries and inventions mentioned therein. All the events predicted have come to pass except that in the last two lines.

Carriages without horses shall go,
And accidents fill the world with
    woe.

Around the world thoughts shall fly
In the twinkling of an eye.

Waters shall yet more wonders do,
Now strange, yet shall be true.

The world upside down shall be,
And gold be found at root of tree.

Through hills man shall ride,
And no horse nor ass be at his side.

Under water man shall walk,
Shall ride, shall sleep, shall talk.

In the air men shall be seen
In white, in black, in green.

Iron in the water shall float,
As easy as a wooden boat.

Gold shall be found 'mid stone,
In a land that's now unknown.

Fire and water shall wonders do,
England shall at last admit a Jew.

And this world to an end shall come
In eighteen hundred and
    eighty-one.

Part Six

GLOSSARY

Chapter 28

The past returns to haunt

OBSOLETE & UNCOMMON WORDS

Many words in common usage last century are long dead and buried as the language lives on and evolves. To aid readers in their journey through yesteryear's idiom, many of the following words have been exhumed from the obsolete word section of unabridged dictionaries, to which the curious are referred for further exploration. Terms not found below may appear in the medical sections (p. 237 and p. 332) or in the Table of Common or Trade Names of Chemicals with Their Chemical Synonyms (p. 388).

Acescent   Turning sour; readily becoming tart or acid; slightly sour.

Æthiop's mineral   Impure black mercuric sulfide prepared by rubbing together mercury and sulfur.

Alkanet   A European plant whose root is used in the preparation of a red dyestuff used to color tinctures, pomades, beverages, &tc.

Aloe, powdered   The dried juice of the leaves of several species of succulent plants of the lily family, used as a purgative, tonic, and emmenagogue.

Amaranth   Any of a large genus of coarse herbs including pigweeds.

Angelica   Any of the genus of herbs of the carrot family, whose roots furnish a flavoring oil.

Annatto   A red or yellowish-red dye prepared from the pulp surrounding the seed of a tropical American tree; used for coloring cheese, butter, &tc.

Ant egg   White egglike pupae or cocoons of ants, popularly thought to be eggs; used for feeding poultry and for making formic acid.

Anti-scorbutic   Counteracting scurvy.

Armenian bole   A soft, clayey, bright-red earth found in Armenia and Tuscany; used formerly in medicine. Usu. colored red by iron oxide, and consisting essentially of hydrous silicates of aluminum, or less often of magnesium.

Arnica   An herb of the thistle family, whose rhizome and roots are used for their stimulant and local irritant effect, as a liniment for bruises, sprains, swellings, &tc.

Arrowroot powder   The powdered root of the arrowroot plant, used as a thickening agent and as a substitute for talcum powder.

Assafœtida/assafetida/asafetida.   A fetid, dark-colored resin, with odor and taste of garlic, from Persian and East Indian plants; used medicinally as an antispasmodic.

Atropia   Atropine, a poisonous crystalline alkaloid from the belladonna plants; used to relieve spasms and to dilate the pupil of the eye.

Bain-marie   The French version of a double boiler for the preparation of food and drugs.

Balm   Any fragrant ointment, used medicinally.

Balm of Gilead   A balsam, obtained from an evergreen African or Asiatic tree, having an aromatic scent and fragrant smell, used in unguents and cosmetics.

Balsam   An aromatic substance flowing spontaneously or by incision from certain plants, but not nec. remaining liquid.

Bayberry   Fruit of the bay tree, which yields an essential oil having a clove-like or cinnamon flavor; lusty herbs used commonly in food preparation.

Bay salt   A very coarse sodium chloride salt, esp. that obtained from sea water by evaporation in shallow pits by the heat of the sun. A present-day substitute is kosher salt.

Bedtick A flat, oblong tick or bag of stout cloth, used for enclosing the material of a bed.

Beet root A large edible root, used as a garden vegetable and as stock feed.

Benjamin/benzoin A fragrant, yellowish gum produced by trees of Sumatra, Java, used esp. in medicine, as a fixative for perfumes, and in incense. Also known as *spicebush, spicewood,* or *benjamin bush.*

Bergamot water Aqueous solution of a pear-shaped orange, *Citrus Bergamia,* whose rind yields an essential oil used in perfumery.

Bird lime An extremely adhesive viscid substance, usu. made from the bark of the holly tree.

Bittersweet Any of several American plants containing a bitter principle; horseweed; sneezeweed. Often causes a poisoning in livestock.

Bladder In the late eighteenth century, the waste-not-want-not farmers at butchering time utilized all of the carcass, except the squeal of the pig, for their family farmsteading needs. Animal bladders (i.e., urinary, gall, &tc) were used much like today's plastic wrap—in pieces as container covers, and in whole as containers for storage of foodstuff, such as lard—hence, referred to as *bladdered* lard.

Blade The leaf of a plant, esp. of an herb.

Blood root A plant of the poppy family with red root and sap, having acrid emetic properties. The rootstock is used as a stimulant expectorant.

Blown Puffed up, as cattle gorged with green food which develops gas.

Bodkin A sharp-pointed implement of steel, bone, or ivory, &tc., for making holes; also a kind of pin used by women to fasten the hair; a large blunt needle.

Bole The trunk or stem of a tree. (*See also* **Armenian bole.**)

Bolster A long, soft pillow, cushion, or pad, used under the bedcovers to relieve pressure on any part of the body, or to fill it out. (A sleeper who drapes his body over a bolster sleeps cooler on a hot night.)

Borage A coarse hairy, blue-flowered European herb used—both flowers and roots—medicinally and in salads.

Bouille Boiled or stewed meats.

Brawn The flesh of a boar; specific, pickled or potted flesh of a boar, as headcheese; also, a pig's head dressed for the table.

Buhach A yellowish powder obtained from the dried and ground flower heads of a species of Chrysanthemum, used for killing noxious domestic insects.

Bullock's gall *See* **Ox gall.**

Bung The stopper of an orifice in the bilge of a cask; also, the orifice itself: the bunghole.

Bungleweed English dialect for *bundweed:* any of the various plants, as the knapweed, ragwort, scabious, and cow parsnip.

Burdock A coarse biennial plant, with burlike heads, which adhere tenaciously to clothing or to the fur of animals.

Cabbage net A small net for boiling cabbages in.

Cajeput Var. of *cajuput:* an East Indian tree, also known as paperbark or white tree. It yields a pungent greenish oil known as *oil of cajuput,* used as a stimulant, antispasmodic, and anodyne.

Calabar bean The highly poisonous seed of a climbing plant of tropical Africa. Its root is used to produce contractions of the pupil of the eye, and in tetanus, neuralgia, and rheumatic diseases.

Calamus A plant of the palm family, also known as *sweet flag,* whose roots are used as a carminative and tonic in dyspepsia and colic.

Camomile/chamomile A common European herb with strong-scented foliage and flower heads that contain a bitter medicinal principle used in coughs, in spasmodic conditions, and as a diaphoretic.

Candy Height An obs. term used in receipts for confections, candy, and sugar sirups, to indicate temperature; usu. between 250–266°F.

Canella alba The cinnamon bark, whitewood, or wild cinnamon tree.

Cantharides A preparation of dried blister beetles. It is a common vesicatory; in internal doses it acts as a stimulant and diuretic. It was formerly considered an aphrodisiac.

Cape wine Wine made in South Africa. *Cape Smoke:* a harsh brandy distilled in the Cape Province from South African wines.

Capillaire A sirup prepared from the maidenhair fern; also any simple sirup flavored with orange flowers.

Capsicum The dried and pulverized fruit of tropical herbs which produce dry, many-seeded, and very pungent berries known as chilies and peppers, used in cooking and as a condiment. Also used extensively in medicines.

Cardamom/cardamum/cardamon An aromatic capsular fruit from the East Indies, used as a condiment, and in medicine as an adjuvant to other aromatics, stimulants and stomachics.

Cascarilla The aromatic bark of a Wést Indian euphorbiaceous shrub. It has a warm spicy, bitter taste, and when burnt emits a musky odor. It is used as a tonic and stomachic. Also called *eleuthera bark* and *sweetwood bark.*

Cassia The long cylindrical pods of East Indian tree, *C. fistula;* also called the *pudding-pipe tree* or *drumstick tree.* The sweet pulp, *cassia pulp,* is a mild laxative.

Catechu Any of several dry, earthy, or resinlike astringent substances obtained by the decoction and evaporation from the wood, leaves, and fruits of certain tropical Asiatic plants, used for tanning and dyeing, and also medicinally as an astringent.

Centaury Any of a genus of low herbs of the gentian family, esp. an Old World herb formerly used as a tonic.

Charge The load of fermented mash placed in the copper boiler, to be distilled by vaporization and condensation into liquor.

Checkerberries The spicy, red, berry-like fruit of the American wintergreen.

Cherry laurel A European shrub, common in shrubberies; also called *laurel.*

Chimney-pot A cylindrical pipe of earthenware or sheet metal, &tc., placed at the top of the chimney to increase the draft and carry off the smoke.

Chincona/cinchona Peruvian tree which yields quinine, and bark which has the same therapeutic qualities as the alkaloid, quinine.

Chin-cups *See* **Cup moss**.

Chow Chow A mixture of all sorts of things; a hodge-podge; esp. chopped mixed pickles.

Clarified butter Butter melted, then decanted from its separated milk solids.

Clyster A liquid injected into the lower intestine; an injection; an enema.

Coal oil Kerosene.

Cochineal A silver-gray, black, or scarlet dyestuff consisting of the ground bodies of female *Coccus cacti,* a scale insect native to Mexico and found on several species of cactus.

Codlin A small, immature apple; hence, an apple of inferior grade, used only for stewing.

Coffee cup A three-quarter-cup measure.

Cogener Var. of *congener:* a thing or person allied in nature, character, or action to another.

Colombo Var. of *calumba:* the root of an African menispermaceous plant. It has a bitter taste, and is used as a tonic and antiseptic in dyspepsia and diarrhea.

Columbia root Var. of *columbo wood:* often called *false calumba,* and used medicinally like calumba.

Comfit A dried sweetmeat; any kind of fruit, root, or seed preserved with sugar and dried; a confection.

Comforter A stuffed and quilted cover for a bed; also called a *comfortable* or *comfort.*

Comfrey A decoction of the mucilaginous root of the common comfrey plant, used in cough mixtures.

Concoction A mixture prepared by the combining of different ingredients.

Copper A vessel, esp. a large boiler, made of copper.

Cos lettuce   A lettuce with long, crisp leaves and columnar head.

Costive   Affected with, or causing, constipation.

Cowslip   A ranunculaceous plant, more usually called *marsh marigold;* in England, the common primrose.

Craw/crop   The pouched enlargement of the gullet of many birds that serves as a receptacle for food and its preliminary mastication.

Cruciferous   Any of a family (*Cruciferae*) of plants including the cabbage and mustard.

Cullis   A strong clear broth of meat, as for invalids; also, a savory jelly.

Cup moss   Any of the cup lichens having cup-shaped stalks or podetia.

Cupping   The act of drawing blood to the body's surface by use of a glass vessel evacuated by heat.

Cutis   The derma, or deeper layer of the skin.

Damiana   A Mexican drug, obtained from several different plants, used as a stimulant, tonic, and aphrodisiac.

Deal   Pine or fir wood.

Decoction   An extract made by placing herbs or fruit in cold water, then boiling or simmering over low heat ten to fifteen minutes, usually in proportion of one part herb to fifteen parts water.

Diachylon plaster   A plaster originally composed of the juices of several plants, but now made of an oxide of lead and oil, consisting essentially of glycerin mixed with lead salts of the fatty acids. It is used for excoriated surfaces and wounds, &tc.

Dinner   The principal meal of the day, eaten by most rural people about midday.

Dogbain   Any of a genus comprising chiefly tropical and often poisonous plants with milky juice and usu. showy flowers.

Dort   Sulkiness.

Dover's powder A powder of ipecac and opium, compounded in the U.S. with sugar and milk, but in England with potassium sulfate. It is an anodyne diaphoretic.

Drachm A one-eighth ounce measure.

Dragon's blood A dark red color, derived from the resin exuding from the fruit of the Malayan rattan palm tree.

Drawn butter Butter melted, clarified, then usually mixed with flour and hot water for a sauce. (*See also* **Clarified butter.**)

Drench A medicinal drink for domestic animals.

Drilling A heavy twilled fabric of linen or cotton.

Echinacea A small genus of coarse herbs of the thistle family. The dried rhizomes and roots are used in the treatment of ulcers and boils.

Elixir A sweetened liquid usu. containing alcohol that is used as a vehicle for medicinal agents.

Embrocations Liniments.

Ergot The dried ergot fungus grown on rye grain, which contains alkaloids used medicinally for their contractile effect on smooth muscles.

Eschalot Var. of *shalot* or *shallot:* a bulbous perennial herb that resembles an onion and produces small clustered bulbs used in seasoning; also, a green onion.

Essence A constituent or derivative (as an extract or essential oil) possessing the special qualities (as of a plant or drug) in concentrated form; also, an alcoholic solution of an essential oil.

Euphorbium A yellow or brownish, very acrid gum resin derived from Old World species of *Euphorbia,* an immense genus of herbs or shrubs. It was formerly employed medicinally as an emetic and cathartic, but is now used chiefly in veterinary medicine.

Eyebright A small European plant, including the scarlet pimpernel, Indian pipe, and Indian tobacco varieties, formerly much used as a remedy for diseases of the eye.

Faints *See* **Feints.**

Fauces The narrow passage from the mouth to the pharynx, situated between the soft palate and the base of the tongue.

Feints Var. of *faints:* the weak and impure spirit which comes over last in the distilling of whisky or liquor and is caught separately. It contains fusel oil and must be rectified. The first runnings or *low wines* are called *strong faints,* and after the runnings, *week faints.* (*Also see* **Tailings.**)

Fennel   A perennial European herb of the carrot family, cultivated for its aromatic seeds and its foliage used in cooking.

Fiat lotio   A matrix lotion vehicle used for the application of medicinal drugs.

Fine   To purify, to clarify, or to make wine fine.

Firkin   A small wooden vessel or cask of indeterminate size, used for butter, lard, &tc., its weight varying with the commodity: for butter, 56 pounds.

Fomentations   The application of hot moist substances to the body to ease pain, and the materials so applied.

Forcemeat   Finely chopped and seasoned meat or fish that is either served alone or used as a stuffing; also called *farce*.

Fo'Ti   An herb grown and used in China, said to induce longevity.

Frontignac   A variety of muscat grape; also, the rich sweet wine produced from muscat grapes near Frontignac, Hérault, France.

Frosted meats   Frozen meats.

Fusa   Fusion: the state of being melted or dissolved together by heat.

Galbanum   A yellowish or brownish gum resin of aromatic odor and unpleasant taste derived from certain Asiatic plants, resembling *asafetida* and used for similar medicinal purposes.

Galled   *See* **Windgall**.

Galvanism   Dynamical or current electricity, esp. as produced by chemical action.

Gammon   A ham or flitch of bacon salted and smoked or dried; also, the lower end of the side of bacon.

Garget   Pokeweed, a coarse American perennial herb; both the berries and roots are emetic and purgative. The root is poisonous, but the young shoots are sometimes eaten like asparagus. Also a disease of swine and cattle marked by inflammation of the head, throat, and mammary (cattle) glands.

Gaultheria   An herb of the American wintergreen family.

Gilead   *See* **Balm of Gilead**.

Gimp   To notch or indent; to shape.

Ginseng   An aromatic plant grown in China and the United States, whose root is highly valued as a medicine. It has a sweet taste like that of licorice, but is of little use except as a demulcent. Highly valued in China as an aphrodisiac.

Gold thread   A small ranunculaceous plant, so called from its fibrous yellow roots.

Golden seal   A perennial Amer. herb with a thick knotted rootstock and large round leaves, whose dried roots and rhizomes are used as an alterative and tonic.

Granulation   One of the minute red prominences, made up of new tissue, which form on the raw surface, as of a wound or ulcer, and are the active agents in the process of healing.

Gravel   Kidney stones or gall stones.

Guage   Obsolete spelling of *gauge* or *gage*.

Gum guaiacum   A resin with a faint balsamic odor, obtained as tears or masses from the trunks of tropical American trees and shrubs of the caltrop family; used medicinally as a remedy for gout, rheumatism, and skin diseases.

Gutta percha   A substance resembling rubber, but containing more resin, from the latex of several Malaysian trees. An electrical insulator; also, used formerly by chemists as a material for making bottles, carboys, baths, &tc.

Gyle   The amount of one brewing of beer or ale. Also, the fermenting wort, or a tun, or vat, for it.

Handful   About a three-fourths to one cup measure.

Handles   Drying trays.

Haricot   The ripe seed, or the unripe pod, of the common string bean.

Harvest bug   Harvest tick: a larval form of certain ticks, which are found in grass and bushes, and attach themselves to men and animals, burrowing under the skin and causing intense itching.

Hasty-pudding   A batter or pudding of flour or oatmeal stirred into boiling water or milk; also, Indian meal mush in the U.S.

Hide-bound   Having the skin adhering so closely to the ribs and back as not to be easily loosened or raised—said of an animal.

Higdum/higdon   A kind of chopped, mixed pickle. Local U.S.

Hight   Obsolete for *height*.

Hoarhound/horehound   An extract or confection made from a bitter mint plant.

Horse-bean   A variety of the common broad bean; varieties are used as a vegetable and for feeding stock.

Humors   Any chronic cutaneous affection supposedly arising from a morbid state of the blood.

Hyoscyamus   Leaves of the henbane, used in neuralgic and pectoral troubles.

Hyssop   A European mint that has highly aromatic and pungent leaves, sometimes used as a potherb.

Iceland moss   An edible lichen found in the arctic regions of the North Temperate Zone. It yields a nutritious jelly and is used in pulmonary complaints and as a demulcent.

Infusion   The steeping or soaking of any substance in water to extract its virtues; also, the liquid extract obtained by this method.

Irish moss   Carrageen; also, a blancmange of it; a seaweed; agar-agar derived from such seaweed.

Iris root   *See* **Orris root.**

Isinglass   A semitransparent, whitish, and very pure form of fish gelatin obtained from the sturgeon. Used for making jellies, glue, and as a clarifier.

Jacob's ladder   A variety of Solomon's seal, perennial European herb.

Kernels (of beef)   Testicles of beef cattle.

Kino   A dark-red or blackish tanniferous product similar to catechu, obtained from various tropical trees. It is commonly used in medicine as an astringent and hemostatic.

Knotted margaram/margeraim/marjoram   Origanum, whose globose heads of small flowers form a compact, knotted mass; used for seasoning foods.

Larding pin   A pin used to insert lardons of bacon or pork into the surface of meats or fowl before cooking.

Laurel leaves   Bay leaves, used as seasoning in cooking.

Lavender   European mint, cultivated for its aromatic oil; also, used to perfume clothing, bed linens, &tc.

Lock Jaw   A variety of tetanus in which the jaws are locked rigidly together.

Logwood   Dye from heartwood of the logwood tree.

Loosestrife   A widely distributed genus of herbs of the primrose family.

Lovage   A European herb cultivated in old gardens as a domestic remedy.

Mallow   A plant with mucilaginous leaves and stalks used as dressings for burns and skin irritations, and as a soothing remedy for colds and sore throat.

Mash   Crushed malt, or meal of rye, wheat, corn, &tc., steeped and stirred in hot water to produce *wort*.

May-duke   A well-known sour cherry of the duke race, with dark-red skins.

Middlings   The medium-sized particles separated in the sifting of ground grain.

Mother of vinegar   A slimy membrane which develops on the surface of alcoholic liquids undergoing acetous fermentation, composed chiefly of yeast cells and bacteria. It is added to wine or cider, as a starter, to produce vinegar, hence, its name. It is also called *vinegar plant.*

Motherwort   A bitter Old World mint, used as domestic remedy.

Moth patches   Chloasma, a cutaneous affection characterized by yellow or yellowish-brown pigmented spots on the skin.

Murrain   A pestilence or plague affecting domestic cattle and plants.

Muscatel   A rich, sweet wine made from the muscat grape or its vine.

Mushroom flaps   Mushroom heads, tops, or buttons.

Must   The expressed juice of the grape, or other fruit, before fermentation; new wine.

Myrrh   A yellowish-brown to reddish-brown aromatic gum resin with a bitter, slightly pungent taste, obtained from African and Arabian trees.

N.O. molasses   A molasses called in the trade *New Orleans Molasses,* which is lighter and of larger sugar content than that called *Porto Rico Molasses,* which has a rummy flavor.

Nitre/niter   Saltpeter/petre (*see* Chemical Table) .

Noyeau   Var. of *noyau:* a liquor made from brandy and flavored with, or in imitation of, cherry or peach kernels. There are two varieties, white and pink.

Oil nuts   The buffalo nut; also, any of several nuts yielding oil, as the cocoanut, the oil palm fruit, the butternut, &tc.

Oleum   Oil.

Oleum lini   Linseed oil; also called *flaxseed oil.*

Oleum terebinth   Turpentine; also called *oil,* or *spirit, of turpentine, gum spirit,* &tc.

Ointment   An unctuous substance, usually medicated and melting readily when applied to the skin; an unguent, a salve.

Opodeldoc   Any of various soap liniments; esp. in American use, the unofficial camphorated soap liniment, of a soft, semisolid consistence.

Origanum   A genus of Eurasian aromatic mints; wild marjoram. Its oil was formerly used in perfumery and medicine.

Orris root   The fragrant rootstock of the Florentine iris: a fixative used in dusting powders, toilet water, dentifrices, &tc., when dried.

Osnaburg   A species of coarse linen, originally made in Osnaburg, Germany.

Oswego corn   Oswego (brand) cornstarch.

Ox gall   The fresh gall of the domestic ox.

Oxymel   A mixture of honey, water, and acetic acid, used as an excipient.

Paregoric   A medicine that mitigates pain, an anodyne; specifically, camphorated tincture of opium.

Paroxysm   A fit, attack, agitation, convulsion of a disease that occurs at equal or unequal intervals; a severe, sudden attack of coughing.

Pearlash/pearl ash   *See* Chemical Table.

Pearline   A soap-like substance used as a soap substitute.

Peghole   Var. of *bunghole:* a vent in a beer cask, closed with a peg or bung.

Pennyroyal   A perennial mint plant; its oil is used as a culicifuge to repel insects.

Persic oil   Oil obtained from apricot kernels or pits.

Philadelphia brick   A scouring compound.

Picklette   Fine chopped pickles.

Pie plant   Garden rhubarb.

Pimpernel root   The dried rhyzome and roots of the burnet saxifrage, used as a diaphoretic and diuretic.

Pipkin   A small earthen pot, usu. one having a horizontal handle; a piggin: a wooden pail or tub with an upright stave as handle.

Pippin   A seedling apple.

Plaster   An external application of a consistency harder than ointment, prepared for use by spreading it on linen, leather, silk, or the like; it is adhesive at ordinary body temperature.

Pomatum   A perfumed unguent esp. for the hair; a pomade.

Pot ale   The residue of fermented *wort* left in a still after the whisky or alcohol has been distilled off, and used for feeding swine.

Potass/potassa   Potash (*see* Chemical Table) .

Porter   A dark liquor made with browned malt, rich in saccharine matter and extract and containing about four or five percent of alcohol; also, a kind of weak, sweet stout.

Poultice   A soft composition, as of herbs, bread, bran, or the like, usu. heated and spread on a cloth to be applied to sores, inflamed parts of the body, &tc., to supply warmth or moisture, or act as an anodyne, emollient, antiseptic, counterirritant, &tc.; often medicated.

Probang   A slender elastic rod, as of whalebone, with a sponge on the end for removing obstructions from the esophagus, making applications, &tc.

Proof spirit   100 proof alcohol.

Pure spirits   Neutral spirits, ethyl or grain alcohol.

Quassia   A drug extracted from the wood of certain American tropical trees, used medicinally as a bitter tonic and a remedy for threadworms in children, as an insecticide, and in brewing as a substitute for hops.

Quill   The rounding fold of a ruff or ruffle; also (pharm.) , a roll of dried bark, as a *quill* of cinnamon.

Race   A root, esp. of green or dried ginger.

Radish pod   Radish root, the edible fleshy portion; used as relish.

Raisin wine   Wine usu. made from the fermentation of dried muscat, or raisin, grapes.

Rape   A turnip, similar to cabbage, grown in the Old World as a forage crop for sheep, and in the United States as a forage crop for hogs and sheep and as a cover crop for orchards. Its seeds yield rape oil and are a food for birds.

Rasp   To scrape.

Resin   Various solid or semisolid natural organic substances, usu. transparent or translucent, which are formed in plant secretions; soluble in organic solvents, but not soluble in water; used in varnishes, inks, plastics, sizes, and in medicine.

Rheum   A watery discharge from the mucous membrane, esp. from the eyes and nose, as when due to a cold; hence, a cold; catarrh.

Rhodium (wood)   The fragrant root and stems of a shrub native to the island of Teneriffe, which yields rhodium, or rosewood, oil.

Rings   Muffin tins or rings.

Rose hips   The fruit, often brightly colored, of the rose.

Rosin   A translucent amber-colored to almost black, brittle friable resin.

Rotgut   Bad liquor, esp. when adulterated.

Rue   A European, strong-scented, woody herb with a bitter taste and used in medicine. From association with *rue* meaning repentence, the rue was formerly known as *herb of grace* or *herb grace*.

Sack   Any of a variety of strong, white wines imported to England from Southern Europe.

Sadiron   A heavy iron, with detachable handle, for smoothing clothes.

Saffron   A deep orange-colored substance consisting of the aromatic, pungent, dried stigmas of a species of crocus; widely used to color and flavor food; was formerly used in dyeing and as a stimulant antispasmodic emmenagogue in medicine. Still used in the Far East as a tonic, stomachic, and aphrodisiac.

Sago   A dry, granulated starch prepared from the trunks of the Sago palm, used in puddings, as an article of diet, and for stiffening textiles.

St. John's wort   A large-flowered herb formerly used in treatment of respiratory diseases and urinary infections.

383

Salamander   A cooking utensil of metal with a plate or disk, heated and held over pastry, &tc., to brown it.

Saleratus   Literally, aerated salt, potassium bicarbonate or sodium bicarbonate, now commonly the latter; baking soda.

Sal prunella/sal prunellae/sal prunelle   Saltpeter (postassium nitrate) fused and cast in balls, cakes, and sticks.

Salt rheum   Any of various cutaneous eruptions, esp. those of eczema.

Salt spoon   A one-quarter teaspoon measure.

Salve   *See* **Ointment**.

Samphire   A fleshy plant growing along the seacoast, sometimes pickled.

Sassafras   The dried bark or the root of a large genus of aromatic trees of the laurel family, used as a diaphoretic, a flavoring agent, aromatic bitters; it yields an aromatic volatile oil used in perfumes.

Sarsaparilla   A Mexican, Central and South American plant whose dried cord-like roots are used in the form of decoction, infusion, fluid extract, or sirup, as a mild tonic or alterative. Also a carbonated beverage of water, sugar, and sarsaparilla flavoring.

Savoy   A race of cabbage having a compact head with wrinkled and curled leaves.

Saxifrage   Any of a genus of mostly perennial herbs with showy flowers and tufted leaves, thought at one time to break up bladder stones. *Also see* **Pimpernel root.**

Scours   Black, yellow, or white diarrhea or dysentery in livestock.

Scrag   The back and neck bones of meat, usu. mutton.

Scummings   Skimmings of scum.

Shapes   A mold for shaping jelly; a jelly mold.

Sheep rot   Sheep'sbane, a marsh pennywort plant, supposed to produce rot in sheep.

Shorts   The coarse middlings from flour milling.

Sippet   A small bit or piece of toast, soaked in milk, broth, &tc., or a small piece of toast or fried bread used for garnishing.

Slip elm bark   Var. of *slippery elm:* the fragrant mucilaginous inner bark of the North American elm, used as a demulcent and as a treatment for diarrhea, dysentery, and chilblains.

Sloths   The waste skins of peeled fruits, vegetables, etc.

Smallage   Wild celery, parsley; *also see* **Galbanum.** One form is *tape grass:* a submerged aquatic plant with long ribbonlike leaves. In the southern U.S. where it is a favorite food of the canvas-back duck, it is called *wild celery.*

Soapine   A soap-like substance used as a soap substitute.

Solomon's-seal   A native plant of the North Temperate Zone, having thick scarred rootstock used medicinally as an astringent, demulcent, and tonic.

Sorrel   A genus of plants having sour leaves and juice.

Soufflé   To fill with air by beating.

Soul   An obs. variant of *sole,* meaning pure, unmixed or unalloyed.

Souse   A pickle made with salt; something steeped in pickle, as fish or pig's feet; the ear, esp. a hog's ear.

Southernwood   A shrubby European wormwood used in brewing of beer; also used today by some to eliminate pinworms from the body.

Spavin   A disease of the hock of horses, marked by a small bony enlargement inside of the leg, due to a sprain or a violent effort.

Spermaceti   A yellowish or whitish waxy solid which separates from the oil obtained from the sperm whale; used in making candles, ointments, cosmetics.

Sphincter   A ring-like muscle surrounding, and able to contract or close, a natural opening or passage of an animal.

Spike oil   Oil from spike lavender, a European mint; used in perfumes.

Spile   A small plug or wooden pin or stake used to stop a vent.

Splint   A bony enlargement on a horse's leg, below the knee joint and on the inside of the leg, due to periostitis.

Spirit of wine   Ethyl, or grain, alcohol (84%).

Sponge   Dough after it has been raised or converted into a light, porous mass by yeast or leaven; a porous pudding usu. made of gelatin, water, sugar, fruit juices, and beaten egg whites.

Spring of pork   The lower part of the forequarter, which is divided from the neck, and has the leg and foot without the shoulder.

Squills   The cut and dried fleshy inner scales of the bulb of the white variety of a bulbous herb of India, which contains physiologically active gluosides and is used as an expectorant, cardiac stimulant, and diuretic.

Stavesacre   A Eurasian larkspur whose seeds contain a violent emetic and cathartic and which are used locally as a fish poison. A tinture or ointment prepared from the seeds is used to kill head and body lice.

Stone   An English unit of weight equal to 14 pounds.

Storax   A balsam obtained from the bark of an Asiatic tree, *Liquidambar,* as a grayish-brown, fragrant, honeylike liquid containing resin, styrene, cinnamic acid, &tc., and used as an expectorant and in perfumery.

Stramonium   The thorn apple, esp. the Jimson weed. Its dried leaves are used medicinally as is belladonna, esp. in asthma.

Succi Expressed vegetable juices usually preserved by the addition of alcohol.

Sugar, clarified Refined white granulated sugar made usu. from cane or beets. (Can be used in lieu of loaf, yellow, brown, &tc., sugars used by our forebears.)

Sumac/sumach A material used in tanning and dyeing, consisting of dried and powdered leaves, peduncles, etc., of various species of sumac shrub or tree valued chiefly for their tannin content (10–30 per cent).

Supper The meal taken at the close of day, when dinner is taken at mid-day.

Suppuration Pus or pus condition.

Sweet bone Bone from fresh meat, not salted or pickled, cured or corned.

Syncope A sudden pallor, coldness of the skin, and partial or complete unconsciousness; a fainting or swooning.

Syrup/sirup Originally, a thick liquid made from the juice of fruits, herbs, &tc., boiled with sugar. Medicinally, a concentrated aqueous solution of sucrose containing either medicinal agents or flavoring agents.

Tailings In the distillation of neutral spirits from fermented mash, those portions which distill over last and are of inferior quality.

Teacup, large A one-cup measure.

Teacup, small A one-half-cup measure.

Tetter Any of various vesicular skin diseases, as ringworm, eczema, psoriasis, and herpes. Also obsolete for a pimple, pustule, ulcer; a blister.

Thoroughwort Also called *boneset* and *agueweed;* an asteraceous herb with diaphoretic and tonic properties.

Tincture Alcohol solution of drugs, prepared either by maceration, percolation, or solution. The alcoholic strength is variable and the drugs generally nonvolatile. The drug strength, where the drug is potent, is usu. 10%; where the drug is not very potent, the strength is usu. 20%.

Tolu Also called *Tolu balsam;* said to have been first brought from Santiago de Tolú, in Colombia.

Tow The coarse or broken part of the flax of hemp, separated by the hatchel or swingle, and ready for spinning; narrowly, the short fibers of hackled flax or hemp.

Treacle Obsolete term for *molasses;* sometimes specif., the molasses which drains from the sugar-refining molds; hence, called *refiners' sirup* and *sugarhouse molasses.*

Triturate To rub or grind, bruise or thrash to a very fine or impalpable powder.

Tun A vat to hold fermenting mash in brewing.

Turf fire Fire fueled by dried peat moss, as practiced in Ireland.

Tw. A density scale, for liquids heavier than water measured on the *Twaddell hydrometer,* named after its inventor.

Ultramarine Blue pigment, having a tinge of violet.

Unbolted   Said of *meal* not bolted or sifted; hence, unrefined, coarse, gross.

Underback   In brewing, the vessel which receives the wort as it flows from the mashing tub.

Uva ursi   The *bearberry;* a trailing evergreen plant of the heath family with tonic, astringent foliage and glossy red berries much loved by bears.

Valerian   A drug consisting of the dried rootstock and roots of the common valerian plant; used as a mild tonic and stimulant, esp. in nervous affections.

Vetiver   An East Indian fragrant grass; its sandlewood-scented roots are much used in making mats and screens, and yielding an essential oil. It is a good fixative and its oil is used in perfumery.

Vinegar plant   *See* **Mother of vinegar.**

Wash   The fermented wort from which spirit is distilled; also, a mixture of dunder, molasses, water, and scrummings, used in the West Indies for distillation of rum.

Wheat meal   Coarsely ground whole-wheat flour; also, *farina:* a creamy-colored, granular, protein-rich meal made from hard—but not durum—wheat.

Whiffletree/whippletree/singletree/swingletree   The pivoted or swinging bar to which the traces, or tugs, of the harness of a team of horses are fastened, and by which the carriage, wagon, plow, or the like is drawn.

Winchester bushel   The English bushel measure, being the volume of a cylinder 18½ inches in inside diameter and 8 inches in depth.

Windgall   A soft tumor or swelling generally found on the fetlock joint of horses, so called because formerly thought to contain air.

Wine glass   A one-quarter-cup measure.

Witch hazel   An alcoholic solution of the distillate of the bark of the witch hazel tree, used as a tonic and a soothing and mild astringent lotion.

Woorara   Var. of *curare.* It is used medicinally to produce muscular relaxation.

Work   The fermenting, as of a liquid, by yeast in the brewing process.

Worm   The condensing tube, usu. copper, of a still, often curved and wound to economize space.

Wort   The sweet infusion of malt which ferments and forms beer.

Chapter 29

COMMON OR TRADE NAMES OF CHEMICALS WITH THEIR SYNONYMS

Common or Trade Name	*Chemical Synonym*
Acid of sugar	Oxalic acid
Acorn sugar	Quercitol
Air saltpeter	Mixed calcium nitrates and nitrites
Alcohol, wood	Methyl alcohol
Alum, Alum flour, Alum meal	Potassium aluminum sulfate
Alumina	Aluminum oxide
American ashes	Crude potassium carbonate
Amide powder	Explosive powder
Aniline	Aminobenzene
Aniline salt	Aniline hydrochloride
Anise camphor	Anethole
Antimony bloom	Antimony trioxide
Antimony black, Antimony glance	Antimony trisulfied
Antimony red, Antimony vermilion	Antimonous oxysulfide
Antimony white	Antimonous oxide
Antimony yellow	Basic lead antimonate
Apple oil	Amyl valerate

Common or Trade Name	Chemical Synonym
Aqua fortis	Nitric acid, applied esp. to the weakened grade of commercial acid
Aqua regis	Mixture of nitric and hydrochloric acid
Arsenic glass	Arsenous oxide
Azurite	Basic copper carbonate
Baking soda	Sodium bicarbonate
Ballistite	Smokeless powder
Baldwin's phosphorus	Fused calcium nitrate
Barium white	Barium sulfate
Barium yellow	Barium chromate
Baryta	Barium oxide
Baryta water	Barium hydroxide solution
Barytes	Barium sulfate
Bauxite	Hydrated aluminum oxide
Beet sugar	Sucrose
Bichrome	Potassium or sodium dichromate
Bitter salt	Magnesium sulfate
Black ash	Impure sodium carbonate
Blanc-fixe	Barium sulfate
Blau gas	Blue gas
Bleaching powder	Calcium chloro-hypochlorite
Blende	Natural zinc sulfide
Blue copperas / Blue stone / Blue vitriol	Copper sulfate
Blue salts	Nickel sulfate
Blue verditer	Basic copper carbonate
Bone ash	Impure calcium phosphate & carbonate
Bone black	Animal charcoal
Boracic acid	Boric acid
Borax	Sodium tetraborate
Bremen blue	Basic copper carbonate
Brimstone	Sulfur
Burnt alum	Anhydrous potassium aluminum sulfate
Burnt lime	Calcium oxide
Burnt ochre / Burnt ore	Ferric oxide
"Butter of"	Chloride of
Cadmium yellow	Cadmium sulfide
Calamine	Zinc carbonate
Calomel	Mercurous chloride

Common or Trade Name	Chemical Synonym
Cane sugar	Sucrose
Carbolic acid	Phenol
Carbonic acid ⎫ Carbonic anhydride ⎭	Carbon dioxide
Carborundum	Silicon carbide
"Caustic"	Hydroxide of
Chalk	Calcium carbonate
Chili niter ⎫ Chili saltpeter ⎭	Sodium nitrate
China clay	Hydrated aluminum silicate
Chinese red	Basic lead chromate
Chinese oxide	Zinc oxide
Chloride of lime	Calcium chloro-hypochlorite
Chloride of soda	Sodium hypochlorite solution
Chrome alum	Potassium chromium sulfate
Chrome green	Chromium oxide
Chrome red	Basic lead chromate
Chrome yellow	Lead chromate
Cinnabar	Mercuric sulfide
Cobalt black	Cobalt oxide
Cobalt green	Cobalt zincate
Cologne spirit	Pure ethyl alcohol
Colonial spirit ⎫ Columbian spirit ⎭	Pure methyl alcohol
Common salt	Sodium chloride
Copper glance	Natural copper sulfide
Copperas	Ferrous sulfate
Corn sugar	Glucose
Corrosive sublimate	Mercuric chloride
Corundum	Aluminum oxide
Cream of tartar	Potassium hydrogen tartrate
Dehydrite	Magnesium perchlorate
Derby red	Basic lead chromate
Dextrose	Glucose
Dipping acid	Sulfuric acid
Disulfuric acid	Fuming sulfuric acid
Dung salt	Sodium arsenate
Dutch liquid	Ethylene chloride
Emerald green	Copper aceto-arsenite
Emery powder	Impure aluminum oxide
Epsom salts	Magnesium sulfate
Essence of bitter almonds	Benzaldehyde

Common or Trade Name	Chemical Synonym
Everitt's salt	Potassium ferrous ferrocyanide
Feldspar	Potassium aluminum silicate
Fischer's salt	Potassium cobaltic nitrite
Flowers of sulfur	Sulfur
"Flowers of" a metal	Oxide of
Freezing salt	Impure sodium chloride
French chalk	Hydrated magnesium silicate
French verdigris	Basic copper acetate
Fruit sugar	Fructose
Fuller's earth	Hydrated aluminum & magnesium silicates
Fulminating mercury	Mercuric fulminate
Galena	Lead sulfide
German silver	Alloy of copper, nickel & zinc
Glauber's salt	Sodium sulfate
Glazier's salt	Potassium sulfate
Glover acid	78% Sulfuric acid
Glucose	Dextrose
Glycerine	Glycerol
Goulard powder	Lead acetate
Grain alcohol	Ethyl alcohol
Grape sugar	Glucose
Green verditer	Basic copper carbonate
Green vitriol	Ferrous sulfate
Gun cotton	Nitrocellulose
Gypsum	Calcium sulfate
Hartshorn	Ammonium hydroxide
Hartshorn salt	Ammonium carbonate-carbamate
Heavy spar	Barium sulfate
Homberg's phosphorus	Fused calcium chloride
Horn silver	Silver chloride
Horse brimstone	Impure, dark native sulfur
Howard's silver	Mercury fulminate
Indian red	Ferric oxide
Iron black	Precipitated antimony
Iron mordant	Ferric sulfate
Iron vitriol	Ferrous sulfate
Japanese antimony	Antimony sulfide
Jeweller's borax	Borax
Jeweller's rouge	Finest calcined ferric oxide
Kalle's salt	Acetone bisulfite
Kaolin	Aluminum silicate

Common or Trade Name	Chemical Synonym
King's yellow	Arsenous sulfide
Klee's salt	Potassium hydrogen oxalate
Kyanol	Aniline
Lac sulfur	Precipitated sulfur
Lampblack	Impure carbon
Land plaster	Ground gypsum
Lanolin	Wool grease (cholesterol)
Laughing gas	Nitrous oxide
Lead vinegar	Basic lead acetate
Leipzig yellow	Lead chromate
Lemon chrome	Barium chromate
Lime water	Calcium hydroxide solution
Litharge	Lead oxide
Liver of antimony	Impure double sulfide of antimony & alkali or alkaline earth
Liver of sulfur	Mixed potassium sulfides
Lunar caustic	Silver nitrate
Lye	Potassium or sodium hydroxides
Macquer's salt	Potassium arsenate
Magister of bismuth	Basic bismuth nitrate
Magister of sulfur	Amorphous precipitated sulfur
Magistery of lead	cf. White lead
Magnesia	Magnesium oxide
Magnesia white	Magnesium oxide or carbonate
Magnesite	Magnesium carbonate
Malachite	Basic copper carbonate
Manganese black	Magnesium dioxide
Marble	Calcium carbonate
Marsh gas	Methane
Meerschaum	Hydrated magnesium silicate
Microcosmic salt	Sodium ammonium hydrogen phosphate.
Milk of barium	Barium hydroxide
Milk of lime	Calcium hydroxide
Milk of magnesia	Magnesium hydroxide
Milk of sulfur	Precipitated sulfur
Milk sugar	Lactose
Minium	Plumbus plumbate
Mitigated caustic	Fused mixture of 1 part silver nitrate and 2 of potassium nitrate
Mixed acid	Mixture of nitric & sulfuric acids
Mixed vitriol	Cupric-ferrous sulfate

Common or Trade Name	Chemical Synonym
Mohr's salt	Ferrous ammonium sulfate
"Muriate of" a metal	Chloride of
Muriatic acid	Hydrochloric acid
Muscle sugar	Inositol
Natron	Sodium carbonate
Natural gas	Mixture of gaseous hydrocarbons
Neutral tartar	Potassium tartrate
Niter	Potassium nitrate
Niter cake	Mixture of sodium sulfate & sodium acid sulfate
Nitro-lime	Calcium cyanamide
Nordhausen acid	Fuming sulfuric acid
Oil of bitter almond	Benzaldehyde
Oil of cinnamon	Cinnamic aldehyde
Oil of garlic	Allyl sulfide
Oil of mirbane	Nitrobenzene
Oil of mustard	Allyl isothiocyanate
Oil of bananas / Oil of pears	Amyl acetate
Oil of pineapple	Ethyl butyrate
Oil of tartar	Deliquescent potassium carbonate
Oil of vitriol	Concentrated sulfuric acid
Oil of wintergreen	Methyl salicylate
Oleum	Fuming sulfuric acid
Orpiment	Arsenic trisulfide
Oxone	Sodium peroxide
Paris blue	Ferric ferrocyanide
Paris green	Copper aceto-arsenite
Paris white	Calcium carbonate
Pearl ash	Potassium carbonate
Perborax / Perborin	Sodium perborate
Permanent white	Barium sulfate
Phosphate rock	Calcium phosphate
Pickle alum	Aluminum sulfate
Pickling acid	Sulfuric or acetic acid
Pink salt	Ammonium-stannic chloride
Plaster of Paris	Calcium sulfate
Plate sulfate	Double salt of potassium-sodium sulfates
Plumbago	Graphite
Potash	Potassium carbonate

Common or Trade Name	Chemical Synonym
Potash, caustic	Potassium hydroxide
Precipitated chalk	Calcium carbonate
Producer gas	An artificial heating gas
Prussian blue	Ferric ferrocyanide
Prussic acid	Hydrocyanic acid
Pure scarlet	Mercuric iodide
Putty powder	Impure stannic oxide
Pyrites	Ferrous sulfite
Pyroligneous acid	Crude acetic acid
Pyroligneous spirit	Methyl alcohol
Quick lime	Calcium oxide
Quicksilver	Mercury
Rectified spirit	90–95% Ethyl alcohol
Red antimony	Antimony oxysulfide
Red lead	Plumbus plumbate
Red liquor	Aluminum acetate in water
Red precipitate	Mercuric oxide
Red prussiate of potash	Potassium ferricyanide
Rochelle salt	Potassium sodium tartrate
Rock salt	Sodium chloride
Rouge	Ferric oxide
Ruby	Aluminum oxide
Sal alembroth	Mercuric ammonium chloride
Sal ammoniac	Ammonium chloride
Sal soda	Sodium carbonate
Sal volatile	Ammonium carbonate
Saleratus	Sodium acid carbonate
Salt cake	Impure sodium sulfate
Salt of amber	Succinic acid
Salt of hartshorn	Ammonium carbonate
Salt of lemon } Salt of sorrel }	Potassium hydrogen oxalate
Salt of tartar } Salt of wormwood }	Potassium carbonate
Saltpeter (Bengal)	Potassium nitrate
Saltpeter (Chile)	Sodium nitrate
Sand acid	Hydro fluosilicic acid
Satin white	Calcium sulfate
Scheele's green	Copper hydrogen arsenite
Schlippe's salt	Sodium thioantimonate
Scotch soda	Impure sodium carbonate
Silica	Silicon dioxide

Common or Trade Name	Chemical Synonym
Slaked lime	Calcium hydroxide
Soda (washing)	Sodium carbonate
Soda ash	Sodium carbonate
Soda crystals	Sodium carbonate
Soda lime	Mixture of sodium hydroxide & calcium oxide
Soft soap	Potash soap
Soluble glass	Sodium silicate solution
Soluble tartar	Potassium tartrate
Souberian's ammoniacal salt	Mercury ammonium nitrate
Spelter	Zinc
Spirit of hartshorn	Ammonia solution
Spirit of salt	Hydrochloric acid
Spirit of wine	Ethyl alcohol (84%)
Stibiated tartar	Potassium antimonyl tartrate
Strontium white	Strontium sulfate
Sugar of lead	Lead acetate
Sugar of milk	Lactose
Superphosphate	Impure calcium hydrogen phosphate
Sylvine	Potassium chloride
Sylvinite	Sylvine with rock salt
Table salt	Sodium chloride
Talc	Hydrated magnesium silicate
Tartar	Crude potassium hydrogen tartrate
Tartar emetic	Potassium antimonyl tartrate
Tin crystals	Stannous chloride
Tin prepare liquor	Sodium stannate
Tin salts	Stannous chloride
Tin white	Stannous hydroxide
Toughened caustic	Fused mixture of silver and potassium nitrates
Trona	Natural sodium carbonate
Turnbull's blue	Ferrous ferricyanide
Ultramarine yellow	Barium chromate
Unslaked lime	Calcium oxide
Vaseline	Soft paraffin
Venetian red	Ferric oxide
Verdigris	Basic copper acetate
Vermilion	Red mercuric sulfide
Vichy salt	Sodium hydrogen carbonate
Vinous alcohol	Ethyl alcohol
Vitriol	Sulfuric acid

Common or Trade Name	Chemical Synonym
"Vitriolate of"	Sulfate of
Washing soda	Sodium carbonate
Water gas	Artificial gas
Water glass	Aqueous solution of sodium silicates
White acid	Mixture of ammonium fluoride & hydrofluoric acid
White alkali	Refined sodium carbonate
White arsenic	Arsenous oxide
White damp	Carbon monoxide
White lead	Basic lead carbonate
White precipitate	Mercury-ammonium chloride
White tar	Napthalene
White vitriol	Zinc sulfate
Whiting	Calcium carbonate
Witherite	Barium carbonate
Wood alcohol / Wood naphtha / Wood spirit	Methyl alcohol
Yellow precipitate	Mercuric oxide
Yellow prussiate of potash	Potassium ferrocyanide
Zinc blende	Zinc sulfide
Zinc powder	Zinc oxide
Zinc vitriol	Zinc sulfate
Zinc white	Zinc oxide
Zinc yellow	Zinc chromate

Part Seven

—•—

SOURCES OF SUPPLY

Chapter 30

Stalking the wild fixings

SUPPLIERS & THEIR INVENTORIES

In her day, the town's apothecary shop or the general store usually supplied the fixings needed for Grandmother Artemisia's receipts and nostrums. It was a commonplace, across-the-counter transaction—whether her need was for potent drugs, exotic herbs, or everyday kitchen paraphernalia.

In today's plethora of regulations, restrictions, and prohibitions against the dispensing of drugs and chemicals to the general public, the consumer may be hard pressed to locate sources of ingredients. Old-time cooking utensils, too, like the kitchen sink pump, have become things of the past—well, almost.

But the diligent and determined can still find hard-to-come-by kitchen tools, ingredients, herbs, and chemicals, &tc. Often, one needs look no farther than the Yellow Pages for listings of the nearest drugstore, pharmacy, chemical supply house, veterinary supply house, health food store, grocery, food market, supermarket—and, of late, the resurrected old-time country general store.

To prime the pump of supply, the following sources are listed. The alert shopper should make initial inquiry about the prices of catalogs—they are not all free—and any pertinent information desired.

Caswell-Massey (mail-order dept.)
320 West 13th Street
New York, New York   10014
Telephone: (212) 675–2210

Caswell-Massey (retail store)
518 Lexington Avenue at 48th Street
New York, New York   10017

Established in 1752, this pharmaceutical house carries colognes, essential oils, soaps, rare herbs, &tc. —not to mention many other items unavailable elsewhere.

Cumberland General Store
Dept MJ.   Route 3
Crossville, Tennessee   38555

The inventory of this store includes coffee mills, kraut cutters, oil lamps, oak kegs, copper kettles, churns, wash pots, wood stoves, cider presses, pumps, plows, harnesses, windmills, hardware and more. The 225-page, illustrated catalog costs about $3.

Glen-Bel's Country Store
Route 5, Box 390 ME
Crossville, Tennessee   38555

The catalog contains fruit presses, coffee mills, butter molds, kraut cutters, wood stoves, wash boards, farm bells, buggies, wagons, oak barrels, churns, stoneware, lamps, hand tools, &tc. The $3 catalog fee is refundable with purchase.

Kiehl Pharmacy
109 Third Avenue
New York, New York   10003
Telephone (212) 475-3400

Opened in the mid-nineteenth century, this pharmacy carries a complete herb inventory and other hard-to-find items.

Mother's General Store (mail-order dept.)
Post Office Box 506
Flat Rock, North Carolina
28731

Mother's General Store (retail store)
101 North Church Street
Hendersonville, North Carolina
28739
Telephone (704) 693-4109

The 50¢ catalog lists more than 150 items in common use in the late nineteenth century—for the farmstead, its kitchen and its food preparation.

Nichols Garden Nursery
1190-ME Pacific
Albany, Oregon   97312

The catalog details a substantial line of herbs, seeds, and plants.

San Francisco Herb Company
367 Ninth Street
San Francisco, California
94103

The inventory includes bulk herbs and spices. Catalog will be sent on request.

Taylor's Herb Gardens, Inc.
Dept. M
1535 Lone Oak Road
Vista, California   92083
Telephone (714) 727-3485

The catalog, for 50¢, offers more than 200 live medical, culinary, and aromatic herb plants.

INDEX